LINGUISTIC AND LITERARY STUDIES

*

LINGUISTIC AND LITERARY STUDIES

IN HONOR OF

ARCHIBALD A. HILL

edited by

MOHAMMAD ALI JAZAYERY
EDGAR C. POLOMÉ
WERNER WINTER

Volume I

GENERAL AND
THEORETICAL LINGUISTICS

LISSE
THE PETER DE RIDDER PRESS
1976

Complete work: ISBN 90 316 0107 1
This volume: ISBN 90 316 0108 X

Printed in Belgium by NICI, Ghent

TABLE OF CONTENTS

FOREWORD

The Linguistic and Literary Studies in Honor of Archibald A. Hill had originally been scheduled to be presented to him at his retirement in 1972, but a number of unfortunate circumstances delayed the publication of the volume until the present date.

The initiative for this volume was taken in the late sixties by Werner Winter and Edgar Polomé, but as they approached some colleagues to obtain their support in their endeavor, they were informed that Leon Dostert was also contacting friends and colleagues of Archibald Hill for contributions to a volume in his honor. Arrangements were immediately made by Edgar Polomé for close collaboration with Professor Dostert, but the untimely death of this dear friend and colleague prevented a collaborative undertaking from taking final shape. Ultimately, the project was continued by Werner Winter and Edgar Polomé, soon joined by Mohammad Ali Jazayery, as prospective editors of the volume. A call for contributions was sent to numerous scholars who had been associated with Archibald Hill in his teaching and research as well as in his long years of service as Secretary-Treasurer of the Linguistic Society of America. The response was tremendous, as could be expected in view of the breadth of activities and involvement of Archibald Hill in the various aspects of linguistics. Seldom, indeed, has a scholar remained active and up-to-date in his field for so long as he has, achieving the *tour de force* of being respected by all schools of linguistics. Furthermore, his scholarly career has been marked by as much deep direct concern for the application of linguistics (to teaching and literary studies) as for linguistic theory and synchronic and diachronic studies.

Being separated by the great distance between Kiel and Austin, and burdened with other heavy commitments, the editors were considerably delayed in completing their task. In addition, a change of publisher at the last moment created further problems. In spite of these difficulties, the work has now reached completion, and the editors are very pleased to present to Professor Hill, and to the readers, this collection of papers covering all the aspects of Archibald Hill's scholarly interests.

An attempt has been made to classify the papers according to broad categories, but in view of the overlap between and among various fields, the inclusion of a given contribution in a particular group may be open to criticism. A distinct effort has also been made to preserve a uniform style, especially in the bibliographical references and footnotes, but, in a few special cases, it appeared impossible to maintain this consistency. Greek terms and quotations are either translated or reproduced in the original alphabet, depending on the choice of the author of the relevant paper. Similarly the system of phonetic transcription used by each author has been retained without change.

Though this volume could not be presented to Archibald Hill in 1972, as originally planned, his retirement has been marked by a series of events that have added particular luster to the completion of a most distinguished and successful university career. The students in the Foreign Language Education Center at the University of Texas, where the study of applied linguistics has grown and thrived in no small measure under his guidance, presented him with a voluminous bound copy of the best papers produced through the years by his students under his supervision. In the Spring of 1972, a series of lectures was sponsored at the University of Texas at Austin, by the Departments of Linguistics, English, and Germanic Languages, and by the Foreign Language Education Center (the paper read by Professor Robert Wilson is published in this volume). On May 1, 1972, a special academic session, presided over by Chancellor Emeritus Harry H. Ransom, honored Archibald Hill. Einar Haugen, past President of the Linguistic Society of America and President of the Comité International Permanent des Linguistes, gave a lecture entitled, "The Curse of Babel". His opening remarks appeared to the Editors as such an excellent characterization of the work and accomplishments of Professor Hill that they could not find better words to describe his achievements. These remarks are accordingly reproduced in this volume. But perhaps nobody could define the significance of his career as a teacher better than Archibald Hill himself, whose address to the graduating class of the College of Humanities of the University of Texas at Austin, at the first convocation of this College on May 20, 1972, provides the best illustration of his views and is reproduced here under the title: Fifty years of English: from comma to full stop.

In completing this volume we would like to thank all the contributors for their papers, as well as for their patience during the long editorial work. The Editors decided, in view of the size of the volume, not to include their own papers. We also wish to express our gratitude to the two secretaries, Ms. Lu Taylor and Ms. Virginia Jones, without whose devoted, strenuous, and accurate work this would never have been accomplished.

THE EDITORS

ARCHIBALD A. HILL:
A BIOGRAPHICAL SKETCH

EDGAR C. POLOMÉ

Archibald A. Hill was born in New York City on July 5, 1902, the son of Dr. Alexander Hill and Mary Dorsey Anderson Hill. His parents were, at that time, the directors of a social settlement on 8th Avenue, which was founded and is still supported by the Rockefeller Foundation, in the western part of lower New York. His parents had previously been the directors of a social settlement in Louisville, Kentucky, which is, again, still in existence under the name of 'Neighborhood House'.

Archibald Hill grew up in California, where his mother taught school for many years after the death of his father in 1908. He attended Pomona College (Claremont, California) where he received his A. B. in 1923; Stanford University, where he got his A. M. the next year; and Yale University, where he was awarded the Ph. D. in 1927. All of these degrees were with a major in English, but his teaching career has been at least equally concerned with Linguistics, which was "something that, in the Twenties, one went into because one was interested, and not something in which one could get an integrated education".

He has been very happily married since 1928 to the former Muriel Louise Byard of Ellsworth, Maine, whom he met while he was a graduate student at Yale University, and who was, at that time, Secretary of the Graduate School. Undoubtedly, the thing of which Archibald is perhaps most proud is his eighteen years as Secretary of the Linguistic Society of America, but as he has stated: "it is obvious to those who know the way in which we operated that I could not have been Secretary of the Society during the years mentioned without Muriel's very loyal and extremely industrious help." A person of rather retiring temperament, Mrs. Hill has never been given the proper recognition that the Linguistic Society should have given her for many years.

Having served as President of the Linguistic Society in 1969, Archibald Hill has continued to maintain a very active interest in the Society.

Professor Hill began teaching at the University of Michigan in 1926 and taught there for four years as instructor and, in his last year, as assistant professor, "since (as he put it) that was the way things were done in the Twenties". He then went to the University of Virginia as an associate professor of English philology in 1930 and stayed there until 1952, with an interval of four years' leave to serve with the U. S. Naval Reserve as Lieutenant Commander and, finally, as Commander during the Second World War.

In 1952 he joined Georgetown University as Vice-Director of the Institute of Languages and Linguistics and was there for three years, coming to the University of Texas in 1955 as Professor of English, later, Professor of English, of Linguistics, and of Education, which was the title he held until June 1972, at which time he became Professor Emeritus.

In the course of his academic career, he has received growing national and international recognition, chairing the conference on English as a Second Language at Ann Arbor in 1957; organizing the three Texas Conferences on Problems of English Analysis as well as editing the contributions to those conferences; directing the Linguistic Institutes in 1960 and 1961; spending several months as linguistic consultant to the English Language Exploratory Committee in Tokyo under the auspices of the Japan Society; and representing the Linguistic Society of America and the American Council of Learned Societies at the International Congress of University Professors of English at Edinburgh in 1962.

The last decade of his academic tenure was particularly fruitful and eventful: In the summer of 1963, he lectured twice daily to a class of 230 teachers in Taiwan, and in the fall he served as consultant to the English Language Education Council in Tokyo and the Texas AID project in Taiwan. In the summer of 1965, he was senior lecturer in the U. S. Department of State Experts Program in Poznań, Poland. In the Fall of 1966, he acted as co-ordinator of the Voice of America – Forum Series: Linguistics Today. In the spring of 1968, he was Fulbright Professor at the University of Belgrade. In the spring of 1969, he was appointed to the Thord-Gray Lectureship at the University of Lund, Sweden. He has also lectured at numerous prominent universities all over the United States.

Maintaining an outstanding publication record, Archibald Hill has contributed more than any other scholar to the shaping of Linguistics in the United States since its modest beginnings in the Twenties. To Linguistics he has brought the precision of a scientist, the humanistic concern of a scholar, the modesty of a gentleman, and a common sense which is all too infrequently present.

FOR ARCH

REMARKS BY EINAR HAUGEN AT AUSTIN, TEXAS ON MAY 1, 1972

Dear Arch:

I come here neither to bury you nor to praise you – only to express my appreciation of you as a friend and as a fellow worker in the vineyard of linguistics.

It is now many years since we first met at what became our common forum and meeting place, the Linguistic Society of America. I knew your name even before meeting you because of your early writings in the field of English linguistics. The year after I had been president you became secretary – 1951 – and since that time, no meeting of LSA or its Executive Committee was complete without you until your retirement from the secretaryship in 1969. I am sure that others will interpret your incredible contribution to that organization better than I can. No one can know how much of your own time and energy and devotion, and that of your wife Muriel, have gone into the smooth and successful operation of the LSA. Under you it grew from a small to a big organization, and linguistics itself grew from programs in other departments to departments of its own in all major universities.

However, I did not come here to talk about your accomplishments as secretary or as an organizer. In the last two or three days I've had the delight of reading and rereading some of your writings. I found that right in my own library at home, I had over twenty of your articles. So I dipped into these to get an impression of the contribution you have made to the intellectual ferment of our time in the field of linguistics.

I hardly need to tell this audience that your most constant theme of research has been the interface between linguistics and literature. Your studies of *Pippa's Song* and *Windhover* are oft-reprinted classics. The list of your writings is in the hands of this audience, who can duplicate my pleasure by looking the articles up in their own libraries, whether at home or at the university.

What I would like to do is to list three traits that struck me as I read these papers. I jotted down some quotations as I was reading and will cite them from the margins of the bibliography. These quotations will amply illustrate the traits to which I refer.

The first trait that I find in your writings is *commitment*. You committed yourself early to a view of language which based itself solidly on a *scientific position*. In our country this meant above all the views of Leonard Bloomfield, who, as you point out in your 1955 article, was the main intellectual force in what came to be known rightly or wrongly as the 'American' school of linguistics.

This commitment meant a firm rejection of speculative thinking about the unseen and the unknowable – above all the mind of the speaker and hearer – and an emphasis on the basic formal analysis of the message itself, the utterance of the speaker or the poem of the writer.

In your article of 1955 on "Linguistics since Bloomfield", I find a classic statement of the structural view of language as a series of levels, each with its own internal organization and each related to the one above and the one below. I am tempted to call it the 'skyscraper' theory of language, one in which you reach heaven in the top story – the place where you can analyze literature using the same tools as on the lower levels. In your article on *Pippa's Song* of 1956 the levels are specifically stated as pre-literary (which is also the micro-linguistic), the micro-literary (which is also the meta-linguistic), and finally the meta-literary (for which there is no equivalent linguistic level). This article also states your basic conviction that "it is form which gives meaning and not meaning which gives form".

The second trait that I find in your papers and would like to underline here is one that I would label as *concern*. We hear a great deal about 'relevance' these days: you have always been concerned with relevant problems. Much of your energy has gone into a battle against the rigid doctrines of 'school-marm correctness'. I'm thinking of your 1951 essay on "Correctness and Style in English Composition". There you make it clear that correctness is not the same as logic or beauty or history or authority or even Latin grammar. You distinguish between correctness and style and list some delightful examples of bad style from our favorite source of such examples, our students' essays: "A home where unfortunate women who had made mistakes went to have their bastards." I take it that this is not an example of what you mean when you say that "illogical suppleness has always been one of the beauties of English". A succinct statement of your views is found in the sentence "it is better to find the facts and teach them than to rely on a merely convenient myth".

In your concern about demolishing myths you have used the sword of humor and the armor of forthrightness on more than one occasion. I enjoyed your demolition of the myth about the primitive Cherokee in 1951 who had no word for 'washing'. I quote: "This paper will be devoted to trailing the washing Cherokee through books on general linguistics and proving that he is a ghost, though one that still walks, and to laying him once for all." In a review of a book on semantics by one of our colleagues, you write in 1952: "The material presented here is thoroughly unscientific so that there is some obligation for the linguist to discuss the work seriously and thoroughly." In an article in *College English* in 1954, you argued that one cannot condemn language structure, only language use: "Good style, whether artistic or intellectual, is possible in any language structure." In an article of 1957 with the challenging title, "Who Needs Linguistics?", you concluded that everybody needs linguistics, but above all, it is needed by linguists themselves: "We have the task of making linguistics sufficiently adult and its results sufficiently available so that all people of good will, who work within the field of language, language art and language usage, can realize there are techniques and results which are of value to them." Here also you state the goal of linguistics: "The understanding of man in relation to his symbolic activity."

The third and last trait that struck me was also the most important – *perspective*. This is a quality that comes with experience and thinking, one that became inevitable as the winds of opinion changed in linguistic research in the 1960's. I find it especially interesting that you have time and again tried to find formulations that would preserve the older views without denying the new.

I find this quality especially prominent in a paper you gave in Japan in 1961 on the "Nature of Language". There you called for a linguistic indeterminacy, parallel to that which is enshrined in physics, whereby "formulations from differing points of view give differing results, both of which must be accepted". You identified the structural school as being primarily interested in the "speakers' grammar" while the generativists appeared to favor a "hearers' grammar". In 1962 you reviewed the various kinds of phonemes that have been proposed and wrote "I am sure that all three kinds of phonemes are valid, useful, and different. A little tolerance all around would help linguistics." In your 1962 article in *Language*, you proposed a postulate on which structuralists and generativists should be able to agree, what you called "fictitious manipulability" (that the relations between utterances are capable of being stated in the form of manipulations). In 1965 you wrote that "phonology and transformations will not support each other until phonologists and transformationalists wish them to and are willing to learn from each other". In 1967 you admitted that "the higher levels of syntactic and semantic analysis as carried on in 1967 are more exciting than the muddy work of carrying the stones and mixing the mortar for foundations". In 1970 you developed your conception of the "stimulus sentence" and contrasted it with the "perfected sentence", which corresponded to the structuralists' and the generativists' sentences, respectively.

The fact that you have been a firm and consistent anti-mentalist has not prevented you from professing your faith in literature as "the area of language in which man's values are most deeply embedded, the literature which has been the constant creation, companion, and model of his spirit" (1955). Again you write in 1961 : "I believe it is language and its use which more than anything else *is* the human spirit and that there is new as well as old truth in Scripture which says 'In the beginning was the Word'."

Your work has combined a truly scientific outlook with a humanistic approach which I feel is the characteristic of your whole personality. With this I will conclude and merely thank you for what you have given us all through your commitment, your concern, and your perspective.

ARCHIBALD A. HILL:
A BIBLIOGRAPHY

1. Stress in recent English as a distinguishing mark between dissyllables used as noun or verb. American Speech 6 (1931), 443-448.
2. California place-names from the Spanish. American Speech 7 (1932), 317-318, and correction: 8, no. 2 (1933), 75.
3. Diomede: The traditional development of a character. Essays and Studies in English and Comparative Literature, University of Michigan (1932), 1-25.
4. Ilium, the palace of Priam. Modern Philology 30 (1932), 94-96.
5. A note on the division of syllables in present day English. American Speech 8, no. 2 (1933), 59-60.
6. Dialect notes on records of folk songs from Virginia. With Arthur Kyle Davis, Jr.. American Speech, 8, no. 4 (1933), 52-56.
7. Phonetic transcription of Victor phonograph record. American Speech Series No. 68-B, Ellsworth, Maine. With N. M. Caffee and F. B. Duke. American Speech 9 (1934), 140-141.
8. Transcription of phonograph record of the speech of a young Negro handy man without schooling, who has lived all his life in Charlottesville, Virginia. American Speech 9 (1934), 215-216.
9. Transcription of phonograph record of the speech of a successful business man (white), born four or five miles from Charlottesville, Virginia. He is about fifty years old. American Speech 9 (1934), 299.
10. A report on proposed investigations of Southern speech. Dialect Notes 6 (1934), 420-424.
11. Research in Southern speech in co-operation with the Linguistic Atlas. American Speech 19 (1935), 237-240.
12. Phonetic and phonemic change. Language 12 (1936), 15-22.
   A. Reprinted in: Readings in Linguistics, ed. by Martin Joos. Washington: A. C. L. S. (1957), 81-84.
13. A style for theses and dissertations (University of Virginia Library, 1938). Mimeographed. 44 pp.

14. A philologist looks at Finnegan's Wake. Virginia Quarterly Review 15 (1939), 650-656.
15. The sound symbolism of Poe. The Virginia Spectator 101, no. 5 (1940), 3-5.
16. New light on some literary lives [discussion of books on Joyce, Hardy, and E. A. Robinson]. Virginia Quarterly 16 (1940), 450-455.
17. Early loss of *r* before dentals. PMLA 55 (1940), 308-359.
    A. Reprinted, without the appendix listing forms, in: A Various Language [:] Perspectives on American Dialects, ed. by Juanita V. Williamson and Virginia M. Burke. New York: Holt, Rinehart and Winston (1971), 87-100.
18. On incorporation as a type of language structure. Humanistic Studies in Honor of John Calvin Metcalf ... (University of Virginia, 1941), 65-79. See publications edited.
19. New semantics, old philology [discussion of books on semantics by Walpole and Hayakawa, and of The New Testament in Basic English]. The Virginia Quarterly Review 18 (1942), 116-120.
20. The use of dictionaries in language teaching. Language Learning 1 (1948), 9-13.
    A. Reprinted in: Readings in Applied English Linguistics, ed. by Harold B. Allen. New York: Appleton-Century-Crofts (1964), 439-443.
21. Review of An introduction to the phonetics of American English, by C. K. Thomas. The Southern Speech Journal 14 (1948), 55-56.
22. A survey of accomplishments and trends in research in present day English. American Speech 25 (1949), 59-61.
    A. Reprinted in: Essays in Literary Analysis. Austin: Dailey Diversified Services (1965), 1-6.
23. Review of Functional change in early English, by D. W. Lee. American Speech 24 (1949), 59-61.
24. *Now* is the time; *once* is enough [discussion of points of usage]. College English 12 (1950), 168-169.
25. Some postulates for distributional study of texts. Studies in Bibliography 3 (1951), 63-95.
26. Towards a literary analysis. English Studies in Honor of James Southall Wilson, ed. by Fredson Bowers. Charlottesville: University of Virginia (1951), 280-285.
    A. Reprinted in: Essays in Literary Analysis. Austin: Dailey Diversified Services (1965), 19-33.

27. Correctness and style in English Composition. College English 12 (1951), 280-285.
   A. Reprinted in: Readings in Applied English Linguistics, ed. by Harold B. Allen. New York: Appleton-Century-Crofts (1958), 311-317.
   B. Also in: A Linguistic Reader, ed. by Graham Wilson. New York: Harper and Row (1967), 49-55.
   C. Also in: Perspectives on Style, ed. by Frederick Candelaria. Boston: Allyn and Bacon (1968), 35-43.
   D. Also in: Classics in Composition, ed. by Donald E. Hayden. New York: Philosophical Library (1969), 228-236.
   E. Also in: Contemporary Essays on Style, Rhetoric, Linguistics, and Criticism, ed. by Glen A. Love and Michael Payne. Glenview, Ill.: Scott Foresman (1969), 101-107.
28. English metrics, a restatement, mimeographed, 1951.
   A. Printed in: Essays in Literary Analysis. Austin: Dailey Diversified Services (1965), 6-18.
29. Review of The history of inflectional *n* in English verbs before 1500, by D. W. Reed. Language 27 (1951), 594-597.
30. English verb nomenclature – third person singular. Studies in Linguistics 10 (1952), 63-64.
31. A note on primitive languages. International Journal of American Linguistics 18 (1952), 172-177.
   A. Reprinted (abridged) in: Language in Culture and Society, ed. by Dell Hymes. New York: Harper and Row (1964), 86-89.
32. A report on the language-literature seminar. With Harold Whitehall. [Mimeographed for the Linguistic Institute, Indiana University] (1952).
   A. Reprinted in: Readings in Applied English Linguistics, ed. by Harold B. Allen. New York: Appleton-Century-Crofts (1958), 394-397; 2nd. ed. (1964), 488-491.
33. Testing a dictionary [Discussion of Matthews Dictionary of Americanisms]. Virginia Quarterly Review 28 (1952), 131-135.
34. Review of Die englische Sprache, by Karl Brunner. Journal of English and Germanic Philology 51 (1952), 90-91.
35. Review of Maya hieroglyphic writing ... by J. E. S. Thompson. International Journal of American Linguistics 18 (1952), 184-186.
36. Review of The structure of English, by Charles C. Fries. Journal of English and Germanic Philology 51 (1952), 591-593.

37. Review of Semantics, by Julian Bonfante. Language 28 (1952), 256-261.
38. Review of The phonology of the Middle English dialect of Sussex, by Sven Rubin. Language 28 (1952), 276-278.
39. Review of Parataxis and hypotaxis as a criterion of syntax and style ... by Alarik Rynell. Language 28 (1952), 534.
40. Can linguistics be made useful to teachers? Language Learning 4 (1952-53), 117-122.
41. A sample literary analysis. Report of the Fourth Annual Round Table Meeting on Linguistics and Language Teaching (Georgetown University (1953), 87-93.
    A. Reprinted in: Essays in Literary Analysis. Austin: Dailey Diversified Services (1965), 34-38.
42. Review of Shakespeare's pronunciation, by Helge Kokeritz. Language 29 (1953), 549-561.
43. Review of The triumph of the English language, by R. F. Jones. Language 29 (1953), 561-563.
44. Review of Studies in honor of Albert Morey Sturtevant, ed. by L. R. Lind. Language 29 (1953), 547-549.
45. Prescriptivism and linguistics in English teaching. College English 15 (1954), 395-399.
    A. Reprinted in: Readings in applied English linguistics, ed. by Harold B. Allen. New York: Appleton-Century-Crofts (1958), 210-214; 2nd. ed. (1964), 280-293.
    B. Also in: Toward liberal education, ed. by L. G. Locke, W. Gibson, G. Arms. New York: Holt, Rinehart and Winston (1962), 121-126.
    C. Also in: Contemporary English: Change and variation, ed. by David L. Shores. Philadelphia: J. B. Lippincott and Company (1972), 231-236.
46. Juncture and syllable division in Latin. Language 30 (1954), 439-447.
47. That special written dialect – formal written English. CAE Critic (December, 1954), 3-4.
48. The linguistic approach to culture. Understanding other cultures, ed. by William A. Parker. Washington: A. C. L. S. (1954), 1-9.
49. Review of French influence in English phrasing, by A. A. Prins. Language 30 (1954), 171-173.
50. Consonant assimilation and juncture in English: A hypothesis. Language 31 (1955), 533-534.

51. Linguistics since Bloomfield. Quarterly Journal of Speech 41 (1955), 253-260.
    A. Reprinted in: Readings in applied English linguistics, ed. by Harold B. Allen. New York: Appleton-Century-Crofts (1958), 14-23.
    B. Also in: Essays in literary analysis. Austin: Dailey Diversified Services (1965), 39-44.
    C. Also in: The Bobbs-Merrill Reprint series in Language and linguistics. Language no. 45. New York: Bobbs-Merrill, n.d.
52. An analysis of 'The Windhover': An experiment in structural method. PMLA 70 (1955), 972-983.
    A. Reprinted in: Essays in literary analysis. Austin: Dailey Diversified Services (1965), 44-50.
    B. Also in: Englische Lyrik von Shakespeare bis Dylan Thomas, ed. by Walter Koch. Darmstadt: Wissenschaftliche Buchgesellschaft (1969), 333-346.
    C. Also in: The Bobbs-Merrill Reprint Series in language and linguistics. Language no. 44. New York: Bobbs-Merrill, n.d. Together with a reply by William H. Machett, from PMLA 72 (1957), 310-311.
    D. Also in: Strukturelle Textanalyse, ed. by W. A. Koch. Hildesheim: Georg Olms (1972), 197-207.
53. Review of Langage et versification d'après l'œuvre de Paul Valéry, by P. Guiraud, and Allgemeine Stilistik, by H. Seidler. Language 31 (1955), 349-352.
54. Language analysis and language teaching. The Modern Language Association of America, F. L. Bulletin no. 41 (December, 1955).
    A. Reprinted in: Modern Language Journal 40 (1960), 335-345.
    B. Also in: Anthology for use with a Guide for teachers in NDEA Language Institutes, ed. by Simon Belasco. Boston: D. C. Heath (1961), 10-20.
    C. Also in: Foreign language teaching, an Anthology, ed. by Joseph Michel. New York: Macmillan (1965), 91-111.
55. Pippa's song: Two attempts at structural criticism. Studies in English 35 (University of Texas, 1956), 51-56.
    A. Reprinted in: Readings in applied English linguistics, ed. by Harold B. Allen. New York: Appleton-Century-Crofts (1958), 402-406.
    B. Also with Japanese translation and notes by Toshiko Susuki, in: The English Teacher's Magazine 8 (Tokyo, 1959), 370-376.

C. Also in: Essays in literary analysis. Austin: Dailey Diversified Services (1965), 63-67.

D. Also in: Introductory readings on language, ed. by W. L. Anderson and N. C. Stageberg. New York: Holt, Rinehart, and Winston, revised ed., 1 (1966), 266-271.

E. Also in: Browning's mind and art, ed. by Clarence Tracy. Edinburgh and London: Oliver and Boyd (1968), 75-81.

56. Notes on the English language. CEA Critic 18, no. 9 (1956), 3.

57. Proposed phonemically based notation for American English as a second language. Austin (1957), offset.

A. Incorporated as Lesson two in: Oral approach to English, Vol. I. Tokyo: English Language Education Commission (1965).

B. Also translated and annotated by Teruo Kuwahara, in: Kozo Gengo Gaku [Structural linguistics] 2 (Tokyo, 1961), 69-83.

58. Who needs linguistics? Report of the Seventh Annual Round Table Meeting on Linguistics and Language Teaching. Washington: Georgetown University (1957), 75-86.

59. Terminology: Some conflicts and compromises. Report of the Seventh Annual Round Table Meeting on Linguistics and Language Teaching. Washington: Georgetown University (1957), 135-140.

60. The first step in English morphemic analysis. Austin (1957): Offset print for distribution at 1957 meeting of the Linguistic Society of America.

61. Introduction to linguistic structures: from sound to sentence in English. New York: Harcourt Brace (1958), xi + 496 pp.

A. The book has been translated into Japanese in an abridged version, by Masatomo Ukaji, Hushichu Ebunpo Raiburari [Phoenix English Grammar Library], Tokyo (1965), 122 pp.

B. Chapter I "What is Language" has been reprinted in: Aspects of American English, ed. by E. M. Kerr and R. M. Aderman. New York: Harcourt, Brace, Jovanovich (1963), 2-9; 2nd. ed. (1971), 3-11.

C. Also in: First perspectives on language, ed. by William C. Doster. New York: American Book Company (1963), 1-15.

D. Also in: Dimensions in communication, ed. by J. H. Campbell and H. W. Helper. Belmont, California: Wadsworth Publishing Company (1963), 147-158.

E. Also in: Language into literature, ed. by James D. Barry and William U. McDonald. Chicago: Science Research Associates (1965), 3-10.

F. Also in: Comment and controversy, ed. by Gerald A. Bryant Jr. Beverley Hills, California: Glencoe Press (1972), 179-196.

62. A program for the definition of literature. Studies in English 37 (University of Texas, 1958), 46-52.

    A. Reprinted in: Essays in literary analysis. Austin: Dailey Diversified Services (1965), 67-70.

63. Preface to a conference on linguistics and the teaching of English as a foreign language. Language Learning (Special Issue, June, 1958), 1-16.

64. Problems in the recognition of stress phonemes. Language Learning (Special Issue, June, 1958), 47-54.

65. Linguistics and the college teacher of language, literature, or composition. College Language Association Journal 2 (1958), 75-86.

66. Review of Das heutige Englisch, by Ernst Leisi. Language 34 (1958), 144-145.

67. The audibility of /+/. Journal of the Canadian Linguistic Association 5 (1959), 81-82.

68. Principles governing semantic parallels. Studies in Literature and Language 1 (The University of Texas, 1959), 356-365.

    A. Reprinted in: Readings in applied English linguistics, ed. by Harold B. Allen. New York: Appleton-Century-Crofts, 2nd. ed. (1964), 506-514.

    B. Also in: Essays in literary analysis. Austin: Dailey Diversified Services (1965), 71-75.

69. Comment and rejoinder [To G. P. Faust, discussing his review of Introduction to linguistic structures]. Studies in Linguistics 14 (1959), 57-67.

70. Review of Word-order in the Winchester manuscript and in William Caxton's edition of Thomas Malory's Morte Darthur ... by Jan Simko. Language 35 (1959), 561-564.

71. Review of Stress in English words, by G. F. Arnold. Language 35 (1959), 564-567.

72. Review of Ob-Ugric metrics, by Robert Austerlitz. Language 35 (1959), 567-569.

73. Esperanto aŭ Dubanto. The Texas Quarterly 3: (1960), 143-149.

74. Review of Studies in Heroic legend and in current speech, by Kemp Malone. Language 36 (1960), 246-249.

75. Grammaticality. Word 17 (1961), 1-10.

    A. Reprinted in: Readings in applied English linguistics, ed.

by Harold B. Allen. New York: Appleton-Century-Crofts, 2nd. ed. (1964), 163-172.

B. Also translated into Russian in Voprosy jazykoznanija 1962, 104-110.

C. Also in: A linguistic reader, ed. by Graham Wilson. New York: Harper and Row (1967), 281-289.

76. Linguistic principles for interpreting meaning. College English 22 (1961), 566-573.

77. The nature of language. ELEC Bulletin 1 (Tokyo: English Language Education Commission, 1961), 13-22.

A. Reprinted in: Applied linguistics and the teaching of English: Selected articles from ELEC Publications, ed. by Tamotsu Yambe. Tokyo: English Language Education Commission (1970), 7-21.

78. Recent linguistics and the teaching of English. ELEC Bulletin nos. 2 and 3 (Tokyo: English Language Education Commission, 1961), 11-15 and 13-22.

A. Reprinted in: Applied linguistics and the teaching of English: Selected articles from ELEC Publications, ed. by Tamotsu Yambe. Tokyo: English Language Education Commission (1970), 163-178.

79. Suprasegmentals, prosodies, prosodemes: comparison and discussion. Language 37 (1961), 557-568.

80. Review of A dictionary of American proverbs, by Archer Taylor and J. W. Bartlett. Notes and Queries (February, 1961), 75-77.

81. Drill materials and instructor's handbook. Preliminary edition of an intensive course in English for adult Japanese. Austin (1961) offset.

A. Printed in: ELEC English course part I, with annotation by Tamotsu Yambe. Tokyo: English Language Education Commission (1961), 324 pp. Reprinted in 1962 and 1963.

B. Also reprinted as: Oral approach to English, with Japanese translation. Tokyo: ELEC (1965). 2 vols., pp. x and 1-328, and pp. x and 329-634.

C. Also in a Chinese edition, as: The new linguistic method. Drill materials and instructors handbook. Edited, annotated and translated by Paul Lin, and Charles Tang. Taipei: University of Texas and Taiwan Normal University (1964), xxiv + 775 pp.

82. Various kinds of phonemes. Studies in Linguistics 16 (1962), 3-10.

A. Reprinted in: Phonological theory: Evolution and current

practice, ed. by Valerie Makkai. New York: Holt, Rinehart and Winston (1972), 236-240.

83. A conjectural restructuring of a dialect of Ireland. Lochlann 2 (1962), 23-37.

84. A postulate for linguistics in the sixties. Language 38 (1962), 345-351.

    A. Translated and reprinted as: Un postulato per la linguistica negli anni sessenta, in Linguistica Generale, Structuralismo, Linguistica Storica, ed. by Tristano Bolelli. Pisa: Nistri-Lischi (1971), 490-500.

85. The validity of overall patterns. First Texas Conference on Problems of Linguistic Analysis in English, The University of Texas (1962), 113-122. See Publications edited.

86. Literature in language teaching. ELEC Bulletin, Tokyo: English Language Education Commission (1962), 5-15.

    A. Reprinted in: Essays in literary analysis. Austin: Dailey Diversified Services (1965), 76-88.

87. Review of The grammar of English nominalizations, by R. B. Lees. Language 38 (1962), 434-444.

88. Review of Studies in connection of clauses ... by R. Karlsen. College English, 23 (1962), 607.

89. Review of The new Merriam Webster. Roundtable of the South Central College English Association, 3, no. 3 (1962), 3-4.

90. Recent developments and problems in the teaching of English. ELEC Publications, Tokyo: English Language Education Commission, 5 (1963), 21-29.

    A. Reprinted in: Applied linguistics and the teaching of English: Selected articles from ELEC Publications, ed. by Tamotsu Yambe. Tokyo: English Language Education Commission (1970), 179-189.

91. A history of the Linguistic Institute. Indiana University Press (1963; repr. 1964), 15 pp.

    A. Reprinted in: ACLS Newsletter 15, no. 3 (1964), 1-12.

92. Review of Dictionaries and THAT dictionary, ed. by James H. Sledd and Wilma R. Ebbitt. Roundtable of the South Central College English Association 4, no. 4 (1963), 2.

93. Review of Bibliographisches Handbuch zur Sprachinhaltsforschung, Teil I, ed. by Gipper and Schwartz. Journal of English and Germanic Philology 62 (1963), 477-478.

94. The locus of the literary work. English Studies Today (Edinburgh, 1964), 41-50.
    A. Reprinted in: Essays in literary analysis. Austin: Dailey Diversified Services (1965), 89-94.
95. Three examples of unexpectedly accurate Indian lore. Texas Studies in Literature and Language 6 (1964), 80-83.
96. The tainted ain't again. College English 26 (1965), 298-303.
    A. Reprinted in: Aspects of American English, ed. by Elizabeth M. Kerr and Ralph M. Aderman. New York: Harcourt, Brace, Jovanovich (2nd. ed., 1971), 276-283).
97. Post-nominal modifiers: transformations and phonology. Acta Linguistica Hafniensia 9 (Copenhagen, 1965), 37-49.
98. English language study and the college English teacher. Texas College English 1, no. 4 (1965), 2 and 5.
99. Process and form in language and poetry. Proceedings of the Regional Conference on the Arts and Humanities in College Education (University of California, Los Angeles, 1965), 3-12.
100. Essays in literary analysis. An informal collection of essays for student use. Austin: Dailey Diversified Services (1965), 115 pp.
    The collection contained reprints of numbers 22, 26, 28, 41, 51, 52, 55, 62, 68, 83, and 91.
    The collection also contained preprint versions of the following:
    A. Poetry and stylistics, delivered as a public lecture, the University of Virginia (1956).
       Reprinted in: Essays on the language of literature, ed. by Seymour Chatman and Samuel Levin. New York: Houghton Mifflin Co. (1967), 385-397.
    B. Some points in the analysis of Keats' Grecian Urn, 95-105. This was reprinted in: Studies in language, literature, and culture of the Middle Ages and later. The University of Texas (1969), 357-66. See Publications edited.
    C. The Windhover revisited. Linguistic analysis of literature re-assessed, 106-115.
       Reprinted in: Texas Studies in Literature and Language 8 (1966), 349-359.
101. The nature and origin of language. ELEC Publications, Tokyo: English Language Education Commission 15 (1965), 1-11.
102. Review of The phonemic structure of English words, by Yi-Chin Fu, and Consonant Patterning in English, by Yasui Minoru. Language 41 (1965), 167-168.

103. Review of Ulster dialects: an introductory symposium, ed. by G. B. Adams, J. Braidwood, R. J. Gregg. Journal of American Folklore 78 (1965), 367.

104. Elmer Bagby Atwood, Obituary. Orbis 14 (1965), 283-285, with W. P. Lehmann, J. J. Jones, and J. W. Neal.

105. Review of English syntax, by Paul Roberts. Harvard Educational Review 36 (1966), 77-83.

106. Review of Trends in modern linguistics, ed. by C. Mohrmann, F. Norman, and A. Sommerfelt. International Journal of American Linguistics (1966), 198-201.

107. The promises and limitations of the newest type of grammatical analysis (Lectures in memory of Louise Taft Semple, The University of Cincinnati, 1966), 38 pp.
    A. Reprinted (revised and abridged) in: TESOL Quarterly 1, no. 2 (June, 1967), 10-22.

108. Non-grammatical prerequisites. Foundations of Language 2 (1966), 319-337.

109. A re-examination of the English articles. 17th Annual Round Table, ed. by F. P. Dinneen, S. J., Number 19 (Georgetown University, 1966), pp. 217-231.

110. Some further thoughts on grammaticality and poetic language. Style 1 (1967), 81-91.

111. The current relevance of Bloch's 'postulates'. Language 43 (1967), 203-207.
    A. Reprinted in: Phonological theory: Evolution and current practice, ed. by Valerie Makkai. New York: Holt, Rinehart and Winston (1972), 241-244.

112. Review of A phonology and prosody of modern English, by Hans Kurath. Journal of English Linguistics 1 (1967), 74-75.

113. Tennessee's Partner by Bret Harte: Literature and the system of values in the language classroom. ELEC Publications 8 (Tokyo, 1967), 20-25.

114. Analogies, icons, and images in relation to semantic content of discourses. Style 2 (1968), 203-227.

115. Preface. Linguistics today, New York: Basic Books (1969), ix. See Publications edited.

116. Summary and a peek at the future. Linguistics today, New York: Basic Books (1969), 270-283. See Publications Edited.

117. A phonological description of poetic ornaments. Language and Style 2 (1969), 99-123.

118. Some speculations on tempo in speech. Southern Speech Journal 34 (1969), 169-173.
119. Imagery and meaning: a passage from Milton, and from Blake. Texas Studies in Literature and Language 11 (1969), 1093-1105.
120. Review of An introduction to general linguistics, by Francis P. Dinneen, S. J. Lingua 22 (1969), 237-244.
121. Review of Recurrence and a three-modal approach to poetry, by Walter A. Koch. Lingua 22 (1969), 244-248.
122. Review of Investigating linguistic acceptability, by Randolph Quirk and Jan Svartvik. Language 45 (1969), 622-624.
123. The hypothesis of deep structure. Studia Linguistica 24 (Lund, Sweden, 1970), 1-16.
124. How does rhythmic prose work? Essays in honor of Claude M. Wise, ed. by Arthur J. Bronstein, Claude L. Shaver, and G. Stevens. Hannibal, Mo.: Standard Printing Co., for the Speech Association of America (1970), 36-48.
125. Towards a parsing procedure for simple sentences in English. Studies in general and Oriental linguistics presented to Shiro Hattori on the occasion of his sixtieth birthday, ed. by Roman Jakobson and Shigeo Kawamoto. Tokyo, TEC Co. (1970), 235-245.
126. Review of An essay on language, by Robert A. Hall, Jr. Lingua 24 (1970), 295-299.
127. Trees of descent in linguistics and textual critisicm. Studia Anglica Posnaniensia 3 (Poznań, Poland, 1971), 3-12.
128. Review of Charisteria Iosepho Vachek sexagenario oblata, ed. by Jan Firbas and Josef Hladký. Language 47 (1971), 451-453.
129. Sound-symbolism in lexicon and literature. Studies in linguistics in honor of George L. Trager, ed. by M. Estelle Smith. The Hague: Mouton (1972), 142-147.
130. A defense of the audio-lingual method in TESOL. Fifteenth Anniversary Volume of ELEC Publications. Tokyo: English Language Education Commission (1972), 69-79.
131. Jury testing in analysis of contemporary language. Studies in linguistics in honor of Raven I. McDavid, ed. by Lawrence M. Davis. Birmingham: University of Alabama Press (1972), 285-291.
132. The green knight's castle and the translators. Canadian Journal of Linguistics 17 (1972), 141-157.
133. A theory of speech errors. Studies for Einar Haugen, ed. by Evelyn Scherabon Firchow, Kaaren Grimstad, Nils Hasselmo, and Wayne O'Neill. The Hague: Mouton (1972), 296-304.

A. Reprinted in: Speech errors as linguistic evidence, ed. by
Victoria A. Fromkin. The Hague: Mouton, (1973), 205-214.

134. Some thoughts on segmentation of lexical meaning. Annals of the
New York Academy of Sciences 211 (1973), 269-278.

135. A hierarchy of drills. TESOL Quarterly 7 (1973), 381-394.

136. Verb and particle combinations. Review of The phrasal verb in
English, by Dwight Bolinger. American Speech 44 (published in
1973, dated 1969), 210-215.

137. Word stress and the suffix -ic. Journal of English Linguistics 8
(1974), 6-20.

138. Figurative structure and meaning. Two poems by Emily Dickenson.
Texas Studies in Literature and Language 16 (1974), 195-209.

139. Method in source study: Yeats' Golden Bird of Byzantium as a
test case. Texas Studies in Literature and Language. 17 (1975),
525-538.

FORTHCOMING

140. A history of the Linguistic Society from 1951 to 1969. To appear
in: The Fiftieth Anniversary History of the LSA, along with sections
by Martin Joos and Thomas A. Sebeok.

PUBLICATIONS EDITED

141. Humanistic studies in honor of John Calvin Metcalf. Charlottesville: University of Virginia (1941), x + 338 pp.
Contains number 18.

142. Report of the Fourth Annual Round Table Meeting on Linguistics
and Language Teaching. Washington, D.C.: Georgetown University
(1953), iii + 116 pp.
Contains number 41.

143. The First Texas Conference on Problems of Linguistic Analysis in
English. Austin: The University of Texas Press (1962), iv + 162 pp.
Contains number 85.

144. The Second Texas Conference on Problems of Linguistic Analysis
in English. Austin: The University of Texas Press (1962), ii + 162 pp.

145. The Third Texas Conference on Problems of Linguistic Analysis in
English. Austin: The University of Texas Press (1962), iv + 186 pp.

146. Linguistics today. New York: Basic Books (1969), xii + 291 pp.
     The book stems from 25 lectures broadcast by the Voice of America
     in its Forum series. It is available overseas under the title Lin-
     guistics, Voice of America Forum Lectures (1969), 317 pp.
     Contains numbers 115 and 116.
147. Studies in language, literature and culture of the Middle Ages and
     later. A volume in honor of Rudolph Willard, edited jointly with
     E. Bagby Atwood. Austin: The University of Texas Press (1969),
     viii + 398 pp.
     Contains number 100 B.

FIFTY YEARS OF ENGLISH:
FROM COMMA TO FULL STOP

ARCHIBALD A. HILL

An Address to the Convocation of the College of Humanities,
The University of Texas, on May 20, 1972

Very nearly half a century ago, as a bewildered, eager, and very nervous
Teaching Assistant, I stood before my first class, one in Freshman
Composition, of course. I had been trained for the mysteries of the
Composition Handbook by seminar-level courses in the Elizabethan
Drama, Old English, Chaucer, and one course regarded as practically
the same thing as contemporary literature – a course in 18th century
prose. All were excellent courses, and even in this year of 1972 I am glad
for what I learned in them. But no one told me and my fellow TAs what
we were supposed to teach our Freshmen, so that we were left to rely on
the common folk-beliefs of the day. Most of us supposed that we were
to protect the English language from the inroads of change and ignorance,
and to see that our students were able to spell and punctuate at least
as accurately as Noah Webster. There was, however, a contrary body
of opinion that held that the teacher of composition was to guide his
students in logical thinking, and see to it that they became good citizens.
Since the holders of the two opinions could scarcely communicate with
each other (not a very encouraging indication of success for composition
courses) we TAs were left severely to ourselves, with no direction at all. I
remember a myth that was circulated among us, which accurately pictures
how lost we were. One of us was supposed to have had such an attack
of stage-fright in his first class, that he could not recall the word comma.
He met the crisis by drawing a picture on the board, and waiting for one
of the Freshmen to supply the missing word. I am afraid that the situation
was not much clearer for all of you when you were Freshmen, nor will it
be much clearer for those of you who begin teaching next Fall. I know,
of course, that here at Texas as well as elsewhere, many devoted colleagues
have labored to bring about improvement, but somehow it does not
come.

The belief that the English language has to be protected from its users is still flourishing, and those who pronounce a phrase like 'cup of coffee' with only a vowel to represent the preposition are condemned as not merely lazy, but to use a phrase I have seen recently, are accused of committing 'linguistic pollution'. Without wishing to sound too much like a characteristically permissive linguist, I can at least point out that dropping the consonant in the particle *of* before a word beginning with a consonant, is to apply the same rule that covers the variation between the two forms of the indefinite article. Dropping the consonant from *of* is not laziness, but unconscious regularization.

The advocates of logical thinking and good citizenship are certainly still with us, and are now in a more commanding position than they were before. Nowadays straight thinking and good citizenship are commonly identified with desire for social change. In fact, many of our teachers are so insistent on social awareness, that it seems to me they believe that the way to teach any English course is to pour a cupful of hot politics over a spoonful of freeze-dried emotion, and thus get instant relevance. Furthermore, the extreme liberals of composition now often hold that to teach what we used to regard as 'correctness' is to use a dominant dialect as a means of keeping the minorities under. If, for instance, Black English employs two deviant sentences, one in the shape 'he be sick' and the other in the shape 'he sick' with differing meaning, where the dominant dialect has only 'he's sick,' dialectologists now point out to us that Black grammar makes a useful distinction which White grammar does not make. I think it is necessary to agree with dialect students at least to the point of saying that it is wrong to judge either the intelligence or the moral character of anyone by the dialect he uses. We ought to remember that good style and clear communication can occur in any dialect. Teaching correctness should surely be limited to helping students to understand the forms and distinctions of formal English, not towards eradicating the forms and distinctions that all of us use in relaxed and easy speech.

The situation today is complicated by a new body of opinion, one that holds that teaching composition is useless, and that individuals achieve a good style (if they do) only by growing older. The holders of this view believe that learning to write is a process of 'cognitive maturation', to use the currently fashionable jargon. Any such statement is surely a counsel of despair. If there is any truth in it, the teacher of composition ought to be able to prevent any interference with the process of cognitive ripening. Yet there is some evidence that writing skills grow worse with the passage of time. There is a recent and impressive survey of writing skills in various age groups, and probably the most discouraging statistic yet turned up is that adults punctuate worse than do seventeen-year-olds. If the adult group has been exposed to more composition teaching than the youngsters, we can only say that the teaching has been counter-productive.

If I have watched the confusion in composition teaching, and shared in it, perhaps I can be pardoned an attempt to describe a way of handling the problems of composition which might, just possibly, be better than the past in which I have shared. I should want to see the Freshman composition course set for itself a limited and reachable goal, and then insure that the goal is reached in as short a space of time as possible. It seems to me clear that the primary goal for a composition course is set by the fact that Freshmen have entered into the process of college education, a process which takes four years if they are successful in staying in it. That is, a Freshman must either have or acquire the kind of skill in writing which will enable him to pass his later courses. If bad spelling and punctuation interfere with passing later courses, spelling and punctuation must be improved. If bad logic interferes, bad logic must be improved. I suspect, however, that bad spelling and bad punctuation are more important than bad logic, since I am afraid that many of us senior establishment academicians might not always recognize bad logic with the same ease that we can recognize bad spelling and punctuation. In short, I believe strongly that the primary aim of Freshman composition is to impart a skill in communication needed for academic work. It is not to purify the language, to eradicate dialect, or to create literary artists. There is, however, a second aim which probably has more long-range importance. The student should be shown something about how to construct complex sentences out of the simple noun-verb-noun sentences we all use in conversation. The more complex sentences are those which have aesthetic qualities of various kinds, and ability to construct them is therefore a necessary preliminary to appreciating the style of our great works of literature. These are, I believe, reasonable and limited aims for a first course in composition, and I also think that if colleges limited the aims to these, they could be reached within the space of a single semester, leaving later English courses for profitable and intelligent study of literature, with all its values for members of our culture. As the study of literature goes on in these later courses, the student's ability to write should deepen and be enriched. He should be given the task of writing about what he reads (as he is now), and by this process of reading and writing, his abilities and his whole personality should continue to mature.

If such limited goals are accepted, what is the process by which they can be reached? I think it is a multiple one. The first stage is the presentation of a body of rules that have to be explained, and then drilled until they are fully internalized. These are the rules of spelling and punctuation – what are usually called the mechanics of composition. This process of explanation and drill should be much like instruction in a foreign language, though there are also important differences. The resemblance to foreign language instruction is in the fact that the instruction is in easy stages which lead each student almost inevitably to the right answer. No student advances from one application of a rule to another unless he has given the right answer, and before the instruction ends, every student should have given right answers to everything presented to him. This kind of instruction in establishing a habituated skill differs from instruction in any kind of problem solving. In problem solving, not all students are equally successful, and grades are given as a measure of differing success. In the spelling and punctuation type of drill, no grades beyond pass and fail should be given, and no student should be given a pass unless he has acquired the skill perfectly.

The first rules for drilling are those of spelling, and a successful presentation requires that the instructor have a clear comprehension of the problems involved. There are several kinds of difficulties in English spelling, a system that I like to call the second worst in the civilized world, exceeded only by the multiple writing systems of Japanese. One difficulty is that we spell every word as if it were pronounced loudly and firmly all alone, not at all as words are pronounced in connected speech. That is, if there is a simple phrase like *cold day*, we spell *cold* with a final *d* though when the phrase is pronounced there is only one *d*, which occurs in the initial position of the noun *day*. A second difficulty is that we use so-called 'silent letters' in a partially systematic fashion to indicate pronunciation. One rule is that a single consonant followed by a vowel, whether pronounced or not, indicates that the vowel before the consonant is long. Thus the adding of a 'silent *e*' to the sequence *writ* changes the pronunciation from /rit/ to /rayt/. A doubled consonant or a single final consonant indicate a short vowel, as in *written*, or *writ* just cited. The system might not be a bad one if carried out rigorously, but unfortunately there are many exceptions, like the short vowel of some three syllable words, for instance the /æ/ sounds of *national*, and *rational*, where by the general rule we should expect /ey/ *nātional* and *rātional*, as in *rationing*. A third difficulty in our spelling system can be illustrated by the words *system* and *atom*. The pronunciation of the second syllable of each is exactly alike, so that pronunciation is no guide to the occurrence of *e* in the first word, and *o* in the second. Both words can be modified by addition of the ending *-ic*, and when this is done, the pronunciations become *sysTEMic* and *aTOMic*, with differing vowel sounds which justify the spelling. The spelling of the base forms of the words has the somewhat dubious value of predicting how the words will be pronounced when *-ic* is added.

But the last and greatest difficulty in English spelling is that we have many alternate spellings for the same sound or sequence of sounds, and these alternate spellings are semantically distributed. For instance, the syllable /sayt/ has three spellings, *sight*, *site*, and *cite*. The syllable /ber/ has two, *bear* and *bare*. These various spellings identify the word as that appropriate to a given sentence, as in 'a sight for sore eyes', or 'a fine site for a building'.

The spelling drills should be progressive, with very simple rules, like the childhood '*i* before *e* except after *c*' as the first stage. Rules governing the spelling of vowel length might be next, with drill on the correspondence between semantic identity and spelling last of all. The spelling drill can not hope to cover all the variant spellings there are for the same structure of sounds, since to do so would be a practically endless task. What the drill should do is acquaint the student with the alternative spellings, and the principle of semantic distribution. That is, if a student hears a syllable like /meyd/ he should know the possibilities, and sort them out properly in each of the phrases 'well made', and 'old maid'.

Punctuation, also, can and should be drilled in much the same way as spelling, though in terms of sentences, of course, instead of isolated forms. There is an unfortunate dispute over whether punctuation can be taught by ear alone, logic alone, or both. In my experience, at least, if the drill is designed so as to avoid patterns of pitch and pause which are ambiguous, punctuation instruction works best if the marks are put in by ear. I have never heard of a group of native speakers of English (of no matter what dialect) who did not recognize that the two following utterances are different, and that one of them should contain a comma:

> We'll call him Arthur.
> We'll call him, Arthur.

An even more striking pair, where there is difference in spelling as well as punctuation in accord with pitch and pause, is

I don't know.
I don't. No.

I pass over the booby-traps of restrictive and non-restrictive clauses with a general comment and discussion of one example. The general comment is that teachers, in trying to teach this distinction by ear have often chosen ambiguous pitch and pause patterns. Suppose the sentence given for punctuation is the following, in which there is only a slight pause after *houses*, and after *brick*, and no pitch modification is given:

The houses / which were of brick / were sold.

Whenever I have tried such sentences on groups of native speakers, some interpreted the sentence to mean that all the houses were of brick and all were sold, others understood that only some of the houses were of brick, and only these were sold. If the sentence is given with the final pitch fall and long pause which marks most sentence ends, and these final markers are placed after *houses* and *brick*, then the meaning is clear:

The houses # which were of brick # were sold.

A native jury always says that all the houses were of brick, and all were sold. It is a minor, but still vexatious, detail that we can not punctuate this second sentence with some relatively stronger mark than a comma, which so often marks merely minor breaks.

The types of instruction that I have been describing are often called remedial, in that in an ideal situation students could be expected to have mastered these skills before coming to college. I doubt, however, if that supposition was ever accurate. It certainly was not true of my college mates, and the survey of writing skills I have mentioned above suggests that it is not true today. But of course, there are always Freshmen who have good practice in writing and who need no such instruction as this. As is always done, such Freshmen should be excused the drill practice, and be allowed to go on to more advanced work. There is a second stage of instruction something like the drill in spelling and punctuation, but certainly more advanced. This is drill in sentence combining, and construction of complex sentences out of the simple kernel of noun-verb-noun-adverb types. It seems to me reasonably certain that there are many students who need drill here, even though their spelling and punctuation are perfect. As an instance of failure in sentence combination I can use a commercial recently heard on the air:

We have tried TO, and succeeded IN, getting the best quality.

The sentence is clear enough, but the fact that the deleted form is *get* in the first half, instead of the *getting* that occurs in the second half, makes the sentence awkward in the extreme. The same principle of combination and deletion is what is responsible for the only dangling modifier which I ever found in student compositions, that seemed to me genuinely funny. It was

This factory is five miles beyond Lynchburg, going south.

This section of the course is obviously much the same as what used to be called 'rhetoric'. In it should go practice in producing patterns characterized by various forms of ornamentation, such as repeated vowel and consonant patterns, even rhythmic patterns like Kipling's once famous

"Not always was the Kangaroo as now we do behold him, but a different animal with four short legs."

A single example of sentence combination and construction will serve to illustrate how simple sentences can be reworked. The stylistic effect sought is that of balance, and starts with the following sentences about pagan Rome:

"Various modes of worship prevailed in the Roman world. The people considered them true. The philosopher considered them false. The magistrate considered them useful. They were all equal in these respects."

From some such set of simple sentences, Gibbon constructed his famous sentence of the second chapter of *The Decline and Fall*:

"The various modes of worship which prevailed in the Roman world, were all considered by the people, as equally true; by the philosopher, as equally false; and by the magistrate, as equally useful."

Other types of sentence structure could be explained and imitated like the simple linking style of Hemingway or the parenthetical style of James. Paragraphs could be presented for study on the basis of redundancy, of concreteness, of emotionally loaded vocabulary, and so on.

It is above all necessary, in this stage of instruction, that the students be given constant practice, under constant guidance. If the practice and guidance are actually given, it seems to me inevitable that the student would emerge with a feeling for style, as well as mastery of mere correctness. He should in consequence be prepared for reading literature in greater depth than merely for content alone, or to see what happens to the heroine.

It is time to end this description of a Freshman Composition course at the University of Utopia with some description of the teaching methods and devices that could be used. For all the drill in mechanics, the devices are already available. The drill would be given by teaching machines, in which taped material is heard by the student, and the student is required to produce a written answer, which the machine then immediately corrects. If the word is spelled correctly, or the comma in the right place, the student goes on to the next item. If his response is not correct, he goes back again and tries it over. The machine is meant to give him explanation, response, and constant reinforcement for all correct responses. However, it is the devices for the second phase of the course which are more interesting to me, and which do not exist as yet, at least in entirety. What I should wish for this phase of instruction is first of all a projector sufficiently bright so that it could be used without darkening the room, and into which the student's actual paper could be put, without previous copying onto a transparency. In other words, what I want is projection of the paper with all its misspellings, blots, erasures, whatever occurred in it. The paper could then be flashed onto a permanent, smooth, and hard white screen at the front of the classroom. As the paper is on the screen, the instructor writes corrections on the white board, so that the student sees the correction immediately and fully, without waiting until the paper has been corrected by a reader, read over by the instructor, and a consultation arranged.

Utopia? No, not quite. It is what could be accomplished if we decide on what we want, and work to get it. I know of one great American University which has given up required Freshman English in despair. I would hope that we would avoid the scylla of exploitation of Teaching Assistants, and the charybdis of despairing abandonment, by setting up a course which can reach a limited but attainable goal, and leaves time for the goal which I think we all agree is most important: the study, understanding, and appreciation of literature.

STRUTTURE FORMALI
E STRUTTURE SEMANTICHE
NELLA COMPARAZIONE LINGUISTICA

RICCARDO AMBROSINI

1. Delle fasi ricostruite delle lingue – ed è ovvio che, cosí dicendo, mi riferisco in particolare alla ricostruzione delle lingue indo-europee – ritengo che, a volte, ci si possa chiamare fortunati se, tramite l'indagine comparativa, si raggiunge una certa struttura formale, di cui, però, il comparatista dovrebbe essere consapevole che, oltre che oggettivamente parziale e metodologicamente convenzionale, è soprattutto scarsamente pertinente. Per lo piú, infatti, sono stati confrontati elementi simili tra loro, presupponendo che la somiglianza formale fosse indizio di altre, ben piú remote, importanti e veritiere somiglianze, mentre è ormai ovvio che nel rapporto tra organizzazione strutturante (per cosí dire, profonda) e singoli elementi strutturati la individualità di questi ultimi è in funzione della prima, perché il sistema precede gli elementi onde è composto, e questi non sarebbero quello che sono in un sistema diverso da quello che li accoglie. Sicché la somiglianza sia di forme particolari sia delle cosiddette "categorie" è sovente illusoria, a meno che la si inserisca in un quadro generale di funzioni, e il confronto tra quelle è tanto superficiale quanto quello di chi paragonasse tra loro tessere eguali di mosaici diversi.

Ciò che generalmente è sfuggito all'indagine ricostruttiva è stata l'attenzione per quelli che si potrebbero, appunto, chiamare "nessi strutturanti di elementi strutturali". Si è detto, è vero, che dell'indo-europeo ricostruito sarebbe stato necessario studiare la sintassi: ma, tranne in pochi e ben noti casi illuminanti e illuminati, non mi sembra che si sia andati al di là di buoni proposti. D'altronde, nella stessa formulazione del tema ("Si studi la sintassi dell'indo-europeo") si celava un equivoco, se non un'aporia sostanziale: cosa si intendesse per sintassi, dato che, ancora, non erano stati recepiti a sufficienza i princìpi, sui quali oggi tanto si discute, della morfonologia e, in genere, i rapporti tra intenzione-organizzazione espressiva e forma.

1.1 La crise dell'indo-europeistica – oggi difficilmente negabile se non da parte di chi preferisca immaginare che vedere la realtà – trae la sua origine da ciò, non certamente dal presunto grado di saturazione del conoscibile: ché il conoscibile è in funzione delle forme e delle modalità della conoscenza e non viceversa, l'ipotesi teorica precedendo la scoperta bruta e dando a questa un senso.

Si tratterebbe di chiedersi, anzitutto, quale funzione abbiano talune 'categorie' (ad es., i casi del nome, i modi e i tempi del verbo) e se di queste si possa veramente cosituire una serie di archetipi, e secondo quale gerarchia. Che ciò, pur in una prassi diversa, non si discosti radicalmente da concezioni generativo-trasformazionali, forse non sarà da alcuni ritenuto elemento positivo: è tuttavia probabile, oltre che degno di attenzione, il fatto che ciò ne sarebbe – come forse ne è stata – una verifica fattuale.[1] E' chiaro che una buona parte dei problemi tradizionali dell'indo-europeistica si troverebbe di nuovo sul tavolo, per essere vagliata nella stessa validità dei problemi, oltre che nelle soluzioni sinora offerte che, come avviene negli spostamenti metodologici, rischierebbero di essere ritenute non soluzioni ma disorganici e provvisori approcci. Eppure, nonostante le apparenze di astrazione contenute in queste proposte, ritengo che da una metodologia organico-funzionale verrebbe in primo luogo confortata l'esigenza di concretezza storica e di aderenza al documento che la comparazione tradizionale, generalmente astratta e formalistica,[2] ha preteso di nutrire, mentre, in realtà, ne è stata sovente estranea. Si parlerà ancora di remoti popoli, di queste incognite etniche, spesso sconosciute nelle loro dimensioni numeriche e socio-culturali, cui è stato attribuito l'uso di lingue trasmesse da serie limitate e parziali di documenti? Si preferirà, invece, trattare del rapporto tra testo e contesto, pur nei limiti della determinazione storica del secondo, e anche se in molte circostante lo strumento e l'oggetto dell'analisi necessariamente si identificheranno tra loro, l'analizzatore, non potendo analizzare altro che il documento linguistico, sarà tuttavia consapevole della duplice dimensione di ciò che sta studiando, del testo – cioè – come processo. Cadranno, forse, numerosi idoli, ma si comprenderà finalmente l'incongruenza di imporre certe determinate coordinate semantiche a determinate forme in base ad una presunta conoscenza di 'realia': magia, tabú, eufemismo acquisteranno un rilievo particolare, concreto, e non saranno soltanto un comodo ripostiglio di dubbi non risolti. Anzitutto, però, si dovranno affrontare problemi di carattere funzionale, pur cercando di evitare le pericolosissime secche della questione del primato ontologico della semantica o della sintassi e di non affrontare direttamente un problema teorico di cui, tuttavia, si terrà presente l'importanza. Ottimisticamente, si potrebbe persino dire che anche questo problema potrebbe essere risolto con i modi di indagine che qui si prospettano[3]: anche se non risolto, su questa base il problema potrebbe trovare un'esemplificazione almeno utile, se non sempre completa e persuasiva.

1.2 Pur dando come presupposta la parzialità – e spesso la frammentarietà – della documentazione, che costringe il corretto indagatore a non parlare, ad es., genericamente di greco, ma di lingua dell'epica, della lirica, della prosa greca, per ogni forma analizzata è necessario definirne la funzione[4] all'interno del singolo sistema in cui è attestata, e controllare se ed entro quali limiti tale funzione si ripresenta in forme superficialmente comparabili di altre tradizioni linguistiche; si può dare il caso che a funzioni analoghe corrispondano forme diverse.

1.2.1 Come funzione si intenderà il rapporto tra una categoria della lingua in questione – anch'essa, ovviamente, funzione di una serie ulteriore di categorie – e lo specifico ruolo ricoperto, in questo àmbito, dalla forma studiata. Ad es., se si stabilisce che l'accordo tra soggetto e predicato è una categoria ed esso si realizza diversamente in greco, in latino e nelle lingue nordiche, non tanto andranno ricercati i motivi delle differenze, le categorie non essendo che aprioristicamente le stesse, quanto le possibilità strutturali di queste; cioè, pur attribuendo la categoria 'accordo' ad una sibillina e semanticamente anodina struttura profonda, ci si dovrà chiedere quali condizioni semantiche concrete abbiano permesso determinate trasformazioni sintattiche, quali modificatori si debbano supporre nell'àmbito di determinati nuclei. Che questo complesso modello definitorio-processuale si colga anche con lo studio delle stratificazioni e delle analisi di cronologia relativa, può darsi: ma l'indagine 'tradizionale' non può valere che come mezzo da sottoporre a verifica preventiva. Proprio in ciò si rivela la crisi della validità stessa di alcune ricerche, oltre a quella di un metodo che ha creduto di superare con la perizia e gli accorgimenti tecnici problemi ben più gravi, collegati con l'esigenza di concretezza in analisi sintattica e semantica.

1.3 Dovendosi procedere dalla constatazione di variabili – perché le forme confrontate altro non sono, se le si considerano come proiezioni particolari di una struttura profonda –, le costanti si dovranno attribuire a quest'ultima, ma per evitare i rischi di una concezione esclusivamente logica, da un lato, e scarsamente organica, dall'altro, si dovrà anche usufruire delle proposte metodologiche della tipologia linguistica[5]. In sostanza, si dovranno prospettare le possibilità di serie di combinazioni, e queste accogliere nel modello trasformazionale, non come astrazioni dedotte dalla riduzione all'unitario di ciò che è fenomenicamente diverso, bensí come schemi operativi, presenti – o meglio, immanenti – nei fenomeni linguistici analizzati.

1.3.1 Ciò che qui si propone è, pertanto, l'utilizzazione trasformazionale di un modello ricostruito, con particolare riferimento alla morfologia e alla sua valutazione non formale ma sintattica: di organizzazione sintattica, in sede di ricostruzione, non si può parlare in assoluto, perché non è dato averne una competenza tale che si proietti in esecuzione, ma soltanto una competenza scientifico-probabilistica.

1.4 Implicito in queste proposte è il trasferimento della indagine dal livello fenomenico a quello della produzione dei fenomeni stessi: siamo però consapevoli della complessità estrema di questo punto, che ingloba l'analisi formale in altre analisi, tra cui principalmente quella stilistica, e che non permette di studiare separatamente la lingua come comunicazione e come espressione. Tuttavia, se sulle motivazioni delle eguaglianze e delle differenze non si possono fare che ipotesi, sulle loro modalità si possono, invece, presentare analisi fornite di sufficiente evidenza; a sua volta, l'analisi comparativa di queste modalità potrà gettare lumi sulle loro cause.

2. Come esempio dei problemi sollevati dalle osservazioni precedenti si tratterà del cosiddetto 'infinito'.

La somiglianza tra le forme che si definiscono di 'infinito' è affatto incompleta, tant'è vero che, notoriamente, l''infinito' è stato considerato un caso limite del procedimento comparativo: mentre si può ricostruire un nominativo singolare in *-s ed un accusativo singolare in *-m, ed una forma di terza persona singolare uscente in *-t (i), dell'infinito non si riesce a dare una formula di struttura omogenea. Anche presupponendo un'identificazione attraverso il tempo tra nome di azione (o nome verbale) e infinito propriamente detto, rimangono insoluti i problemi della suffissazione prevalentemente difforme, della scelta del tema – del presente e/o di altri tempi – e la generale incertezza – tranne nel vedico – sui rapporti con i sistemi casuali delle lingue rispettive.

Le spiegazioni della sostanziale eterogeneità formale dell'infinito sono diverse: l'infinito, non come categoria ma come forma, può essersi formato in sedi diverse o può aver rinnovato in queste una struttura che, casualmente, una lingua può aver conservato, senza peraltro che un tale tratto arcaico si imponga con peculiare rilievo. Effettivamente, se ripercorriamo la storia di alcune lingue, ci avvediamo che il rinnovamento formale è stato notevole: ad es., la prosa greca del V-IV sec. a.C. ha rinunciato alle forme uscenti in -μεναι, -μεν, che invece fiorivano nella lingua dell'epica e della lirica (anche se, in questa, in misura minore e tramite quella) accanto a quelle in -ειν, rimaste vitali; le forme latine in -*ier* sono un fossile della poesia epica, sopraffatte da quelle in -*ī*; il sanscrito classico ha ridotto ad una, forse in relazione ad una riduzione generale delle sfumature semantiche collegate esplicitamente con opposizioni morfo-sintattiche, la ricca serie di infiniti vedici; le lingue romanze non recano traccia dell'infinito perfetto latino, sebbene – sia pure con funzioni anche diverse da quelle originarie – del sistema del perfetto abbiano conservato l'indicativo perfetto (in misura ridotta, anche il piuccheperfetto) e il congiuntivo piuccheperfetto, sicché, se non possedessimo il latino, non potremmo attribuirgli un infinito perfetto, ma soltanto quello presente: si trascura qui di considerare l'infinito futuro latino che – diversamente, ad es., dalle condizioni del futuro greco – con la flessione del futuro indicativo non ha nulla a che vedere, ma si allinea con la cosiddetta coniugazione perifrastica e, in certo modo, con la struttura perifrastica del futuro sanscrito – non vedico – in *nomen agentis* in -*tā* (/-tar/) + *asmi*. La veste dell'infinito germanico si distingue affatto da quella dell'infinito slavo che, invece, ha qualche analogia con l'infinito tocario.[6] E' certamente difficile ricostruire una forma funzionale che vada al di là del confronto tra due lingue, ove può essere rimasta come una conchiglia fossile travolta dal sommovimento degli strati; ma che dire della corrispondenza funzionale? Nel miglior dei casi, si tratta di un parallelismo nell'utilizzazione anche nominale di un tema ben più diffuso e comparabile nella flessione verbale: se la formula *esmi* si può ricuperare alla base di quasi tutte le forme di lingue indo-europee di prima persona singolare del verbo *essere*, dell'infinito di *es-* non esiste una formula comune, neppure nel grado radicale, normale in latino, *es-se*, in greco, *es-men(ai)*, *es-nai*, ma ridotto negli antenati del ted. mod. *sein*.

3.1 Quanto ai rapporti presumibili tra questa forma nominale del verbo ed altri temi nominali – i cosiddetti nomi verbali e astratti –, essi variano moltissimo tra lingua e lingua, come, d'altronde, varia l'uso delle forme infinite del verbo. Sintagmi come l'italiano *al sorgere* e *al calar del sole, col passar del tempo, con l'andar degli anni*, indubbiamente confrontabili con sintagmi francesi (cfr. *le coucher du soleil*) e inquadrabili nell'àmbito di fenomeni neoromanzi – e, come tali, da studiare in una particolare motivazione sociologica e culturale –, rivelano una sensibilità per l'aspetto verbale, che non è messa altrettanto in rilievo da forme sinonimiche e sintagmi omosemantici, formati con sostantivi astratti: ché mentre *all'alba* e *al tramonto, col tempo, con gli anni* indicano dei punti o dei periodi nel tempo, anche se connotativamente implicano una nozione di durata, i sintagmi con l'infinito sopra ricordati indicano, invece, un processo, una continuità esplicitamente denotata. Ma come interpretare funzionalmente questi infiniti? Che il fenomeno sia antico, possono dimostrare attestazioni dantesche,[7] nelle quali l'uso degli infiniti rivela il senso di una continuità che non sarebbe espressa da nomi astratti sinonimici – i quali, oltre tutto, non sempre ci sono. Inversamente, nell'uso dell'inifinito tedesco preceduto da articolo (*das Sein, das Werden der Menschen, das Wesen*), la funzione dell'infinito è più quella di un sostantivo astratto che di forma del verbo. Da ciò si può desumere che nell'equivalenza teorica tra 'nome verbale' e 'infinito', si deve fare attenzione a dove batte l'accento, se su 'nome' o su 'verbale', e poi valutare la funzione, tutto compreso più semantica che sintattica, dell'infinito.

3.2 Ma su un piano comparativo assoluto, indipendentemente dalle relazioni cronologiche (praticamente eluse, d'altronde, nella prassi indo-europeistica, quando si confronta una tradizione come l'ittita con quella lituana, con un salto di quasi tremila anni), il confronto tra le funzioni che l'infinito ha in italiano in sintagmi affini a questi e l'uso dell'infinito in greco, in latino, in indiano antico è insostenibile; semmai, in alcune fasi di queste lingue (specialmente di greco e indiano antico), si constata in costrutti di tal valore l'uso preferenziale del participio. Si tratta, quindi, in primo luogo di definire le funzioni sintattiche e i parametri semantici in cui possono entrare quegli infiniti. Anche l'inglese distingue, notoriamente, tra l'uso di forme uscenti in -*ing* e infinito, e alcuni degli esempi italiani di cui sopra potrebbero trovare il loro corrispondente in sintagmi inglesi con NV (-*ing*) + SN.[8] Ma se il chiedersi i motivi delle differenze sposta il problema verso considerazioni più semantiche che sintattiche, ed insieme storicizza la questione, ciò non deve considerarsi se non un aspetto del problema: nel passaggio dalla comparazione alla ricostruzione non ci dovremmo, infatti, trovar di fronte ad una comparabilità approssimativa, anche se formalmente appariscente, ma ad una effettiva, anche se non totale, sovrapponibilità teorico-funzionale. Si giungerà così a concludere che la base della comparazione non è data dalla somiglianza della struttura formale ma da quella semantica, intendendo questa come il parametro della utilizzabilità funzionale di dati morfemi in determinati contesti sintattici. Da ciò si deduce che la comparazione dovrebbe concepirsi in ordine gerarchico, dalle funzioni alle forme e non viceversa. Che in uno schema di corrispondenze funzionali rientrino immediatamente talune desinenze (del nom.sg., dell'acc. sg., ad es., come sopra si è accennato), è ovvio; ma è ovvio anche che in una serie gerarchica queste categorie dovrebbero occupare i livelli più alti, in quanto su esse si fondano numerosissime altre relazioni.

4. Paradossalmente ci si potrebbe anche chiedere se è legittima, e se ha un senso, la comparazione stessa, se non come accertamento di differenze. Orbene, se queste differenze fossero varie epifanie di un processo unitario – ad es., se le varie forme di infinito rivelassero un comune concetto categoriale –, la comparazione, e la ricostruzione che ne segue, avrebbe veramente un senso, e forse avrebbe ancor più senso di un confronto tra forme simili appartenenti a organizzazioni categoriali diverse. Se però i termini in questione risultano refrattari ad un collegamento funzionale, la comparazione stessa cade e, per tornare al nostro esempio, dell'infinito si può soltanto constatare che è concepibile, in base a nostri schemi pregiudiziali e a certi nostri usi di interpretazione grammaticale, come forma non finita del verbo: il che, in verità, è assai poco.

4.1 Ma ancora: se l'infinito greco è declinabile, l'utilizzazione ne è in qualche modo comparabile con quella dell'infinito e del gerundio latino? Ma al rapporto tra gerundio e gerundivo latino, cosa corrisponde in greco? Le strutture formali e quelle semantiche, in questo caso, si escludono a tal punto che in latino non si può rendere con un infinito il gr. καλὸς ἰδεῖν e in greco non si può dire con mezzi formali affini a quelli latini *viri legibus scribundis creati*. Inoltre, anche se si tenta di confrontare il -*se* degli infiniti latini con *-ε-σεν degli infiniti greci (ammettendo per valida l'ipotesi e non ritenendola un frutto del tentativo esasperato di ridurre all'unità due realtà diverse),[9] la stessa distribuzione formale dei due suffissi e l'uso delle forme che rispettivamente ne risultano, discordano totalmente tra loro.

4.2 Eppure, sinché è possibile, è legittimo rintracciare eventuali corrispondenze. Dove trovarle, nel caso dell'infinito? Secondo J. Kuryłowicz[10], in tal caso esse sarebbero offerte dalla cosiddetta frase oggettiva. Anche qui si dovrà tuttavia tentare di fissare i limiti dell'uso: in greco le costruzioni predicative con il participio sono notoriamente più diffuse che in latino, e la coincidenza più forte non si noterà nella frase oggettiva propriamente detta (ove il greco può avere ὅτι + modi finiti e non richiede il soggetto espresso), quanto nella dipendenza di 'infiniti' da 'verbi modali' (volō/ βούλομαι, possum/δύναμαι), pur con le differenze di campi semantici che contraddistinguono anche questi verbi. La concordanza di fondo è da cogliere, però, nel fatto che una forma nominale può reggere un complemento, e particolarmente un accusativo (in questo caso, le condizioni del latino classico sono diverse da quelle del latino arcaico, ove era usabile un *procuratio rem*, con un sostantivo suffissato in *-tiōn-, cioè in una coppia di suffissi conglobata, *-ti-, confrontabile con suffissi slavi di infinito, e *-ōn-, confrontabile con suffissi germanici di infinito). La struttura profonda comune è data dalla riduzione nominalistica di una frase, in quanto la frase trasformata conserva le caratteristiche verbali della frase da trasformare e riduce – o, come in latino, trasforma – taluni elementi pronominali della proposizione trasformata. Se l'uso dell'infinito, in questi casi, può simboleggiarsi come:

$$\{SN + Vmodale\} + \{SN + V(\pm SN')\},$$

ove SN sia eguale a se stesso ma diverso da SN',

$$\rightarrow \{SN + Vmodale + Vinf (\pm SN')\},$$

d'altra parte si deve tener presente la regola per cui:

$$\{SN + V(\pm SN')\} \rightarrow \{Vinf (\pm SN')\} \text{ dopo verbo modale.}$$

L'utilizzazione di HABEŌ come verbo modale (solo parzialmente di VOLŌ) nella formazione del futuro e del condizionale nella maggior parte delle lingue romanze, dimostra che il processo sopra teorizzato non soltanto è esemplificabile, ma si è effettivamente sviluppato attraverso il tempo: nell'it. *leggerò il libro* (o nel fr. *je lirai le livre*), *il libro* (o *le livre*) continua ad essere complemento di /legger-/ (o di /lir-/), trasformato da Vinf a semantema verbale, perché altrimenti si assisterebbe al contrasto tra *vengo* (o *je viens*) intransitivo al presente e *verrò* (o *je viendrai*) transitivo al futuro, perché *ho* (*j'ai*) è transitivo (cfr. *io ho un libro, j'ai un livre*).

4.3 A proposito di quest'esempio occorre, tuttavia, chiedersi perché una determinata forma sia potuta entrare a far parte di una perifrasi, e cercare la motivazione della somiglianza tra questo fenomeno romanzo con quello che si osserva nelle lingue germaniche. Indubbiamente è facile alludere ad una tendenza comune, ad uno sviluppo parallelo, e, nel caso di infiniti gotici seguiti da *haban*, anche ad un contatto linguistico, se non ad un prestito.[11] Però il motivo fondamentale, formalizzabile in una struttura generativa profonda,[12] fornita di particolari possibilità trasformazionali, è da cercare nella funzione sintattica di un 'infinito', neoromanzo da un lato e germanico dall'altro, proiettato nelle perifrasi in cui è documentato e fornito delle funzioni cui queste hanno adempiuto – e che, prima che si compiesse questo processo formale, forse neppure esistevano, almeno nelle connotazioni semantiche di certi valori sintattici.

E' chiaro, infatti, che se non possiamo fare a meno di tradurre ed interpretare con schemi nostri – e quindi, secondo la nostra competenza – un determinato fenomeno, dobbiamo fare ogni sforzo per recuperare un'organizzazione semantica che pur tende a sfuggirci. Per questo, appunto, oltre a spesso fallaci strutture formali si debbono recuperare, nella comparazione sì da renderle esplicite nella formalizzazione della ricostruzione, ben più complesse strutture del significato, desumendo da ciò che è eguale e diverso, comune e specifico, una gerarchia di organizzazioni, di nessi strutturanti che, a ben vedere, sono l'unica realtà procedurale che meriti di essere studiata e, se possibile, raggiunta.

Università di Pisa

NOTE

[1]   Come ho fatto notare recentemente (Ambrosini 1970:346), nelle mie "Concordanze nella struttura formale delle categorie verbali indo-europee" (Ambrosini 1962:33-7 e 36, fn. 9) mi riferivo all'applicabilità di criteri trasformazionali nell'àmbito di problemi linguistici indo-europei. Rapporti tra l'opera di J. Kuryłowicz e la grammatica trasformazionale sono stati notati anche da E. Coseriu (1968:275, fn.3), mentre dei rapporti tra linguistica storica e grammatica generativa si interessano un recente libro di R. D. King (1969), dedicato in buona parte a problemi fonologici (di *Transformational Syntax in Historical Problems* trattano soltanto le pp. 150-3, in cui si tiene particolarmente presente un lavoro di P. Kiparsky (1968)), uno di R. Katičić (1970), che ammette: "We can say but little about syntactic correspondences in comparative linguistics" (90), pur precisando *(ib.)* che "In recent time very interesting and stimulating results have been achieved in comparative syntax especially on the basis of Anatolian data" e riferendosi ad una ricerca di V. V. Ivanov (1965), e uno di N. E. Collinge (1970:102-27, 157ss).

[2]   Sull'ipotesi che "comparative linguistics not only presupposes description but also contributes very substantially to its completion by stating the interrelationships of the data obtained by the description of single languages", sicché "comparative research is not in kind and scope from descriptive linguistics", cfr. R. Katičić (1970:99). In questo àmbito anche la tanto discussa ipotesi delle laringali acquista una giusta dimensione di accettabilità; si veda, oltre a E. Polomé (in W. Winter 1965:1-65), N. E. Collinge (1970:97 e 67-97).

[3]   V. 1.2., 1.2.1., 1.3. et 1.3.1.

[4]   V. 1.2.1.

[5]   Cfr. R. Katičić (1970: 113).

[6]   Cfr. R. Ambrosini (1962:46-7, fn. 40).

[7]   Oltre a *Purgatorio* i.115-6 *di lontano / conobbi il tremolar de la marina,* si ricordi

il movimentato inizio del son.lxi delle *Rime, Sonar bracchetti, e cacciatori aizzare, lepri levare, ed isgridar le genti, | e di guinzagli uscir veltri correnti, | per belle piagge volgere e imboccare | assai credo che deggia dilettare | libero cor.*

[8] Sull'opposizione 'latente' in alcuni casi tra l'uso dell'infinito ed del participio in -*ing* in inglese moderno, cfr. R. Kempson e R. Quirk (1971:551-6).

[9] Se le forme di infinito greco e vedico si possono distinguere nei tipi in *-*(e)-m-en*, *-*(e)-s-en*, *-*(e)-w-en* (cfr. V. Pisani (1949:172)), e se di *-*(e)-s-en* si presume una somiglianza strutturale con il lat. *legere* < *leg-e-s-ĭ e di *-*(e)-w-en* con l'itt. -*wan* (specialmente se da *-*w-ṇ*), avremmo in questi infiniti forme coniugabili del verbo, perché *-*m(e)* e *-*s(e)* ricordano gli elementi pronominali (e desinenziali?) di I[a] e II[a] sg. (e di III[a] riflessivo) e *-*w(e)* quello di I[a] e II[a] plur. (oltre al lat. *vōs*, ai. *vas*, asl. *vy*, gr. ὐ-μεῖς, cfr. anche le desinenze ai. -*va(s)* e itt. -*wen(ı)*). In queste lingue si hanno, forse tracce di quel rapporto tra nome verbale e persona che sembra formalmente più chiaro in greco e vedico, e che, a distanza di secoli, si trova, ad es., in età rinascimentale nel napoletano e, ancor oggi, nel portoghese (cfr. C. Tagliavini (1964:381, n. 183 e 184; J. Kuryłowicz 1964:163-4).

[10] Cfr. J. Kuryłowicz 1964:159.

[11] In estrema analisi, causa delle somiglianze linguistiche è sempre un prestito, per remoto che sia: ma questa spiegazione, valida in sé, può portare ad un certo semplicismo nelle applicazioni, soprattutto se non si esclude che la recezione di un fatto linguistico sia totalmente passiva, priva di una necessaria rielaborazione da parte del pur sprovvedutissimo recettore.

[12] Sulla scarsezza delle ricerche sinora compiute in sede di grammatica storica generativa, cfr. King 1969:217.

BIBLIOGRAFIA

Ambrosini, R. 1962. Concordanze nella struttura formale delle categorie verbali indo-europee. Studi e Saggi Linguistici 2.33-97.

—, 1970. Strutture e parole. Palermo: Flaccovio.

Collinge, N. E. 1970. Collectanea linguistica, The Hague: Mouton.

Coseriu. E. 1968. Sincronía, diacronía y typología. Actas del xi Congreso internacional de Lingüística y Filología Románicas. Madrid.

Ivanov, V. V. 1965. Obščeindoevropejskaja, praslavjanskaja i anatoličeskaja jazykovye sistemy. Moskva.

Katičić, R. 1970. A Contribution to the General Theory of Comparative Linguistics. The Hague: Mouton.

Kempson, R., Quirk, R. 1971. Controlled activation of latent contrast. Language 47.548-572.

Kiparsky, P. 1968. Tense and Mood in Indo-European Syntax. Foundations of Language 4.30-57.

King, R. D. Historical Linguistics and Generative Grammar. New Jersey: Prentice-Hall.

Kuryłowicz, J. 1964. The Inflectional Categories of Indo-European. Heidelberg: Winter.

Pisani, V. 1949. Glottologia indoeuropea. Torino: Rosenberg e Sellier.

Tagliavini, C. 1964. Le origini delle lingue neolatine. Bologna: Patron.

Winter, W. (ed.) 1965. Evidence for Laryngeals. The Hague: Mouton.

PSYCHOLOGISMUS UND OBJEKTIVISMUS IN DER SPRACHWISSENSCHAFT

LÁSZLÓ ANTAL

Die Auffassung des gegenwärtigen Artikels steht in einem diametralen Gegensatz zu den seit Aufkommen der generativen Sprachtheorie üblich gewordenen sprachphilosophischen (d.h. mentalistischen) Ansichten von Chomsky, Katz, usw. Diese Tatsache hat den Verfasser gezwungen, im Interesse einer einleuchtender Darlegung bestimmte 'elementare' Analogien anzuwenden. Hoffentlich verzeiht der Leser diesen quasi-didaktischen Charakter der Ausführung.

1. Die Donau ist ein Fluß, und als solcher besteht sie aus Wasser. Ihre Eigenschaften scheinen – auf den ersten Blick – Wassereigenschaften zu sein. Man spricht z.B. darüber, daß die Donau hier schnell, dort aber langsam ist. Es ist offenbar, daß eine Wassereigenschaft in diesen Feststellungen impliziert ist – nämlich die Geschwindigkeit des Wassers. Weiterhin spricht man darüber, daß die Donau kalt oder warm ist. Damit bezeichnen wir wieder eine Wassereigenschaft – nämlich die Temperatur des Wassers. Häufig erwähnt man, daß die Donau hoch oder niedrig ist — damit geben wir wieder eine Wassereigenschaft an, und zwar eine quantitative Eigenschaft, nämlich die Menge des Wassers. Auf den ersten Blick ist die Donau Wasser, sie scheint nicht mehr als eine bloße Summe von Wasser zu sein. Auf den zweiten Blick aber erweist sich diese Auffassung als grundfalsch. Dasselbe Wasser, das bei Regensburg relativ schnell wegfließt, strömt in Jugoslawien oder Bulgarien wesentlich langsamer. Dasselbe Wasser, das bei Regensburg vielleicht nur 16 Grad hat, hat bei Wien 18 oder 20 Grad. Es klingt paradox, aber es ist unleugbar, daß die Geschwindigkeit des Wassers in der Donau nicht eine Eigenschaft des Wassers ist, sondern eine Eigenschaft des Flusses. Die Temperatur des Wassers in der Donau ist eigentlich nicht eine Eigenschaft des Wassers, sondern eine Eigenschaft der Umgebung des Flusses. Weiterhin: jenes Wasser, das die vorige Woche bei Regensburg weggeflossen ist, hat schon Wien zurückgelassen – aber der Fluß ist in Regensburg derselbe Fluß geblieben. Das Wasser verändert sich in der Donau schnell; die Donau selbst verändert sich langsam. Obwohl auf den ersten Blick die Donau nicht

mehr zu sein scheint als eine mechanische Summe von Wasser, ist sie in Wirklichkeit wesentlich mehr als Wasser. Was für uns besonders wichtig ist: die Donau hat solche Eigenschaften, die aus den Eigenschaften des Wassers, das in ihr fließt, unableitbar sind. Unter anderem hat sie ein Flußbett, einen Lauf und eine geographische und wirtschaftliche Bedeutung. Damit die Donau ihre Fluß-Existenz verwirklichen kann, ist Wasser unbedingt notwendig, aber nicht nur Wasser. Die Donau hat eine Geschichte — und diese Geschichte ist keineswegs eine Summe der Teilgeschichten jener Wässer, die in ihr jahrhundertelang weggeflossen sind. Die Donau ist mehr als ein bloßer Haufen von Wassermolekülen, genauso wie eine Armee mehr ist als eine Gruppe von Soldaten, ein Trinkglas mehr als ein Haufen von Glasmolekülen; andernfalls nämlich wäre der Unterschied zwischen einem Trinkglas und einem Glasaschenbecher unerklärbar. Summa summarum: Aschenbecher, Trinkgläser, Flüsse, Armeen usw. sind Erscheinungen, deren Eigenschaften aus den (Teil)eigenschaften ihrer Elemente unableitbar sind. Sie haben eine Geschichte, und ihre Geschichte ist nicht eine reine Summe der Teilgeschichten ihrer Elemente. In einer alten Armee dienen junge Leute. Eine Armee kann ganz jung sein, auch dann, wenn ihre Soldaten alt sind. Würden wir nicht annehmen, daß das Ganze mehr ist, als eine mechanische Summe seiner Teile, dann würden wir eo ipso das Prinzip des Strukturalismus zurückweisen, und zwar im weitesten Sinne, nicht nur als linguistischen Strukturalismus, sondern als Strukturalismus überhaupt. Die Entwicklung der modernen Physik, Biologie und die Entwicklung zahlreicher Sozialwissenschaften berechtigen eine solche Zurückweisung nicht. Jetzt aber müssen wir von der Donau Abschied nehmen und unseren Blick auf die Gesellschaft lenken.

2. Eine Gesellschaft ist mehr, als ein Haufen oder Gruppe von Individuen. Weiterhin ist es ganz offenbar, daß die Eigenschaften einer Gesellschaft aus den Eigenschaften der Individuen, die in dieser Gesellschaft leben, unableitbar sind. Z.B. kann niemand leugnen, daß tiefgehende und rasche gesellschaftliche Veränderungen nach 1945 in den osteuropäischen Ländern vorgegangen sind. In derselben Zeit ist die grundlegende Masse jener Individuen, die diese Veränderung mitmachten, identisch geblieben. Jede Gesellschaft hat eine Geschichte. Die Geschichte einer Gesellschaft ist aber nicht eine Summe der persönlichen Lebensbahnen ihrer Mitglieder. Ähnlich wie der Wasserbestand der Donau sich ständig und rasch erneuert, während der Fluß im Wesentlichen identisch bleibt, verändert sich der Stand der Individuen in

einer Gesellschaft relativ schnell, während die Gesellschaft sich im Wesentlichen langsamer umgestaltet. Es kann leicht vorkommen, daß die Zahl der Kranken in einer 'kranken' Gesellschaft niedriger ist als in einer 'gesunden' Gesellschaft. Eine große Gesellschaft besteht manchmal aus winzigen Individuen. Wie im Falle von Aschenbechern, Flüssen, Armeen usw. so ist auch im Falle der Gesellschaft klar, daß sie mehr ist, als eine Summe von Menschen, daß sie wichtige Eigenschaften hat, die aus den Eigenschaften ihrer Individuen nicht entstehen konnten. Wenn zu einem gegebenen Zeitpunkt zwei Individuen, ein altes und ein junges, nebeneinander leben, leben sie in der gleichen Phase der Gesellschaft, aber in zwei verschiedenen Phasen ihres Lebens. Was für uns besonders wichtig ist: das Verhältnis des Individuums seiner Gesellschaft gegenüber ist dasselbe, wie das Verhältnis des Wassers seinem Fluß gegenüber.

Aber müssen wir noch bei der Gesellschaft oder, genauer, bei dem Verhältnis von Gesellschaft und Individuum bleiben? Obwohl es unleugbar ist, daß das Leben der Gesellschaft, d.h. die Geschichte derselben nicht eine Summe der individuellen Lebensbahnen ist, und, obwohl es unleugbar ist, daß das Leben des Individuums der Gesellschaft gegenüber als etwas Gesondertes, etwas anderes erscheint, ist es doch eine wichtige Tatsache, daß das Leben des Individuums von der Gesellschaft nicht unabhängig ist. Das Individuum hat eine Meinung (im weitesten Sinne) über die Gesellschaft, in der es lebt. Das Individuum kennt die Gesellschaft, in der es lebt. Jedes Individuum hat also bestimmte Kenntnisse bezüglich der Gesellschaft, in der es lebt. Aber es ist hier etwas, was für uns besonders wichtig ist:

a) Jene Kenntnisse, die bezüglich der Gesellschaft als Vorstellungen im Bewußtsein der verschiedenen Individuen vorhanden sind, unterscheiden sich von Individuum zu Individuum.

b) Jene Wissenschaft, die die Gesellschaft beschreiben soll, kurz, die Soziologie, interessiert sich nicht für jene subjektiven Vorstellungen, die im Hirn der Individuen vorhanden sind, sondern betrachtet als ihr wahres Objekt jene außerindividuelle, objektive, gesellschaftliche Realität, von der das Individuum als von einem Gesonderten, mit ihm nicht Identischen umgeben ist. Es kann manchmal vorkommen, daß auch die Art und Weise der Widerspiegelung der objektiven gesellschaftlichen Realität bei den verschiedenen Individuen dem Soziologen als aufschlußreich erscheint, aber immer nur unter dem Vorbehalt, daß diese Untersuchung neben dem wahren Forschungsobjekt der Soziologie, d.h. der Gesellschaft selbst, nur etwas Sekundäres ist.

Die Gesellschaft kann nicht eine Summe von Individuen sein, da die Gesellschaft ihre Individuen überlebt. Bis zu einem gewissen Grad ist sie unabhängig von ihren Individuen – unabhängig in jenem Sinne, dass die konkreten Eigenschaften der Individuen sie nicht interessieren. Ähnlich wie dem Flusse vollkommen gleichgültig ist, was für ein Wasser in ihm fliesst – wichtig ist nur, dass es überhaupt Wasser ist – ist es auch der Gesellschaft gleichgültig, welche konkreten Individuen in ihr leben.

Wenn es uns gelungen ist, zu verstehen, dass die objektive Realität auf der einen Seite, und die subjektive Widerspiegelung dieser Realität auf der anderen Seite zwei verschiedene Erscheinungen sind, die sich mindestens so zueinander verhalten wie ein aufgebautes Haus zu seinem Bauplan, dann können wir weitergehen, und statt die Gesellschaft als Ganzes zu betrachten, können wir unsere Aufmerksamkeit einem ihrer wichtigsten Aspekte, nämlich der Sprache widmen.

3. Der erste, schon moderne Versuch, über das Wesen und die Natur der Sprache Rechenschaft zu geben, stammt von Hermann Paul. Der Kern seiner Auffassung lautet: Die Sprache ist irgendeine Kenntnis in der 'Seele', d.h. im psychologischen Mechanismus des Sprechenden. Die Auffassung, wonach die Sprache etwas Psychologisches sei, die im Kopfe des Sprechenden residiert und nur dort, ist – auf den ersten Blick – von zwei sog. 'Argumenten' unterstützt:

a) Trennt man dem Sprechenden den Kopf vom Rumpfe ab, dann spricht er ganz bestimmt nie mehr.

b) Wenn ein ganzes Volk ausstirbt, verschwindet auch seine Sprache.

Die beiden Argumente sind wirkungslos. Wenn dem Sprechenden der Kopf vom Rumpfe abgetrennt wird, hört nicht nur seine Sprachtätigkeit auf, sondern auch seine Verdauung. Wagt jemand ernsthaft zu behaupten, dass seine Verdauung eine psychologische Tätigkeit ist? Wenn ein Volk ausstirbt, verschwindet nicht nur seine Sprache, sondern seine ganze gesellschaftliche Existenz, seine Produktionsverhältnisse, der ganze Prozess seiner gesellschaftlichen Produktion. Wagt jemand ernsthaft zu behaupten, dass die gesellschaftliche Produktion eines Volkes, d.h. die Erzeugung neuer materieller Güter, eine psychologische Tätigkeit ist?

Wenn ich annehme, dass die Sprache primär und wesentlich im Individuum und nur im Individuum existiert, dann muss ich annehmen, dass der Begriff 'Sprache', Sprache als solche, z.B. deutsche Sprache, englische Sprache, usw., eine blosse Fiktion ist, die keine Realität ausdrückt. Eben diese Auffassung hat Paul vertreten: "Wir müssen

eigentlich so viele Sprachen unterscheiden als es Individuen gibt"
(1909:37) – wie er in seinen Prinzipien darlegt. "In Wirklichkeit gibt
es eigentlich soviel Sprachen wie Individuen" – wiederholt er dieselben
Gedanken in einem Vortrag (1910:368).

Gehe ich nicht von einer überindividuellen Sprache aus, sondern von
vielen Individualsprachen, dann behaupte ich, dass in Wirklichkeit
keine wesentliche Verbindung, kein wesentlicher Zusammenhang
zwischen diesen Individualsprachen existiert – nur eine Ähnlichkeit.
Dieser Auffassung nach ist die Sprache eine private Erscheinung, genauso
wie die Verdauung.

Jede anspruchsvolle Sprachtheorie muss einen wichtigen Gegensatz
erklären können. Wir können sagen, dass eine adäquate Sprachtheorie
die Sprache in ihrer Totalität, d.h. in ihrer geschichtlichen Wirklichkeit
erklären muss. Oder: Eine wissenschaftliche Theorie der Sprache muss
den Gegensatz auflösen können, der zwischen der relativen Stabilität
der Sprache auf der einen Seite und ihrer geschichtlichen Veränderung
auf der anderen Seite vorhanden ist. Paul, zwar ein Psychologist, jedoch
ein brillanter Geist, dazu noch ein sprachgeschichtlich geschulter Wissen-
schaftler, hat das erkannt und versucht. Sein Versuch, die erbitterte
und hoffnungslose Anstrengung eines Gelehrten, der die Konsequenzen
seiner falschen Prämisse ehrlich ziehen wollte, ist gescheitert. Wenn
für jemanden wie für Paul die Sprache eine individualpsychologische
Erscheinung ist, dann muss sich eigentlich jede sprachliche Veränderung
so viele Male abspielen, wie es Individuen gibt.[1] In diesem Falle aber
bleibt nur ein einziger, schwacher theoretischer Rettungsgürtel – nämlich
die Theorie der Nachahmung; also jene Auffassung, dass die Quelle
jeder sprachlichen Veränderung – letzten Endes – ein gewisses, wenn
auch unbekanntes Individuum ist. Mit Rücksicht auf die Massenhaftig-
keit und Einförmigkeit der sprachlichen Veränderungen auf der einen
Seite und auf die grosse Zahl der sprechenden Individuen auf der anderen
Seite, ist diese Überzeugung unbeweisbar und unannehmbar. Aber ich
muss nocheinmal unterstreichen, dass Paul in jeder Hinsicht konsequenter
war, als seine heutigen Nachfolger, die amerikanischen Mentalisten,
vor allem Chomsky und Katz, die noch nie versucht haben, die Konsequenzen ihrer psychologistischen Grundprämisse bezüglich der
sprachlichen Veränderung zu ziehen.

Wundt, der grosse Gegner von Paul, hat erkannt, dass Stabilität
und Veränderlichkeit in der Sprache, d.h. jene Tatsache, dass die sprachlichen Veränderungen fortwährend im Gange sind, ohne dass sie von den
Sprechenden, die sie verwirklichen, bemerkt würden, uns zwingen, neben

den Individualsprachen noch ein weiteres Phänomen vorauszusetzen. So hat er festgestellt, dass "... die völkerpsychologischen Entwicklungen das individuelle Leben überdauern, dabei aber doch, da sie durchaus von den psychischen Eigenschaften der Einzelnen getragen sind, mit dem Wechsel der Generationen eigenartige Veränderungen erfahren, die prinzipiell jeder Vergleichbarkeit mit dem individuellen Seelenleben entrückt sind" (1904:10-11).[2]

Wundt hat den Begriff 'Volksseele' vorgeschlagen. Wenn dieser Begriff metaphorisch verstanden ist, habe ich nichts dagegen. Versteht man ihn wörtlich – und Paul hat ihn absichtlich so verstanden – dann ist er natürlich unannehmbar. Auf jeden Fall: Wie Fluss und Wasser, Gesellschaft und Individuum, Armee und Soldat sich gegenüberstehen und einander beiderseitig voraussetzen, so stehen sich gegenüber und setzen einander beiderseitig voraus Individualsprachen auf der einen Seite und objektive oder gesellschaftliche oder geschichtliche oder überindividuelle Sprache auf der anderen Seite. Die Sprache, nämlich diese gesellschaftliche Sprache, ist ein Teil der objektiven Realität; sie ist eine solche Realität, die von den sprechenden Millionen durch ihre Sprachtätigkeit täglich wiedererzeugt und aufrecht erhalten wird.

Früher, dort, wo wir vom Verhältnis von Gesellschaft und Individuum gesprochen haben, haben wir gesehen, dass das Individuum Vorstellungen in seinem Bewusstsein von der umgebenden gesellschaftlichen Realität entwickelt. Diese Vorstellungen sind die subjektiven Widerspiegelungen der Gesellschaft. Die Wissenschaft der Gesellschaft, d.h. die Soziologie, betrachtet als ihr wahres Objekt nicht diese Vorstellungen, sondern die widergespiegelte Realität – die Gesellschaft selbst.

Es ist evident, dass auch die objektive, überindividuelle Sprache sich im Bewusstsein des Sprechenden widerspiegelt. Und zwar als eine notwendige Kenntnis – die subjektive Sprachkenntnis der objektiven Sprache. Es ist charakteristisch und tragisch für die Sprachwissenschaft, dass die objektive, gesellschaftliche Sprache, d.h. das wahre Objekt der Linguistik mit der subjektiven Kenntnis, oder, genauer, mit den subjektiven Kenntnissen dieser Sprache wiederholt und wiederholt verwechselt worden ist.

4. Eben jetzt haben wir festgestellt, dass die subjektive Kenntnis der Sprache mit der objektiven Sprache in der Geschichte der Sprachwissenschaft auf Schritt und Tritt verwechselt worden ist. Dies bedeutet natürlich nicht, dass niemand diese zwei grundverschiedenen Erscheinungen unterscheiden konnte. Wir können sogar von zwei gegensätzlichen Richtungen sprechen. Die eine Richtung, die als individualistische,

psychologistische, oder, schweren Herzens, als idealistische bezeichnet werden könnte, hat solche Vertreter gehabt wie Paul, Baudouin de Courtenay, Vossler, Bally, Chomsky, Katz, usw. Die andere Richtung, die ich als soziologische, oder realistische, oder objektive, oder, vielleicht, als materialistische bezeichnen könnte, hat solche Vertreter wie Wundt, Meillet,[3] Hjelmslev,[4] und Bloomfield.

Chomsky ist der Auffassung, dass eine adäquate Sprachtheorie die sprachliche Kompetenz des Sprechenden erklären und modellieren muss. Die Kompetenz ist nicht mehr und weniger, als die subjektive Kenntnis der Sprache. Das bedeutet, dass das wahre, primäre Objekt der Linguistik für Chomsky nicht die reale, gesellschaftliche Sprache ist, sondern ihre subjektive Widerspiegelung. Natürlich weiss Chomsky auch sehr gut, dass diese Widerspiegelung sich von Individuum zu Individuum ändert. Eben darum muss er einen idealen Sprecher bzw. Hörer voraussetzen. Der Begriff 'Kompetenz' ist in der Sprachwissenschaft keineswegs neu. Er ist identisch mit der wohlbekannten Kategorie *langue* von Saussure. Auch die Performanz ist eine Saussuresche Kategorie: *parole*. So dass man ruhig aufschreiben kann:

> *langue* – Kompetenz (d.h. die Kenntnis der Sprache)
> *parole* – Performanz (d.h. die Anwendung der Sprache)

Aber weder bei Saussure noch bei Chomsky finden wir etwas, das unserer Sprache entsprechen würde. (Der Begriff *langage* bezeichnet bei Saussure nicht eine dritte Einheit, sondern die Gesamtheit von *langue* und *parole*.) Man könnte einwenden, dass Saussure, wenn er den Begriff *langue* erörtert, häufig das Beiwort 'sozial' gebraucht. Nun zeigen seine eigenen Feststellungen ganz klar, dass die Kategorie *langue* seiner Auffassung nach nicht etwas Objektives sein kann.[5]

Die Unzulänglichkeit der individualistischen Sprachauffassung – geschichtlich betrachtet – ist zum erstenmal offenbar geworden, als Paul auf Grund dieser Auffassung die Art und Weise der sprachlichen Veränderungen erklären wollte. Die heutigen Vertreter des Psychologismus oder Mentalismus haben nie versucht, die historische Realität der Sprache in Betracht zu ziehen. Statt die ganze Sprache, d.h. ihren synchronischen und diachronischen Aspekt zu untersuchen, untersucht Chomsky und seine Schule nur den synchronischen Aspekt, aber auch dort nicht die reale, die objektive Seite der Sprache, sondern ihre idealisierte, idealistisch verallgemeinerte subjektive Widerspiegelung. Wenn Chomsky die Wirklichkeit der Sprache in das subjektive Bewusstsein, in das Hirn des Sprechenden versetzt, ist er jenem Soziologen ähn-

lich, der, statt die Gesellschaft zu untersuchen, jene Ansichten, Aberglau-
ben und Ideen untersucht, die bezüglich dieser Gesellschaft in der
Volksmeinung üblich sind. Zur gleichen Zeit beraubt er die Sprache ihres
Objektes und weist sie in den Bereich der Psychologie. Katz spricht
darüber, dass die Sprache eine 'psychologische Realität' sei.[6] Leider x
hat er versäumt uns zu sagen, was eigentlich eine psychologische Realität
ist, und, wenn sie nur im Hirn des Individuums existiert, wie sie überhaupt
real sein kann. Dann sind auch unsere Träume Realitäten, da sie in
unserem Bewusstsein existieren, und nur dort.

Wer die Realität der Sprache leugnet und ihr nur irgendeine psychologische Existenz zuschreibt, ist gezwungen, zu versuchen, die Eigenschaften der Sprache aus den Eigenschaften des menschlichen Hirnes
abzuleiten. Diese Phase ist bei Chomsky gesetzmässig eingetreten.
Was können wir von diesem Versuch sagen? Seine 'Bedeutung' kann am
besten mit einer kleinen Analogie erleuchtet werden. Stellen wir uns
einen Soziologen vor, der die Grussformen einer Gesellschaft untersucht.
Nun, unter anderem muss er auch den Händedruck als einen Spezialfall
der Grussformen irgendwie deuten. Meine Frage lautet: Können wir die
soziale Funktion des Händedrucks aus den anatomischen Eigenschaften
des Armes ableiten? Berechtigt uns jene Tatsache, dass der Händedruck
mit unserem Arm verwirklicht wird, zu behaupten, dass der Händedruck
ein biologischer Akt ist?

Die sprachliche Tätigkeit des Individuums ist ein Teil seiner gesellschaftlichen Tätigkeit. Die Sprache selbst ist eine Sammlung von Normen,
die diese gesellschaftliche Tätigkeit bestimmen oder vorschreiben. Diese
Normensammlung ist weder physikalisch noch psychologisch – sie ist
gesellschaftlich. Die einzige Erscheinung, woraus die Sprache ableitbar
ist, ist die Gesellschaft selbst. Die Sprache aus dem menschlichen Hirne
abzuleiten, bedeutet die Gesellschaft aus dem menschlichen Hirn ableiten zu wollen.

5. Die individualistische Auffassung war unfähig, die prinzipielle
Möglichkeit und den Ablauf der sprachlichen Veränderung zu modellieren. Mit einer Dualität, nämlich mit der Dualität von *langue-parole*
bzw. Kompetenz-Performanz bemühen wir uns vergebens, das grosse
Problem der Veränderung zu lösen. Nehmen wir neben *langue* und *parole*,
d.h. Kompetenz und Performanz, auch einen dritten Faktor an, nämlich
die Sprache, dann gewinnen wir ein solches Schema, das das grosse
Dilemma, nämlich den Gegensatz von Stabilität und Veränderung in der
Sprache wesentlich besser zu modellieren erlaubt. Es ist eindeutig,

dass die subjektive Kenntnis der Sprache, d.h. die Kompetenz, die objektive Sprache widerspiegelt. Die Kompetenz ist von der objektiven Sprache determiniert. Auch das kann kaum bezweifelt werden, dass die Anwendung der Sprache, d.h. die Performanz, auf der Kenntnis der Sprache beruht, so dass ihr Verhältnis die folgende Richtung zeigt:

SPRACHE

↓

KOMPETENZ

↓

PERFORMANZ

Setzen wir aber nur eine 'einbahnige' Richtung oder Wirkung voraus, dann sind wir noch immer unfähig, die sprachliche Veränderung zu erklären. Gleichzeitig ist es eine unleugbare Tatsache, dass sich die Sprache fortwährend verändert. Eben darum müssen wir voraussetzen, dass die Performanz auf die Sprache zurückwirkt. Es ist klar, dass die Kompetenz nie eine vollkommene Widerspiegelung der Sprache ist. Weiterhin müssen wir annehmen, dass die Performanz nie eine vollkommene Realisation der Kompetenz ist. Zwischen Sprache und Performanz ist also eine doppelte Phasenverschiebung vorhanden. Nun, wenn irgendeine Verschiebung von vielen Performanzen allgemein in eine bestimmte Richtung erfolgt, dann wirkt diese Verallgemeinerung auf die Sprache zurück. Die Sprache modifiziert sich; diese Modifizierung spiegelt sich in der Kompetenz wider. Nach dieser Modifizierung der Kompetenz ist die frühere Verschiebung zwischen Sprache und Performanz aufgehoben. Dadurch wird die Neuerscheinung, die vom Gesichtspunkt einer früheren Kompetenz als Ausnahme, als Unregelmässigkeit, als Fehler galt, ein normaler oder regelmässiger Akt der Performanz. Die ganze geschichtliche Entwicklung der Sprache könnte vielleicht so charakterisiert werden, dass immer wieder neue Gegensätze zwischen Sprache und Performanz, beziehungsweise zwischen Kompetenz und Performanz entstehen und danach aufgehoben werden, vielleicht in jener Weise wie wir das soeben geschildert haben, nämlich:

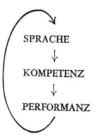

SPRACHE

↓

KOMPETENZ

↓

PERFORMANZ

6. Häufig wirft Chomsky den 'Verhaltenswissenschaften' vor, dass sie nur die oberflächlichen Erscheinungen erklären wollen bzw. können. Was das Wesen und die Natur der Sprache anbelangt, bleibt uns nur eine der folgenden zwei Möglichkeiten offen: Entweder betrachten wir die Sprache als ein ausserindividuelles Phänomen. In diesem Falle hat die Sprache mit der Psyche nicht mehr zu tun als jede andere gesellschaftliche Tätigkeit des Menschen. Oder wir nehmen an, dass die Sprache etwas Mentales sei. In diesem Falle berauben wir die Sprachwissenschaft ihres Objektes und überweisen die Sprache in den Bereich der Psychologie. Wir haben versucht zu zeigen, dass mit mentalen Individualsprachen allein die sprachliche Veränderung unerklärbar ist. Eben darum können wir feststellen, dass die folgende Behauptung Bloomfield's auch heute noch ihre volle Richtigkeit hat: "We can pursue the study of language without reference to any one psychological doctrine" (1933:vii).

Eötvös University, Budapest

NOTEN

[1] Paul hat das klar erkannt und formuliert: "... jedes Individuum seine eigene Sprache und jede dieser ihre eigene Geschichte hat..." (1909:39).
[2] Wenn auch nicht eindeutig und in jeder Hinsicht klar, hat Wundt doch erkannt, daß die Sprache selbst dem Individuum gegenüber eine solche Kontinuität bildet, "die prinzipiell jeder Vergleichbarkeit mit dem individuellen Seelenleben entrückt" ist, d.h. ihre Eigenschaften aus den Eigenschaften der Individuen unableitbar sind. Nun nichts ist charakteristischer, als jene Tatsache, daß H. Paul, der größte Theoretiker der Sprachgeschichte, eben jene Kontinuität zu verneinen gezwungen worden ist (als eine unvermeidliche Folge der Prämisse, daß nur Individualsprachen existieren), die das Wesen jeder Geschichte bildet: "Denn eben diese Bezeichnung (die Völkerpsychologie) täuscht eine geistige Kontinuität innerhalb der menschlichen Gemeinschaften vor, wie sie in Wirklichkeit nicht besteht, und verführt dazu, Faktoren zu übersehen, die für das Verständnis aller geschichtlichen Entwicklung von höchster Bedeutung sind." (1910: 366).
[3] "... le language est donc éminemment un fait social. En effet, il entre exactement dans la définition qu'a proposé Durkheim; une langue existe indépendamment de chacun des individus qui la parlent, et, bien qu'elle n'ait aucune réalité en dehors de la somme de ces individus, elle est cependant, de par sa généralité, extérieure à chacun d'eux; ce qui le montre, c'est qu'il ne dépend d'aucun d'entre eux de la changer et que toute déviation individuelle de l'usage provoque une réaction..." (Meillet 1921:230).
[4] "... le grammairien n'a pas besoin d'avoir recours au phénomène subjectif constitué par le sentiment linguistique des sujets parlant; au contraire la considération de ce facteur variable et fuyant ne servirait qu'à troubler le résultat. Le système linguistique et les valeurs dont il consiste ne sont pas des faits psychologiques. Le système et les valeurs sont indépendants de l'individu..." (Hjelmslev 1935:86).
[5] "... la langue n'est pas une entité, et n'existe que dans les sujets parlants" (Saussure

1931:19); "... les associations ratifiées par le consentement collectif, et dont l'ensemble constitue la langue, sont des réalités qui ont leur siège dans le cerveau." (*ibid.*: 32); "C'est un trésor déposé par la pratique de la parole dans les sujets appartenant à une même communauté, un système grammatical existant dans chaque cerveau..." (*ibid.*:30).

[6] Unter anderem hat er festgestellt, "that the linguist ... claims that his theory describes a neurological mechanism" (Katz 1964:129). Diese Behauptung von Katz ist mehrmals scharf kritisiert worden. Cowan z.B. hat bemerkt: "If physiologists were to discover that and how neurological mechanisms produced speech acts, whatever this might mean, then they might be said, in one sense at least, to have explained these. But one certainly does not explain or justify grammatical rules simply by supposing, as I for one certainly should, that speaker-hearer performances might have some sort of physiological basis, nor yet by supposing that this basis might somehow be precisely isomorphic to the grammar explained – just or even approximately how being left quite obscure". (Cowan 1970:32). In seinem bedeutenden Buch geht Esper noch weiter: "If the 'mechanism' whose properties the 'mentalist' seeks to discover is a 'brain mechanism', then the use of such terms as *mental, mentalism, innate ideas,* seems extremely unfortunate; they would hardly be adopted by anyone familiar with the history of psychology and aware to the historical connotations of these words. Moreover, it is not a part of the competence of a linguist to 'look inside people's heads', and I doubt whether a neurophysiologist would be justified in attaching heuristic value to a linguist's prescriptions concerning the properties which are to be identified in the 'brain mechanisms'." (Esper 1968:223). Später schreibt Esper: "... the figurative terminology in which the Chomskyan hypotheses have been expressed – 'device', 'mechanism', 'deep structure' – in which hypothesized *functional* relationships, the products of a particular kind of linguistic analysis, masquerade as – biological? – *structures* – this terminology is both pretentious and a nuisance" (*Ibid.*:224).

REFERENCES

Bloomfield, Leonard. 1933. Language. New York: Holt.
Cowan, J L. 1970. The myth of mentalism in linguistics. Studies in thought and language, ed. by J L. Cowan, 11-34. Tucson: University of Arizona Press.
Esper, Erwin A. 1968. Mentalism and objectivism in Linguistics. Foundations of Linguistics, 1. New York: Elsevier.
Hjelmslev, Louis. 1935. La catégorie des cas. Étude de grammaire générale. Acta Jutlandica. Aarhus, 8. 1-184
Katz, Jerrold J. 1964. Mentalism in linguistics. Language 40. 124-137.
Meillet, Antoine. 1921. Comment les mots changent de sens? Linguistique historique et linguistique générale. 1.230-271. Paris: Edouard Champion.
Paul, Hermann. 1909. Prinzipien der Sprachgeschichte. 4th ed. Halle: Max Niemeyer.
Paul, Hermann 1910. Über Völkerpsychologie. Rede gehalten beim Stiftungsfeste der Universität München. Süddeutsche Monatshefte. 7:10.
Saussure, Ferdinand (de). 1931. Cours de linguistique générale, ed. by Charles Bally & Albert Sechehaye. Paris: Payot.
Wundt, Wilhelm. 1904. Völkerpsychologie. Die Sprache. 2nd ed. Stuttgart: Alfred Kröner.

WHO IS A STRUCTURALIST?

RAIMO ANTTILA

It is general practice today to divide the history of Western linguistics into three main periods: the prestructuralist (or traditionalist), the structuralist, and the generative-transformationalist period. Such practice is certainly convenient, for it does not seem to distort the situation any more than the tripartition of English into Old, Middle, and Modern, or the partition of a year into four seasons. In all cases the actual division points are not as drastic as the names appear to imply. But there is an enormous difference in connotation, because in the hands of the generative-transformational grammarians the term 'structural' has turned into an insult, a term of abuse. This practice is unjust and has a strong element of propaganda in it, in general agreement with Marxist history according to which the past is evaluated according to present-day criteria. Similar connotations have been assigned to the term 'Neogrammarian' by both structuralists and generative grammarians, and so on, which displays the same lack of understanding for historical explanation.

The reverse connotation is that generative-transformational grammar is something quite different from structuralism, and that the latter should be replaced in toto by the former. Of course, on the contrary, generative-transformational grammar is a natural outgrowth of structuralism, a particular variety of structuralism. This more accurate evaluation of background is easily available in many surveys, either in terms of structuralism in general (Piaget 1968, Schiwy 1969), or structural linguistics in particular (Lepschy 1970). For the latter topic a standard reference would also be Bierwisch 1965. Its English translation (1971) seems to imply that some of the modern variants need not be classified as 'structural linguistics', and the danger of misinterpretation is great. Thus the original title is superior, because it cannot easily be misread. We must keep in mind Bloomfield's maxim that "it is not enough to write so that everybody understands, one has to write so that nobody can misunderstand" (personal communication of Bernard Bloch's). The inclusion of generative-transformational grammar in structural linguistics has of course been specifically made also in other connections (e.g. Coseriu 1970:221, 223), and "transformational grammar as propounded most rigidly is an extreme form of structuralism" (Lehmann 1971:37). Somehow such statements have been systematically ignored, and the resulting notion of scientific continuity has been replaced with one of discontinuity. Such stray statements may not seem to carry any weight, although they certainly should. A balanced discussion of this topic is given by Chafe (1970: §§1, 7-8). Also he shows quite clearly how generative-transformational grammar changed 'structuralism' into an equally rigid 'syntacticism' whose main basis and bias still was the phonetic output of utterances. One moved, so to speak, the center pole of the tether, but kept the restrictive mechanism. Such a syntactic model has no more to say about language use than any other variety of structuralism, and thus a rigid partition into competence and performance became a necessity. This resulted in a deeply ingrained structuralism, whose position in the language model was only slightly different, but whose scope remained about the same as before. We must note, for instance, that both variants shun semantics (Chafe 1970, Anttila 1970:268). This led logically to the quite unexpected situation where Chomsky can be called "the inveterate structuralist" (Ehrmann 1970:23). My intention is not to defend a particular form of structuralism, but to show that all varieties have and have had weaknesses that can be compared and criticized. By looking at a few selected aspects we can add some historical depth both to structuralism in general and to its recent developments in particular. Emphasis of known facts can be beneficial.

One of the most prevalent criticisms against structuralism by the generative-transformational grammarians has been the former's emphasis on classification or taxonomy, thus making 'taxonomic' a term of abuse. A science without taxonomy is hardly a science, and neither is a science that is only concerned with taxonomy. It is hard to see how the explanations of evolutionary biology would be possible without an exact taxonomy. Generative-transformational grammar claims (or has claimed) that it can now replace taxonomy with explanation. But what has actually happened is that the new notational devices have led to new taxonomies. These have been as rigidly observed as previous structural taxonomies. In fact, they have largely remained as taxonomies, even though they are given out as explanations (Anttila 1972). Notational flexibility is in itself of course no explanation even if it is prerequisite to it and is an aid to it in some ways. Structuralism too, especially the variation called functionalism, which was derived from the practice of the Prague School, has provided very good explanatory hypotheses. The structuralists have been blamed for using a notation geared to surface units. This is offered as proof that they really did not know how language worked. In the first place, it is quite illegitimate to criticize the notational usages of the past according to present-day criteria. The basic principle of good historical explanation forbids this. In the second place, the generativists actually tend to use their notation in exactly the same way the structuralists did. Why should it automatically be unacceptable in the one case while quite legitimate in the other? Note how little difference there is between the following quotations when read sensitively to get behind the notational razzle-dazzle, or flim-flam:

Psychologists sometimes object to this formula, on the ground that the speaker is not capable of the reasoning which the proportional pattern implies. If this objection held good, linguists would be debarred from making almost any grammatical statement, since the normal speaker, who is not a linguist, does not describe his speech-habits, and, if we are foolish enough to ask him, fails utterly to make a correct formulation. Educated persons, who have had training in school grammar, overestimate their own ability in the way of formulating speech-habits, and, what is worse, forget that they owe this ability to a sophisticated philosophical tradition. They view it, instead, as a natural gift which they expect to find in all people, and feel free to deny the truth of any linguistic statement which the normal speaker is incapable of making. We have to remember at all times that the speaker, short of a highly specialized training, is incapable of describing his speech-habits. Our proportional formula of analogy and analogic change, like all other statements in linguistics, describes the action of the speaker and does not imply that the speaker himself could give a similar description (Sturtevant 1947:98, quoting Bloomfield 1933:406).

Suppose that someone succeeds in writing a grammar which correctly enumerates the sentences of a language and assigns them the right structural descriptions. Such a grammar would ipso facto correctly represent the substance of a fluent speaker's knowledge of this language. But it would not necessarily represent the form of this knowledge in the sense of actually corresponding to the system of rules which is internalized by the speaker and constitutes part of what enables him to produce and understand arbitrary utterances in the language (Kiparsky 1968:171).

In fact, the functionalists accuse transformational grammar of being surface linguistics. Vachek (1968) thinks that Chomsky's rigid competence-performance axis falls only within Saussure's *parole*, where no motivation can be found; i.e., this is taxonomy rather than explanation. But also Coseriu maintains that Humboldt's generative grammar was truly functional, and that transformational grammar covers only Humboldt's *Erzeugtes*, not *Erzeugung*. The object of transformational grammar is not *langue*, but very much a surface grammar (Coseriu 1970:215-222; cf. also Chafe's criticism mentioned above).

In other words, 'structuralism' does not just entail surface linguistics, as is often assumed or claimed. Structuralism has its roots in Marxism (Leach 1970:7) with its 'deep structure' and 'surface structure' corresponding to 'infrastructure (*Struktur, Basis*)' and 'superstructure (*Überbau*)'. And it is the infrastructure that is 'real', not the superstructure. Marxism was one of the major influences on Lévi-Strauss, the main exponent of structuralism today; the other two were psychoanalysis and geology (Leach 1970:5, Schiwy 1969:37). All three show stratification. Any structure is a system of transformations (Piaget 1968:6, 121, 124). The notion of transformation causes structuralism to encompass all philosophies not strictly empirical, even certain forms of empiricism like logical positivism, which uses syntactic and semantic forms to explicate logic. Logic itself does not – at least not yet – easily fall into such structures of transformation blocs (Piaget 1968:7), and in this sense generative-transformational grammar might be considered nonstructural, depending on its degree of reliance on logic. The Gestalt psychologists added much to the concept of structure. We must note that K. Bühler even had a notion of the consciousness of the rule that intervenes in relational structures (*Regelbewusstsein*) (Piaget 1968:46). And Lévi-Strauss developed a structuralism of abstract underlying global systems from which one can transform other systems or the actually attested systems (Schiwy 1969:16). In other words, Lévi-Strauss quite independently developed generative and transformational rules for myth analysis (Leach 1970:233), which are taken by current nonlinguistic structuralists as paragons of structuralism; generative-transformational grammar displays many rules similar to Lévi-Strauss'. Structuralism has often developed in the direction of transformationalism (e.g. Guillaume, Merleau-Ponty, Tesnière), even if we would not go as far as Coseriu (1970:787): "Alles Wesentliche der Transformationstheorie, soweit diese überhaupt gültig ist, kann man schon in den Arbeiten verschiedener europäischer Gelehrten auffinden (Porzig, Bally, Kurylowicz, Frei u.a.)" (from the Spanish of 1965). Coseriu goes on to point out that he has treated most of the theoretical problems treated by transformational grammarians in his earlier work: questions of language as creative activity, language as creation, language systems as systems of possibilities, degrees of grammaticality, the character and meaning of the speaker's intuition.

He admits that he did not use a coherent philosophical foundation, nor did he have much success. I know that for many his statement would sound megalomaniac, although what he says here is highly relevant in the present context, for it shows that functional structuralism is by no means a mere taxonomy. We also see how generative-transformational grammar is a sort of structuralism that could have been expected. Chomsky helped break the unilateral emphasis (Piaget 1968:118); but this gave of course a new and uncalled-for unilateralism.

The great enigma of history is this: When can a particular line of thought start to develop in full swing and gain the ascendency? Somehow earlier attempts to expand structuralism (e.g. Coseriu's) did not really get off the ground. There must be the right amount of fashionableness involved to ensure success. Schiwy 1969 treats structuralism as fashion, method, and ideology. The breakthrough of French structuralism happened in the mid-sixties when it became the dominating intellectual fashion. It has tended to degenerate into a *Weltanschauung*, and therein lies its danger, since it is scarcely permissible to ideologize scientific knowledge and cognition and then to promote this ideology into a science (Schiwy 1969:86-93). The same relationship between fashion and ideology has accompanied the history of generative-transformational grammar, reflecting what happened to American structuralism in its heyday. In both of these camps one's own ascendency and vigorous research was interpreted as the same: one's own bias is taken as proof of the correctness of one's activity and as an indication of what future holds. Generative-transformational grammar showed how wrong the American structuralists were on this score, but its practitioners maintained the very same attitude toward their own doctrine. History ought to teach us more: The rise of British empiricism 1690-1740 (cf. also various other 'cultural revolutions') and its complete dominance of the scientific scene for a time did not mean that empiricism was the only truth to be had. And now linguistics is turning toward semanticism (Chafe 1970). This is only another kind of structuralism with antecedents in glossematics and stratificationalism.

The strength of structuralism is in its method, whatever that is exactly. We are all aware of its basic manifestations and I have to leave it at that here (see Bierwisch 1965:147-50, Schiwy 1969:43-45). In principle this means part-total relations, transformations, and self-regulation (Piaget 1968:8-16). Transformations are indeed statements of relations. Methodological structuralism tries to get at underlying structures which explain the surface attestations using a deductive method that requires the construction of logico-mathematical models. In this sense the structure does not enter the domain of the observable 'facts' and remains 'un-conscious' in the individual members of the group considered (Piaget 1968:83). The application of the method entails new ways of looking at familiar facts (Leach 1970:3). The method was indeed quite good, but it was often applied without sensitivity, that is to say, carried either too far or not far enough. The general principle tended to be 'once right, then always right'. Thus, e.g., the various schools of structuralism have upheld Proto-Indo-European schwebeablaut till our own day. Because in a very few cases there is clear alternation in the position of the vowel in a string of consonants, this alternation was made with no other justifi-cation a central point in Proto-Indo-European phonology, just for the sake of neat structuralizing (Anttila 1969). In the case of the Gothic vowels Vennemann 1971 takes the structuralists' own method and shows that it was not adequately applied before to this problem. But structuraliz-ing for the sake of structuralizing is still with us. In 1951 Allen (1951:132-133) criticized 'modern aphonetic phonology' which was a retention of Saussure's (1960:11) position: "Le linguiste n'a nul besoin d'être un phonologiste consommé; il demande simplement qu'on lui fournisse un certain nombre de données nécessaires. ..." Most variants of generative phonology follow this to the letter. Generative grammarians also retain the principle 'once right, always right' (all doctrinaire positions are drastic oversimplifications, i.e. distortions): If some changes cannot be gradual, no changes can be gradual. This is an obviously false induction (Andersen 1972, Itkonen 1970, 1971). The principle has been used in reverse between different schools if the competition is once wrong, it is always wrong. Synthesis has been very difficult, because loss of face seems to be worse than loss of faith. In some areas the structuralists are patently wrong, hence always wrong, and the same holds for the generativists, as seen from the other camp. This is another facet of what Kaplan has called 'the drunkard's search': it is easier to look for a lost key under a lamp, because 'it is lighter there' than where the key was lost. Thus scientists formulate problems in a way which requires for solution just those techniques they are most familiar with. This leads to Kaplan's 'law of the instrument': give a small boy a hammer, and he will find that everything he meets needs pounding (Kaplan 1964:28-29, 277, Garvin 1970:3). Different linguists have different lamps and hammers, but they certainly use them the same way.

In terms of theory building, syntacticism and semanticism are superior to other varieties of structuralism. I find it difficult to draw a line between theory and method, because in practice they merge to a great degree.

American structuralism created a theory by elevating its method into a theory (Teeter 1964); in other words, the method was used as a theory. Now, generative-transformational grammar has used its theory largely as a method for scouting for evidence to justify the theory.

If American structuralism shunned universals – a position most strongly propounded by Boas – Lévi-Strauss' structural anthropology compensates it with the other extreme. He tries to get at the human mind, the universals of human culture (Leach 1970:1, 22, 40). In fact, he even tries to establish a semantic algebra, a very modern idea indeed (Leach 1970:32). The goal is everywhere a species of superrationalism which fixes the goals everywhere (cf. Schiwy 1969:37). These human universals must be innate at some deep level. We must not assume that this is Chomsky's innatism (Piaget 1968:93), for the latter is philosophically rather loose (Coseriu 1969:26-27, 50). Lévi-Strauss, on the other hand, has a strictly deductive model; according to Piaget (1968:90) it is the most strikingly so ever used in a human science, since it is an algebra of possibilities, rather than observance of empirical fact (Leach 1970:43). What at first was generalization only (Leach 1970:127) has turned into a strict dogma of rather uncertain universals, difficult of proof. Such universals are posited on the basis of a rather superficial knowledge of a few Brazilian tribes. In 'modern' linguistics English has been a similar model for the determination of 'universals'. It must be emphasized that Lévi-Strauss' method or approach is linguistic rather than psychological. One sees the same Jakobsonian heritage at work as in the transformational camp. Also Lévi-Strauss seems to always be able to find what he is looking for, and counterevidence is overlooked or dismissed with powerful invective (cf. Leach 1970:12-13). It is no wonder that both offshoots end up in the same cul-de-sac. One obvious lack is the neglect of biology, both in Lévi-Strauss and Chomsky, for in fact Piaget says that only by ignoring biology can we accept Chomsky's innate reason and Lévi-Strauss' permanence of the human intellect (Piaget 1968:122). It is exactly here that Chafe's semanticist model has more to offer. Ultimately the key to all structures might well be found in the structure and function of the biological organism (cf. Piaget 1968:40).

This leads us directly into the notion of history. Lévi-Strauss has not carried out any diachronic studies, and he generally equates the study of history with the study of cross-cultural anthropology (Leach 1970:7-9, 98). History has nothing to teach the Marxists or other Hegelians because they already know what has happened and what will happen. Lévi-Strauss' idea of history is contrary to Marxist dogma (Leach 1970:5), because the present epoch in its vantage point is not superior to any other epochs (Leach 1970:7), for history as a matter of fact cannot affect the universal level he posits (Piaget 1968:90-91). This tends to be true also of transformational grammar as far as language itself is concerned, whereas in the interpretation of other linguistic schools purer Marxist principles are applied, as was mentioned above. Since the rise of a scientific school is partly dependent upon fashion, it should not be a random coincidence that the rise of transformational grammar has coincided with the increase in the appeal of Marxism.

Some of the sources of structuralism lie in Marxism to begin with. However, there are other sources that stretch back to Pāṇini and the tradition of Hindu grammar. This fact reveals that endeavors to prove that Pāṇini was a structuralist or transformationalist are at best didactic exercises. The prestructural structuralists par excellence were the Neogrammarians. Their sins were legion (sinless persons are boring; and Terence Wilbur points out to me a maxim of Meister Eckhardt's: to come upon great things, one must go astray a little), and generative grammarians have tended to lump them together with the later, full-fledged structuralists. For a number of reasons this is justified, but the same case can be made for a similarity between the Neogrammarians and generative grammarians. The following points have been picked out of Wilbur's (1972) highly readable account of the Neogrammarian era, and I suggest that they apply as they are also to the transformationalists. Part of the Neogrammarian myopia was to misinterpret deliberately and to oversimplify. Furthermore, a highly emotional tone accompanied the Neogrammarian contention, and the Italians in fact called it the *nuova fede*. The Neogrammarian position on sound change eliminated all need for explanation (cf. the same on analogy by generative-transformational grammarians through various strict rule taxonomies). There were also rhetorical bows to the past just as today great praise is granted to Port-Royal and sundry other predecessors. In general, observation was named explanation and mistaken for causal factors, exactly like today. The whole Neogrammarian controversy occupies a much greater position in the history of the field than it clearly deserves, and this should be the judgment we pass on many modern controversies as well. It is possible to draw many more parallels but these will suffice to show how history repeats itself and how no particular school is as pristine as it fancies itself to be. We must note also how Bloomfield and Chomsky agree in their low estimation of the eighteenth century (an observation of Peter Maher's). Both are wrong also in their view that language is a rigid system (cf. Lepschy 1970:118). This is also what Hockett (1968) claims: Transformational grammar has on many points gone back to Bloomfield.

Structuralism thus has a long history, although it has only recently been combined with both deduction and experience (Piaget 1968:117). Most variants have retained many of the negative aspects. Perhaps M. Foucault goes farthest in his structuralism without structures, with its scorn for history and genesis and contempt for functions (Piaget 1968:114). The devaluation of these aspects is shared to a certain degree by the generative-transformational school. It is very curious that Gödel's theorem about the weakness of structures (*Unvollständigkeitssatz*) has been completely ignored in modern linguistic theory and in the evaluation of its historical development. Structures are always imperfect, and higher-level formalizations have to build on the weaker structures in the fashion of a pyramid (Piaget 1968: 29-32, 120-122). J. Bechert is now investigating the implications of Gödel's findings for linguistics (personal communication); in the meantime we will have to be satisfied with Sapir's dictum 'all grammars leak'. It is safe to say that all linguists – no matter how brilliant and original – only stand on the shoulders of their intellectual ancestors (cf. Lepschy 1970:37-38, 91, 137). Those who claim that they started ab ovo are indulging in the worst sort of narcissism.

I have presented these few informal remarks and observations to lessen the dangers of distortion and oversimplification in the comparison of rival models. The current crop of students has no access to such elementary notions, and there is danger for them to fall prey to their own lack of perspective. Therefore I have kept my references to basic treatments only. In particular, I have pointed out both the time axis in the development of structuralism and a breadth axis which shows that there is more to structuralism than the so-called post-Bloomfieldians who are by no means all of one mind. Above all, this should be taken as a footnote to Starosta's well-argued and inspiring exposition of the polarities working in science and linguistics (Starosta 1971; see also Garvin 1970). Such polarities were considered from quite a different angle by William James, and I am submitting a plea for the same sort of orientation in linguistic analysis (Anttila 1972). I must repeat what has been said above: structuralism is a method and not a doctrine. When it becomes a doctrine it creates a number of schismatic sects. As a method it is open, and it is best when used in conjunction with other methods (Piaget 1968:124, Schiwy 1969:71). Such a method implies refined techniques, intellectual honesty, and progressively closer approximations (Piaget 1968:117-118). As linguists every last one of us is a structuralist, and many of us who put up disclaimers are even more so than some others. This makes the term superfluous. I have suggested the same for 'generative' (Anttila 1972). We should finally learn humility and show respect for those whose theoretical commitments are not identical to ours, for our field of endeavor covers such a wide variety of concerns. Sciences form a circle and not a straight line (Piaget 1968:119; cf. Lepschy 1970:120).

University of California, Los Angeles

REFERENCES

Allen, W. S. 1951. Phonetics and comparative linguistics. Arch. Ling. 3.126-136.
Andersen, Henning. 1972. Diphthongization. Lg. 48.11-50.
Anttila, Raimo. 1969. Proto-Indo-European schwebeablaut. UCPL 58. Berkeley and Los Angeles.
—, 1970. Review of Bach – Harms (eds.), Universals in linguistic theory. UAJb 42.268-271.
—, 1972. Are we gradually where we started out from? UAJb 44. 222-226.
Bierwisch, Manfred. 1965. Strukturalismus. Geschichte, Probleme und Methoden· Kursbuch 5.77-152 (Mai).
—, 1971. Modern linguistics. Janua linguarum, Series minor 110. The Hague: Mouton.
Chafe, Wallace L. 1970. Meaning and the structure of language. Chicago, University of Chicago Press.
Coseriu, Eugenio. 1969. Einführung in die transformationelle Grammatik. Tübingen, University Book Store.
—, 1970. Sprache: Strukturen und Funktionen. XII Aufsätze. Tübinger Beiträge zur Linguistik 2. Tübingen.
Ehrmann, Jacques (ed.). 1970. Structuralism. Anchor Books A719. Garden City (N.Y.): Doubleday.
Garvin, Paul L. 1970. Moderation in linguistic theory. Language Sciences 9.1-3 (February).
Hockett, Charles F. 1968. The state of the art. Janua linguarum, Series minor 73. The Hague: Mouton.
Itkonen, Terho. 1970. Ovatko äänteenmuutokset vähittäisiä vai harppauksellisia? (Summary: Gradual or sudden sound changes?). Virittäjä 4/1970:411-438.
—, 1971. (More on the above). Virittäjä 2/1971:199-206.
Kaplan, Abraham. 1964. The conduct of inquiry. Methodology for behavioral science. San Francisco: Chandler.
Kiparsky, Paul. 1968. Linguistic universals and linguistic change. Universals in linguistic theory, ed. by Emmon Bach and Robert T. Harms, 170-202. New York: Holt.
Leach, Edmund. 1970. Claude Lévi-Strauss. Modern Masters M5. New York: The Viking Press.
Lehmann, Winfred P. 1971. Grammatischer Wechsel and current phonological discussion. Generative studies in historical linguistics, ed. by Mária Tsiapera, 9-43. Current Inquiry into Language and Linguistics 2. Edmonton: Linguistic Research, Inc.

Lepschy, Giulio G. 1970. A survey of structural linguistics. London: Faber and Faber.

Piaget, Jean. 1968. Le structuralisme[3]. Que sais-je? 1311. Paris: Presses Universitaires de France.

Saussure, Ferdinand de. 1960. Cours de linguistique générale. Paris: Payot. (1st ed.: 1916).

Schiwy, Günther. 1969. Der französische Strukturalismus. Mode, Methode, Ideologie mit einem Textanhang. Rowohlts deutsche Enzyklopädie 310-311. Hamburg: Rowohlt.

Starosta, Stanley. 1971. Linguistics and anti-science. Philippine Journal of Linguistics 2.13-27 (June).

Sturtevant, Edgar H. 1947 (1960). An introduction to linguistic science. New Haven: Yale University Press.

Teeter, Karl V. 1964. Descriptive linguistics in America: Triviality vs. irrelevance. Word 20.197-206.

Vachek, Josef. 1968. A note on future prospects of diachronistic language research. Lingua 21.483-493.

Vennemann, Theo. 1971. The phonology of Gothic vowels. Lg. 47.90-132.

Wilbur, Terence H. 1972. Hugo Schuchardt and the Neogrammarians, in: Schuchardt, the Neogrammarians, and the transformational theory of phonological change (Theo Vennemann, T. H. Wilbur, eds.), pp. 73-119. (Linguistische Forschungen 26). Frankfurt/M.: Athenäum.

ON INTERROGATIVE MOVEMENT
IN ENGLISH

EMMON BACH

I am concerned here with two alternative accounts of the fronting of interrogative phrases in English. In one account – which we may call SWOOP – a single application of a 'movement' transformation applies at the point in a derivation when the full domain of the movement is reached, either on the last cycle for direct questions, or on some intermediate cycle in indirect questions:

1.   Who did you see at the fair?
2.   John asked me when I was leaving for Kelsey Bay.

In the other account (HOP), successive applications of the rule on each cycle move the WH-phrase step by step to its final resting place. To settle the question should be of some interest since a number of conclusions depend crucially on the assumption of one or the other rule.[1]

The original direct argument for SWOOP was given in Postal (1971, but versions of this monograph were circulated considerably earlier). Postal pointed out the following facts (which also apply to the movement of relative pronoun phrases): when a WH-phrase occurs in a prepositional phrase, English allows the option in many instances of moving the preposition along with the noun phrase. But once the choice is made the preposition must be carried along to its target position and not 'stranded' at some intermediate place on its journey, or else the grammar will incorrectly predict that sequences like (3) are grammatical:

3.   *Who did you say that with Harry was traveling?

What we have to get is either (4) or (5):

4.   With whom did you say that Harry was traveling?
5.   Who did you say that Harry was traveling with?

Jackendoff (1969) and Bresnan (1971) both mention a counter-proposal (due to Chomsky, see now Chomsky 1973) to meet this difficulty: one might mark either the interrogative noun phrase itself or the prepositional phrase in which it stands with a special feature and then formulate the rule to apply to the constituent so marked. Postal (1972) argues against this proposal on general grounds: the use of such arbitrary feature marking should not be allowed by linguistic theory. He then gives independent arguments that HOP is incorrect. Given the relative unconstrainedness of linguistic theories at present it is important to look for as many independent arguments as possible and the following defense of SWOOP is presented in that spirit.[2]

Before turning to some new arguments for the correctness of SWOOP it may be worthwhile to pursue Postal's stranding argument and Chomsky's counter-proposal a bit further. In general, I accept Postal's objections completely. But let us assume the feature-marking analysis anyway. It can be seen that this proposal, taken together with HOP, is inadequate even to describe the distributional facts correctly. The reason why it will not work is very simple. In essence, the feature-marking proposal is simply a way of coding a prepositional phrase so that it will move as a whole (i.e. will 'pied-pipe' in Ross's sense [1967a]). But not all sentences will allow movement of the preposition and not all sentences will allow it to be left behind, and the crucial environment for determining the possibilities may not be present until one or several cycles later than the first cycle on which HOP could apply.

Consider first the difference between direct and indirect questions. In a direct question prepositions may be carried along, in indirect questions they may not:

6.   With whom are you going?
7.   Who are you going with?
8.   I know who I'm going with.
9.   *I know with whom I'm going.

But we cannot know until we have passed the cycle on which HOP would operate whether we are in a direct or indirect question.[3]

Further, the sentence in which the WH-phrase is directly contained may be embedded at an indefinite depth:

10.   With whom did Sally say Harry thought ... you were going.
11.   I know who Sally said Harry thought ... you were going with.

Now a proponent of the feature-marking analysis might try to save HOP by claiming that the feature-marking took place by means of a precyclic rule which could look at enough of the superstructure of the question to get the correct output. But this proposal would merely amount to a way of coding a tree so that it would operate as if the rule were not a hopping rule. Similarly, some way could be arranged to block the improper derivations at a later stage when the determining environment is reached. But again, this would amount just to doing a swooping rule in several stages.

But we can counter these counter-proposals even so. Suppose we try to determine at the beginning of the derivation whether the preposition can move with the NP, and mark it accordingly. Thus, we would code the phrase marker so as to ensure these results:

12.   I wonder what I should put the ice-cube on top of.
13.   *I wonder on top of what I should put the ice-cube.

However, there is an optional rule which allows the parenthetical insertion of phrases like *I wonder*. If this rule is applied, the sentence corresponding to (13) is O.K.:

14.   On top of what should I put the ice-cube, I wonder.

This rule follows the HOP rule (as it must on any derivation, by definition of HOP), hence it will have to be made obligatory in an ad-hoc way for just those cases where we have marked the PP (or else the feature-marking rule must not only know the environment of the question but its entire derivational history).[4]

The second argument against the feature-marking proposal applies only if it is claimed that the same rule is involved in shifting an interrogative phrase and a relative pronoun. It has been known for a long time that the possibilities for pied-piping differ according to whether relativization or interrogative fronting is involved.[5]

15.   Reports the covers of which the government prescribes the height
        of the lettering on always put me to sleep. (= Ross's 4.163b)
16.   *The covers of what does the government prescribe the height of
        the lettering on?

But if the internal structure of the clauses is the same we cannot know whether or not to pied-pipe at the point where a successive cyclic HOP rule would operate.

In each of the above arguments the difficulties of a HOP analysis arise because facts about preposition shifting depend on structure external to the first clause on which HOP would apply. Difficulties of this sort are actually much more general. Let us consider two examples.

Ross (1967a) has noted that extraction of a NP (whether by interrogative movement or relativization) must be blocked in *that*-clauses that have not been extraposed. Thus, we have:

17.   Who is it likely that Oscar will marry?
18.   *Who is that Oscar will marry likely?

Ross proposed that results like this were to be explained by a general movement constraint on extraction from sentential subjects. But this constraint cannot, by definition, apply to the application of HOP, since it depends on structure above the clause in question. To save the HOP analysis we would have to make Extraposition on the higher clause obligatory just in case the embedded sentence had undergone HOP, a completely ad-hoc device that would again just ensure that things turned out as if we had applied a SWOOP rule.[6]

Again, interrogative movement is optional (in many dialects) in direct questions, but not indirect questions:

19.   Now you're going to do what?
20.   He asked me what I was going to do.
21.   *He asked me that (if?) I was going to do what?

(These examples are intended as regular interrogatives with falling intonation, not as echo-questions.) But as we saw above the determination of the direct-indirect distinction depends on knowledge of higher structure. To save HOP we might make it optional, but then we would have to add a new obligatory rule for indirect questions which would exactly duplicate the effect of a swooping rule.

The final argument against HOP is of a different nature. Bresnan (1971) has shown that normal stress (and intonation) can be accounted for in an elegant way by assuming that the stress rule(s) operate at the end of every syntactic cycle. Thus she is able to give an account for the difference between pairs like these:

22.   George left dírections to follow.
23.   George left directions to fóllow.

(22) has a relative clause interpretation (= directions which we were supposed to follow) while (23) is interpreted as a complement structure (= directed us to follow). Now on the assumption that interrogative movement follows the application of the stress rule (this is ensured in Bresnan's treatment by her syntactic analysis of interrogatives) she also accounts for these normal patterns:

24.   What bóoks has Helen written? (= Bresnan's (32))
25.   What has Helen wrítten?

The Nuclear Stress Rule assigns strongest stress to *what books* in (24) when it is still the last lexical phrase in the sentence, but not to *what* in (25) since it is derived from a pronoun. But it is crucial for this account that interrogative movement work as Bresnan assumes in a single step at the point in the derivation where the proper environment for movement is met. Given a rule like HOP (and assuming the correctness of Bresnan's ordering hypothesis that stress assignment comes at the end of every syntactic cycle) we would have the following derivation (omitting irrelevant details):

$$\text{Q you think [COMP Helen has written WHAT books]}$$

S_1 HOP: Q you think [COMP WHAT books Helen has written]

Stress rules: Q you think [COMP WHAT books Helen has written]
$$\qquad\qquad\qquad\qquad\qquad\qquad 2\qquad\quad 2\qquad\qquad\quad 1$$

S_0 HOP   WHAT books you think Helen has written
$$\qquad\qquad\quad 2\qquad\qquad 2\qquad\quad 2\qquad\qquad\quad 1$$

Stress assignment WHAT books do you think Helen has written
$$\qquad\qquad\qquad\quad 3\qquad\qquad\qquad 2\qquad 3\qquad\qquad\quad 1$$

That is, the normal intonation is supposed to be something like this

26. ^{2}What books do you think Helen has ^{3}written^1 #

(where the numbers refer to pitch levels, and the final double-cross a clause juncture, see Hill (1958) for an explanation of the notation and an account of English stress and pitch). But surely this sentence can only have a contrastive or emphatic interpretation.[7]

I think that it can be concluded that the weight of evidence, whether from general theoretical considerations or from a variety of different facts about English, is on the side of SWOOP as opposed to HOP. There is no doubt in my mind that given the wide possibilities offered by current linguistic theory in just about any of its formulations, a successive cyclic account could be patched up to work, but I believe it would then just amount to a kind of mechanical variant of a single movement rule. Obviously, if we allow ourselves to code information about higher environments into a structure, and ensure that the WH-phrase keeps moving as long as it is supposed to (and no further) without trailing any bits and pieces along the way, we can convert any unbounded movement rule into a successive cyclic rule and vice-versa. In the remainder of this paper I will note some implications of the assumption of a single movement rule.

The main implication of retaining SWOOP as the correct interpretation of interrogative movement are for various alternative treatments of pronominalization.

Within the tradition of treating pronoun-antecedent relationships as the result of a rule of English grammar (in the widest sense) there are two independent distinctions: (1) whether pronouns are transformationally derived by a rule of NP-replacement, or are present more or less as such in the base and coreference relations are assigned by interpretive rules (the first in Ross 1967b, the second in Jackendoff 1969, 1972, for example), (2) whether the rule (of whatever sort) is ordered cyclically, last-cyclically, or defined on surface structure, optional or obligatory, and so on. For the following conclusions, (1) is irrelevant. In general, it is very difficult to tell any difference between accounts in terms of a replacement transformation or an interpretive rule that reconstructs, in effect, what would have been replaced by a transformation, if we are arguing in terms of rule-ordering and so on. Thus, the choice between transformational and interpretive treatments must be made on the basis of other considerations. Discussions of pronominalization have been muddied somewhat by a failure to keep these distinctions clear.

Ross (1967b) provided an elegant argument for the cyclic and obligatory nature of pronominalization on the basis of sentences like this:

27.   Realizing that *he* was unpopular didn't bother *Oscar*.

If we interchange the pronoun and the noun we will have a perfectly grammatical sentence, but one in which the noun and the pronoun *him* cannot be coreferential.

28.   *Realizing that *Oscar* was unpopular didn't bother *him*.

Note that if the rule were optional, we could choose not to apply it until the last cycle and then derive the non-reading of (28). Thus, (27), (28) seem to show that the rule (whether interpretive or transformational) must be obligatory.

Postal (1971) exhibited sentences like the following to show the untenability of the obligatory cyclic account[8]:

29.   Which of the men who visited *her* do you think *Betty* criticized?
30.   Which of the men who visited *Betty* do you think *she* criticized?

Both of these sentences are good, but there is no way to derive (30) by a cyclic obligatory rule, since at the point of the derivation where it would apply, the sentence would have the following shape:

31.   You think [Betty criticized which of the men who visited Betty]

and pronominalization could only work forwards to derive (29). As Postal noted, this conclusion follows only if WH-movement takes place on a later cycle (not necessarily the last cycle), that is if SWOOP is correct and not HOP. Since we have shown HOP to be incorrect, we can conclude that it is not correct that pronoun-antecedent facts can arise from a cyclic *and* obligatory transformation or interpretive rule.

If HOP were correct we could get both derivations by a cyclic obligatory rule, since the *which*-phrase would be positioned at the head of the embedded sentence and pronominalization could work in either direction. On the other hand, if the rule establishing pronoun-antecedent relations were optional, we could derive both (29) and (30) by choosing to apply the rule on the first applicable cycle (for (29)) or on the last cycle after WH-movement (which could yield an alternative derivation for (29) as well as a derivation for (30).

Let us next note that any cyclic rule together with HOP will lead to incorrect derivations. Consider (32):

32.   *Which boy is *she* likely to marry that *Betty* likes?

I assume that the extraposition rule that gets (32) from its source applies after the WH-movement rule and is in fact a last-cyclic rule (Ross 1967a). Since there is a derivation of (33) (the immediate source of (32), cf. (29)), on the assumption that HOP is correct, there is no way to prevent the application of Extraposition from NP to get (32):

33.   Which boy that *Betty* likes is *she* likely to marry.

There is, on the other hand, a way to block (32) with an optional rule, but only if we assume a SWOOP rule. Assume again that sentences like (30) or (32) can only be derived by application of a rule of pronoun-antecedent assignment on a later cycle than the one on which the first possible derivation of (29) takes place. All we need do is assume that this rule is ordered after Extraposition from NP (and hence after SWOOP) and there will be no way to derive (32). Unfortunately, further sentences can be found which will escape this solution:

34.   Which boy that Betty likes is likely to marry her?

This sentence has a straightforward derivation by the optional rule, but since the rule can work on an earlier cycle, there is no way to prevent the later-cyclic application of Extraposition from NP to yield[9]

35.   *Which boy is likely to marry *her* that *Betty* likes?

Since the interrelationships among the various hypotheses we are considering are rather complicated, let me summarize the discussion in the form of a chart

Pronoun-antecedent rules	WH-movement	Inconsistent with facts illustrated by
cyclic optional	HOP	(27) (28) (32) (33)
,,	SWOOP	(35)
,,	HOP or SWOOP	(35)
,,	SWOOP	(30)
,,	HOP	(32)
,,	HOP or SWOOP	(35)

It thus seems that no cyclic rule can account for all the examples we have noted. On the other hand, there are many sentences which show, like Ross's (27), that a last-cyclic or surface-structure rule will not work. The inadequacy of a surface-structure rule is especially clear from examples like the following ambiguous sentences which differ in their coreferentiality possibilities according to the interpretation:

36.   Crashing into Harold's house, he saw an elephant.
37.   What he discovered was a proof of Descartes' existence.

Since neither a cyclic nor a last-cyclic rule will do the job it is evident that there is no single rule of pronominalization. Jackendoff's interpretive account comes the closest to meeting all the requirements of the data, since he is able to handle cases like (27) by a last-cyclic interpretive rule that assigns a non-coreferentiality relation to any pairs of anaphoric elements and possible antecedents that have not been marked as coreferential by some previous interpretive rule. No account that I know of is consistent with all the sentences we have considered. It is interesting that the problem arises in cases like (32) and (35) because of the assumption that the extraposition rule follows the fronting of the interrogative phrase and is hence later or last-cycle. If this assumption can be successfully challenged then Jackendoff's account would work, as far as I can see.[10]

Finally, if our conclusions about the SWOOP formulation of interrogative movement (and by implication relative clause formation) are correct, some other explanation for the facts that led Chomsky to adopt the successive cyclic analysis must be found.

University of Massachusetts
Amherst, Mass.

NOTES

[1] The problem has been discussed most recently in Chomsky 1973 and Postal 1972. The SWOOP formulation was assumed in Bach 1971, the HOP rule in Jackendoff 1969 (but not 1972). A number of other discussions will be referred to below. It should be noted that the formulations mentioned are independent of whether the rule is last-cyclic or ordinary cyclic. Postal (1972) calls rules like HOP 'successive cyclic' and rules like SWOOP 'higher-trigger cyclic'.

[2] Postal's independent argument is based on facts of the grammar of English. The argument is that if HOP is assumed, then rules like Tough-movement and Raising, which operate on the next cycle, would have to be complicated in an ad-hoc way to allow possibilities like (i) and (ii):

i.   What do you think would be difficult for Melvin to find?
ii.   Who does John seem to love?

The proper formulation of both rules is a matter of considerable controversy. For Tough-movement, see Postal 1971, Postal and Ross 1971, Akmajian 1972, Lasnik and Fiengo forthcoming; for Raising, Postal 1974, Chomsky 1973.

[3] That direct and indirect questions have the same internal structure is shown by Baker (1970). Barbara Hall Partee has pointed out to me the discussion of this restriction in Fowler (s.v. *Preposition at end*).

[4] This part of the argument, by itself, is not very decisive, since it would be possible to claim that such facts should be captured by a surface-structure constraint. But as far as I can see there is no independently needed surface-structure constraint. Since any version of interrogative movement will have to ensure that the WH-phrase ends up at the right place in terms of the direct-indirect distinction and the presence of the right sort of environment (e.g. an interrogative verb), separating out this aspect of the construction as a surface-structure constraint would involve an ad-hoc complication of the grammar.

[5] These facts are pointed out in Stockwell, Schachter, and Partee (1973:606) and attributed to Ross (1969a), although I have been unable to find the reference in Ross. But they have certainly been part of the lore of transformational grammar for a long time.

[6] Extraposition, as against Intraposition, as in Emonds 1972, is defended in some detail in Bach forthcoming. But a completely parallel argument can be constructed for analyses like Emonds'.

[7] This argument is implicit in Bresnan 1971. Chomsky (1973, fn. 50) cites Bresnan and suggests another conclusion (if I understand him correctly): WH-movement and possibly other rules are ordered in a separate cycle after most of the 'regular' cyclic rules but still apply in a successive cyclic fashion. Since stress assignment would take place presumably within the first set of cyclic rules, with the WH-phrase still in place, the correct assignment to cases like (26) would result. However, the earlier arguments given here would apply just as well to this alternative treatment of HOP. I have assumed that the stress rules will be fixed up to apply in such a way as to yield (in Bresnan's notation) *What books do you think Helen has written?* As far as I can see the rules, with Bresnan's analysis, will yield a contour (surely incorrect) with the primary stress on *books*, next highest stress on *think*, and least heavy stress on *Helen* and *written*:

  1   2   3   3
What books do you think Helen has written (or 1 2 4 4).

[8] Actually, Postal cites the examples as counterevidence to a cyclic account, but what they show is that the cyclic rule cannot be obligatory, as we will see.

[9] The fact that such sentences are incompatible with any optional cyclic assign-

ment of coreferentiality or optional transformation of pronominalization was pointed out to me by Stanley Peters.

[10]   This is one point then in which there appears to be a real difference between the rules of pronominalization and interpretive rules of coreference assignment. Jackendoff has two separate rules, one which optionally marks possible anaphors as coreferential with antecedents and an obligatory non-coreferentiality rule which operates on the final cycle. There is no natural analogue in a transformational account to this latter rule. What the pair of rules does, in effect, is say on the last cycle "If any pair of noun phrases and pronouns cannot have been marked coreferential anywhere in a derivation then they can't be so marked on the end of the derivation either." The closest analogue in a transformational account would be a derivational constraint saying just that but restricted to the last cyclic operation of the pronominalization rule. Slightly different predictions would arise from these two accounts. The class of cases that provide difficulties for both are those like (32) and (35) where an optional rule puts a pair into an impossible configuration from an earlier possible configuration. It seems likely to me that no account in terms of rules of the sort we have been considering in the particular framework of transformational theory will be able to handle all the facts. The solution will perhaps come by changing the framework, as in Partee 1972, or Fauconnier 1973, or by working within a discourse theory as in Kuno 1972.

REFERENCES

Akmajian, Adrian. 1972. Getting tough. Linguistic Inquiry 3:373-7.

Bach, Emmon. 1974 Syntactic theory. New York.

Baker, C. L. 1970. Notes on the description of English questions: the role of an abstract question morpheme. Foundations of Language 6:197-219.

Bresnan, Joan. 1971. Sentence stress and syntactic transformations. Language 47:257-81.

Chomsky. Noam. 1973. Conditions on transformations. In Stephen Anderson and Paul Kiparsky, eds., Festschrift for Morris Halle.

Emonds, Joseph. 1972. A reformulation of certain syntactic transformations. In Stanley Peters, ed., Goals of linguistic theory (Englewood Cliffs).

Fauconnier, Gilles. 1973. Cyclic attraction into networks of coreference. Language 49:1-18.

Fowler, H. W. 1960. A dictionary of modern English usage. Oxford.

Hill, Archibald A. 1958. Introduction to linguistic structures. New York.

Jackendoff, Ray S. 1969. Some rules of semantic interpretation for English. M. I. T. Ph. D. dissertation.

Jackendoff, Ray S. 1972. Semantic interpretation in generative grammar. Cambridge, Mass.

Kuno, Susumu. 1972. Functional sentence perspective: a case study from Japanese and English. Linguistic Inquiry: 3:269-320.

Partee, Barbara Hall. 1972. Opacity, coreference, and pronouns. In Donald Davidson and Gilbert Harman, eds., Semantics of natural language (Dordrecht).

Postal, Paul M. 1971. Crossover phenomena. New York.

Postal, Paul M. 1972. On some rules that are not successive cyclic. Linguistic Inquiry 3:211-22.

Postal, Paul M. 1974. On raising. Cambridge, Massachusetts.

Ross, John R. 1967a. Constraints on variables in syntax. M. I. T. doctoral dissertation.

Ross, John R. 1967b. On the cyclic nature of English pronominalization. In To Honor Roman Jakobson (The Hague) II, 1669-82.

Stockwell, Robert P., Paul Schachter, and Barbara Hall Partee. 1973. The major syntactic structures of English. New York.

RULES AND COUNTER-RULES
IN HISTORICAL PHONOLOGY

WILLIAM COWAN

Since the publication of Halle 1962, there have been a significant number of publications in which the basic approach introduced by Halle – the expression of linguistic change, and phonological change in particular, by changes in the set of rules that operate upon underlying phonological structures – has been expanded, revised, elaborated upon, and otherwise used as a springboard for discussion of historical considerations in language. Whether or not all change is best handled via rule manipulation, it cannot be doubted that such manipulation or such expression can give penetrating insights into at least some of the processes that play a part in linguistic change. One such insight is the realization, in cases like Lachmann's law in Latin or root-final consonantal gemination in Maltese, that morphophonemic alternation may be a decisive factor in phonological change. A more traditional approach that works only or primarily with autonomous phonemes would fail to uncover this pertinence of the morphophonemic level, or at least would have difficulty in expressing it as cogently.

It has become apparent since Halle's article appeared that not all rules are of the same type. My observations have been restricted to their setting in a historical frame of reference, but there does not seem to be any reason that different types of rules could not be recognized in a synchronic frame as well. Rules can differ in their internal construction and range of application, as well as in the extent and rapidity of their spread, so that we have, for example, chorded rules like Lachmann's law that have morphophonemic information built directly into the rule, so to speak, and which apply simultaneously at various levels in a derivation, similar to the way in which a chord in music specifies notes simultaneously at various levels in a musical scale; and we can have sluggish rules, like the one that specifies the change of [xw] to [w] in Welsh (Sommerfelt 1962, quoted by Chen and Hsieh 1971), that, whatever their shapes, are diffused slowly across a lexicon or a dialect area, or across both. It is the purpose of this article to point out some of the ways in which rules differ among themselves, and to point out a conclusion to be reached from the appreciation of this diversity. In some ways, rules can be viewed in the same way one views phonemes, either autonomous or systematic; some, perhaps all, rules can be of various types at the same time, just as some phonemes are both obstruants and stops, or both resonants and nasals. Whether one wants to discuss rules as, say, chorded or sluggish or whatever, may depend upon the strategy followed at a certain point, and what the purpose of the discussion is. Similarly, it may well turn out that rules can be analysed into their distinctive features or component parts, such as sluggishness or persistence, with appropriate pluses and minuses, again according to the depth of analysis and the purposes to which such an analysis is to be put. These further investigations are not attempted here, but merely adumbrated as a suggestion for further work. Let me add at the outset that I, as many others interested in this field, conceive of rules as artifacts of linguistic analysis, pale reflections, as it were, of actual processes like analogy or assimilation, not having any reality outside the description of the language. I mention this only because in the discussion that follows it appears that rules not only do have this independent existence denied here, but indeed have traits and characteristics that verge on the anthropomorphic. By viewing rules as if they had these characteristics we may gain some insights into the processes of language change, therefore such a procedure is defensible; but it can be done only if we keep in mind the disclaimer mentioned above.

In terms of internal structure, I am aware of the following three types of rules: persistent, chorded, and sudden death. In terms of external relationships or applications, I am aware of the following three types of rules: underground, sluggish, and lenticular. There are undoubtedly other types, both internally and externally defined, that have escaped my attention, but these will do to begin with.

The first type of rule given a definition and brought to the attention of those working in historical linguistics is the persistent rule, first discussed by Chafe (1968), and later applied to a problem in Maltese by Cowan (1970). Briefly, a persistent rule is one whose effect is not cancelled by the rule or rules that come after it either in real time or in a derivational construct, but which persists for a shorter or longer time in the language. Persistent rules tend to show their effect time and time again, coming into operation each time that a change elsewhere in the system produces forms that fit their structural descriptions – lying in wait, so to speak, with their nets spread to catch the appropriate forms. The well-known diphthongization of /ee/ in Finnish is a good example of a persistent rule, although it has not been recognized as such. Kiparsky (1968), who first presented the example, considered it a case of rule reordering. Campbell (1971) considered it a case of rule addition with the same rule being added before and after an intervening rule; that is, the rule was added to the language twice. The facts are as follows: in Finnish, the sequence /ee/ was diphthongized to /ie/; for example /vee/ → /vie/ 'take'. A form like /teɣe/ 'do', contemporaneous with /vee/, was not affected. However, at a later date, the /ɣ/ in /teɣe/ was elided, and the resulting /tee/ became diphthongized to /tie/, coinciding with /vie/ with respect to the vowel sequence. Kiparsky's solution is to posit that at an earlier stage, the order of rules was:

(1) ee → ie   (/vee/ → /vie/)
(2) eɣe → ee   (/teɣe/ → /tee/)

but that at a later date the order became:

(1) eɣe → ee   (/teɣe/ → /tee/)
(2) ee → ie   (/tee/, /vee/ → /tie/, /vie/)

This reordering of rules ties in with Kiparsky's generalization that rules tend to shift into the order that allows their maximum utilization in the grammar: in the first order, the diphthongization rules catches only one form, whereas in the second order it catches two. Campbell, claiming that all rule change is really rule addition, presents the following solution:

(1) ee → ie   (/vee/ → /vie/)
(2) eɣe → ee   (/teɣe/ → /tee/)
(3) ee → ie   (/tee/ → /tie/)

in which Rule 1 is added as Rule 3 after an intervening Rule 2. Both Kiparsky's solution and Campbell's are sophisticated and account for the facts, but it seems to me that a more realistic solution is to recognize that the diphthongization rule entered the language before the rule that elided /ɣ/, and simply remained there when the elision rule came in, coming into operation a second time after the elision rule produced the appropriate input. It could be schematically presented as follows:

(1P) ee → ie   (/vee/ → /vie/)
  ┆
(2) eɣe → ee   (/teɣe/ → /tee/)
  ↓
    ee → ie   (/tee/ → /tie/)

However presented, there seems to be no reason to suppose that just because a rule enters a language after another rule the first rule ceases to operate. In fact, it is possible to envision that all rules are persistent unless and until they are cancelled by a later rule, either entering immediately after the rule in question, or at a later date with any number of intervening rules. The task, then, would be not to specify persistent rules but to specify rules that are not persistent, or rules that are later cancelled.

The second type of rule to be considered here is the chorded rule. It was pointed out, but not named, by Campbell (1971) in his discussion of Lachmann's law. Rather than recognize this law as a result of a rule inserted into a language at other than the end of the phonological component, as is done by Kiparsky (1968), King (1969), and others, Campbell considers it a rule added at the end, but with morphophonemic specification reaching back, or up, into the derivation, which specification correctly generates the long vowel of the pertinent forms, even though the vowel occurs before a voiceless consonant in the actually spoken forms. This not only seems an intuitively correct analysis of the situation, but also seems to be what Halle had in mind when he first analysed the Great Vowel Shift in English in terms of rule addition as a method of outlining phonological change, since it allows the possibility that two phonemes might fall together at one stage of the language, but become separate again at a later stage on the basis of the morphophonemic effects left by the earlier coalescence. The second change is the one that can be expressed by the addition of a chorded rule. Lachmann's law could be noted as follows:

$$(1) \text{ ag} + \text{past participle} \rightarrow \text{agtum} \quad (\rightarrow /\text{agtum}/)$$

$$\begin{array}{l}
\cdots \\
(2) \text{ g} \rightarrow \text{k}/\_\text{t} \\
(3) \text{ a} \rightarrow \bar{\text{a}}/\_\text{g}
\end{array} \Bigg] \qquad \begin{array}{l} (\rightarrow /\text{aktum}/) \\ (\rightarrow /\bar{\text{a}}\text{ktum}/) \end{array}$$

in which the added Rule 3, lengthening the /a/, is marked with a chord tie to the place in the derivation where it gets its conditioning.

In general, whenever there are grammatical prerequisites to a phonological change, this change can be expressed by means of a chorded rule that extends back in the derivational structure to the grammatical nexus that is the prerequisite. Another example of this would be the development of one prototone in Atsi to the high short falling tone in verbs and to the low falling tone in nouns, with no further phonological conditioning (Burling 1967). In such a case, the chord notation would be extremely long, and a direct tying is not feasible; a variant notation would be simply a parenthetical reference to the higher nexus:

(x) Verb → po^2, lo^2, ...
(y) Noun → nwa^2, lei^2, ...

.

.

.

(z) V^2 → $\acute{V}$/rule x
→ $\tilde{V}$/rule y

However noted, the chord effect seems to be fairly widespread in historically significant rule structure.

The third type of rule noted here is what might be called sudden-death rules. They are rules that in effect prevent a condition from coming about in that they act simultaneously with a rule that creates the input or environment favorable to their being triggered, and which operate upon that input to produce a changed output. I now believe that the reduction of final geminate consonants in Maltese (and all other dialects of Arabic known to me) is a rule of this nature. With the elision of final short vowels in Arabic, forms like /yaḥibbu/ 'he loves' and /xaddu/ 'cheek' would have become /yaḥibb/ and /xadd/. However, there is no evidence that these forms ever existed in Arabic, and it seems more likely that a sudden-death rule had previously entered Arabic, and, since sudden-death rules are also generally persistent, lay dormant, waiting for the elision of final vowels which enabled it to come into operation. That is, the sudden-death rule operated simultaneously with the vowel elision rule in real time, even though in a logical derivation it had to come after the vowel elision. The difference between a sudden-death rule and a persistent rule is this: The persistent rule enters the language as a regular rule, and just stays around. The sudden-death rule enters covertly, and does not operate until the sudden-death situation is opportune. That is, the reduction of final geminates in Arabic did not come in as a regular rule operating on final geminates – there were none of these in the language – but entered as a prohibition on the appearance of the final geminates.

Turning our attention to rules that seem to be primarily of external significance in historical development, we can isolate what I have called elsewhere underground rules (Cowan 1971). These are rules that create exclusively underlying forms. The only fairly sure case of an underground rule that I have observed is the one that creates root final gemination in

...CVC# forms in Maltese and other Arabic dialects. Since the ...CVC# forms never exhibit the results of the gemination rule – these results occur only in forms of the structure ...CVCC + V... (where + marks the division between the root and the following morpheme) – the rule produces no surface forms, and hence remains underground. Another possible underground rule is the one in Swahili that converts underlying /u/ to /w/ before the relative particle /o/, since the /w/ goes to zero before this /o/ and never appears at the surface. For example, underlying and historically prior /uliuo/ 'the (tree) which' becomes /uliwo/ by the underground rule, then /ulio/ by the w-elision rule. Note that this is underground in only some instances in Swahili, since there are cases where the /w/ resulting from /u/ remains /w/ before /o/: /nilimuona/ 'I saw him' becomes /nilimwona/, with no elision of the /w/. This situation is complicated by other historical changes, like an earlier /βona/ 'see' becoming /ona/ due to loss of /β/, but I believe that the small portion isolated in this discussion does exhibit underground behavior.

Sluggish rules are those which, whatever their internal structure, travel slowly across a lexicon or dialect, or both. It is different rates of spread or diffusion that give rise to irregularities noted by Wang (1969) and Chen and Hsieh (1971) for Chinese, as well as those mentioned earlier in this article for Welsh. Some rules are more sluggish than others. This difference could be noted as an n-ary feature of this type of rule. An example of a rule spreading slowly across a lexicon is possibly the one specifying the change k → t/kV_# in Narragansett (Cowan 1969), since we have forms like *wekick* 'to the house' (from /wiikeŋki/), where the final /k/ is preserved, as well as forms like *keesaqut* 'to Heaven' (from /kiišekenki/), where final /k/ has become /t/. The rule had reached the lexical item for 'Heaven', but not the lexical item for 'house'. Rules travelling slowly across a dialect area produce isoglosses, and are too numerous to need exemplification here. Sluggish rules immediately suggest a sociolinguistic field of reference: the sluggishness or lack thereof of a rule may well be a reflex of its acceptability to the speakers concerned – the more acceptable, the more rapidly it spreads.

The last type of rule to be surveyed here is what Newton (1971) has called lenticular rules. These begin as regular rules, indistinguishable from other rules, but after a certain amount of time begin to taper off in the range of their domain, or in their intensity. A graphic notation of their effect would thus describe half a lens-shaped figure. The example that Newton presents is nasal assimilation in Greek: from /Nθx/ we would expect a rule of nasal assimilation to produce /θθx/, but in fact it does not, being overridden by a historically later rule of cluster simplification that produces /Nx/. The nasal assimilation rule was more intense or stronger at an earlier stage, but by the time the cluster simplification rules entered the language it had lost its force and yielded to the later rule. Newton's formulation is within a model of linguistic change that he calls line phonology, a model that he characterizes as more reflective of the facts than the point phonology of previous formulations. In this he is obviously correct, but his model still does not preclude that some changes consist of a line that is a single point: some changes occur definitely after an immediately preceding change, and cease operating when followed by a later change. Newton's model can include both line rules and point rules.

There are no other rules that have come to my attention at the present time. However, each of the types mentioned here can have a converse, thus arranging themselves into binary units similar to the distinctive features of phonology: persistent rules can be opposed by evanescent rules; chorded rules by single-note rules; sudden-death rules by lingering rules; underground rules by establishment rules; sluggish rules by lively ones; and lenticular rules by, say, point rules.

If it is true that these different types of rules exist, and if it turns out that there are even more waiting to be discovered, then, since rules are but reflections of processes at work in language change, this diversity will be ample evidence of the multiplicity of the processes of change. Language, it seems, does not change in only one way; it changes in many ways, and any theory that attempts to characterize what goes on will have to account for this diversity.

Carleton University

REFERENCES

Burling, Robbins. 1967. Proto Lolo-Burmese. Indiana University Research Center in Anthropology, Folklore and Linguistics. Publication 43.
Campbell, Lyle. 1971. Review of Historical linguistics and generative grammar, by Robert D. King. Lg. 47.191-209.
Chafe, Wallace. 1968. The ordering of phonological rules. IJAL 34.115-36.
Chen, Matthew, and Hsin-I Hsieh. 1971. The time variable in phonological change. Journal of Linguistics 7.1-13.
Cowan, William. 1969. PA *a, *k and *t in Narragansett. IJAL 35.28-33.
—. 1970. A persistent rule in Maltese. Canadian Journal of Linguistics 15.122-8.
—. 1971. An underground rule in Maltese. Journal of Linguistics 7.245-51.
Halle, Morris. 1962. Phonology in generative grammar. Word 18.54-72.

King, Robert D. 1969. Historical linguistics and generative grammar. Englewood Cliffs: Prentice-Hall.
Kiparsky, Paul. 1968. Linguistic universals and linguistic change. Universals in linguistic theory, ed. by Emmon Bach and Robert T. Harms, 170-202. New York: Holt, Rinehart and Winston.
Newton, B. E. 1971. Ordering paradoxes in phonology. Journal of Linguistics 7.31-52
Sommerfelt, Alf. 1962. Diachronic and synchronic aspects of language. The Hague: Mouton.
Wang, William S-Y. 1969. Competing changes as a cause of residue. Lg. 45. 9-25.

THE USE OF COMPUTERS IN THE STUDY OF MEDIEVAL GERMAN: TWO SUGGESTIONS

WILLIAM C. CROSSGROVE

Although American linguistics in the late sixties and early seventies has been dominated by the discussion of the linguistic theories of Noam Chomsky, computational linguistics has also achieved some recognition. By computational linguistics I mean advances in linguistics which would have been unlikely without the use of the computer, an early example being the development of a quantitative measure of phonological relatedness between pairs of languages (Kučera 1964, Kučera and Monroe 1968). Since the formation of the Association for Machine Translation and Computational Linguistics in the early sixties – the Association for Computational Linguistics since 1968 – there has been an established niche in the American academic scene for linguists working with the computer.

The computer has also proven to be a valuable tool for relieving linguists of certain tasks which had previously been done by hand. Large-scale lexicographical undertakings have benefited from the use of the computer; a good example is the plan for a new dictionary of Old English (Leyerle 1971). The computer has proven especially useful to philologists, the scholars who lay the foundations on which historical linguistics is built. Specifically, the ability of the computer to alphabetize rapidly and accurately has led to the planning of word-indexes and concordances to medieval texts. New plans are continually being announced in the "Directory of scholars active" published twice yearly in the journal *Computers and the Humanities*. In my field, medieval German, the computer is being used to prepare a series of concordances and indexes in which three volumes have already been published and many more are planned (Wisbey 1968a, 1968b, 1969; see also Scholler 1966a and Wisbey 1967). A listing similar to the "Directory of scholars active" has just been initiated for medieval German by the *Zeitschrift für deutsche Philologie* (Lutz 1971 and a note on page 475 of the same issue). As has been pointed out by Scholler (1966b), these indexes for individual texts are useful to literary scholars for a variety of reasons; and one might argue that any editor of a text could in the future be expected to provide some form of word-index or concordance as a by-product of his editorial labor. At the very least a machine-readable version of the finished text could be produced since editing usually involves typing the manuscript several times, and it is no more difficult to type with a key punch than with a standard electric typewriter. In fact, in the long run a machine-readable version of the text may be more useful than published results.

Technological feasibility and scholarly value are not necessarily enough, however, to insure that future editions of medieval texts will automatically be processed by the computer. First of all, computers are still not equally available at all institutions, and funds for computer operation may or may not be available even when computers are. But I think that a more fundamental problem is involved here. Alphabetization of indexes and concordances is so routine and trivial that it is of little interest to people who work full-time with computers. It is at best a traffic problem for a computer center when lengthier alphabetizations may tie up some equipment for substantial blocks of time. From the vantage point of those who work with the computer, it may seem that anyone can use the machinery if he is willing to spend a few hours learning about the basics of computer science so as to understand in general what is going on, and if he learns the simplest control instructions which enable him to submit his material in the proper form and format for processing.

Nonetheless, there is not much evidence to indicate that large numbers of philologists and literary scholars are using the computer for routine alphabetization. A comparison of the persons attending the conference reported on by Beatie (1967) with those planning to attend a symposium announced in the May 1971 issue of *Computers and the Humanities* (p. 277) indicates that three of the four American participants in the 1971 meeting were already participants in the one held in 1967. In other words, a relatively small group of scholars has become deeply involved in computer work. Many others appear to be reluctant to take the necessary steps to penetrate the mysteries of a large university computing center in order to carry out tasks that seem peripheral to their main interests, even though the tasks may be far less peripheral than they seem. The kind of simplified access most frequently offered to computer users involves time-sharing or some other system designed to make the largest high-speed computers economically feasible by keeping them running as steadily as possible. The managers of a university computing center have a vested interest in encouraging users who can keep their machinery going even if the work itself is uninteresting to them, but the whole apparatus is likely to seem too complex and 'scientific' to interest many who could otherwise benefit from it. The widespread use of computers in literary studies could probably be more readily encouraged by the mass production of machinery which is slow, limited in function, simple to operate, and inexpensive. The basic operations involved in alphabetization are so simple that a machine with a small logical unit and a modest number of readily accessible storage units might be technologically feasible at a price which would enable it to be installed wherever a group of scholars would have frequent, but not necessarily constant, use for it as an aid in their research and teaching. Such a machine could be designed with a few simple instructions for a limited range of indexing and concordance-making tasks so that users could learn how to operate it in a few minutes. Then a library of texts in machine-readable form could be available for use as need arises.

It might be argued that remote terminals hooked up to a large computer will serve the same purpose, but I am doubtful of this for two reasons: such terminals are not well adapted to the inputting of large amounts of data, and the state of the art is such that new ground rules must be learned every few months or years, something which will be tolerated only by those genuinely interested in the computer. I would argue instead that only a special-purpose computer which becomes a stable office fixture, like an electric typewriter or a copying machine, will find wide acceptance among literary scholars.

So far our discussion has been limited to work with single texts. Linguists are of course also interested in working with individual literary texts – the scholar to whom this volume is dedicated has repeatedly demonstrated in his research and teaching how linguists can contribute to the study of literary texts –, but more frequently linguistic research implies processing material from a variety of texts: texts from an entire group whether it be defined historically, geographically, or sociologically. Here little progress has been made in the study of medieval German with the computer although the work described by Lenders (1971) is aimed at solving some of the problems. The difficulties can perhaps best be illustrated with an example. A computer-produced index of the main manuscript of *König Rother*, a twelfth-century German epic, turns up the following entries for Middle High German *unz(e)* 'until': *vnz* (four times), *vnze* (three times), and *vnzer* (once, with enclitic *er* 'he'). While the entries vary somewhat in spelling, they could readily be found

in an alphabetical index because they occur in succession. If we then looked for the same item in *Reinhart Fuchs*, a twelfth-century German epic
about Reynard the Fox preserved in a thirteenth-century manuscript,
we would find no entries at all. The scholar who knew Middle High
German would suspect what could have happened, so he would look
under *biz*, Modern German *bis*, a variant which gradually replaced *unz*
in the meaning 'until' during the Middle Ages. Here one finds two entries,
but closer examination reveals that only one is the desired lexical item
while the second occurrence is a first-person-singular-optative-present
verb in the phrase *er biz ich in* 'if I would bite him to death'. The lexical
item *biz* with the meaning 'until' also occurs in *König Rother*, and here
one finds the following entries: *biz* (21 times), *bit* (three times, along
with 15 occurrences which are variants of *mit* 'with'), *biez* (once), and
miz (once). Since people bite less frequently than animals in epics, the
homography in the *Reinhart Fuchs* entry is avoided here. As is obvious,
however, finding the 26 entries for *biz* in *König Rother* requires extensive
knowledge of the orthographical pecularities of the text. More detailed
examples of the kind discussed here are given by Schröder (1969:389-92).

   The user of a word-index or concordance must therefore know a good
deal about his material if he plans to use it properly; he must know where
to look for variants. If the index is parsed, then this difficulty is avoided,
but a considerable amount of additional effort must be invested in the
preparation of a parsed index. The arguments for and against parsing are
old, having been stated in connection with hand-prepared indexes
(Schröder 1962) and repeated for computer-produced ones (Wisbey
1962:171-2, Schröder 1969:388-91). Presumably the lack of parsing is
more an inconvenience than a fatal flaw for most indexes to individual
texts, and one which is even less troublesome in the case of a concordance;
but extreme orthographical inconsistency, such as we have in *König
Rother*, greatly mitigates the usefulness of either.

   The inconveniences to users of individual indexes are nearly insur-
mountable difficulties to projects involving groups of texts. There is no
program, short of a complete algorithm for analyzing the language,
which would enable a lexicographer to retrieve relevant items from a
variety of texts for an entry *biz* in making a Middle High German
dictionary. Since an algorithm of this kind is unlikely to be forthcoming,
the answer lies in additional hand work. The major question is simple
to pose: should linguists attempting multi-text analysis work from indexes
and concordances of individual works, or should a standardized corpus
be created as the foundation for such work? The only alternative now

available is the first, but in the long run it is less appealing because every analysis will require a new examination of the existing indexes or concordances. The linguistic study of medieval German will profit from computers only in an eclectic and highly limited fashion.

The second alternative, a standardized corpus, is a much more attractive long-range goal, but there are enormous problems. Should standardization be in terms of the idealized Middle High German of courtly literature as devised by nineteenth-century scholars, or should it be in terms of Modern Standard German orthography? The former will appeal more to medievalists who like the familiar look of normalized editions, but the latter would make the corpus accessible for historical studies without a conversion algorithm (Lenders 1971:329). Naturally, I would expect that in either case manuscript spellings would be preserved along with normalizations so that the normalized form would be available for alphabetization while the actual form would be available for analysis and printing out. The work on Late Middle High German described by Lenders (1971) is in some sense an attempt at a compromise between the possibilities of working from individual indexes or from a standardized corpus. The starting point is a single text which is indexed and normalized in Middle High German and in Modern Standard German orthographies, and which is marked for simple grammatical categories. The goal is gradually to build a dictionary by using this information to analyze further texts. The project should lead to interesting results for future work, but it appears to be directed more at perfecting techniques of automatic analysis than at the actual production of a dictionary. Schröder (1969:393-5) also discusses some of the problems of normalization of medieval German texts.

A second difficult question is whether a series of relatively homogeneous mini-corpora, comparable except in size to the one used by Kučera and Francis (1967) for written English, should be produced; or whether a single large corpus should be constructed with as much information as is available on regional, temporal, and sociological provenance. I suspect that only the latter will be feasible.

Finally, it must be decided whether one or a few scholars will undertake such a project on their own, as in the case of the planned dictionary of the Old High German glosses (Wells 1970), or whether a large-scale international undertaking might not be the best way to resolve these questions. There is a desperate need, for example, for an up-to-date Middle High German dictionary (Scholler 1966b:162-3) which does not appear to be in the offing. It seems to me that the time has arrived for a major cooperative effort by linguists, literary scholars, and philologists working with Middle High German on a project using texts from many manuscripts in a standardized form. Exchange of information alone will not lead to a significant breakthrough.

Brown University

REFERENCES

Beatie, Bruce A. 1967. Computer study of medieval German poetry: A conference report. Computers and the Humanities 2.65-70.

Kučera, Henry. 1964. Statistical determination of isotopy. Proceedings of the Ninth International Congress of Linguists, Cambridge, Mass., August 27-31, 1962, ed. by Horace G. Lunt, 713-21. The Hague: Mouton.

Kučera. Henry, and W. Nelson Francis, 1967. Computational analysis of present-day American English. Providence: Brown University Press.

Kučera, Henry, and George K. Monroe. 1968. A comparative quantitative phonology of Russian, Czech, and German. Mathematical linguistics and automatic language processing, 4. New York: American Elsevier.

Lenders, Winfried. 1971. Lexikographische Arbeiten zu Texten der älteren deutschen Literatur mit Hilfe von Datenverarbeitungsanlagen. Zeitschrift für deutsche Philologie 90.321-36.

Leyerle, John. 1971. 'The dictionary of Old English': A progress report. Computers and the Humanities 5.279-83.

Lutz, Hans Dieter. 1971. Übersicht zur maschinellen Analyse altdeutscher Texte. Zeitschrift für deutsche Philologie 90.336-55.

Scholler, Harald. 1966a. Word index to the *Nibelungenklage*. Ann Arbor: University of Michigan Press.

—. 1966b. Über die Förderung der Nibelungenforschung durch Elektronenrechner. Zeitschrift für deutsches Altertum 95.149-65.

Schröder, Werner. 1962. Review of Collected indexes to the works of Wolfram von Eschenbach, ed. by R.-M. S. Heffner, and A word-index to the texts of Steinmeyer *Die kleineren althochdeutschen Sprachdenkmäler*, by R.-M. S. Heffner. Anzeiger für deutsches Altertum 73.133-7.

—. 1969. Der Computer in der deutschen Philologie des Mittelalters. Beiträge zur Geschichte der deutschen Sprache und Literatur (Tübingen) 91.386-96.

Wells, J. C. 1970. 'Die althochdeutschen Glossen' after fifty years. Colloquia germanica (no volume numbers) 185-91.

Wisbey, Roy A. 1962. Concordance making by electronic computer: Some experiences with the 'Wiener Genesis'. Modern Language Review 57.161-72.

—. 1967. Vollständige Verskonkordanz zur *Wiener Genesis* mit einem rückläufigen Wörterbuch zum Formenbestand. Berlin: Erich Schmidt.

—. 1968a. A complete concordance to the Vorau and Strassburg *Alexander* with a reverse index to the graphic forms, an index of rhymes, and a ranking list of frequencies. Compendia, 1. Leeds: W. S. Maney.

—. 1968b. A complete word-index to the Speculum ecclesiae. Compendia, 2. Leeds: W. S. Maney.

—. 1969. A complete concordance to the *Rolandslied* (Heidelberg Manuscript) with word indexes to the fragmentary manuscripts by Clifton Hall. Compendia, 3. Leeds: W. S. Maney.

THE ROLE OF
METAPHOR IN LINGUISTICS

ROBERT J. DI PIETRO

Although much has been written about metaphor, linguists have not been among those who have made great use of the concept in their work. For the most part, reference to metaphor in general linguistics texts, whenever it occurs, is limited to a few passing remarks concerning its possible impact on language change (Hall 1964, Martinet 1964) or its role in building figures of speech (Hall 1964). Some linguists (Jakobson and Halle 1956, Hill 1968) have discussed the role metaphor plays in literature and in the nature of linguistic signs in general. Only a few recent attempts, such as that of Lambert (1969), have been made to place metaphor in a position of prominence in linguistic theory. Within these pages I shall attempt to support an assertion that any theory of language which does not account for metaphor is severely limited and quite possibly misled.

Metaphor can be discussed in a number of ways. Various authors have addressed themselves to one or more of the following questions: (1) what purpose does metaphor serve (Embler 1966), (2) how does it work within a system of language (Brooke-Rose 1958, Thomas 1969, Lambert 1969), and (3) how does it originate (Abse 1971, Lewin 1970). Metaphorical transference of meaning may be intimate and personal or it may be openly shared by a community of speakers. In the former case, metaphor can provide a key to unconscious thought (Voth 1970). In the latter case, it forms the basis of idioms.

The failure to give an accounting of metaphor in linguistic theory has placed great restrictions on the productivity of generative models. Elsewhere (Di Pietro 1970), I have shown how creative sentences with metaphors such as those found in poetry would be rejected as non-grammatical within the framework of Chomsky's *Aspects* (1965) model or, for that matter, within the framework of any similar generative model. In a manner of speaking, the sentences produced and analyzed by generative grammars as we know them have only 'literal' senses.

There is an important reason for this state of affairs. If a sentence has only one 'literal' sense, it is deemed unambiguous. If it has more than one, it is ambiguous. Metaphors, however, are not necessarily ambiguous, although they do not 'literally' mean what they appear to say. Not even Chafe's (1970) model, which seems to have certain advantages over Chomsky's in this respect, handles the problem satisfactorily. With reference to idioms (which we could term loosely as 'dead' metaphors), Chafe has developed a procedure for 'literalization' through a 'post-semantic process' which attaches the proper 'literal' meaning where context requires it. The outcome of the literalization procedure is that a meaning different from the one usually associated with an expression is generated. In this way, the expression *he kicked the bucket* acquires the sense of 'he died', where context would not permit the usual trans-formations, such as the passive, to be activated. Chafe's procedure requires that we know how to distinguish, in every case, between literal and nonliteral senses. Unfortunately, it is no clearer in Chafe's model than it is in any of the others how we can unequivocally retrieve the literal sense of every word and expression. Is *leg* in *the leg of the table* being used idiomatically or literally? Is *foot* in *foot of the mountain* as idiomatic as *leg* in the preceding example? While I would say in my own speech either *the leg of the table* or *the table's leg*, I would hesitate to do the same with *the foot of the mountain*. Is it possible that all uses of *leg, foot, arm,* and other such terms would be idiomatic whenever they do not refer to parts of the human anatomy? If so, how do we know it? Have we applied more than purely grammatical criteria in sorting out literal senses from idiomatic ones?

It is of some comfort to know that linguists do not stand alone with their lack of empirical foundations in the determination of literal senses. Many philosophers and literary analysts merely assume that literal senses exist and that the principle task involves studying how new senses may be associated. Thomas (1969) gives some notable examples of how types of metaphor and figurative language emerge from extensions of meaning from literal to nonliteral. He never appears to question the validity of the opposition 'literal / nonliteral'. In the same vein, Browne (1971, 12) describes metaphor as involving a discontinuity, i.e. "a conflict between the conventional meaning of an expression ... and its rhetorical meaning in a given speech ...".

With regard to its logical operations, metaphor is simply described. In essence, a metaphorical statement is one which can be symbolized as A → B, or A is B. Simile, which I prefer to interpret as a kind of metaphor, is an operation in which A is said to be like B. In linguistics, we have a parallel distinction with respect to 'context free' and 'context sensitive' rules. The basic metaphor operates as a 'context free' rule (or at least as one in which context is not overtly specified), while the simile explicitly states that a term can be considered as another term only under specified or delimited conditions, ie. A → B in context X. With this distinction in mind, it is easy to see why Robert Burns might prefer to use a series of similes in his well-known poem which begins with the line 'My love is like a red, red rose'. Use of this simile sets the stage for others, e.g. 'My love is like a melody'. Had he framed his opening line in terms of a 'context free' metaphor, he might have implied unlimited equations of his love with roses – some of them quite thorny and aphid-like in their appeal! It has been pointed out, incidentally, that metaphors do not usually take the surface form of a simple *be* predication in poetry. Preferences are for stylistic variants such as apposition, apostrophe, and address (Brooke-Rose 1958, 105ff.). Various literary genres may tend to favor some figures of speech over others. Jakobson and Halle (1956), for example, find metonymy to be prevalent in realistic fiction, where a concern for detail is evident. Browne (1971) finds metonymy frequently used in Gothic fiction, as well. Whatever their surface structure may be, each figure of speech contains an underlying *be* predication somewhere in its derivation.

In my opinion, metonymy, synecdoche, hyperbole, conceit, oxymoron, and other figures of speech all stem from either simile or metaphor. Expressions such as *I like Brahms, All hands on deck!, I've got a terrible cold, He's the emperor of ice cream*, and *She succumbed to the cold fire of his eyes* all seem to involve a metaphorical operation at some stage of their generation. Each appears to require us to be capable of perceiving some sort of change or aberration in a system of associated meanings. The metonymic value of *Brahms* in *I like Brahms* derives from our ability to perceive that the composer's name can represent his music. Metaphorical transference of senses is just as evident in the synecdoche *All hands on deck!*, where *hands*, since they are attached to *sailors*, can stand for them. Whether a figure of speech is effective or not seems to depend not on the operation itself, but on how well the hearer or reader accepts the relationship of the terms involved in the operation.

As a matter of fact, both metaphorical and literal expressions utilize the same kind of operation. There is no difference between the predication of *Water is liquid sunshine* (an apparent metaphor) and *Water is H_2O* (a supposedly literal statement). To determine whether a predication is literal or metaphorical depends on judgements relating to the universe of discourse in which it occurs. To say that water is liquid sunshine is to make an association of senses ('liquid' with 'sunshine') which does not occur according to a supposed system of natural perceptions. To say that water is H_2O invokes a system of cognition about chemical elements in which water literally consists of two atoms of hydrogen and one atom of oxygen. Yet, to equate water to sunshine is to bring out the importance of both in making plants grow. If we say that one of the expressions is 'poetic' while the other is 'scientific', then we have classified them according to different universes of discourse, rather than draw a distinction between literal and metaphorical sense. As Shibles (1971) has pointed out, each universe of discourse, such as art, poetry, science, and religion, carries with it a different set of presuppositions, and reality is at least as diverse as are the various universes of discourse. By making allusions to different contexts, we are open to gaining deeper insights into the world as we conceive of it. The metaphors which invite empirical validation we think of as 'facts'. We build our sciences by a careful selection of factually based metaphors (Wheelwright 1962:164-5). Thus, geneticists refer to a genetic 'code' and biologists to a 'tree of evolution' – metaphors which help them to arrange their research in meaningful ways. It is only when metaphorical statements are not related to empirical fact that scientists reject them. A good example of the scientist's attitude can be found in Cohen's (1971) review of Rosen's *Dynamical system theory in biology*. Rosen speaks of 'dynamical metaphors' which comprise a "system of ordinary differential equations of specified form the qualitative behavior of which in some way resembles the qualitative behavior of a class of biological phenomena" (as quoted by Cohen 1971:674). These dynamical metaphors are to stand as explanations of the phenomena they resemble, according to Rosen. Cohen's criticism of Rosen is unrelenting: "Because the elaboration of language is, for some people, much easier than the labor of establishing concordance or tension between general principles and experience, there is an enormous temptation to spin out language that has the sound and syntax of general principles and to declare it scientifically satisfying without scrupulous regard to its relation to reality" (Cohen 1971:674).

Linguists, at least the prominent ones, are apparently not so firm in requiring experimental support for their theories. Compare the following from Chomsky regarding the correlation of linguistic theory to the structure of the mind: "It seems to me that the most hopeful approach today is to describe the phenomena of language and of mental activity as accurately as possible, to try to develop an abstract theoretical apparatus that will as far as possible account for these phenomena and reveal the principles of their organization and functioning *without attempting, for the present, to relate the postulated mental structures and processes to any physiological mechanisms or to interpret mental function in terms of "physical causes"*. We can only leave open for the future the question of how these abstract structures and processes are realized or accounted for in some concrete terms ..." (Chomsky 1968:12; italics mine). Since Chomsky leaves unsaid what 'concrete terms' might be involved, it is difficult to see how we are to understand the principles whereby language is organized. The term 'mind', itself, has provided a useful metaphorical framework in which to cast much of the discussion of generative grammar. Yet, psychotherapists, who might rank themselves among the most frequent users of the term, appear not to use it in their technical discussions because of its vagueness.

Perhaps a useful distinction to make in understanding how people use metaphor in language and how linguists use it in writing grammars is the one between 'tool' and 'artifact'. Language can be interpreted as the product of man's creativity, as important as other products such as his societal structure and his technology. At the same time, language is also the instrument by which man shapes his system of communication. When language is interpreted as product or artifact, it is equatable to grammar. We have no linguistic term with which to label language as tool, but it is intimately connected with man's general powers of perception and his ability to affect objects. What complicates research in language is the interrelationships between linguistic tool and artifact. Whenever man creates a tool, that tool also comes to play a part in determining the work performed. Just as an auto mechanic who acquires the tools necessary to repair foreign-made cars is not likely to be inclined toward working on American vehicles, so the users of a particular language often find it difficult to discuss topics not commonly touched upon in that language. I have frequently observed that foreign students of linguistics often prefer to discuss the subject in English among themselves because English has been the language of instruction and has provided them with the necessary tools and phraseology – not to mention the culturally-determined contexts to which linguistics is appropriate. This is not to say, of course, that appropriate tools and contexts could not be developed in other languages. On the contrary, men readily do so, aided by their facility to make metaphors.

When we talk about grammar, we are focussing on language as an artifact. When we say that grammar consists of such terms as 'nouns, verbs, definite articles and numbers', all of which interact systematically, we are establishing a universe of discourse in which these terms are to be taken literally and are not supposed to have metaphorical value. Thus, the modern 'scientific' grammarian is not satisfied with a definition of noun as the name of a person, place, or thing, which, even though it may be true, is not relatable to other units in the grammatical framework which he has established. If anything, calling a noun 'the name of a person, place, or thing' would be metaphorical with regard to contemporary grammar. The generativist, for example, would much prefer to define noun in terms of its relationship to other constituents in syntax.

Once the presuppositions for the grammatical universe of discourse are determined, it is labeled 'grammatical theory' and a sizeable number of terms, otherwise metaphorical, can be admitted and considered to be literal. In transformational generative grammar, for example, many of the terms derive metaphorically from plant imagery. 'Trees' are produced, with 'branches' that can be 'pruned' or attached, as if grafted, to other trees. There are 'kernel' sentences. Just as birds nest in real trees, so do constructions in grammar trees. Other metaphors come from mathematical logic, such as 'transformation' and 'recursion'. Still others derive from the engineering sciences: 'power of generation', 'simplicity' of design, and so on.

In the process of rejecting earlier theories of grammar, the metaphors of those theories are devalued. No one in transformational grammar draws 'box diagrams' as did the structuralists. Whereas 'trees' are supposed to reflect a reality of language design, boxes do not. The advocates of each school defend their metaphors vigorously. Lakoff, when attempting to reconcile the notion of transformational rule with the observations of researchers in language-related fields, avers that "... there is a very good reason to believe that transformations do exist" (Lakoff 1970:637), and proceeds to make such rules more inclusive or global. He apparently believes that when the metaphorically-derived rules of a grammar are made to be more general, their literal senses will no longer be questioned. Regardless of how sophisticated we make our grammars, we shall do nothing more than postpone the day when an empirical foundation must be found for them (cf. remarks on Chomsky, above).

Contemporary linguists, for all their sophistication, have not veered from the age-old dichotomy of discourse into rhetoric and logic. The belief that language is essentially logical and non-emotive in its organization and function has led linguistic analysts to ignore the importance of metaphor and affect. Linguistic theory remains almost exclusively centered on questions of how language as artifact (i.e. 'grammar') can be described. An even greater limitation is self-imposed by the linguists in neglecting the force of metaphor used as a tool in shaping the artifact. If metaphor involves the interrelating of universes of discourse, then it is likely that language, in its everyday use, is far more usually metaphorical than it is literal. The users of a language are constantly called upon to respond in some verbal way to novel situations. The logically consistent and thematically restricted discourse of science and philosophy is far more infrequent than the short responses to requests for information, verbal reactions to pain and pleasure, and so on, for which people use language. We accept metaphorical language almost without question. If we are shown a picture of a rabbit, we are more likely to respond: *That's a rabbit* than *That's a picture of a rabbit*. In other words, we willingly accept the contextual framework of pictorial description in order to respond without making overt reference to it. (Hill 1968 has supplied a general discussion of the nature of signs and icons in linguistic terms.)

If the reason produces literal sentences and the system to understand them, then the imagination yields metaphorical ones and has the power to change the system. Probably without a perception of system, men would not be able to function nor be able to recognize metaphors (see Thomas 1969:35). But the perception of system is not an answer to the quest for truth. What sounds 'intuitively true' to us is what is in harmony with our perception of the state of affairs. If this is so, then what we consider literal in meaning depends upon the systems of beliefs we have built for ourselves. Grammar is just this type of system. But man changes his systems just as he creates them. The attempts by Labov (1966) and others to 'explain' language change by charting the variation in language through social strata have resulted, perhaps, in a clearer picture of the ways in which change may affect a system. But since no capacity to predict new changes has been gained, the contributions of sociolinguistics are perhaps best considered to be descriptive rather than truly explanatory.

To the students of cognitive development in man, I would make a plea to give equal importance to research in man's affective development. Psychotherapists have long recognized the importance of both dimensions of language in their work. Baker (1950), for example, provides an interesting example of how cathexis may arise from the human psyche and take universal forms of metaphors in language. Working as a psychoanalyst among the Maoris, he observed that importation of the domesticated European house cat into Maori culture has given rise to the same sort of dream symbolism associated with the cat in other languages even though the animal was new to the Maoris. Baker's conclusion was that these associations arose from universally shared sexual motifs in the unconscious. To support his thesis, he provides a long list of 'phallic symbol-complexes' in various languages of the Malayo-Polynesian group. Abse recognizes a degree of affect underlying even literal language. The evolution of discursive language, according to Abse, involves "partial repression of the original mnemic image of the percept, of closely related conceptual elaborations, of directly connected (aroused) instinctual derivatives and emotional reactions, and to a lesser extent, of the figurative reference which had continued to carry elements of the former" (Abse 1971:26). Further down on the same page, he writes: 'live metaphor arises via a flexible and regulated derepression and regression to sensorial imagery with subsequent establishment of word connections'. An example of regression with projective identification may be found in Western Apache where anatomical terms are extended to describe the parts of an automobile: *wos* 'shoulder' and 'front fender'; *kai* 'thigh, buttock' and also 'rear fender'; *inda* 'eye' and 'headlight'; *ji* 'heart' and 'distributor'; and so on (data from Basso 1967).

If linguistics is to make important strides in this decade, it will have to move to a study of how man uses his emotive as well as his cognitive powers to build and change the artifact he calls grammar. In brief, linguistics will have to focus sharply on how language functions metaphorically. Man is a wondrous maker of metaphors, and perhaps it is for this reason that his language is really distinct from all other systems of communication on this earth.

REFERENCES

Abse, D. Wilfred. 1971. Speech and reason. Charlottesville: University of Virginia Press.
Baker, Sidney J. 1950. Language and dreams. International Journal of Psycho-Analysis 31.171-8.
Basso, Keith H. 1967. Semantic aspects of linguistic acculturation. American Anthropologist 69.471-7.
Brooke-Rose, Christine. 1958. A grammar of metaphor. London: Secker & Warburg.
Browne, Robert M. 1971. The typology of literary signs. College English 33.1-17.
Chafe, Wallace. 1970. Meaning and the structure of language. Chicago: University Press.
Chomsky, Noam. 1965. Aspects of the theory of syntax. Cambridge: MIT Press.
—. 1968. Language and mind. New York: Harcourt, Brace.
Cohen, Joel E. 1971. Review of Dynamical system theory in biology, by Robert Rosen. Science 172.674-5.

Di Pietro, Robert J. 1970. Notes on 'innovation' and 'creativity'. Languages and Linguistics Working Papers 1.30-3. Washington: Georgetown University Press.

Embler, Weller. 1966. Metaphor and meaning. DeLand, Florida: Everett/Edwards, Inc.

Hall, Robert A., Jr. 1964. Introductory linguistics. Philadelphia: Chilton.

Hill, Archibald A. 1968. Analogies, icons, and images in relation to semantic content fo discourses. Style 2.203-27.

Jakobson, Roman, and Morris Halle. 1956. Fundamentals of language. The Hague: Mouton.

Labov, William. 1966. The social stratification of English in New York City. Washington: Center for Applied Linguistics.

Lakoff, George. 1970. Global rules. Lg. 46.627-39.

Lambert, Dorothy Mack. 1969. The semantic syntax of metaphor: a case grammar analysis. Univ. of Michigan dissertation.

Lewin, Bertram D. 1970. The train ride: a study of one of Freud's figures of speech. The Psychoanalytic Quarterly 39.71-89.

Martinet, André. 1964. Elements of general linguistics. Chicago: University Press. [Original French version 1960.]

Shibles, Warren A. 1971. An analysis of metaphor in the light of W. M. Urban's theories. The Hague: Mouton.

Thomas, Owen. 1969. Metaphor and related subjects. New York: Random House.

Voth, Harold M. 1970. The analysis of metaphor. Journal of the American Psychoanalytic Association 18.599-621.

Wheelwright, Philip. 1962. Metaphor and reality. Bloomington: Indiana University Press.

NOTES ON LANGUAGE RECEPTION
AND VARIATION

GEORGE P. FAUST

This paper uses A. A. Hill's 1970 account of his reception of language as a springboard. As always, he makes great good sense, so that there is little or nothing to take issue with in his report on his idiolect. His article, however, leaves the rest of us free to make our own extensions. My concern here is a double one. First, we need if possible to learn how to make pandialectal statements in describing a language, which means learning how to take language variation into account without setting up any one idiolect or dialect as the norm to which all others are referred. Second, we need to ask if the same operations that produce language should be expected to receive it, whether by matching or reversal. At the points of junction with the outside world, sensory impressions are certainly different from motor activities. Listening is not speaking.

It is not surprising that the investigation of speech reception should be a relatively recent concern of linguists. After all, the development of articulatory phonetics preceded that of acoustic phonetics, and auditory phonetics is still in its infancy. It follows from the history of linguistics and the present state of our knowledge that the major approaches to linguistic analysis, no matter what their proponents claim, should be biased in favor of speech production. This is self-evident in analyses with a unidirectional flow toward utterance, but it is just as much true of a corpus-based analysis which mainly aims to account for the utterances used as a starting point. No valid neutrality as between speaker and listener has yet been achieved by a major analysis, for the obvious reason that no one knows enough yet to manage it. Claims to such neutrality are statements of goals, not of achievements. Extensive discussion of language reception, as distinct from original language acquisition, is simply non-existent. For the present we must resort almost entirely to educated guesses, based on what seem to be reasonable inferences.

My first guess is about the nature of the phonetic signal in transit, and the perception of it by two or more auditors. We know from acoustic phonetics that the speech spectrograph and other pieces of hardware can register features of the signal that are significant to linguists, but at the same time we are reasonably sure that machines do not capture everything. Nor, of course, is everything they do capture linguistically significant. If the producer of the signal is a trained phonetician, he may be able to tell us something about it in terms of its articulation. But after the machines and phonetician have had their say, it is still quite possible that certain features of the signal will go unrecognized until they reach a listener equipped to perceive them.

This bit of speculation rests substantially on the belief that no two idiolects have identical organizations of phonology – in short on the belief that Hill 1958 was basically right in distinguishing between idiophonemes and diaphonemes. Linguists today might perhaps be more inclined to differentiate subphonemically, in terms of phonetic components or features – point or manner of articulation, voice, and the like. But while the terms used in phonological discussion have changed, the main point stands. Just as Trager and Smith 1951, Hockett 1958, Hill, and others maintained through the 1950s, an overall pattern must be posited if we are ever to make pandialectal statements. However, because of variable inner and idiolectal arrangements, an analysis intended for the whole of a language must be flexible enough to allow for assignments that appear to violate the goals of correctness, simplicity, and generality that most responsible linguists set for themselves.

Let me illustrate with glottal stop and postvocalic *h* in English, generally represented in the literature of the early and middle 1950s as [ʔ] and /h/. The standing accorded glottal stop by various linguists has ranged all the way from paralinguistic through allophonic to phonemic: [ʔoʊ] instead of [oʊ] signals the speaker's surprise or other disturbed condition and is linguistically nil; [maʊnʔn̩] and [baʔl̩] show that [ʔ] is an allophone of /t/; [səmʔm̩], [maʊnʔn̩], and the interrupted nasal signifying negation combine to demonstrate that [ʔ] is /ʔ/. Since glottal stop is easily perceptible to a trained ear and since it is described in articulatory terms, linguists have felt called upon to assign it a specific role in the phonology. But it seems to me quite possible that if three auditors with appropriately differing idiolects – or perhaps dialects – listen to the same phonetic signal containing a glottal stop effect, they might quite properly interpret it phonologically in different ways, since each auditor would process the signal according to his own system. As a corollary, it is evident that a statement about glottal stop for the English language must allow for all interpretations of it by linguists working with native speakers.

Postvocalic *h* poses a markedly different problem. Let us set aside at once, as irrelevant here, the vexed question of whether it is allophonic with prevocalic *h*. The most prominent variants that are germane presumably register as either a centering vocalic glide or as additional length. The third possibility, to be considered for those with idiolects like my own, is that postvocalic *h* may fail to register at all in ordinary speech. For example, we can probably agree that anything we would spell *sorry* is the same lexical item regardless of the pronunciation of its stressed vowel nucleus. In Trager-Smith notation, apparently at least half a dozen variants occur: /ɑ, ɔ, o, ɑh, ɔh, oh/. Probably many Americans distinguish five or all six before /r/, but I for one register only two: one with a central vowel as in *starry* and one with a back vowel as in *story*. This state of affairs can be explained only in terms of my lacking a productive distinction between /o/ and /ɔ/ and between /V/ and /Vh/, since the difference between *sorry* as [sɑ́ri] and *sari* as [sɑ́:ri] is clear when they are offered in isolation as a minimal pair. In other words, there is a something in the phonetic signal which can register (for me) as additional length but which is ordinarily ignored or blocked because it does not fit into my phonological system. More generally, postvocalic *h* may be heard as a centering glide producing diphthongization, as length (perhaps interpretable as tenseness?), or as what Hockett 1958 refers to as noise in the channel. The point to be emphasized here is that all may be simultaneously valid in the language and that all but the last may be interpreted by an analyst as either a separate segment [h] /h/ or as a feature or component of the vowel.

The slight evidence adduced here by way of illustration and the much more extensive evidence available elsewhere suggest that in ordinary use, as distinct from trained phonetic discrimination, the speakers of a language hear utterances in terms of their own phonological systems used in production. This means that only a part, and perhaps a relatively small part, of the phonetic signal in transit registers with any one individual. But since other parts do exist, it may well be that the whole can never be accounted for systematically. The operation seems to be one of selection (probably combined with some distortion) governed by the possibilities of matching with an idiophonology. If linguists are to aim at a diaphonology, they will have to allow for variation both laterally at a given level and vertically (hierarchically) at two or more levels. Whether such requirements can be met within the framework of any linguistic theory so far proposed is obviously open to question.

The illustrations already given immediately raise questions about

correctness in analysis, particularly for those approaches that view
morphemes and lexemes as ordinarily composed of sequences of phonological units.[1] In the language designs which explicate the approaches,
the units predictably differ: classical phonemes and morphophonemes
(or morphophones) for Sapir, Bloomfield, and their followers; systematic phonemes for Chomsky and other generative-transformationalists;
and basic phonemes for Lamb and the stratificationalists. But the same
general question arises no matter what the unit is called or just where it is
located in its system: What non-arbitrary way is there of choosing among
the half-dozen stressed vowel nuclei that can appear in *sorry*? The surface
manifestation need not, of course, be identical with or unique to the
underlying phonological vowel, but presumably all the variants realized
in utterances must be derivable from whatever phonological unit is
chosen as part of the composition of the lexeme. The problem of choice
is there not only for *sorry* but for all lexical items that have more than
one pronunciation, sometimes within the same supposed dialect, as with
either. On occasion even a single idiolect – if it is like mine – will vacillate
between *advértisement* and *advertísement*.

But all this is not to say that choices are not made in one way or
another. The least reputable way, of course, is to assume that one's
own favorite pronunciation is basic and all others are to be explained
as deviations from this 'norm'. On such a basis I might select /sáriy/,
/íyðər/, and /əd+vártizmint/ as the sequences of which lexical items
sorry, *either*, and *advertisement* are composed. A better way would be to
consult convenience in analysis, which often implies simplicity of statement. The variations in the stressed vowel of *sorry*, for instance, are most
simply accounted for by starting from a morphophonemic ᵐ/ɔ/ and
allowing for single-unit movement in either direction – shift to either
nonround or nonlow, if you prefer – and the addition of length or centering glide.[2] A third way of choosing is to "see underlying forms and
phonological processes as closely paralleling historical forms and phonetic changes" (Chafe 1970:7). On the productive side, this certainly can
lead to a multidialectal set of contemporary results, though it is not clear
how far back into history we must go for the underlying form – to OE
sārig or beyond to reconstructed forms. Unfortunately, the implication
of the historical basis is that whole dialectal systems, not just single items,
would have to be traced. It is simply impossible at present even to conjecture how this or any other type of analysis can account for the experience
of native speakers perceiving the phonological composition of morphemes
and lexemes. There may be no such thing as a single correct analysis.

To show that language variation is not limited to the phonological component of language, let me turn to that essential part of the syntax which concerns the arrangement of constituents and at times the identification of them. In the discussion of *sorry* as a lexeme, there was a tacit understanding that the variant realizations all referred to the same item in the language. So also it is now to be assumed that the auditors may get the same meaning from a sentence even when their interpretations of its constituent structure differ. It is obvious from the literature which has accumulated that the determination of constituents and the establishment of their mutual relations is much too big a subject to be dealt with here in substantial detail.[3] But whereas the literature is mostly devoted to showing the grammatical pertinence of constituent structure and how best to account for differences in meaning dependent on it (e.g. Wells 1947 and the now celebrated *old men and women*), the discussion here is limited to illustrating how different interpretations of the constituents of a given utterance may often result in producing substantially the same meaning.

We can assume a class of utterances which, like the example below, will be universally interpreted as SVO sentences with an optional locative:

S	V	O	Loc
David	joined	his friend	at the inn

We must also assume that there are no significant discrepancies in the understanding of the lexical items, so that the only differences will be in the assignment (not the identification) of the major divisions of the sentence as constituents.[4] The question at issue is whether substantial differences in understanding will accompany differing interpretations of the constituent structure. If we focus on the role of *Loc* as a modifier (by fiat), there are five arrangements of constituents which are either traditional or likely:

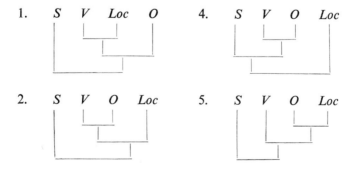

3.   *S*   *V*   *O*   *Loc*

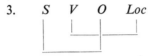

Only the first arrangement, which reflects traditional school diagramming, requires tacitly rearranging the order of the divisions. The last in effect makes *Loc* a part of *O*, thus reducing the number of divisions from four to three. It is probably significant that the last arrangement is also the only one that excludes *V* from the immediate constituency of *Loc*, directly as in Nos. 1 and 3 or indirectly as in Nos. 2 and 4. Provided the first four arrangements produce the same meaning, we may justifiably suppose that agreement is unimportant as long as *V* stands above the horizontal line marking the immediate constituent(s) with *Loc*. If this is so, there can be no one correct analysis of the constituent structure of the example from the point of view of language reception.

So far, no question has been raised about the identification of constituents, but in English, at any rate, there is often disagreement among analysts. The point can be demonstrated by simply changing the verb of the example already given:

S	V	?	O	Loc
David	looked	for	his friend	at the inn

The *for* could be assigned to the verb or the object, or it could conceivably be classed as a major division by itself. This last seems too improbable to merit serious consideration here, though it would have to be explored in a full-dress study; but each of the first two assignments has had many proponents. My own suggestion is that both can be right at the same time – that is, that two auditors of the example can differ in their assignments without disagreeing about the meaning of the whole. My impression (which can be no more than an impression) is that as listeners we are normally prepared for both assignments to constituents, so that we probably have little or no idea which interpretation we use if, as in the example, both are likely. Incidentally, such conditioning may account for our ease in understanding both of the following related sentences, even though productively we may have a decided preference for one:

> For whom did you look?
> Who(m) did you look for?

The tenacity with which both placements of *for* are maintained in English argues for a syntactic flexibility in the language as a whole that analysts rarely stress.

It is now time to sum up. Throughout this paper I have argued that an adequate linguistic theory and mode of analysis must take into account the variable interpretations that are commonly present when speakers of the same language listen to one another. In straight phonology, they seem to be restricted by the design of their idiophonological systems. At the same time, they are apparently equipped to accept, without much hesitation or confusion, limited but sometimes quite noticeable variations in the shapes of morphemes and lexemes. And finally, listeners can differ about the structure of what they hear without missing the speaker's meaning.

All this has a serious bearing on the principles by which linguists are presumed to operate. It suggests that the belief in unique correct solutions of language problems should be abandoned. It questions whether simplicity in description is a valid criterion for deciding between two grammars. It doubts that much generality of statement can be attained except at the cost of precision or by imposing a sort of dogmatic rigidity on the analysis. Accountability remains, but to the prime goals of linguists should be added comprehensiveness and flexibility. Meanwhile, pending serious and extensive investigation, it is asking too much to expect detailed answers to my questions about pandialectal statements and the mechanisms that account on a community-wide basis for language reception.

Lexington, Kentucky

NOTES

[1] The use of *ordinarily* allows for the possibility of morphemes and lexemes which have no realizations. A single phonological unit may be considered a minimal sequence. But cf. Lamb 1966 on phonology.

[2] Chomsky and Halle 1968 start from an underlying [ɔ] to produce a surface-structure [ä] (205). But they limit themselves "to the phonetics of a single, prototype dialect, passing over much phonetic detail and dialect variation that are beyond the scope of this study" (206). The limitation prevents their derivation from being germane in an overall frame of reference.

[3] Postal 1964 is still the most complete treatment I know.

[4] The *Aux* of generative grammar is ignored for simplicity.

REFERENCES

Chafe, Wallace L. 1970. Meaning and the structure of language. Chicago and London: University of Chicago Press.

Chomsky, Noam, and Halle, Morris. 1968. The sound pattern of English. New York, Evanston, and London: Harper and Row.

Hill, Archibald A. 1958. Introduction to linguistic structures. New York: Harcourt, Brace and Co.

—. 1970. Toward a parsing procedure for simple sentences in English. Studies in General and Oriental linguistics: Presented to Shiro Hattori on the occasion of his sixtieth birthday, ed. by Roman Jakobson and Shigeo Kawamoto, 235-245. Tokyo: TEC Co., Ltd.

Hockett, Charles F. 1958. A course in modern linguistics. New York: The Macmillan Co.

Lamb, Sydney M. 1966. Prolegomena to a theory of phonology. Language 42:536-573.

Postal, Paul, 1964. Constituent structure: A study of contemporary models of syntactic description. Indiana University Research Center in Anthropology, Folklore, and Linguistics, Publication Thirty.

Trager, George L., and Smith, Henry Lee, Jr. 1951. An outline of English structure. Studies in Linguistics. Occasional Papers, No. 3. Norman, Okla.: Battenburg Press.

Wells, Rulon S. 1947. Immediate constituents. Language 23:81-117.

TESTING AUDITORY DISCRIMINATION OF SUPRASEGMENTAL FEATURES

DAVID M. FELDMAN

1. INTRODUCTION

The importance of auditory discrimination testing both as an indicator of aptitude for foreign language learning and as a measure of proficiency in foreign language acquisition has long been appreciated.[1] The literature abounds in evidence of the essential nature of auditory discrimination ability in the habilitation of persons with auditory, phonatory and language deficits.[2] Moreover, numerous studies offer substantial proof of a reliable correlation between auditory discrimination ability and pronunciation skill.[3] With few exceptions, however, extant prognostic and diagnostic tests of auditory discrimination ability are exclusively oriented toward the segmental phones of the language in question (or, in the case of second-language learning emphases, of the target language in contrast with the source language). This bias, aggravated by the customarily superficial treatment accorded to non-segmental features in most teaching and habilitational materials, would seem to undervalue the real importance of suprasegmental features in both the hearer's and the speaker's grammar of the language being treated.

It has been suggested that English-speaking students who are generally unable to perceive the difference among certain prosodic features of other non-tone languages, such as pitch level and syllabic stress, in the basic sentences of the instructional dialogues, are often unable to produce the same features when articulating the sentences. However, when the same sentences aremodelled in a controlled *recitative* style, in which, for example, the intonation contour are suppressed, these same students quickly perceive the patterns of stress and their subsequent oral production of the utterances improves considerably.

In devising a successful measure of auditory discrimination at the prosodic level, we faced an essential preliminary issue in determining the ultimate value of isolating these features from the segmental phones and sequences with which they co-occur in normal language behavior (Lehiste 1970:2-5). Such isolation seemed justified on the basis of the informal observations reported above, but also because phonemic perception ultimately depends upon the simultaneous recognition of the individual significant features which, in bundles, make up the acoustic identity of the specific sound patterns (Jakobson 1965:1-15). Obviously, the isolation of such features is not accomplished in normal language behavior and, consequently, must be achieved by electromechanical means. If, however, we wish to make an eventual comparison between the electromechanically-generated features (EGF) and the same features in normal language behavior (HGF), the EGF parameters should, we felt, in turn duplicate as closely as possible those of the same isolated feature when it occurs in normal language behavior. Such a comparison lies, of course, at the heart of our objective: to determine to what extent the subject's ability to perceive correctly the isolated EGF's bears upon his subsequent ability to perceive the same features accurately in normal language behavior.

The research and resulting test which are the subject of the present paper have sought to respond in some degree to the above problems. Although the prototype of the test described here is designed for Spanish, its form is adaptable for other non-tone languages.

2. SELECTING THE CORPUS

As a first step, it was necessary for us to analyze Spanish in terms of those of its prosodic features which could clearly be identified as suprasegmental. This task was complicated by the very term *suprasegmental* itself. Customarily, the term *segmental* is applied to those phonetic features which occur as articulations in a linear time-sequence, such as vocoids and contoids. *Suprasegmental*, on the other hand, is applied to those phonetic features which in normal language behavior do not appear except in co-occurence with one or more segmental features (e.g., syllabic stress, which presupposes the existence of some segmental phone or sequence which is articulated with, among other things, a greater airflow to produce an acoustic feature of intensity). Thus, at the outset, the suprasegmental features may be viewed as overlaid functions of inherent features.

The phenomena of *juncture* and *duration*, however, differ from such features as stress, pitch level, etc., in that they can be interpreted as occurring within the segmental line. Yet they are customarily treated as parts of the suprasegmental system of a language. For our purposes, we insisted upon a non-literal interpretation of the term *suprasegmental*. In that in broad and narrow transcription we customarily mark features of pitch level, stress, etc., *above* the symbols for the phones with which they co-occur, the literal value of the prefix *supra-* is emphasized. The fact that features of juncture and duration are noted within the segmental line, however, cannot but de-emphasize the literal value of the term *suprasegmental*. Still, these two last features have at least one vital similarity with those which we can easily categorize as suprasegmental in the literal sense: they are not realized in normal language behavior except in conjunction with segmental phones. It was necessary, then, at least for the purpose of the present experiment, for us to interpret the term *suprasegmental* as referring to those phonetic features of a language which are not realized in normal language behavior except in certain specific co-occurrence with segmental phones. Given the entrenchment of the term *suprasegmental* in contemporary linguistic terminology, it seemed more prudent to continue to use the term, rather than suggest a replacement, but to do so in the sense proposed by Lehiste (1970:3): "... suprasegmental features are features whose arrangement in contrastive patterns in the time dimension is not restricted to single segments defined by their phonetic quality."

In consonance with the above principle, then, a generalized inventory of some of the major prosodic features of Spanish can be made:

> intensity;
> duration;
> pitch level;
> terminal contour.

Juncture does not appear on the list, since its allophonic realizations can be subsumed either under categories already established elsewhere in the list (such as *duration*, in examples such as /bá+á+ablár/ > [bà:βlár̥]), or as a more purely segmental phenomenon involving pause, syllabic division, or the specific quality of adjacent segmental phones.

On the basis of the generalized inventory we can proceed to establish some information concerning the relative frequency, functional load, and functional value of each feature. Also, we need to consider the extent to which these features occur independently of one another in normal language behavior. Finally, we must establish the essential acoustic parameters of each in order to generate then in isolated form by electro-mechanical means.

3. THE CORPUS

In response to the first need, and for the present purpose, existing phonemic analyses of Spanish are adequate indicators of the frequency and functional value of each feature.[4] In response to the second, however, existing acoustic studies were insufficient to provide all the needed data for Spanish, so a corpus of twelve utterances was devised, within which all the most frequent patterns of the above suprasegmental features occurred. Each of these utterances was then analyzed spectrographically. The combination of the phonemic analysis and the acoustic studies together yielded sufficient information to begin the construction of the test. Specifically, four prosodic features seemed appropriate for inclusion in the test:

1. INTENSITY. Four distinct levels of intensity were perceptible in our corpus, although only the binary contrast between +intensity and —intensity is phonemic. Intensity co-occurs in the corpus irregularly with a variety of specific durational quantities and pitch levels. Below, we shall indicate these four levels by the symbols ´, `, ^, and ᵕ, in descending order of intensity as measured in watts/cm² and in decibels. The fourth level can also be viewed as the occurrence of intensity.

2. DURATION. A feature of length is present in Spanish, but is not phonemic. It results regularly as a realization of phonemic juncture (/+/) but also irregularly as a result of the superposition of nonlinguistic features under individual emotional stimulus. In some dialects of Spanish, e.g. Porteño, some degree of duration can be noted as a phonetic feature of stressed vowels in prosodically stressed positions. Below, we shall indicate duration by the symbol [:] and express its acoustic nature in terms of chronological duration.

3. PITCH LEVELS. Four comparative pitch levels appear in the corpus, although they are phonemic not as static levels in isolated syllables, but as contours. Contours for the present purpose may be defined as movements from one static pitch level to another and can be labelled as *intonation* to distinguish them from *pitch levels*. In Spanish, pitch levels may co-occur with intensity, duration, or both. Below we shall indicate pitch levels by means of numbers (1, 2, 3, 4) in ascending order of pitch as expressed in the wave frequency measured in Hz.

4. TERMINAL CONTOURS. Three phonemic terminal contours are present in the corpus. They co-occur in predictable patterns with specific immediately-preceding pitch levels or intonation contours. Below, we note them as / ↑ / (rising), / ↓ / (falling), and /||/ (sustained). They are expressed acoustically as movements of wave frequency, measured in Hz.

The next step was to determine the most frequent ways in which the above four suprasegmental prosodic features occur and co-occur in the language in order to build the contexts within which the features were to be tested.

1. INTENSITY. *Acoustic features*: Realized as a greater output of energy in terms of watts/cm^2 and as measured in decibels relative to a particular fundamental frequency and to a constant of 0.0002 dynes/cm^2. It is recognizable in relation to the preceding or following intensity levels in the utterance. The preceding intensity level is dominant, but the following level is significant if the most intense level occurs in the initial position.

Occurrence: The fundamental perceptual focus is the distinction between +intensity and —intensity. Since intensity does not always, but may occasionally, co-occur with a particular pitch level or quantity of duration, it is necessary to include several of these types of possible co-occurrence in the test.

2. DURATION. *Acoustic features*: Based upon the relative, rather than absolute, length of the phoneme in the given sequence, duration is, however, measurable in the absolute at specific speech tempi. It is recognized in terms of chronological length of an articulation, from its onset through its coda.

Occurrence: Duration may co-occur with any vocoid or with contoids of the nasal, lateral, vibrant, or continuant categories. It is often present as a realization of juncture. In the test, then, it must appear both as a pure phenomenon of chronological length without phonemic consequences and as an allophone of juncture.

3. PITCH LEVELS. *Acoustic features*: Again recognizable in relation to preceding or following pitch levels, but measurable in given utterances in terms of frequency, as expressed in Hz.

Occurrence: In Spanish, pitch levels can occur as static or contoured forms. The former is less common in normal language behavior, but, in that the contour can best be described in terms of general rising, falling, or sustained progression between two static pitch levels, both the static and contoured forms must be included in the test.

4. TERMINAL CONTOURS. *Acoustic features*: Recognizable in relation to the immediately preceding pitch level or to the immediately preceding

intonation contour as a movement from higher to lower, lower to higher, or unchanging Hz level.

Occurrence: In Spanish, the terminal contour is independent of any specific preceding intonation contour. Thus, rising terminal contours may occur after falling intonation contours, etc. The function of the terminal contour is to indicate to the hearer the specific reaction expected by the speaker. In the test, then, terminal contours must appear in the context of all possible preceding intonation contours and pitch levels. The corpus of the test, then, includes first each of the suprasegmental features described above, as distinct from one another. Thereafter, the four features are presented in their most frequent patterns of co-occurrence.

4. PRODUCTION AND RESPONSE MODES

Just as in contemporary audiology the results obtained from pure-tone as opposed to language audiometry differ, so should we expect that, in language audition, the suprasegmental features should be perceptible in at least two forms: (1) as purely acoustic phenomena and (2) as language behavior. Moreover, our continuing interest was to discover to what extent the correct auditory perception of these features as purely acoustic phenomena would lead to increased acuity in the perception of the same features in normal language behavior. Thus, the experiment is designed to generate the features electro-mechanically. As a check on the relationship between the perception of the EGF and that of the same features in language, the same features were then generated by human voices in language context using actual Spanish utterances. In the HGF, first only male voices occur. Then only female voices occur. The final mode involves the appearance of male and female voices in random sequence.

> Production Mode 1: electro-mechanical generation
> Production Mode 2: human generation
> > Mode 2A: male voices
> > Mode 2B: female voices
> > Mode 2C: male and female voices, random sequence

In terms of response mode, it is essential to eliminate as many uncontrollable elements as possible (including spelling conventions, some knowledge of the target language vocabulary, general mental ingenuity, etc.), so that the production mode is entirely 'oral' and the response mode entirely 'aural'. In order that intelligence might not affect performance, the only intelligence required in the experiment is enough to make marks on an answer sheet and to understand simple spoken directions in the subject's own native language. The response mode is, then, passive and takes the form of differentiating among several choices and marking an answer sheet accordingly.

5. ACOUSTIC REALIZATION

The first issue to be resolved concerned the overall rate for the generation of each set of models. That is, in presenting a sequence of more vs. less intense segments in a test designed to measure the perception of the highest degree of intensity, the EGFs should equal the number generated by a native speaker over the same durational period. The figure of eight syllables per second has long been considered the upper threshold (Hudgins-Stetson 1937). We did, however, perform our own measurements specifically with regard to Spanish and, more essentially, with the key utterances which we used in establishing the corpus. We thus asked each informant to produce from memory each of the target utterances at three velocities, corresponding to what each informant considered to be slow, normal, and fast.[5] We found that, when the individual rates of each of the seven informants were averaged, a tempo characterizable as 'slow' averaged 2.5 syll/sec; 'normal' 3.4 syll/sec; and 'fast' 5.6 syll/sec. Thus we established the overall presentation rate in the EGF as 3.0 syll/sec.

The following data are stated in order of their occurrence in the test as specified in section 3 above:

INTENSITY. Using a reference level of 60 db. relative to 10^{16} watts/cm², our informants consistently recognized syllable nuclei at a fundamental frequency of 200 Hz as being 'stressed' when produced at a range between 76 and 83 db. Differences between 'stressed' and 'unstressed' syllable nuclei of less than 16 db, at 200 Hz were perceived, although inconsistently. When the difference fell below 10 db, it would not be recognized consistently in any regular pattern by our informants.[6] Consequently 'stressed' vs. 'unstressed' contrasts, with regard to intensity, were produced on the test as no less than differences of 16 db, depending upon the fundamental frequency. In that the perception of 'stressed' vs. 'unstressed' is based upon the first syllable in the utterance, it was important to ensure that the pattern produced included the feature of intensity in varying positions in each utterance.[7]

DURATION. Using an overall reference velocity of 3.0 syllables per second, EGF syllables were generated ranging from a minimum length of 8 centiseconds to a maximum of 18.5 centiseconds. Following Navarro,[8] the average duration of a given stressed syllable was fixed at 14.1 centiseconds, while the duration of a given unstressed syllable was fixed at 11.3 centiseconds. Thus, subjects are asked to identify durational contrasts between syllables of from 8 to 12 centiseconds in length and syllables of from 14 to 19.5 centiseconds in length.

PITCH LEVEL. Based upon an average fundamental frequency for declarative material of 223 Hz for female voices and 132 Hz for male voices,[9] at 40 db intensity, pitch level distinction for the EGF were fixed at fundamental frequency changes of 20 Hz ($PL_1 = 135$ Hz; $PL_2 = 155$ Hz; $PL_3 = 175$ Hz; $PL_4 = 195$ Hz). This guaranteed that all four pitch levels would fall within the average range of both the male (134 Hz – 146 Hz) and female (199 Hz – 295 Hz) voices as established by Cowan (1936).

TERMINAL CONTOURS. Terminal contours 31 ↓, 13 ↑ arbitrarily established as rises or falls of 100 Hz from the immediately preceding pitch levels, while the contours 21 ↓ and 23 ↑ were established as rises or falls of 60 Hz from the immediately preceding pitch levels.

6. RESULTS, IMPLICATIONS AND CONCLUSIONS

In determining the results of our experiments, it is necessary to bear in mind that the evaluative instrument which we sought to develop is not a 'test' in the usual sense of the term. It is, rather, an evaluative device which was employed to help provide some information bearing upon the following questions:

1. What correlation is there between an individual's perception of the EGF's and his perception of the same features generated in context by human speakers;

2. Does exposure to the EGF's have any bearing on an individual's rate of progress in duplicating the correct features in normal language behavior; and

3. Does an individual's performance on the present evaluative instrument have any implications for the measurement of aptitude for language study.

To verify the experiment's possible bearing on the above issues, it was necessary to administer it to three distinct groups of language learners.

The first group (I) took the test only once, in an attempt to measure the correlation between their performance on the EGF's in comparison to their performance on the human-generated sections. The second group (II) took the full test once at the beginning of a semester and only the HGF section at the end of the semester. A control group took only the HGF section at the end of the same semester. We then attempted to measure the final results of both groups to determine to what extent the early exposure of the one group to the EGF-HGF correlation affected their classroom performance. The third group (III) took the test only once at the beginning of the semester. A control group did not. At the end of the semester, the grades assigned by the instructor in the areas of listening comprehension and speaking for each of the two groups were compared.

The resulting statistical data show an average of between 18% and 20% improvement in the overall performance in listening comprehension and speaking for the group having participated in the experiment. This is, of course, only one of the conclusions which may be drawn from this study. It would seem to suffice, however, to indicate that:

1. The features in question are more easily perceived as EGF than as HGF.

2. The exposure to the EGF leads consistently to the improved accuracy of perception of the HGF.

3. Once exposed to the HGF, individuals tend to perform at a higher level in the aural and oral phases of second language learning.

It is our conclusion, then, that sufficient evidence exists to warrant extensive further development of auditory discrimination practice based on EGF methods as an integral part of the initial stages of second language learning.

California State University, Fullerton
and Universidad de Santiago (Vigo)

NOTES

[1] Cf. Pimsleur, Paul. Programming Acoustic Discriminatory Skills. In: F. R. Morton, Programming Audio-Lingual Skills (Ann Arbor: University of Michigan, 1962); Rivers, Wilga. Listening Comprehension. Modern Language Journal 50.196-204 (1966), and chap. vi in her Teaching Foreign Languages (Chicago: University of Chicago Press, 1968); and Newmark, Gerald, and Diller, Edward. Emphasizing the Audio in the Audio-Lingual Approach. Modern Language Journal 48.18-20 (1964).
[2] Cf., for example, Louis de Carlo, The Deaf p. 87 (Englewood Cliffs: Prentice-Hall, 1964), Feldman (1973b).

[3] Cf. footnotes 1 and 2.
[4] For example, Bowen and Stockwell 1965, with allophonic and articulatory data as provided in Navarro 1957.
[5] Cf. Harris 1970.
[6] Cf. Lehiste and Ivić 1963.
[7] Cf. Westin 1966.
[8] Navarro 1916, 1917, 1918, 1921, 1957. In general, it is felt that the duration of speech sounds varies between 30 and 300 milliseconds. Lehiste 1970 reports that it is probably impossible to perceive durational differences of less than 40 milliseconds. Frequency has no effect on the perception of duration, whereas intensity increases up to a certain level tend to improve the listener's capacity for discrimination (Lehiste 1970:17).
[9] Cf. Petersen and Barney 1952.

REFERENCES

Cowan, J. M. 1936. Pitch and Intensity Characteristics of Stage Speech. Archives of Speech (Supplement). State University of Iowa.

Delattre, Pierre. 1962. A Comparative Study of Declarative Intonation in American English and Spanish. Hispania 45.233-241.

—. 1965. Comparing the Phonetic Features of English, French, Spanish, and German. Philadelphia: Chilton.

Durand, Marguerite. 1946. Voyelles longues et voyelles brèves. Paris: C. Klincksieck.

Feldman, David. 1973a. On Syllable-final /l/ and /u/ in Portuguese. In A. Valdman, ed., Papers in Linguistics and Phonetics to the Memory of Pierre Delattre. The Hague: Mouton.

—. 1973b. Auditory discrimination of suprasegmental features in Spanish. International Review of Applied Linguistics in Language Teaching 9:3.195-209.

Hammarström, G. 1956. Problèmes phonométriques et autres concernant la durée en suédois. Revista do Laboratório de Fonética, Coimbra. 3.17-37.

Harris, James. 1970. Spanish Phonology. Cambridge: MIT Press.

Hudgins, C. V., and Stetson, R. H. 1937. Relative Speed of Articulatory Movements. Archives Néerlandaises de phonétique expérimentale 13.85-94.

Jakobson, Roman et. al. 1965. Preliminaries to Speech Analysis. Cambridge: MIT Press.

Lafon, Jean-Claude. 1964. Le test phonétique et la mesure de l'audition. Paris: Dunod.

Lehiste, Ilse. 1970. Suprasegmentals. Cambridge: MIT Press.

Lehiste, Ilse, and Ivić, Pavle. 1963. Accent in Serbo-Croatian. Michigan Slavic Materials 4. Ann Arbor: Department of Slavic Languages and Literatures.

Navarro, Tomás. 1916. Cantidad de las vocales acentuadas. Revista de filología española 3.387-408.

—. 1917. Cantidad de las vocales inacentuadas. Revista de filología española 4.371-388.

—. 1918. Diferencias de duración entre las consonantes españoles. Revista de filología española 5.367-393.

—. 1921. Historia de algunas opiniones sobre la cantidad silabica española. Revista de filología española 8.30-57.

—. 1957. Manual de pronunciación española. 5th ed. New York: Hafner.

Peterson, G. E., and Barney, H. L. 1952. Control Methods in a Study of Vowels. Journal of the Acoustical Society of America 24.175-184.

Peterson, G. E., and Lehiste, Ilse. 1960. Duration of Syllable Nuclei in English. Journal of the Acoustical Society of America 32.693-703.

Rosenblith, W. A., and Stevens, K. N. 1953. On the DL for Frequency. Journal of the Acoustical Society of America 25.980-985.

Westin, Kjell et al. 1966. An Experimental Study of the Relative Importance of Pitch. Language and Speech 9.114-126.

THE COLLECT AS A FORM OF DISCOURSE

CHARLES A. FERGUSON

Linguists and grammarians through the centuries have generally regarded a grammar as a characterization of the possible (i.e. grammatical, pronounceable, writable) utterances of a particular language.[1] Sometimes this aim has been reduced, as when a linguist has tried to characterize only a limited corpus; sometimes it has been expanded, as when a linguist has tried to characterize a set of dialects or languages by the same grammar. Recently the notion of grammar has been consciously extended, in a direction sometimes implicitly suggested in the past, to a characterization of the utterances appropriate or acceptable under various sociolinguistic, psychological, or communicative conditions. No matter which of these views is taken, the linguist faces the same crucial question. What is the locus of the grammar, exactly what is this this 'language' which he is characterizing? The problem of how to define a language as opposed to a dialect or a family of languages is an old one which remains inadequately resolved (see, for example, Ferguson and Gumperz 1959, or many other treatments), but it will not be examined here. An even more troublesome problem is the existence of systematic conditions on grammaticality or acceptability which cut across what every linguist would regard as separate languages or seem to have a quite nonlinguistic locus. We will examine this question by making some observations about a particular form of discourse, a very slight example, but one which may nevertheless be instructive: the collect.

Contemporary attempts at discourse analysis have generally been intended to show features of a particular language which should be incorporated in a total grammar of the language, although some also have been intended to suggest universal features of grammar. Only rarely have linguists been interested in characterizing the changes in a particular form of discourse as it continues through time, or tracing the features of a form of discourse as it passes from one language to another. These latter interests have been more evident in the work of folklorists and students of comparative literature. The present paper is intended as a very small exercise in showing continuity of a form of discourse across a language boundary and through the history of a language. As such, it may serve as slight but deeply-felt tribute to Archibald Hill, whose devotion to linguistics would recognize in this kind of study a legitimate problem for linguists and a possible contribution to the analysis of literature.

The form of discourse to be discussed is the traditional brief prayer, uttered by the minister on behalf of the congregation near the beginning of the mass, which generally sets the theme for the day or season being observed. This prayer, which is a characteristic of the Western Church, apparently first emerged in Latin sometime in the third to fifth centuries of the Christian era, the earliest known collection being the Leonine Sacramentary (named after Pope Leo the Great, A. D. 440-61). From the earliest examples to the present day, this prayer, called simply THE PRAYER (*oratio*) or THE COLLECT (*collecta, collectio*, origin disputed), has exhibited a very clear structure of form and content. A full collect has five parts: 1) an invocation, i.e. an address to God; 2) a basis for petition, i.e. some quality of God or some action attributed to him; 3) the petition or desire itself; 4) the purpose or reason for making the request, i.e. the good result which would follow the granting of the petition; and 5) a formulaic ending. Of these five parts, the second or the fourth is sometimes absent, and occasionally both are missing. This structure is represented by Formula 1.

(1)   Collect → Invocation (+ Basis) + Petition (+ Purpose) + Ending

Details about the range of variation possible within each part and correlations among the form or content of the parts will be discussed only to the extent necessary for our purpose here, but there is a sizeable literature on these matters and they are evidently amenable to rigorous formal analysis.[2]

The collects have had a long and complex history in the Roman Church, in some places or at some times being greatly expanded, but always the basic structure outlined above has been present, and in fact many collects have been retained without change since the Leonine Sacramentary.

At the time of the Reformation those churches which kept the main features of the mass, such as the Church of England and the Lutheran Churches of the continent, translated and adapted the historic collects for use in vernacular services of worship. The first collection of these prayers to appear in English was in the Prayer Book of 1549, and many of them appear in the same form – apart from modernization of spelling and punctuation – in Anglican, Lutheran, and other English-language service books in use at the present time. Translations and adaptations of Reformation collects are also to be found in dozens of other languages, sometimes dating back to the 16th Century, often prepared in the 19th Century in connection with Protestant missionary efforts.

In recent decades, movements of liturgical renewal have given rise to new collects and new variations of old collects in many different modern languages, for use by Christians of many denominational affiliations. In this paper we will pay some attention to all three major layers of collects: Latin, Reformation, and contemporary.

1. DISCOURSE GRAMMAR

Formula 1 above could be regarded as a kind of phrase-structure rule specifying the base form of a collect. If we assume that the constituents are ordered as listed, we could then identify possible expansions and appropriate lexical categories, and we could devise transformational rules which would characterize the full range of acceptable orders and constructions which appear in collects.[3]

For example, in Latin collects the Invocation may consist of a single word, e.g. *Deus* 'God', as in the collects for Christmas (midnight), Ash Wednesday, Epiphany, 1st, 2nd and 4th Sundays in Lent, etc., or it may be expanded in typical noun-phrase fashion, e.g. *Omnipotens sempiterne Deus* 'Almighty everlasting God' as in the collects for Christmas (early), 2nd and 3rd Sundays after Epiphany, Palm Sunday, etc.

The Invocation may be preceded by certain other elements outside the noun phrase, most commonly an imperative (sometimes followed by a pronominal object), less commonly a direct object with its modifiers (very rarely a direct object alone). Another preposeable element *quaesumus* 'we beg', 'please'.' is quite rare as the first word, but frequently appears in second position between the preposed imperative or direct object and the Invocation.

As a kind of surface constraint, we may note that the maximum amount of material that may precede the noun of the Invocation seems to be
$\left\{\begin{array}{l}\text{direct object}\\\text{imperative}\end{array}\right\}$ + *quaesumus* + Adjective, and, in this case, apparently only a single adjective occurs, not two or more.

Illustrative examples:

Excita, Domine ... 'Stir-up, O-Lord' (2nd Sunday in Advent)
Converte nos, Deus salutaris noster ... 'Change us, God salvation our'
(1st Monday in Lent)
Ecclesiam tuam, Domine ... 'Church your, O-Lord' (St. John)
Concede, quaesumus, omnipotens Deus ... 'Grant, we-beg, Almighty God'
(Christmas)
Preces nostras, quaesumus, Domine ... 'Prayers our, we-beg, O-Lord'
(Quinquagesima)

In spite of the fact that indefinitely many different collects may be composed, it is abundantly clear that there are severe, systematic constraints on order and constructions, and the form of the collect could probably be captured by some kind of sentence grammar.

It is not immediately apparent, however, where this particular sentence grammar belongs in a full grammar of Latin sentences, since some of its rules would be closely related to, or even subsumed under, rules of very general applicability, while others would be limited to related forms of discourse (e.g. prayers in general) or only valid for the collect itself. The collect poses one of the dilemmas of the sentence-vs.-discourse issue in a very clear way. Theoreticians have tended to see the function of grammar writing as the characterization or generation of SENTENCES, and discourse analysis as concerned with utterances larger than sentences. Elsewhere (Ferguson 1967) I have given a clear example of grammaticality of the typical sentence-syntax sort which goes beyond a single sentence. Here I draw attention to a piece of discourse analysis which is limited to single sentences. Sentencehood is not the crucial differentiator between grammar in the usual sense and discourse grammar, or else the differentiation itself is questionable.[4]

2. TRANSFER GRAMMAR

When Archbishop Cranmer and his associates undertook to render the Latin collects into English equivalents for use in public worship, they faced all the usual problems of the translator. The two languages – like any pair of languages – differed in phonology, syntax, and lexicon, and in the relations between semantic value and the respective linguistic systems. The whole question of the commensurateness of linguistic systems has been discussed from many points of view, e.g. contrastive analysis, machine translation, language universals, and it will not be treated here. Also, of course, the existence of doctrinal differences interfered with direct translation. But in this section let us examine differences which are neither narrowly linguistic nor theological.[5]

One important difference between the Latin collects and Reformation English collects is the question of style, or perhaps better, register. What special features of the respective languages are appropriate for use in public prayers as opposed to other uses of language? Some stylistic features are common to both, such as the use of paranomasia or word-play in which, for example, the same stem or root appears in several places with different endings or an affix is echoed with different stems. This will of course differ in detail: for example, the Early Modern English prayer register had more alliterative repetition while Latin had more complex interlocking patterns of word order. Also, a word-play in one language often cannot be reproduced in the other simply because of the lexical and phonological differences.

The feature which we will examine here is the EME practice of word pairing, in which two synonymous words or phrases are used in direct coordination or in a parallel or chiastic position apparently to express a single notion. This is part of a more general registral difference of conciseness vs. elaboration in the Latin and EME prayer Language. The Roman collect, like some other parts of the liturgy, tended to be very terse: a minimum of words tightly arranged with clause-final cadences (*cursus*); the Reformation English collect, like the vernacular devotional literature on which it was based, was free and expansive; somewhat wordy, with a rhythmic flow involving sequences of short and long words. Latin collect style also had characteristic word pairs but they were fewer in number and more often antitheses rather than synonyms. The word pairing which characterizes Reformation English collects and Prayer Book style in general may have originated in the pairing of Romance loanwords with the Anglo-Saxon glosses attested for Middle English, but in any case it was a striking feature of elaboration compared to the Latin originals. An example cited by Brooks illustrates these registral differences (traditional collect for 1st Sunday after Epiphany, now replaced in Roman usage): ... *ut et quae agenda sunt videant et ad implenda quae viderint convalescant* ... '... that they may both perceive and know what things they ought to do and have grace and power faithfully to fulfil the same ...' Word play: *videant*: *viderint*; *faithfully*, *fulfil*. Pairs: perceive and know; grace and power (Brooks 1965:129-30).

It is of some interest to note that this English pairing, whatever its origin, is very similar to the word pairing found in the poetic portions of the Old Testament, particularly the Psalms[6] and in all likelihood the two kinds of pairing were mutually reinforcing in the development of LITURGICAL ENGLISH.

What is of particular interest in this paper, however, is where the description of registral features belongs in a grammar. Registral and stylistic features may cut across the various components of a grammar (e.g. phonology, syntax, lexicon) in complex ways, but clearly the identification of registers begins very early in child language development[7] and some of the fundamental registral differences may be universally present in the linguistic competence of the members of a speech community. In any case, we need to try experimental versions of registral 'grammars' either in the form of tagging appropriate elements and rules of a conventional grammar or in the direct formulation of registral constraints and regularities.

3. DIACHRONIC GRAMMAR

Collects have been translated into English or composed directly in English since medieval times, and English collects are still being produced at the present time. As mentioned above, the two great periods of English collect composition are the 16th Century and the 20th. During the course of the four centuries between these periods, the English language changed in many respects, not only in linguistically well-recognized ways such as phonology or syntax but also in the characteristics and distribution of registers and styles. As an example of more narrowly linguistic change, we may note that second-person relative clauses, which were perfectly acceptable in 16th Century English, now are marginal or nonexistent for most speakers of English. As an example of registral and stylistic change, we may note that the current preference in prayers is for greater simplicity, in the sense of fewer words and fewer subordinate clauses.

The commonest way of expressing the Basis component of the collect in Latin is a relative clause dependent on the noun of the Invocation. For example, the collect for Epiphany begins as follows: *Deus qui hodierna die unigenitum tuum gentibus stella duce revelasti* ..., which was translated into EME: 'O God, who on this day by the leading of a star didst reveal thine only-begotten Son to the Gentiles, ...'. In modern English this kind of clause is at the very margins of acceptability. When second-person relative clauses appear in contemporary liturgical texts they often have third-person agreement, e.g. 'Almighty God, who know*s* us to be ...'; usually they are avoided altogether. A contemporary Roman Catholic version of the Epiphany collect reads: 'O God, on this day you revealed your Son to the peoples of the earth through the guidance of a star ...' The syntactic change eliminating such second-person clauses is relatively unimportant in the total historical syntax of English, but it has a great effect on the collect as a form of discourse.[8] In the first place, it often results in breaking the collect into more than one sentence, and, in some cases, it is probably the direct cause of the elimination or revision of the Basis in a collect. Some contemporary versions of collects have even removed the Basis from the collect and set it separately as a kind of introductory statement or 'bid' to prayer preceding the collect itself, and this change is chiefly due to the unacceptability of second-person relative clauses. Thus, two experimental versions of a new collect for the Thursday after Ash Wednesday begin:

I   Lord, our God,
    you walk before us and give us guidance in everything we do.

    Stay with us, and be our ...

II Let us pray to the Lord, our God,
    who walks before us
    and gives guidance in everything we do.

    Stay with us, and be our ...

Once a new format with preceding bid is attempted, it then becomes possible to set the Purpose in that position rather than the Basis, as is done in some contemporary versions, and this move toward a major alteration in the basic structure of the collect was apparently triggered by the syntactic change.

The general preference for simplicity, interestingly enough, tends to take contemporary English collects nearer to the original Latin forms in wordiness and total length, although the grammatical structure of English is still a bar to the kind of tight arrangement typical of the Latin style. The use of word pairing, however, has become so much a part of liturgical English that it frequently persists in contemporary collects, and the simplification comes more from omission of adjectives and adverbs and the dropping of other elements such as the resumptive 'the same' (e.g. 'through the same thy Son, Jesus Christ our Lord, ...' in the ending formula for collects in which Christ has been mentioned).[9]

The writing of diachronic grammar is often viewed as the specifying of successive stages, and this may be done by providing relatively static grammars and statements of relationship between them or by giving a baseline grammar and a succession of changes. In writing a diachronic 'grammar' of the English collect, both of these procedures would be possible and instructive, but at least one other kind of grammar would be of obvious value: a characterization of the structure common to all periods. Such a grammar would serve to place the English collect within the universe of all collects and at the same time specify its differences from non-English collects.

Perhaps the fundamental problem here, as in all treatments of variation, is how to recognize and present the significant equivalences. At one level, the second-person relative clause of EME is equivalent to the contemporary independent declarative sentence, but at another level it is different and the EME structure is closer to the Latin. The attempt to write a diachronic grammar of a small form of discourse such as the collect might be revealing and instructive for the writing of larger-scale diachronic grammar, whether of sentence type, discourse type, or more pronounced sociolinguistic focus.

4. LOCUS OF THE GRAMMAR

In each of the preceding sections we have commented on structural regularities which could be presented in the form of a grammar, but in each case the locus of the grammar has not been a homogeneous, full, natural language. It has been a form of discourse in a particular language, a form of discourse in two languages, or a form of discourse at different stages of the same language. Indeed, a very natural object-language for a grammar would be the class of all possible collects in any language of Christian worship at any time from third to twentieth centuries. The definition of this LANGUAGE is hardly more problematic than the definition of a homogeneous, full, natural language, and like the latter requires a sociological component.

Among the many variables of interest are code (i.e. which language or language variety is used), time period (e.g. century), doctrine, day or occasion, liturgical setting. We have already seen how different languages and different historical periods would correlate with differences in collect grammars. Differences in doctrine explain, for example, the radical shift in collects for saints' days between Latin collects and Reformation collects in any language, all reference to intercession of saints being removed from the latter. Differences in day or season account for such general textual differences as the alleluia qualities of collects in the Easter season, and are, of course, a crucial factor in determining the wording of particular collects. Differences in liturgical setting refer to the relation of the collect to other variable parts of the liturgy, to the formulaic expressions which precede and follow collects, to whether the collect is intoned or spoken by the minister or read aloud in unison by the congregation, and many other similar phenomena. Differences in this realm are also related to variations in the actual texts of collects.

In the point of view adopted here, much of the basic grammar of the collect is independent of the variables given above, but the range of variation to be covered by the total grammar must be in terms of variables such as these. Perhaps the most novel point for the linguist is the notion that most of the basic grammar and even some fairly superficial details of this form of discourse are essentially language independent. For the collect as a form of discourse we might start with a definition of the sociolinguistic setting (assembly of Christians, leader, theme-prayer of day or season, etc.) and then construct a grammar and a set of conditions under which specified variation takes place.

In her important early paper on sociolinguistic variables, Ervin-Tripp noted: "One of the major problems for sociolinguists will be the discovery of independent and reliable methods for defining settings" (Ervin-Tripp 1964). This problem is just as difficult as ever, but it still holds as much promise now as it did then. The present paper has merely restated it, giving a simple example, and has suggested that sociolinguists might regard the setting as the locus for a kind of grammar. A sociolinguistically located grammar, although at present far beyond our techniques of analysis and presentation, must be an ultimate goal for linguists who see themselves as students of language in society.

Stanford University

NOTES

[1] The points made in this paper emerged from work done on the Sub-committee on Prayers of the Liturgical Texts Committee of the Inter-Lutheran Commission on Worship during 1970-71, and I would like to express my appreciation of the opportunity to work with the members of these bodies as they create and adapt liturgical texts.

[2] Cf. Suter 1940, Reed 1947:277-87, 567-622, Kulp 1955, and the references they cite.

[3] For a sample generative grammar of Early Modern English based on the text of the Lord's Prayer, see Bloomfield and Newmark 1963: 237-285. The presentation there alludes to forms of discourse but its aims are different from those of the present

study and it does not make explicitly the four points offered here. For a basic analysis somewhat different from Formula 1 see Kulp 1955:388ff. and references.

[4] See Traugott 1975 for a stimulating discussion of discourse analysis in relation to current sentence-based grammatical models. Although her discussion is focused on literary texts and the stylistics of particular works or authors, her approach has many points of contact with the approach suggested here.

[5] For a recent discussion of the problems involved in translating Latin collects into the English of the Prayer Book, see Brook 1965:126-36.

[6] This word pairing is a striking feature of early Canaanite poetry, well attested in Ugaritic and Hebrew poetic texts. Cf. Dahood 1966-70 I xxxiii-xxxv, III 445-56, and references.

[7] Cf. Weeks 1971.

[8] The status of first- and second-person relative clauses may well be an important typological question, of value in cross-language analysis following the research strategy of 'language universals', as in Schwartz 1971. For example, how widespread is the repetition (or non-suppression) of the second-person pronoun in the relative clause, which is obligatory in German and hence a feature of German collects?

[9] The formulaic ending of the collect has generally been the most rigidly constrained part. In one tradition of Reformation English collects, for example, the basic form is "... through Jesus Christ thy Son our Lord, who liveth and reigneth with thee and the Holy Ghost, one God, world without end, ..." and this has prescribed variants if the Son or the Spirit is addressed or mentioned in the prayer, and a shortened form for when the collect is used as a secondary prayer or 'commemoration'. Luther, in the numerous translations and adaptations of collects he himself made, used a great variety of endings, but Lutheran usage soon stabilized again. It is interesting to note greater variety again in some contemporary collects. Cf. Prayers of the Day and Season 1971.

REFERENCES

Bloomfield, Norton W., and Leonard Newmark. 1963. A linguistic introduction to the history of English. New York.

Brook, Stella. 1965. The language of the Book of Common Prayer. New York.

Dahood, Mitchell, 1966-70. Psalms I, II, III (The Anchor Bible).

Ervin-Tripp, Susan M. 1964. An analysis of the interaction of language, topic and listener. Amer. Anthr. 66:86-102.

Feltoe, Charles L. (ed). 1896. Sacramentarium Leonianum. Cambridge.

Ferguson, Charles A. 1967. Root-echo responses in Syrian Arabic politeness formulas. Linguistic studies in memory of Richard Slade Harrell, ed. by Don G. Stuart. Washington, D.C. 35-45.

Ferguson, Charles A., and Gumperz, John J. 1960. Introduction, Linguistic diversity in South Asia, ed. by Charles A. Ferguson and John Gumperz. International J. Amer. Linguistics 26.3 Pt. III 1-18.

Kulp, Hans-Ludwig. 1955. Das Gemeindegebet im christlichen Gottesdienst. Leiturgia XX, ed. by K. F. Muller and W. Blakenburg. Kassel. 355-419.

Prayers of the Day and Season. 1971. Multilithed. Distributed by the Inter-Lutheran Commission on Worship. New York.

Reed, Luther D. 1947. The Lutheran liturgy. Philadelphia.

Schwartz, Arthur. 1971. General aspects of relative clause formation. Working papers on language Universals, 6.139-71. Stanford.

Suter, John Wallace, Jr. 1940. The book of English collects. New York.

Traugott, Elizabeth Closs. 1975. 'Style' as chameleon: Remarks on the implications of transformational grammar and generative semantics for the concept of style. In the present festschrift.

Weeks, Thelma. 1971. Speech registers in children. Child Development 42.1119-1131.

THE SEGMENTED SENTENCE:
BALLY'S THEORY RECONSIDERED[1]

HENRI FREI

1. TOPIC AND COMMENT

Bally last defined the segmented sentence (1941:36) as an utterance divided into two parts separated by a pause, one of which, designated by Z, is the aim of the utterance, its psychological predicate, its *propos (comment)*, whereas the other, designated by A, forms the psychological subject, or *thème (topic)*, that serves as a basis for the propos. Examples:

> *Cette lettre* (A), *je ne l'ai jamais reçue* (Z).
> *Does he bite* (Z), *your dog* (A)?

The order of the segments may be AZ or ZA.

2. RECIPROCAL CONDITIONING VS. UNILATERAL DEPENDENCE

Bally's view of the relations between the two segments leads to a troublesome paradox, unknown to himself and unnoticed by others up till now.

On the one hand, he asserts that there is between A and Z a relation of interdependence, of complementarity, of reciprocal conditioning (1965: §§90, 155). But he admits, on the other hand, as did Sechehaye (1926:165), that Z is a grammatically independent sentence with an autonomous intonation, and able to stand alone, without A, whereas the latter, which does not have an autonomous intonation, is closely dependent on Z and cannot stand alone (1965: §§62, 82, 1941:36). Cf. the examples above. I shall call A in this respect a satellite, and Z a nucleus; their relation is one of unilateral dependence: N is independent of S, but there can be no S without N.

Although, applied to the same examples, the relation AZ is true, and the corresponding relation SN equally unquestionable, they show conflicting properties: A and Z are reciprocally complementary, whereas

SN is a relation of unilateral dependence. This contradiction is explainable by the fact that AZ belongs to parole, and SN to langue.

A theory that founds its distinctions on facts proper to speaker or hearer belongs to the science of parole. According to Bally, the propos (Z) is what one wants to make known, and the thème (A) the topic on the basis of which the propos is uttered (1965:§ 61). Further, the propos is what matters to the speaker, the thème what is useful to the hearer (1941:36). The distinction SN, on the contrary, is independent of any reference to the speaker or hearer.[2]

3. WORD SATELLITE, SENTENCE SATELLITE, DETACHED SATELLITE

Bally rightly insisted on the fact that the relation is between the whole of A and the whole of Z (1965:§§ 90, 91). For example, in *On ne fume pas, ici* (ZA), the relation is not between *ici* and the verb; it is between *ici* and the whole sequence *On ne fume pas* (1941:38).

The same is true if this example, viewed from the standpoint of langue, is analysed as a case of unilateral dependence: *ici* depends, as a sentence satellite, on the whole nucleus *On ne fume pas*. If it were dependent on the verb alone, the sentence would be a non-segmented one, and the satellite a word satellite: *On ne fume pas ici. You can't smoke here.*

Strictly speaking, the concept of sentence satellite is not yet sufficient to enable one to distinguish a segmented sentence. There are sentence satellites within non-segmented sentences: *Il est* MALHEUREUSEMENT *absent. Arthur has* UNFORTUNATELY *failed his exam.*

In order to obtain a segmented sentence, the sentence satellite has to be separated from the nucleus by a pause; in other words it must be a detached satellite: *Il est absent,* MALHEUREUSEMENT (or: MALHEUREUSE-MENT, *il est absent*); *Arthur has failed his exam,* UNFORTUNATELY (or: UNFORTUNATELY, *Arthur has failed his exam.*).[3]

We cannot examine here how far the segmented and non-segmented types are synonymous. The incorporation of *malheureusement* in the non-segmented sentence may be a variant (allotagm) of the segmented type.

4. SEGMENTED SENTENCE DEFINED FROM THE POINT OF VIEW OF LANGUE

We now have all the elements required to define the segmented sentence from the point of view of the langue.

If, like every sentence (Frei 1962: §1, 2, p. 130 top, Martinet 1960: §1-9, p. 19), the segmented sentence is a sign, the definition will have to take account of both faces of the sign, the *signifié* (syntactic relations) and the *signifiant* (syntactic processes).

From the standpoint of the *signifié*, the segmented sentence is a relation of unilateral dependence between a sentence (= nucleus) and a sentence satellite. From the standpoint of the *signifiant*, sentence and sentence-satellite are divided by a pause. This junctural feature seems to be a language universal, whereas the use of intonation for labelling the detached satellite, a process which plays such an important role in the Indo-European sphere, is in some languages a secondary phenomenon (Bearth 1971: §16.1, p. 386 top).

5. DEPENDENCE VS. IDENTIFICATION

We have seen above (§ 3) that a detached satellite is a sentence satellite. According to Bally, it is the medial pause that shows that, grammatically, the segment A is not a 'complement' of Z, within which it is, moreover, often represented by a pronoun: *Cet homme, je ne* LE *connais pas.* An analysis based on the non-segmented syntax would in this case be fallacious as A would become an internal element of Z (1941:38).

Bally's argumentation needs clarifying:

5.1 We shall not return to the affirmation that A is not a complement of Z. This belongs to the psychology of parole, whereas, according to the proportion $A:Z = S:N$, the corresponding relation within the sphere of langue is a relation of dependence SN.

5.2 Even if A is not an internal element of Z, it is nevertheless undeniable that there is a relation between A (*Cet homme*) and the pronoun *le*, which is part of Z. The difficulty is explainable by the fact that this relation is not a relation of dependence, but of identification, and that therefore it does not form a syntagm: the sequence *Cet homme, ... le* is not a syntagm, while the segmented sentence, forming a relation of dependence DS-N, is one, which is the case for every relation of dependence.

5.3 As soon as one leaves the sphere of *parole*, to analyse AZ as a *langue*-relation, it becomes inconsistent to say that the satellite is 're-presented', or 'taken over' (in case of the order DS-N), or 'announced' (in the case of the order N-DS) by a pronoun belonging to the nucleus. Like the concepts of topic and comment, which succeeded those of psychological subject and predicate (Bally 1965: §32n.1), this is a remnant of the pre-Saussurean psychology of language. As a matter of fact, we have here a relation between identifier and identified: the detached satellite (*Cet homme*) identifies the pronoun *le*.

6. ANAPHORICAL VS. EPIPHORICAL

Bally has not attempted to give any general classification of segmented sentences and, except perhaps for the order of segments (AZ vs. ZA) or their degree of complexity (the segments can themselves be segmented sentences), one will not find in his writings any hints pointing towards such a classification.

All segmented sentences fall into two classes, anaphorical and epiphorical, according to whether the detached satellite is, semantically, included in the nucleus or not. *Cet homme, je ne le connais pas* belongs to anaphorical segmentation. Conversely, *Il est absent, malheureusement* or *He's busy, of course* is a case of epiphorical segmentation.

A segmented sentence can belong to the anaphorical type without containing any anaphorical pronoun: *Très mal tissée, cette étoffe! Rather nice, that!* (N-DS), but all segmented sentences whose nucleus contains a pronoun that is identified by the satellite are anaphorical. Of course, no epiphorical segmented sentence can contain an anaphorical pronoun.

7. DIRECTION OF TRANSPOSITION: FROM NON-SEGMENTED TO SEGMENTED

Bally did not think of elaborating a transpositional theory of segmentation. He merely approached the problem from the standpoint of genetical linguistics. As a rule, he considers the segmented sentence as resulting from the condensation of two coordinated sentences (or quasi-sentences), as a stage in the progress from coordinated syntax toward non-segmented syntax: *Il viendra. Peut-être.* (C_1 C_2) → *Il viendra, peut-être* (N-DS) → *Il viendra peut-être* (1965:§ 67, 1941:38; examples mine). English examples: *He died. Yesterday.* → *He died, yesterday.* → *He died yesterday.*

Whether it is called transposition (Bally) or transformation (Chomsky), moving a sign from one class to another is an individual and momentary act of speaking and therefore dependent on *linguistique de la parole*, but the process is bound up with the code of langue, principally with some kind of relation between departure and arrival classes. In order to understand this division into *parole* and *langue*, one may draw a comparison with the phenomenon of analogy. The analogical process by which a speaker creates a new sign or by which he reproduces an already existing one, is a process of *parole*, but the proportional relation that he takes as a model (e.g. *decode : encode = decamp : encamp*) forms a part of the system of *langue*.

Of the 'three characteristic forms of enunciation' treated by Bally: *coordination, phrase segmentée, phrase liée* (1965: §§61-109), we may, from the standpoint of synchrony, lay aside the first from the outset. *Coordination*, as it always implies two sentences or quasi-sentences at least, presupposes the other forms of enunciation and is therefore not a primary phenomenon.

As to the other two, transposition is from non-segmented to segmented. This is reflected by the fact that the segmented sentence presupposes the non-segmented one. Arguments:

(a) All segmented sentences contain non-segmented parts. In *Cet homme, je ne le connais pas* (DS-N), N is a non-segmented sentence. If we form a complex segmented sentence by substituting a segmented sentence n-s for N (*Cet homme, est-ce que je le connais, moi?*), the subsegment n is again a non-segmented sentence, as in the following pair of English sentences: *Actually, I've just seen him. Actually, I've just seen him, your brother.*

Conversely, a non-segmented sentence never governs a segmented one. The immediate constituents of *J'aimerais savoir combien ça pèse, cette lettre* are not *J'aimerais savoir* (non-segmented) + *combien ça pèse, cette lettre* (segmented), but *J'aimerais savoir combien ca pèse* (N) + *cette lettre* (DS). This applies equally to the English sentence: *Could you tell me how much it weighs, this parcel?*

(b) Statistical data obtained so far (Bennett, Lauberte) indicate that while practically all segmented sentences can be reconverted into non-segmented ones, only a part of the non-segmented ones is transposable into segmented sentences[4].

Université de Genève

NOTES

[1] I am indebted to T. J. A. Bennett for revising the English of this article and providing the English examples. Abbreviations: A = *thème*, topic; Z = *propos*, comment; S = satellite; N = nucleus; DS = detached satellite; C = coördinated.

[2] Although Bally himself admits that, in the case of the non-segmented sentence, A and Z belong to parole (1941:35), he extends his theory of reciprocal conditioning between thème and propos to the whole of syntagmatics (1965:§§ 154, 155). A troublesome consequence of this confusion of parole and langue is that he feels compelled to exclude the relation of coördination, with the collocations that depend on it, from the sphere of syntagmatics (Frei 1948)

[3] The concept of sentence modifier (as a rule an adverb) is narrower than that of detached satellite: *My Uncle Willy, he doesn't trust anybody*; *Myself, I prefer the red one*; *If it rains, we'll play the match tomorrow*; *You do that again, and I'll smack you!*

[4] For yet another demonstration, cf. Bearth 1971: § 16, p. 385.

REFERENCES

Bally, Charles. 1941. Intonation et syntaxe. CFS 1.33-42 [repr. in Godel 1969:101-109].

—. 1965. Linguistique générale et linguistique française. 4th ed. Berne: Francke. [*Phrase segmentée*: §§ 79-98, repr. in Godel 1969:77-87].

Bearth, Thomas. 1971. L'énoncé toura (Côte d'Ivoire). Geneva dissertation. Norman: Summer Institute of Linguistics of the University of Oklahoma, Publication No. 30.

Bennett, Thomas. 1973. The segmented sentence in the spoken English of a South-Eastern Englishman. Geneva dissertation.

Frei, Henri. 1948. Note sur l'analyse des syntagmes. Word 4.65-70.

—. 1962. L'unité linguistique complexe. Lingua 11.128-40.

Godel, Robert, ed. 1969. A Geneva School reader in linguistics. Indiana University studies in the history and theory of linguistics. Bloomington & London: Indiana University Press.

Lauberte, Emma. La phrase segmentée dans le letton parlé d'aujourd'hui. Geneva dissertation (in preparation).

Martinet, André. 1960. Eléments de linguistique générale. Collection A. Colin, 349. Paris: Colin.

Sechehaye, Albert. 1926. Essai sur la structure logique de la phrase. Collection linguistique publiée par la Société de linguistique de Paris, 20. Paris: Champion.

SOME FUNDAMENTAL INSIGHTS OF TAGMEMICS REVISITED

PETER H. FRIES

In its development over the past two decades, tagmemic theory has been strongest in dealing with relations which hold on or near the surface.[1] But even on this level tagmemicists have had difficulty in integrating their insights into a coherent system. Longacre (1965), for example, attempts to present some of the fundamental insights of tagmemics in the realm of grammar. He deals in particular with the concepts TAGMEME, SYNTAGMEME, LEVEL, HIERARCHY, and FIELD.[2] In spite of his efforts, however, the concept of hierarchy remains weakly motivated and the concept of field is not really integrated within the system. This paper is an attempt to integrate these two concepts into tagmemic theory in a theoretically well motivated way and in a way which is consistent with the actual practice of tagmemicists. I attempt this topic in the hope that a more coherent and explicit theory of surface grammar will make it easier to develop useful theories of deep structure and semantic structure, as well as to relate these structures to the surface structure.

Since the portion of tagmemic theory I am trying to formalize deals with surface structure, the elements, relations, and contrasts discussed are (unless otherwise noted) elements, relations, and contrasts of the surface structure. In other words, it is not necessary to refer to deep-structure relations in order to motivate surface-structure grammar. It is true that a large number of contrasts which obtain on a surface level do correlate with contrasts on a deeper level as well. Thus, an interrogative clause differs from a declarative clause on both the surface and the deep levels of structure. But other surface level contrasts (say the difference between *John saw the dog* and *what John saw was the dog*) do not correlate with a difference on the deep structure level of analysis.

TAGMEME

A tagmeme is an association of a grammatical function with the set of items which may fill that function. As Longacre (1965:65) has said, "Tagmemics makes grammatical functions focal, but associates such functions with sets of items and constructions". The primacy of grammatical function arises because the various functions contribute a type of meaning. Thus the subject of a clause is the topic of the clause. *John saw Bill* is a statement about John, while *Bill was seen by John* is a statement about Bill. Similarly, *the dented fender* is not an exact paraphrase of *the fender dented. (The dented fender was the left one. The fender dented was the left one.).* When the participle occurs before the noun it characterizes the noun in a relatively permanent way. When the participle follows the noun it modifies no such permanence is implied.[3] The difference in the relationship between modifier and head in the two examples above is a result of the difference in the grammatical functions the two modifiers fill.

Differences in functional relationships are formally demonstrable in that they correlate with differences in form: e.g. different filler classes, permutability, transformation potential, agreement, etc. It is important to note, however, that these formal correlates do not define the function but only correlate with the function. A grammatical function is a relationship between a constituent and the construction of which it is a part. The formal correlates of a grammatical function are not the relationship itself, but a result of such a relationship.

SYNTAGMEME AND FIELD

Since a grammatical function is a relationship between a constituent of a construction and the construction itself, to speak of a grammatical function implies the existence of some unit which contains the function. Such units are called syntagmemes. But the units of language are contrastive units; thus syntagmemes are contrastive construction types. Now it is well known in phonology that the way to show contrast is to find examples of minimal pairs, or, if these cannot be found, examples showing contrast in analogous environments. But neither of these situations is a necessary condition for saying that two phones contrast and therefore belong to different phonemes. [h] and [ŋ] are in complementary distribution in English, yet few linguists (and no tagmemicists) have seriously considered them to be allophones of the same phoneme. Similarly, it is impossible to find good examples of contrast between consonants and vowels, yet [a] and [p] are not considered to be allophones of the same phoneme in any language. In other words, contrast in identical environments and contrast in analogous environments are merely manifestations of a more basic kind of contrast: contrast in field. The English phonemes /h/ and /ŋ/, and, for that matter, /p/ and /b/, are considered to be different phonemes primarilly because they play different roles within the system of English phonemes. Contrast in field usually (but not always) correlates with contrast in identical or analogous environments.

Contrast within the grammatical hierarchy has been difficult to define as long as linguists searched for an analog in grammar to the minimal pair in phonology. Once one realizes that the basic contrast is contrast in field, then the inability to find an analog for minimal pairs is no longer so disturbing. A field, in the sense being used here, is a set of language units which differ from each other along a certain finite set of parameters. In the grammatical hierarchy, the units are syntagmemes and the parameters of each field are expressible in terms of grammatical functions.

Though this last statement is not made overtly in statements of tagmemic theory, it can be shown to be consistent with the practice of tagmemicists. On the one hand, no tagmemic grammar, as far as I know, has posited two contrasting syntagmemes solely on the basis of differences in form. While it is true in a number of cases that the differences in form may be the most obvious differences, tagmemicists have always intuitively felt that a difference in grammatical relationship also existed. Thus one might find in the description of a language two clause syntagmemes described as follows:[4]

A) Transitive clause $= +$ Subject: NP $+$ Predicate: VP_{-be}
$+$ Object: NP

B) Equative clause $= +$ Topic: NP $+$ Predicate$_{Link}$:
$VP_{be} +$ Comp: NP

The primary formal difference between A and B lies in the fact that the filler of the predicate in A is all verbs other than *be*, while the filler of the predicate in B is the verb *be*. But this is not the only difference posited between the two clauses. Differences in functions are posited as well. The second NP in A, for example, fills the object function while the second NP in B fills the complement function. Such a situation is typical of tagmemic practice.

A second bit of evidence that the parameters of grammatical fields are grammatical functions arises from the fact that in all cases which I have examined in which an author has attempted to present a system of contrasting syntagmemes, differences in the component functions are the

INDEPENDENT CLAUSES

	Declarative Clause	Imperative Clause	Yes-No Interrogative Clause
Intransitive	+S+Act Intr Decl Pr He ran.	+Act Intr Imp Pr Run!	+S+Act Intr Inter Pr Did he run?
Single Transitive	+S+Act Sg Tr Decl Pr+DO She guided the tourists.	+Act Sg Tr Imp Pr+DO Guide the tourists!	+S+Act Sg Tr Inter Pr+DO Did she guide the tourists?
Double Transitive	+S+Act Db Tr Decl Pr+IO+DO They gave John a book.	+Act Db Tr Imp Pr+IO+DO Give John a book!	+S+Act Db Tr Inter Pr+IO+DO Did they give John a book?
Attributive Transitive	+S+Act At Tr Decl Pr DO At They elected him chairman.	+Act At Tr Imp Pr+DO+At Elect him chairman!	+S+Act At Tr Inter Pr+DO+At Did they elect him chairman?
Equational	+S+Eq Decl Pr+Eq Co She was kind.	+Eq Imp Pr+Eq Co Be kind!	+S+Eq Inter Pr +Eq Co Is she kind?

parameters of the field.[5] A typical case in point is the above matrix adapted from Liem 1966, showing a portion of the system of English clauses.

Each cell in every row has some set of functions (or absence of functions) in common, and each cell in every column has some set of functions (or absence of functions) in common. We can now make an analogy with phonology. If we consider each cell in the field to be a unit – analogous to a phoneme – the distinctive features of that unit are the surface-level grammatical functions which compose it. One might predict a possible difference of opinion as to what the real linguistic unit is, the occupant of the cell (the phoneme or syntagmeme) or the set of features defining each cell (the phonological distinctive features or surface-grammatical functions. This last is usually verbalized as transitive-intransitive, or declarative-imperative, etc.). It is our belief that both unit and feature are relevant.

Once we see that the contrast involved when we say 'a syntagmeme is a contrastive construction type' is contrast within field, and when we realize that the variables of the field are largely functional variables, we see some of the reasons for the heuristics used by tagmemicists. First of all, the heuristics on a syntagmeme level are necessary in order to distinguish differences in function which constitute variables of the system of syntagmemes from those differences in function which do not. Thus, on a clause level, any clause may be modified for time. The presence or absence of a time modifier cannot distinguish one clause from another. Secondly, Longacre's dual criterion[6] for contrasting syntagmemes is merely an affirmation that an IMPORTANT difference (an emic difference) between two clause types should correlate with more than one formal difference.

From the foregoing discussion of system it can be seen that Longacre is being repetitious when he says:

syntagmemic contrast is, then, in reference to three considerations: (1) the internal tagmemic structure of the syntagmeme; (2) the distribution of the syntagmeme (as an exponent of tagmemes) in other (usually higher level) syntagmemes; and (3) the distribution of the syntagmeme within a system of syntagmemes (1968:xiii).

The past few pages have shown that 1 and 3 are, to all intents and purposes, one basic factor – role in system – looked at from two points of view: 1 from the point of view of distinctive features of the system, and 3 from the point of view of system as a whole. Some aspects of 2 are accounted for by the fact that certain tagmemes directly affect the distributional properties of the including syntagmemes. Questions do not have the same distribution as the corresponding declarative or imperative clauses. It remains to be seen, however, whether all significant differences in distribution correlate with differences in the component functions of the contrasting syntagmemes.

LEVEL AND HIERARCHY

A level is a system of contrasting syntagmemes. A hierarchy is a system of contrasting levels. These two definitions in conjunction with what has already been said about system (in particular that the parameters of a system are definable in terms of surface-structure function), imply that the various levels within a hierarchy are to be contrasted and identified by the various functional relations posited for the syntagmemes with each level.

That is, roughly, a clause is a clause because it contains a predicate or predicate-like tagmeme while a phrase is a phrase because it contains tagmemes such as head, modifier, etc. It is worth noting here that in saying this I am merely emphasizing one aspect of the definition of levels, especially the clause and phrase levels already used by tagmemicists. Thus, in Elson and Pickett (1962:64), the definition of clause included the statement: "A clause construction is any string of tagmemes which consists of or includes one and only one predicate or predicate like tagmeme among the constituent tagmemes of the string ..." Similarly Longacre (1964:74) included the following sentence in his definition of phrase. "[A phrase] may be single centered, double centered, or relator-axis; and expresses such relationships as head-modifier, linkage of elements, or relation of an element to the clause by means of an overt relator."

These two statements are examples of the type of statement advocated here. The difficulties with them lie in the fact that the first statement is over-simple, since there are constructions which we may want to call clauses, but which do not contain predicate or predicate-like constructions. Note, for instance, the following examples:

> a) *(I don't like) John playing near the railing*
> b) *With the king safely out of the way, (the barons quickly distributed among themselves the wealth of the commoners.)*
> c) *(I wanted) John to come*

The second statement is more complete, but does not seem to be unified by any underlying principle. One could justifiably ask whether these relations have anything in common which contrast them as a group with relations which are typical of clauses or words. As far as I can tell, Longacre has no answer to such a question other than "that's the way things are". I believe this lack of motivation stems from his emphasis on descending exponence in the definition of hierarchy. Longacre

(1964:74) includes, for example, a statement that phrases are "a class of syntagmemes of a hierarchical order ranking above such syntagmemes as the word and/or stem and below such syntagmemes as the clause and sentence". The definition of each level (sentence, clause, phrase, and word) in Longacre 1964 contains a similar statement locating it within the hierarchy of levels. In this context saying that clause level ranks just above phrase level implies, among other things, that phrases typically manifest clause level tagmemes.

It is clear from the pervasiveness of statements locating construction types within the hierarchy that descending exponence plays an important role in Longacre's definition of hierarchy. He admits, however, that:

Attempts to define hierarchy overly rigidly in terms of exclusively descending exponence can only lead to complete jettisoning of the notion of hierarchy. The exceptions are too glaring to rationalize away successfully for very long (1970:185).

However, we should note that Longacre clearly regards counterexamples to his general rule that higher ranking constructions have constituents which belong to the next lower rank, as nothing more than temporary exceptions to the general rule.

... without the downward thrust of constituent structure [from discourse level to morpheme level – PHF] there could not be hierarchy. Descending hierarchy and level skipping are but different instances here of the same tendency. Furthermore, both recursion and back looping must, eventually, terminate and give way to the downward thrust (1970:186).

Within this model of hierarchy Longacre has no means of explaining why the exceptions to the 'downward thrust' of hierarchy occur when and where they do. Why, for example, do relative clauses fill noun phrase tagmemes but not the tagmemes of a prepositional phrase?

It seems to me that such questions can be answered only if we focus away from descending exponence as a defining feature of hierarchy and search for a more basic defining feature. A good candidate for such a basic defining feature is the kind of function each unit has in a connected discourse.

If we look at the use of language in connected discourse we find certain things assumed, certain things asserted,[7] and relations between assertions expressed. In a clause such as *the old man walked home* the assertion is made that a given individual walked to a particular location. In addition to this assertion, however, the information is given that the individual involved is a man and is old (and probably that he has been mentioned before). The information that he is old and is a man, however, has a different status within the clause from the information which is asserted: it is not asserted. It is brought in in order to supply enough information to the listener so that he can identify the participant in the action. Information which is not asserted takes on roughly the status of features describing the participant.[8] These features may be used to contrast the actual participant with other potential participants (the old man instead of the young one, the old man instead of the old woman), or they may be used to more fully describe a participant in order to explain a further action (and its implications). It can be shown that the clause *the old man walked home* is true whether or not the listener agrees that the man is old. The clause is true if a particular individual (whom I described as old) walked home. It is true that conversations such as (A) *The old man walked home*, (B) *He's not old* may occur but the participants realize that such a sequence of sentences is strange.

Noun Phrases are semantically complexes of features even if they contain restrictive relative clauses. Thus, *I found out that that man I met at the party yesterday is a bank president*, and *Beware of men you meet at parties* both contain noun phrases (with *man* as head) which contain relative clauses. The function of the first relative clause is to contrast one individual with others, while the function of the second is to describe the relevant feature of a given class of men. In both instances, however, the semantic interpretation of the noun phrases will be in terms of a set of semantic features. Thus, when they are considered from the standpoint of the including clause, restrictive relative clauses are to be interpreted as merely adding descriptive/identificational features within the noun phrase. Functions of speech acts and portions of speech acts, such as assertion, and description or identification of participants in an assertion, may be called discourse functions. These functions are signalled in the surface structure and hence may be called surface-grammatical meaning.

If we look at the way these discourse functions are distributed throughout the hierarchy, we see that the various hierarchial levels correlate generally with different discourse functions. Clauses typically express assertions (c.f. Longacre 1964:35), phrases typically indicate participants in the assertions (*the man*), features of the participants (*the very old man*), or restrictions on the assertion such as limitations as to time, place, manner, etc. Within participants of an assertion I must include the action itself (e.g. *will have been completed*), and any modalities and conditions imposed on the action such as aspect, and tense. Relations between assertions such as cause, conjunction, antithesis, and relations between a participant in an assertion and the assertion itself (*I gave the book to Harry*) are expressed by single words.

With such a correlation we are now prepared not only to find a general trend of descending exponence (phrases typically manifest clause-level tagmemes, words typically express phrase-level tagmemes, etc.), but also to find exceptions to this general trend. Exceptions occur, for instance, when a relation between two assertions is overtly expressed, e.g., in *John came downstairs because he wanted some milk* the word *because* fills a sentence-level tagmeme. If, on the other hand, a participant in an assertion is itself an assertion, we expect to find a clause filling a grammatical function within another clause (*That he came early surprised me.*). Similarly, if we wish to identify a participant in one assertion by noting that he also is a participant in a second, the theory would predict that a clause would fill a phrase-level tagmeme. Thus, if a given individual both shot a guard and led a gang, then one could find either *the one who shot the guard led the gang*, or *the one who led the gang shot the guard*. The choice of one or the other alternative depends on what is already known by the listener.

Now if we accept discourse function as the underlying motivation for hierarchy, it seems to me we must ask where the source for discourse functions such as assertion, identification of participants, etc. lies. My answer is that it lies largely in the functional aspect of the component tagmeme of the syntagmemes. That is, clauses predicate because they have tagmemes which interact in such a way as to predicate. (*The dog is barking.*) Noun Phrases do not predicate (*the barking dog, the dog barking in the street*), because they have no tagmemes which interact to make a predication.[9] I do not deny here that the same information is conveyed in *the dog is barking* and *the barking dog*. The two constructions differ in that, in the first, barking is asserted with respect to the dog, while in the second, the fact that the dog is barking is used as an identifying or descriptive feature of the dog.

In summary we now have a system of five terms: TAGMEME, SYNTAGMEME, LEVEL, HIERARCHY, and FIELD (= SYSTEM) which are interrelated largely via the concept of surface structure grammatical function. But this means that functional relations are of crucial importance within this theory of grammar. That is, if we label the functions of *head down* in *Head down, the bull charged* as Subject-Predicate, we imply that this construction is some sort of clause, while if we call these functions Head-Modifier, we imply that the construction belongs on the phrase level.

But basing this aspect of tagmemic theory on surface level grammatical functions offers a direct challenge to tagmemicists. If surface structure grammatical relations are so important to the theory, then tagmemicists ought to develop a coherent theory of surface-structure grammatical relationships. What does it mean when we say that X is the subject or object of a clause? What similarities must subjects in language A share with subjects in a language B? How may subjects differ? In short, what is needed is a kind of etics of surface-level grammatical functions. Tagmemicists have implicitly operated with such a theory for a long time. Velma Pickett for example has told me of long conversations about how best to label certain grammatical functions in her dissertation. It seems to me that it is time for tagmemicists to make such a theory explicit.

NOTES

[1]   Actually it can be shown that tagmemics has no level of analysis which is identical to the level called surface structure by transformational grammarians; specifically through the use of double function, tagmemicists may deal with some of the elements transformationists analyze as being deleted from the string. The level of structure tagmemics does deal with is so shallow, however (especially in comparison to the analysis of Ross and Lakoff, or the case grammar of Fillmore), that in this paper we will use the term surface structure for the level of analysis that tagmemics treats.

[2]   Longacre (1965) uses the term *matrix* instead of *field*. I prefer *field* or *system* for two reasons. First of all, *matrix* refers to a visual n-dimensional array which may be used to represent a system of a language (each dimension of the array representing a parameter of the system). Since I believe the things said here have some relevance for a language system, not merely its visual representation, I prefer to use *system* and *field* which directly refer to the objects being described. My second objection to the use of the term *matrix* is that on a number of occasions within tagmemic literature matrices have been used to represent objects other than systems. Pike (1970:38) presents a "Co-Occurrence Matrix of Bimoba Clauses in Clusters". This matrix is no more than a chart of the various clause types which may co-occur within a clause cluster. No attempt is made to state that this chart represents a system of the language. Neither *field* nor *system* has, to my knowledge, been applied to such a representation. I prefer to use the terms which exclude such charts, hence I will restrict myself to the terms *field* and *system*.

[3]   See Bolinger 1967 for a detailed discussion with many examples.

[4]   While this example does not pretend to describe any actual language, examples similar to the one presented here may be found in Trique (Longacre 1966:244), Lamani (Trail 1970:38, 50-51), and Totonac (Reid, Bishop, Button and Longacre 1968:31, 34, 44).

[5]   In personal conversations, Pike has indicated that the theory allows differences in distribution to be possible parameters of systems. In searching the literature, I have not found any cases in which this possibility has been used. I believe that should such cases occur, the differences in distribution will probably correlate with differences in grammatical function. Hence, it will not be necessary to use distribution as a parameter of a grammatical system.

[6] Longacre's dual criterion unfortunately was initially heralded as a major theoretical advance. Pike (1962:231) calls it a "crucial theoretical advance". In reality, the dual criterion is a very useful heuristic device which derives from a theoretical advance which in the early sixties remained unexpressed.

[7] While the term ASSERT normally refers only to one function of a speech act, one which is closely related to declarative clauses, my use of the term here is to be understood as including other functions of speech acts, such as questioning and commanding. These, of course, are closely related to interrogative and imperative clauses.

[8] The distinction between the information which is asserted and the information which is used as descriptive or identificational features of a participant of an assertion is roughly similar to the distinction Leech (1970:25-28) makes between the including predications, rank-shifted predications, and downgraded predications. Downgraded predications take on the status of features, while the including predications and rank-shifted predications are asserted.

[9] The approach I am suggesting here may also provide a criterion for treating certain clause-like and phrase-like constructions as clauses rather than phrases; e.g.

> *With John gone, (there were only six of us to feed.)*
> *Head down, (the bull charged.)*
> *(John came home) tired.*

Each of the above examples has neither a typical clause-level structure nor a typical phrase-level structure; so internal formal criteria are indecisive. All three express assertions which are independent of the INCLUDING assertion.

REFERENCES

Bolinger, D. 1967. Adjectives in English: Attribution and predication. Lingua 18.1-34.

Elson, Benjamin, and Pickett, Velma. 1962. An introduction to morphology and syntax. Santa Ana: Summer Institute of Linguistics.

Longacre, Robert E. 1964. Grammar discovery procedures. Janua Linguarum, Series minor 33. The Hague: Mouton.

—. 1965. Some fundamental insights of tagmemics. Language 41.65-76.

—. 1966. Trique clause and sentence: A study in contrast, variation, and distribution. IJAL 32.242-252.

—. 1968. Philippine languages: Discourse, paragraph and sentence structure. Santa Ana: Summer Institute of Linguistics.

—. 1970. Hierarchy in language. Method and theory in linguistics, ed. by Paul Garvin, 173-195. Janua Linguarum, Series maior 40. The Hague: Mouton.

Leech, Geoffry N. 1970. Towards a semantic description of English. Bloomington: Indiana University Press.

Liêm, Nguyen Dãng. 1966. English grammar: A combined tagmemics and transformational approach. Linguistic Circle of Canberra Publications, vol. 1, Series C. Canberra, Australia.

Pike, K. L. 1970. Tagmemic and matrix linguistics applied to selected African languages. Santa Ana: Summer Institute of Linguistics.

Reid, Aileen, Bishop, Ruth G., Button, Ella M., and Longacre, Robert. 1968. Totonac: From clause to discourse. Santa Ana: Summer Institute of Linguistics.

Trail, Ronald. 1970. The grammar of Lamani. Santa Ana: Summer Institute of Linguistics.

EINE TRANSFORMATIONELLE GRAMMATIK MIT REKONSTITUENTIELLER KOMPONENTE

CHRISTOPH HAURI

Beside the transformational component of a grammar a reconstituential component is attempted as being superior in information to both dependency structure and constituent structure.

1.1 Was die transformationelle Komponente einer Grammatik ist, muß heute nicht mehr erklärt werden. Beim vorliegenden Versuch ist nur die Erklärung ihrer rekonstituentiellen Komponente nötig. Hier kann versichert werden, daß die Rekonstituenten (R)-Struktur sowohl der Dependenz (D)-Struktur als auch der Konstituenten (K)-Struktur an Information überlegen ist.[1]

1.2 Nach früheren Versuchen (1.3) nehmen wir im Pascalschen Dreieck das Modell einer binären allgemeinen Struktur (2) mit einer rekursiven allgemeinen Adjunktionsregel an. Die Vermutung einer Reduktionsregel ergibt uns die R-Struktur (3), diejenige einer Deletionsregel die D-Struktur (4), bei der die Endkette zuwenig Information vermittelt, und diejenige einer Deletions-Substitutionsregel die K-Struktur (5), bei der die Endkette zuwenig Information und der Baum zuviel Information vermittelt, die ihre Nichtendelemente betrifft. Das Prinzip der Wortstellung (6) lehrt uns die nicht nur theoretische, sondern auch praktische Überlegenheit der R-Struktur.

1.3 Die D-Struktur von Tesnière (1959) und die K-Struktur von Chomsky (1965) sind einander mit verschiedenen Methoden gegenübergestellt worden. Während sie Hays (1964) und Gaifman (1965) miteinander vergleichen, führt sie Lecerf (1961) auf eine allgemeine Struktur zurück, die er G-Syntax nennt. Wenn man in einer allgemeinen Kette alle eckigen Klammern und alle Operationspunkte auslösche, die den Nichtendelementen der K-Struktur entsprechen, gelange man zu einer D-Kette, und wenn man in ihr alle runden Klammern auslösche, zu einer K-Kette. Baumgärtner (1965) deutet diese Methoden. Robinson (1970) erweitert die D-Struktur nach der K-Struktur zu einer R-Struktur, die sie hybride Dependenz-Phrasenstrukturgrammatik nennt. Jede

D-Struktur sei durch die einfache Technik der Zufügung eines unterschiedlichen Duplikats zu jedem Vorkommen einer Kategorie in einem D-Baum in eine K-Struktur umwandelbar.

2.1 Die allgemeine Anfangskette ist von der Form (a)

a)   # A_1 #

wo # = Grenzsymbol, A_1 = erstes Nichtendelement.

2.2 Die allgemeine Adjunktionsregel ist von der Form (b)

b) $A_n \rightarrow a_n (A_{2n+1}{}^\wedge A_{2n})$

wo (+) = potentielle Anwesenheit, $\rightarrow$ = wird ersetzt durch, $^\wedge$ = Verkettungssymbol, a_n = ntes Endelement.

2.3 Eine der durch Anwendung der allgemeinen Adjunktionsregel (b) aus der allgemeinen Anfangskette (a) abgeleiteten allgemeinen Endketten ist (c)

c)   # $a_1{}^\wedge a_3{}^\wedge a_7{}^\wedge a_6{}^\wedge a_2{}^\wedge a_5{}^\wedge a_4$ #

2.4 Der allgemeine Baum (d)

d)

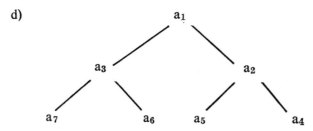

ist aus der allgemeinen Endkette (c) durch die allgemeine Anweisung (e)

e)   Ungeradzahlige Elemente werden von oben nach unten links, geradzahlige Elemente vom nächstmöglichen oberen Knoten nach unten rechts eingetragen.

aufzurichten. In jedem allgemeinen Baum ist von den drei zu einer Gabel gehörigen Elementen das obere die Konstituente, und das untere linke und das untere rechte sind ihre Subkonstituenten.

3.1 Die R-Struktur besitzt im Unterschied zur allgemeinen Struktur eine Reduktionsregel. Die R-Reduktionsregel ist von der Form (f)

f) $a_{2n} \rightarrow a_n$

3.2 Die allgemeine Endkette (c) wird durch Anwendung der R-Reduktionsregel (f) durch die R-Endkette (g)

g) # $a_1^\frown a_3^\frown a_7^\frown a_3^\frown a_1^\frown a_5^\frown a_1$ #

ersetzt. Sie verdoppelt nicht die den Elementen eigenen Indexe, sondern sie selbst. Nicht anders als bei der Parallele der Oktavversetzung in der Musik der 2., 4. und 6. Oberton als Oktavversetzungen des 1., 2. und 3. Obertons, werden in der Sprache die 2., 4. und 6. Konstituente als Rekonstituenten der 1., 2. und 3. Konstituente empfunden. In jeder R-Endkette ist von denjenigen drei zu einer Zeile gehörigen Elementen, bei denen das erste und das dritte miteinander identisch sind, das linke die Konstituente, das nächste rechte ihre Subkonstituente und das nächstmögliche rechte ihre Rekonstituente.

3.3 Der R-Baum (h)

h)

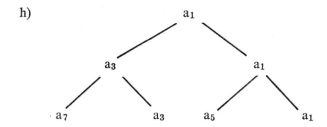

ist aus der R-Endkette (g) durch die R-Anweisung (i)

i) Erstmalige Elemente werden von oben nach unten links, nichterstmalige Elemente vom nächstmöglichen oberen Knoten nach unten rechts eingetragen.

aufzurichten. In jedem R-Baum ist von den drei zu einer Gabel gehörigen Elementen das obere die Konstituente, das untere linke ihre Subkonstituente und das untere rechte ihre Rekonstituente.

4.1 Die D-Struktur besitzt im Unterschied zur allgemeinen Struktur und im Gegensatz zur R-Struktur, die eine Reduktionsregel besitzt, eine Deletionsregel. Die D-deletionsregel ist von der Form (j)

j) $a_{2n} \rightarrow o$

4.2 Die allgemeine Endkette (c) wird durch Anwendung der D-Deletionsregel (j) durch die D-Endkette (k)

k) # $a_1^\frown a_3^\frown a_7^\frown a_5$ #

ersetzt.

4.3 Der D-Baum (l)

l)

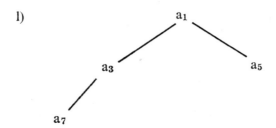

ist aus der D-Endkette (k) durch die allgemeine Anweisung (e) nicht aufzurichten, weil sie die geradzahligen Elemente der allgemeinen Endkette (c) nicht enthält.

4.4 Wegen der Deletion der geradzahligen Elemente statt ihrer Reduktion zu nichterstmaligen Elementen vermittelt die Endkette bei der D-Struktur gegenüber der R-Struktur zuwenig Information. Die D-Deletionsregel (j) bewirkt, daß die Hierarchie der Konstituenten zwar aus dem D-Baum (l) wie aus dem R-Baum (h), aber nicht aus der D-Endkette (k) wie aus der R-Endkette (g) zu erkennen ist.

5.1 Die K-Struktur besitzt im Unterschied zur allgemeinen Struktur und im Gegensatz zur R-Struktur, die eine Reduktionsregel besitzt, eine Deletions-Substitutionsregel. Die K-Deletions-Substitutionsregel ist von der Form (m)

m) $\quad \dfrac{a_n}{2} \rightarrow \left\{ \begin{array}{c} O \\ A_{\frac{n}{2}} \end{array} \right\}$

wo $\{+\}$ = alternative Anwesenheit.

5.2 Die allgemeine Endkette (c) wird durch Anwendung der K-Deletions-Substitutionsregel (m) als mit der D-Deletionsregel (j) reziproke Deletionsregel durch die erste K-Endkette (n)

n) $\quad \# \; a_7 \hat{\,} a_6 \hat{\,} a_5 \hat{\,} a_4 \; \#$

ersetzt. Durch deren Anwendung als gegen die allgemeine Adjunktionsregel (b) redundante Substitutionsregel wird sie durch die zweite K-Endkette (o)

o) $\quad *\# \; A_1 \hat{\,} A_3 \hat{\,} a_7 \hat{\,} a_6 \hat{\,} A_2 \hat{\,} a_5 \hat{\,} a_4 \; \#$

ersetzt. Diese besteht nicht, weil sie Nichtendelemente enthält.

5.3 Der erste K-Baum (p)

p) $\quad *a_7 \; a_6 \; a_5 \; a_4$

besteht nicht, weil er die niedrigerzahligen Elemente der allgemeinen Endkette (c) nicht enthält. Der zweite K-Baum (q)

q)

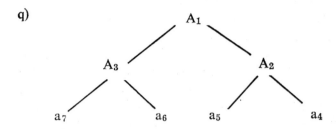

ist aus der zweiten K-Endkette (o) durch die allgemeine Anweisung (e) nicht aufzurichten, weil sie nicht besteht.

5.4 Wegen der Deletion der niedrigerzahligen Elemente statt ihrer Reduktion zu erstmaligen Elementen vermittelt die Endkette bei der K-Struktur gegenüber der R-Struktur zuwenig Information. Wegen der Substitution von Nichtendelementen für Endelemente statt deren Reduktion zu erstmaligen Elementen vermittelt der Baum bei ihr gegenüber der R-Struktur zuviel Information. Die K-Deletions-Substitutionsregel (m) als Deletionsregel bewirkt, daß die Hierarchie der Konstituenten zwar aus dem zweiten K-Baum (q) wie aus dem R-Baum (h), aber nicht aus der ersten K-Endkette (n) wie aus der Endkette (g) zu erkennen ist. Als Deletions- und Substitutionsregel bewirkt sie, daß die K-Struktur nicht wie die R- und D-Struktur einen mit der Endkette biuniken Baum hat.

6.1 Bei der Wortstellung erscheinen zwischen der Tiefen- und Oberflächenstruktur die Ebene der gewöhnlichen Wortstellung und die Ebene der gelegentlichen Wortstellung durch Emphase. Von den vierundzwanzig Anordnungen der vier Glieder Verb, Subjekt, Objekt und Adjektiv des Subjekts sind in den natürlichen Sprachen diejenigen sechs, in denen das Subjekt dem Objekt vorangeht und seinem Adjektiv unmittelbar vorangeht oder folgt, häufiger als die übrigen achtzehn. Die sechs Anordnungen sind von der kanonischen Form (r)

r)   (Verb) (Subjekt) Adjektiv$_S$ (Subjekt) (Verb) Objekt (Verb)

Deren erster bis sechster Typ sind (s) (t) (u) (v) (w) (x)

s)   Verb Subjekt Adjektiv$_S$ Objekt
t)   Verb Adjektiv$_S$ Subjekt Objekt
u)   Subjekt Adjektiv$_S$ Verb Objekt

v)   Adjektiv$_S$ Subjekt Verb Objekt
w)   Subjekt Adjektiv$_S$ Objekt Verb
x)   Adjektiv$_S$ Subjekt Objekt Verb

Der erste Typ, bei dem alle bestimmten Glieder allen bestimmenden Gliedern vorangehen, ist zentrifugal. Der sechste Typ, bei dem alle bestimmten Glieder allen bestimmenden Gliedern folgen, ist zentripetal.

6.2 Das erwähnte Prinzip der Wortstellung hat Greenberg (1963) aufgezeigt. Bei der relativen Anordnung von Subjekt, Verb, das bei Hill (1958)[2] Prädikator heißt, und Objekt, das bei ihm Komplement heißt, sei in Aussagesätzen mit nominalem Subjekt und Objekt die dominante Anordnung fast immer eine, in der das Subjekt dem Objekt vorangehe.

6.3 Die R-Endkette (g) stimmt zur kanonischen Form (r), wobei a_1 = Verb, a_3 = Subjekt, a_5 = Objekt, a_7 = Adjektiv$_S$. Der erste bis sechste Typ (s-x) können durch Deletionen erzeugt werden, wogegen die übrigen achtzehn Anordnungen durch Permutationen erzeugt werden können. Die Erzeugung der englischen Oberflächenstruktur mit dem zweiten (t) und vierten Typ (v) und diejenige der deutschen Oberflächenstruktur mit diesen Typen und dem sechsten Typ (x) ist für die R-Struktur leichter.

6.4 Die D-Endkette (k) stimmt dann zum ersten Typ (s). Der zweite bis sechste Typ (t-x) müssen wie die übrigen achtzehn Anordnungen durch Permutationen erzeugt werden. Die Kongruenz des Verbs mit dem Objekt ist für die D-Struktur weniger leicht.

6.5 Die erste K-Endkette (n) stimmt dann zum sechsten Typ (x), wobei a_4 = Verb, a_6 = Subjekt. Der erste bis fünfte Typ (s-w) müssen wie die übrigen achtzehn Anordnungen durch Permutationen erzeugt werden. Die Kongruenz des Verbs mit dem Subjekt ist für die K-Struktur weniger leicht.

6.6 Hat die kanonische Form (r) die universale Wortstellung, so ist die Behauptung von McCawley (1970), daß die englische Tiefenstruktur den zweiten Typ (t) fordere, und diejenige von Bach (1962), daß die deutsche Tiefenstruktur den sechsten Typ (x) fordere, so falsch, wie die Behauptung von Lakoff (1970), daß die Kongruenz der K-Struktur schwerfalle, richtig ist.

University of Queensland

NOTEN

[1] Eine vorläufige Fassung dieses Papiers wurde an der Tagung der Linguistic Society of Australia vom 23.-24. August 1971 in Melbourne mitgeteilt.
[2] Ich entbiete meinem Lehrer und Kollegen 1962-64 an der University of Texas meine besten Wünsche.

REFERENCES

Bach, Emmon. 1962. The order of elements in a transformational grammar of German. Language 38.263-9.

Baumgärtner, Klaus. 1965. Spracherklärung mit den Mitteln der Abhängigkeitsstruktur. Beiträge zur Sprachkunde und Informationsverarbeitung 5.31-53.

Chomsky, Noam. 1965. Aspects of the theory of syntax. Cambridge, Massachusetts: MIT Press.

Gaifman, Haim. 1965. Dependency systems and phrase-structure systems. Information and Control 8.304-37.

Greenberg, Joseph H. 1963. Some universals of grammar with particular reference to the order of meaningful elements. Universals of Language, hrsg. von Joseph H. Greenberg, 58-90. Cambridge, Massachusetts: MIT Press.

Hays, David G. 1964. Dependency theory: A formalism and some observations. Language 40.511-25.

Hill, Archibald A. 1958. Introduction to linguistic structures: From sound to sentence in English. New York: Harcourt, Brace.

Lakoff, George. 1970. Global rules. Language 46.627-39.

Lecerf, Yves. 1961. Une représentation algébrique de la structure des phrases dans diverses langues naturelles. Comptes rendus de l'Académie des Sciences 252.232-4.

McCawley, James D. 1970. English as a VSO language. Language 46.286-99.

Robinson, Jane J. 1970. Dependency structures and transformational rules. Language 46.259-85.

Tesnière, Lucien. 1959. Eléments de syntaxe structurale. Paris: Klincksieck.

SYNTACTIC RECONSTRUCTION
AND THE COMPARATIVE METHOD:
A UTO-AZTECAN CASE STUDY

RODERICK A. JACOBS

A major goal of syntactic reconstruction is the determination of directions of syntactic change within the language or languages under study and, more ambitiously, those characteristic of human language in general. Where no records of earlier stages of a language are available, little or no internal syntactic reconstruction may be possible. But useful reconstruction is still possible through cross-linguistic comparison if there are two or more sister languages almost certainly with a common origin, and if these languages show little evidence of borrowing either from each other or from other languages. Such is the situation with the Cupan languages, three Uto-Aztecan languages spoken in Southern California southeast of Los Angeles and northeast of San Diego. Moreover, at least two stages in the development of Cupan can be observed indirectly. Anthropological and archaeological evidence supports strong linguistic indications that the ancestors of the present-day Luiseño speakers became separated from other Cupan speakers at a period considerably earlier than a second split separating the groups that became the modern Cupeño and Cahuilla peoples.

Clearly knowledge of the existence of such stages is invaluable for reconstruction. A characteristic noted for only two of the languages might more reasonably be assigned to proto-Cupan if the languages were Luiseño and Cupeño or, even better, Luiseño and Cahuilla, than Cahuilla and Cupeño. However, the possibility of like independent development cannot be ruled out without additional evidence. Luiseño has retained, with some modification, an active enclitic system much like that in Cupeño, whereas in Cahuilla almost all the functions of enclitics in the other languages are carried out by verb inflection and most enclitics are rare. It is reasonable to posit an enclitic system in the proto-language for internal reasons too complex to explore here, but additionally there is good external motivation. Cupan is one of three groups within a larger Uto-Aztecan branch, Takic. Languages from the other two groupings, Serrano and Gabrielino, have very similar enclitic systems, and other less closely related Uto-Aztecan languages, most notably Hopi, are no less similar.

What I shall do here is work out reconstructions for an area of syntax offering few problems for reconstruction and then show how such reconstruction provides valuable information for areas of syntax where reconstruction is far less straightforward. Although there are problems concerning the status of certain relative-demonstrative constituents in underlying structure, relativization in Cupan is remarkably uniform for the three languages, morphologically and structurally. But the verb-tense systems of the languages show a surprising degree of variation, although the major division is the expected one between Luiseño and Cupeño-Cahuilla. Thus, while Luiseño has five past tense paradigms, Cupeño and the mountain dialect of Cahuilla have only two, and these are really a single tense differentiated by the presence or absence of a durative morpheme. Furthermore, the desert dialect of Cahuilla consistently uses so-called present tense forms as unmarked past tense verbs. Indeed the major time-reference contrast in this dialect might better be regarded as a *realized* versus *unrealized* one. Finally, forms which in one language arc past tense forms appear with future reference in another language. Since relativized verbs in the most common relative constructions all appear to have distinct time reference and since these constructions are the only relatives common to all three languages, these should provide evidence about earlier time-reference systems associated with the verb.

Relative constructions in Cupan normally follow their head noun. Immediately after the head noun is a pronominal element not unlike the English relative particle *that*, called here the *relative-demonstrative*. The relativized verbs appear characterizable within a tripartite time reference categorization for past, present, and future time, frequently with the option of durative aspect. Crosscutting this division is one between relatives having subjects coreferential with the head noun and those having object or oblique noun phrases coreferential. Although the examples of the latter group contain only coreferential objects, they differ from those with coreferential oblique noun phrases only in lacking an additional pronoun marked for the particular oblique case.

The following examples are all past or future relative constructions with deleted coreferential subjects:[1]

> *Ca*   1. *'áwal pe' húnwet-i mámayaw-ic*
> *Cu*   2. *'awál pə' húnwət-i mámayəw-ic*

L   3. *'awáal po húnwut-i mámayuw-mokwic*
dog RD bear-ACC help-PAST REL
'the dog that helped the bear'

Ca 4. *'áwal pe' húnwet-i mámayaw-nax(-ka')*
Cu 5. *'awál pə' húnwət-i mámayaw-qat*
L   6. *'awáal po húnwut-i mámayaw-lut*
dog RD bear-ACC help-FUT REL
'the dog that will help the bear'

With the exception of Cahuilla example 4, the relativized verbs all apparently have the absolutive ending *c* or *t*, which are two of the three found on non-possessed nouns. In fact, the final glottal stop on the apparent exception 4 is really an underlying *t*, as the accusative forms show – *-naxti* or *-naxkati*. That these constructions contain nominalized verbs is borne out for Cahuilla and Cupeño at least by the existence of an alternative construction differing only in containing an agentive noun instead of the verb, one which may have any of the grammatical functions and inflections of nouns. However, its form, *mámayawva'ac* in Cahuilla, is that of a verb root plus a suffix *-va'ac* and in relative constructions it may contain not only object prefixes but also a durative affix.[2]

The Luiseño *-mokwic* suffix is likely to be a later Luiseño innovation rather than a proto-Cupan remnant. It differs grammatically from the Cahuilla and Cupeño suffixes in allowing a durative morpheme *qal* to precede it. The *-ic* suffix is found not only in Cahuilla and Cupeño but also in Serrano, and there are rare but significant relative-like constructions containing *-ic* even in Luiseño:

L   7. *caamca kwiil ci'i-ŋi-ic-um   wuko'axon*
we acorns gather-leave-PAST REL – PL arrive
'We who left from acorn gathering are arriving.'

L   8. *pi po' cam-ki kulaw-tal lo'x-ic*
and then our-house wood-with build-PAST REL
'our house made with wood ...'

The Luiseño *-lut* and Cahuilla *-nax* are also probably innovations. Without the *t* absolutive, *-lut* is *-luw* or *-low* (as the *-lut* variant, *-lowut,* indicates), a motion suffix found in all three languages with the meaning 'go in order to V' or 'go and V'. In these circumstances it seems reasonable to regard *-lut* as a later development, especially since the expected form *-kat* or *-kut* is already in use with a different meaning. Furthermore,

the plural form of *-lut* is *-kutum*, not **-lutum*. The Cahuilla form is almost
certainly a future *-ne* plus an element *ax* which appears also as a prefix
and as part of an infrequent enclitic, both with the interpretation
'unrealized action or event'. The corresponding element is an enclitic in
the other Cupan languages, in Serrano, and in Hopi. We assume here
that the enclitic usage is the earlier one. The use in all three languages
of what must have been **-kat* supports the probability of **-kat* as the
proto-form in this construction, especially since the closest Takic language, Serrano, has a like element:

> S   8a. *'ama cicint 'uba'im caatubi-ka' mumuk*
>   the boy tomorrow sing-FUT REL sick
>   'The boy who will sing tomorrow is sick.'

So proto-Cupan past and future relatives with coreferential subjects
must, after the application of certain transformations not relevant to our
discussion, have had an underlying structure rather like this:

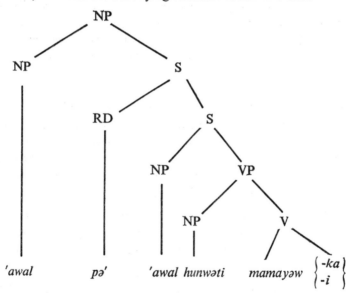

> 9. **'awal pə' hunwəti mamayəw-ic*
>   'the dog that helped the bear'
>
> 10. **'awal pə' hunwəti mamayəw-kat*
>   'the dog that will help the bear'

Figure 1

A nominalization transformation adds the absolutives *t* or *c*, and a
deletion transformation removes the coreferential subject.

Cupan relatives with coreferential objects present few difficulties:

Ca 12. *'awal pe' hunwet mamayaw-ve*
Cu 13. *'awal pə' hunwət pə-mamayəw-və*
L   14. *'awaal po hunwut po-mamayuw-vo*
        dog RD bear he-help-PAST REL
        'the dog that the bear helped'

Ca 15. *'awal pe' hunwet pe-mamayaw-pi*
Cu 16. *'awal pə' hunwət pə-mamayəw-pi*
L   17. *'awaal po hunwut po-mamayuw-pi*
        dog RD bear he help-PAST REL
        'the dog that the bear will help'

Except for 12, the relatives above all seem to have a pronominal subject marker in the form of a possessive. Both Cahuilla examples actually have a deleted subject marker *he-*, which appears only under primary stress. The *pe-* prefix in 15 is an object prefix, inserted under a requirement that a pronominal marker must always appear in surface structure in *-pi* constructions. Structurally these relatives look like regular possessor-possessed nominals. Thus Cupeño *mal* 'hand' loses its absolutive *l* when possessed and must be preceded by a pronominal possessive marker even when there is a noun standing for the possessor. Thus 'the man's hand' is

Cu 18. *naxanic pə-ma*
        man his-hand

and '(that) the bear helped' is

Cu 19. *hunwət pə-mamayəw-və*
        bear his-help-PAST REL

In both cases an absolutive appears if there is no possessive marker. The presence of a possessive marker in 19 identifies the logical subject of the verb as the noun phrase immediately preceding it in the lower sentence, just as in 18 it identifies the preceding noun phrase as its possessor. But verb forms with *-və* and *-pi* are found without possessive markers and hence with absolutive endings. In this case a preceding noun phrase is identified as *not* being the logical subject. Where the verb is transitive, such a noun phrase is the logical object:

Cu 20. *hunwət mamayəw-vəl*
        bear help-PAST
        'The bear was helped.'

Cu 21. *hunwət mamayəw-pic*
bear help-FUT
'The bear will be helped.'

The -*və* and -*pi* here have two roles, as reference to time past or future, and as indicator of switch-reference.

Proto-Cupan past and future relatives with coreferential objects probably had the following underlying structure:

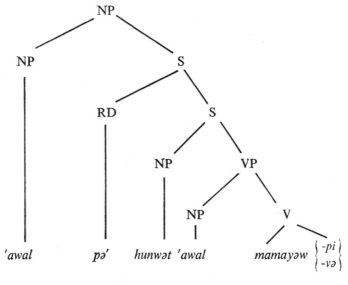

22. **'awal pə' hunwət pə-mamayəw-və*
'the dog that the bear helped'
23. **'awal pə' hunwət pə-mamayəw-pi*
'the dog that will help the bear'

Figure 2

Once again nominalization and deletion transformations convert the structure into the surface forms. Through nominalization the lower-sentence subject becomes a 'possessor' by the prefixation of a pronominal copy of it to the verb. Since the nominalized form is possessed, no absolutive is added.

Relatives with present-time reference might be expected to reveal the same kinds of processer, generating forms differing in the presence or absence of subject markers and in the relative suffixes. This seems roughly true for those with coreferential subjects:

Ca 24. *'awal pe' hunwet-i mamayaw-qalet*
   25. *'a'walem pe' hunwet-i mamayaw-wenetem*
Cu 26. *'awal pə' hunwət-i mamayəw-qalət*
   27. *'awalim pə' hunwət-i mamayəw-wənətim*
L 28. *'awaal po hunwut-i mamayuw-qat*
   29. *'awaalum pomon hunwut-i mamayuw-qatum*

      'the dog that is helping the bear'
      'the dogs that are helping the bear'

Cu 30. *naxanic pə' hawi-qalət*
      man RD sing PRES REL
      'the man that is singing'

Relatives with coreferential objects have exactly the same suffixes as those with coreferential subjects. In Cahuilla and Cupeño, since the relativized verbs have absolutive endings, no subject markers appear. But in Luiseño a subject marker occurs with the final *t*:

L 31. *'awaal po hunwut po-mamayuw-qat*
      'the dog that the bear is helping'

In Luiseño, present-time relatives have become more like past and future ones in that switch-reference is signalled by the presence of a subject marker even though this construction violates the general Luiseño (as well as Cupan) rule restricting absolutives to non-possessed nominals. The other languages, having no subject markers in these constructions, distinguish between coreferential subject and object clauses mainly on the basis of the presence or absence of a lower subject in surface structure. Where the non-coreferential subject is a pronoun, not a noun, an independent pronoun always fills the subject position. And to reduce the possibility of ambiguity further, the alternation of *-qal* with *-wen/wən* depends on the number of the lower subject while the presence or absence of the regular plural suffix is conditioned by the head noun phrase in the higher sentence.

But matters are still more complex. The Cupeño suffixes minus the *-ət* and the Luiseño ones are the same as those for past duratives. The Cahuilla suffixes, taken from Mountain Cahuilla, do not correspond, even when the *-et* is removed, to any tense endings in Mountain Cahuilla. Yet these suffixes are all used for present-time reference.

The Desert Cahuilla tense suffixes corresponding to present tense in the other dialects provide a partial answer. They are *-qal*, singular, and *-wen*, plural. These forms are obviously the underlying ones for the Mountain suffixes -*qa* and -*we* since final-consonant deletion is common in the mountain dialect. Although -*qal* and -*wən* are past tense endings in Cupeño while -*qa* and -*wə* are the present tense suffixes, it is clear that here again -*qal* and -*wən* are the underlying forms for present tense too. The final consonants often appear when the verb is sentence-initial. And the form *hawiqalət* in 30 is not the form one would expect if the relative were formed on the past tense verb. This verb is one of a class of Cupeño verbs having a subject marker infixed (instead of pre-fixed) in its past tense realizations. The expected form would be *haw-pə-qal-ət*. If, as suggested, the underlying forms for the present is *hawiqal*, then *hawiqalət* would be the expected relative form. Synchronically, then, present-tense verbs in Cahuilla and Cupeño are nominalized and the absolute *t* suffixed after an epenthetic vowel – *e* in Cahuilla, *ə* in Cupeño. The corresponding vowel in Luiseño would be *u*.

Indeed, the Luiseño relative suffix -*qat* often occurs as [qu]. Since the Luiseño present-tense-singular suffix may be either -*qa* or -*q*, the alternation of vowel quality in the relative suffix is explainable if it is assumed that the rule for Luiseño is like those for the other languages. A final *t* is added, together with an epenthetic *u* if the present tense suffix has no vowel. The present-tense-plural suffix in Luiseno is -*wun*, so -*wunut* should be the relative suffix instead of -*qatum*. Since such a form does exist – as a suffix in both singular and plural gerundival forms whose time reference must be that of the forms modified – it may have been a relative suffix once, one that became specialized as a gerundive. Gerundival forms in the other languages may have either -*qal* or -*wen*/-*wən* regardless of number. Alternatively, the gerundival function may be the original one.

The latter alternative is more promising for several reasons. First of all, in Cahuilla and Cupeño, although the examples are the forms always given as translations of English present-tense relative clauses, they have in fact a wide time-reference ranging from distant past to ongoing present, the durative aspect being common to all. Secondly, an alternative pair of suffixes in Cahuilla appears more often in such clauses: -*qalive* and -*wenive*. Like forms are found in Cupeño though they are far less common. In these forms, -*ve* is really a marker indicating both *switch-reference* and *realization* of the event referred to in the relative. The Cahuilla and Cupeño evidence suggests that at the stage where Cahuilla and Cupeño were one, *-*qal* and *-*wən* were just durative-aspect markers for *realized* verbs (all three languages have special durative markers for *unrealized* or *future* verbs). This means that, as in modern Desert Cahuilla, there was no true present tense, perhaps just an unmarked [+realized] 'tense'. And there were no present relative constructions. In all three languages many 'relic' uses of -qal and -wen/-wən/-wun survive where the suffixes are either purely aspectual, or the particular form depends not on number but on other contrasts, e.g. animate/inanimate. It is possible, even likely, that this was the situation in proto-Cupan.

Desert Cahuilla appears to have changed least in this respect and Luiseño most. The Luiseño past relative suffix -mokwic, unlike the -ic suffixes in the other language, allows the durative aspect suffix -qal. So the unmarked [+realized] relatives have become specialized as present-tense relatives. This specialization is typical of Luiseño. Many of the past-tense forms developed in like ways. Such a development of a tense system from a more general aspectual system is not unusual in human language. This is not to suggest that normally there are verb-aspect stages of languages and verb-tense stages. The normal situation at any given time is mixed. But here in Cupan it appears that there probably was a stage at which proto-Cupan had a purely aspectual system, one whose primary dimensions were the contrasts *realized* and *unrealized*, *durative* and *non-durative*. The absence of any more specialized time-reference system in proto-Cupan relatives supports such a hypothesis. In one of his discussions of Hopi, Whorf describes his *expective* and *reportive* categories of assertion in terms not inappropriate for proto-Cupan, though his categories are not exactly equivalent to the *unrealized* and *realized* ones discussed here:

The expective declares an expectation or anticipation of a situation. It has nothing to do with time as such. ... There is no distinction in the reportive between past and present, for both are equally accomplished fact. Thus to the Hopi 'he is running' need not be different from 'he was running' .... (1967:114)

University of California, San Diego

NOTES

[1] Examples in this paper are cited in approximate systematic phonemic form, although in this case they are close to systematic phonetic form. Within a word c becomes [č] before a vowel, [š] elsewhere. Stress will be marked only on the first set of forms. Hyphens are used to set off systematic phonemic boundaries relevant to the discussion. Parentheses in examples enclose optional elements.

To stress structural likenesses and differences vocabulary items cognate in Cupan have generally been chosen. Although examples here in one language may be understood by speakers of the others, the languages are not in fact mutually intelligible.

The following special abbreviations are used:

Ca = Cahuilla	ACC = accusative case suffix
Cu = Cupeño	PL = plural number suffix
L = Luiseño	REL = relativizing suffix
S = Serrano	RD = relative-demonstrative

Reconstructed word forms have been worked out in general accord with conclusions reached by Langacker (1970) and Voegelin-Hale (1962), except that where Luiseno *o* becomes [u], it is shown as *u*, and where Cupeno *ə* becomes [i], it is shown as *i*.

[2] Incidentally, the existence of forms like this poses problems for the lexicalist-interpretive versions of generative-transformational theory but is predictable under both the standard theory as formulated in Chomsky (1965) and so-called generative semantics.

REFERENCES

Hyde, V., and others. 1971. Introduction to the Luiseño language. Morongo Indian Reservation: Malki Museum Press.

Jacobs, R. A., and Rosenbaum, P. S. 1968. English transformational grammar. Waltham, Mass.: Xerox College Publishing.

Langacker, R. W. 1970. The vowels of proto Uto-Aztecan. IJAL 36, 3.169-180.

Voegelin, C. F. and F. M., and Hale, K. L. 1962. Typological and comparative grammar of Uto-Aztecan, I. Memoir 17, supplement to IJAL 28.

Whorf, B. L. 1938. Some verbal categories of Hopi. Lg 14:275-268, (Reprinted in: Language, thought, and reality, ed. by J. B. Carroll, Cambridge, MIT Press, 1967, 112-124.)

RULE REPLICATION

ROBERT D. KING

I wish to deal in this paper with certain questions concerning what I take to be a fact of phonological history: that structurally similar rules tend to be innovated more than once in the history of a language or language family. This phenomenon, which I will designate RULE REPLICATION, has often been noted (say in discussions of 'drift), but to my knowledge little has been done to explain it or explore its consequences.

There are in particular three questions that seem worth raising and to which I will propose tentative answers. Is rule replication characteristic of phonological development, or should it be regarded as fortuitous? Should rule replication be rewarded in the evaluation metric of generative phonology? What motivates rule replication?

Certain general types of rule replication are not uncommon. The Slavic palatalizations are a well known example, umlaut processes in Germanic another: early Germanic had a-umlaut (a lowered the vowel in the preceding syllable), most of the attested Germanic dialects had i-umlaut (only Gothic lacked it), and some of the dialects (Old English and Nordic) latterly developed u-umlaut. Lenition processes are common throughout Romance history. Monophthongization and diphthongization have occurred and reoccurred within Germanic.

But, in addition to these cases where a general TYPE of rule is replicated within language families at different times and often independently in different dialects, there are a number of examples in which a specific rule is replicated in almost identical form within a single grammar of a language. It is this kind of rule replication that I will be dealing with in the remainder of this paper.

In an early stage of Middle English two structurally similar rules of epenthesis coexisted in a single grammar:

$$(1) \qquad \emptyset \to e \ / \begin{bmatrix} + \text{ cns} \\ - \text{ voc} \end{bmatrix} \text{---} \begin{bmatrix} + \text{ son} \\ + \text{ cns} \end{bmatrix} \#$$

$$(1') \quad \theta \rightarrow e \, / \begin{bmatrix} V \\ + \text{ stress} \end{bmatrix} \begin{bmatrix} + \text{ cns} \\ - \text{ voc} \end{bmatrix} \underline{\qquad} \begin{bmatrix} + \text{ son} \\ + \text{ cns} \end{bmatrix}$$

Because they were not adjacent in the ordering, but more importantly for other reasons (see King and Cooley 1975 for a complete discussion), the latter rule (1'), innovated in the 13th century, could not have arisen as a generalization of 1, which was a rule of Old English. Notice that both rules have the effect of breaking up Consonant-Resonant sequences.

Halle and Keyser (1971:123-35) discuss a case of rule replication from early modern English stress assignment. Prior to the eighteenth century the grammar of English contained only one rule, the Romance Stress Rule, which operated in accordance with the 'weak cluster principle' that sequences of a lax vowel followed by at most one consonant were skipped over in placing stress. In the eighteenth century, however, a new Stress Retraction Rule making use of the weak cluster principle was innovated; but the two rules, both structurally similar to the extent that they exploit the same weak cluster principle, were separated in the ordering by a third rule. Hence, they could not be collapsed. The two replicated rules (actually rule schemata) are stated below in simplified form:

$$(2) \quad V \rightarrow [1 \text{ stress}] \, / \, [X \underline{\quad} C_0 \left(\begin{bmatrix} V \\ - \text{ tense} \end{bmatrix} C_0^1 \right) \begin{bmatrix} V \\ - \text{ tense} \end{bmatrix} C_0]$$

$$(2') \quad V \rightarrow [1 \text{ stress}] \, / \, [X \underline{\quad} C_0 \left(\begin{bmatrix} V \\ - \text{ tense} \end{bmatrix} C_0^1 \right) \begin{bmatrix} V \\ 1 \text{ stress} \end{bmatrix} C_0 (+ y)]$$

Miller 1969 cites an example from Sanskrit in which two similar – in this instance similar both structurally and functionally – rules were innovated at different times. The first rule (3) replaced old palatal stops (k' g' g'h) by retroflex [ṭ] word-finally and before consonants. This rule was followed later by the addition of rule 3', converting [ṣ] to [ṭ] in the same contexts:

$$(3) \quad \begin{bmatrix} - \text{ son} \\ + \text{ high} \\ - \text{ back} \end{bmatrix} \rightarrow \begin{bmatrix} - \text{ cont} \\ + \text{ retr} \end{bmatrix} \, / \underline{\quad} \begin{Bmatrix} C \\ \# \end{Bmatrix}$$

$$(3') \quad \begin{bmatrix} - \text{ son} \\ + \text{ cont} \\ + \text{ retr} \end{bmatrix} \rightarrow [- \text{ cont}] \, / \underline{\quad} \begin{Bmatrix} C \\ \# \end{Bmatrix}$$

It has also been claimed (Stanley 1972) that Sanskrit, at one stage of its development, had two nonadjacent but structurally quite similar rules of deaspiration:

(4) $[-\text{son}] \rightarrow [-\text{tense}] / \_\_\_ [-\text{son}]$

(4') $[-\text{son}] \rightarrow [-\text{tense}] / \_\_\_ \#$

In Old Icelandic two weakening rules were innovated at different periods (King 1971):

(5)   When unstressed, $\bar{\imath}$ is shortened and i deleted after a long syllable ($\bar{V}C_0$ or VC_2).

(5')   When unstressed, $\bar{\imath}$ is shortened and i deleted after a short syllable ($\breve{V}C_0^1$).

Rule 5', which is the later rule, could not have been simply a generalization of rule 5, as one might plausibly expect, because a third rule, *i*-umlaut, was added (chronologically) between 5 and 5'. (Apparently, rule 5 was lost prior to the innovation of 5' – in any event, not long after.)

I do not see anything especially peculiar or pathological about such cases of what I am calling rule replication, and I believe others could be found without much difficulty. That they are not even more common in the literature I attribute to two factors in particular: (1) they represent, as I will show later, an unstable and hence transitory situation; (2) by the evaluation criteria used prior to 1969 two structurally similar but nonadjacent rules would be nonoptimal, and phonologists would not have been inclined to admit solutions so at variance with the notion of simplicity. Such cases would have been 'analyzed away'. Whatever the reasons for the apparent relative infrequency of instances of rule replication, it seems to me that the examples listed are enough to establish a case: replication of innovations and – a special case of the former – the cooccurrence in the same grammar of structurally similar but nonadjacent rules is certainly not impossible, nor is it excessively rare.

If this claim is correct, then we may raise several interesting questions. One of these is synchronic and involves the problem of how to evaluate a grammar containing two structurally similar but uncollapsible rules. Should the evaluation metric in phonology place a higher value on rules that are structurally similar but nonadjacent than on rules that are completely different? The answer suggested in Kisseberth 1970 is affirmative.[1] The underlying idea is that since the cooccurrence of such rules is characteristic of natural languages, hence not accidental, such cooccurrence should be higher valued in the metric vis-à-vis the cooccurrence of two nonadjacent but structurally dissimilar rules.

I agree that rule replication can hardly be accidental, in the latter section of this paper I will in fact suggest – very tentatively – what might be responsible for the phenomenon. But, I claim, simply to observe that some fact about language is nonaccidental is not sufficient reason to force the simplicity metric to reward that fact – to seek an explanation for the fact in the evaluation metric rather than elsewhere. It is surely no accident that languages don't have rules placing main stress on every vowel of the word; yet we do not seek an explanation for such a datum in the evaluation metric. Presumably, such a rule would be disallowed by some set of phonetic or acoustic constraints on the content of possible phonological rules. A language with a nasal point-of-articulation assimilation rule is doubtless not an accident; yet the grammar of such a language is not reckoned simpler in the current evaluation procedures (correctly, in my opinion). It is no accident that purely phonological rules often become morphologized over time; again the evaluation metric is not revised to explain this fact.

In short, simply saying that something is not an accident does not, it seems to me, force us necessarily to include a clause in the evaluation metric rewarding a language that conforms to the something in question. The explanation for nonaccidentalness may be phonetic, it may be diachronic; in any case, it is not necessarily the evaluation metric that must provide a rationale.

To return to the case at hand, it is far from clear that rule replication within a grammar should be granted any kind of preferred status in the evaluation of that grammar. The reason I claim this is that rule replication within a grammar represents, in the cases known to me, an unstable phonological configuration. It never persists for long; it tends to be removed, soon after its inception, in one way or another. In the Middle English example cited earlier, rule 1' is lost within a century or less of its addition to the grammar. In the example from English stress given by Halle and Keyser, a reordering collapses the two like rules – again within a century. As Miller shows in regard to rules 3 and 3' from Sanskrit, the rule replication does not persist for long. I am unable to comment on the subsequent development of rules 4 and 4'. In the Nordic case recall that rule 5 was either lost before the addition of 5' or, if a grammar containing both rules did in fact exist, shortly thereafter.

The evidence is clear that rule replication, when it does occur, is not allowed to persist for long. But this is exactly what is predicted by the 'ordinary' evaluation metric. This metric would treat the cooccurrence of two structurally similar rules as nonoptimal (not necessarily unrelated, see Kisseberth 1970:292); and given the easy assumption that grammars tend to erase nonoptimal features, we accordingly expect cases of rule replication within a grammar to disappear – to be unstable. Any revision of the metric to reward the cooccurrence of structurally similar but nonadjacent rules vis-à-vis totally dissimilar but nonadjacent rules flies in the teeth of the observation that the former cases are strikingly unstable whereas the latter cases are not.

If not in the evaluation metric, where should we look for an explanation of why rule replication occurs with nonrandom frequency? More generally, why do the same kinds of innovations tend to be repeated again and again during the historical development of a language? It is possible, as Kisseberth (1970:306) proposes, that innovations are conditioned at least in part by what rules are already present in the grammar. It seems to me, however, that this suggestion raises more questions than it clarifies; it is a description rather than an explanation. I do not see any acceptable way to make the rules of a grammar, or morpheme-structure constraints, or both together with simplification, accountable for the observed fact that innovations tend to be repeated. I suggest that an explanation can only be found in recognizing a new subcomponent of the phonology – namely a set of constraints on the possible shapes of words. Only such constraints, it seems to me, could have the effect of inducing similar innovations over a lengthy period of time.

In other words, I am suggesting that we incorporate into phonology a set of surface-phonetic constraints (SPC's) along the lines of those proposed in Shibatani 1973. While there is much that remains to be worked out regarding the theory of SPC's, Shibatani has at least made the beginning of a convincing case that constraints on the possible shapes of words are needed along with morpheme-structure constraints and phonological rules.

Shibatani discusses the possibility that SPC's can motivate the innovation of phonological rules and gives an example from Japanese. Before considering the possible relationship between SPC's and rule replication, I would like to illustrate how the assumption of SPC's sheds light on the unity underlying diverse phonological innovations. During the thirteenth and fourteenth centuries in most Germanic dialects a 'standardization of quantity' took place (Prokosch 1939:140). The facts in German are especially clear. In Middle High German, accented syllables were of four possible types: open with vowel long or short, closed with vowel long or short. Thus, *nāmen* 'took', *name* 'name'; *dāhte* 'thought', *dahte* 'covered'. Two rules then entered the grammar at the same time. One, lengthening vowels in open syllables, was:

(6) $V \rightarrow [+ \text{long}] / \underline{\quad} CV$

The other, shortening vowels in closed syllables, was:

(7)   V → [− long] / ___ CC

There is no way to collapse these two rules without deforming the feature
system or resorting to illicit uses of variables, yet the two rules are clearly
part of a general, unified process requiring syllable balance at the surface
phonetic level. This process can be stated in terms of morae. In Middle
High German accented syllables had one (short vowel without consonant), two (short vowel with consonant, long vowel without consonant),
or three (long vowel with consonant) morae. A surface-phonetic constraint was imposed (or activated): every syllable must have two morae.
And the result in the grammar was the addition of two rules structurally
quite dissimilar but functionally related in their effect on surface structure.
Without the assumption of an SPC one is forced to regard it as an accident that two such rules entered the grammar at exactly the same time.

In the same vein I suggest that SPC's open the door to an explanation
of why rules tend to be replicated. Notice that the effect of replication
in general is to introduce some generalization about surface structure
to a larger set of instances. The Middle English rules of epenthesis,
for example, both have the consequence of replacing Consonant-Resonant sequences postvocalically by Consonant-e-Resonant sequences.
A ...VCC sequence is replaced by ...VCVC, a sequence favored in many
of the world's languages. If we assume that there was in Middle English
an SPC requiring ...VCVC sequences, it becomes apparent why epenthesis rules would tend to be replicated over time. Similarly, in the stress
example from Halle and Keyser, what seems to have motivated the new
Stress Retraction Rule of John Walker, rule 2′, was a surface-phonetic
requirement that the weak cluster principle already active in stress
assignment should also play a role in stress retraction.

Clearly the discussion to this point is unsatisfactory in detail, if not
necessarily in principle. The general principle would be the completely
reasonable one that surface structure plays a crucial and perhaps primary
role in determining the form of innovations in the rule component −
that innovations are, in many cases, a secondary response to a demand for
a certain kind of surface phonetic structure. If this is granted, then certain
facts about change fall out in a natural way: why German innovated
its two rules at the same time, why types of rules tend to be replicated
over time. What is exceedingly unclear is the exact nature
of the SPC's as well as the details of the relationship between SPC's and
the inducement of innovations on a grammar. Given that the notion of

SPC has hardly been developed beyond the most primitive stage, it is premature to make any extravagant claims about the implications of this nascent quasi-theory for diachronic change. However, it does seem profitable to me to entertain the possibility that phonological change consists of a complicated symbiosis between phonological rules and SPC's, not simply of an alteration in the phonological rule component. Several kinds of interrelated changes – of which rule replication is only one – seem to be best accounted for by the assumption of SPC's.

I will conclude with a few comments concerning DRIFT. Rule replication in the sense used here conforms to one of the senses in which Sapir 1921 used his famous term. It has always seemed clear to me that there was something correct about Sapir's notion of drift – that similar processes persist and reappear in languages that are genetically related. And it is equally clear that the received theory of diachronic generative phonology does not adequately account for drift. The only mechanism available in this theory for drift-type phenomena is simplification (see King 1969: 202). Simplification will account for certain 'outbreaks' of a shared feature, e.g. loss of final devoicing both in standard Yiddish and certain dialects of Swiss German.

But simplification, in any of its normal senses, will not account for rule replication. I have suggested that surface-phonetic constraints will. One kind of drift, and possibly others as well, thus seems to have some hope of an explanation provided generative theory is extended to include surface-phonetic constraints, and provided the theory of phonological change is extended to include change motivated by these constraints.

University of Texas at Austin

NOTE

[1]   Kisseberth deals only with functionally related rules as distinct from structurally similar ones. I assume, as do Halle and Keyser (1971:50, n. 21), that Kisseberth's arguments clearly imply that structural similarity, even in nonadjacent rules, should count for something in the metric.

REFERENCES

Halle, Morris, and Samuel Jay Keyser. 1971. English stress. New York: Harper and Row.
King, Robert D. 1969. Historical linguistics and generative grammar. Englewood Cliffs, N. J.: Prentice-Hall.

—. 1971. Syncope and Old Icelandic *i*-umlaut. Arkiv för nordisk filologi 86.1-18.
—. and Marianne Cooley. 1975. An ordering problem in early Middle English. Glossa 9.3-12.
Kisseberth, Charles W. 1970. On the functional unity of phonological rules. Linguistic Inquiry 1.291-306.
Miller, D. Gary. 1969. The role of derivational constraints in analogical restructuring. Unpublished paper.
Prokosch, Eduard. 1939. Comparative Germanic grammar. Philadelphia: Linguistic Society of America.
Sapir, Edward. 1921. Language. New York: Harcourt Brace.
Shibatani, Masayoshi. 1973. The role of surface phonetic constraints in generative phonology. Language 49.87-106.
Stanley, Patricia C. 1972. Topics in Sanskrit verb phonology. University of Texas dissertation.

ON USING PRUNING IN
ARGUING FOR EXTRINSIC ORDER

ANDREAS KOUTSOUDAS

Postal (1971) argues that WH-Q-MOVEMENT must be extrinsically ordered to apply after REFLEXIVIZATION. My purpose here is to show that Postal's rule ordering argument provides a basis for questioning the adequacy of Ross's (1968) pruning convention:

S-Pruning: delete any embedded node S which does not branch (i.e. which does not dominate at least two nodes). (26)

Postal (74-79) argues that we can explain the ungrammaticality of sentences like 2 by assuming that the structure underlying 1 is 3, and by assuming that REFLEXIVIZATION can apply only within a single S-domain.

(1) You_1 saw someone stab you_1
(2)   *You_1 saw someone stab $yourself_1$

(3)

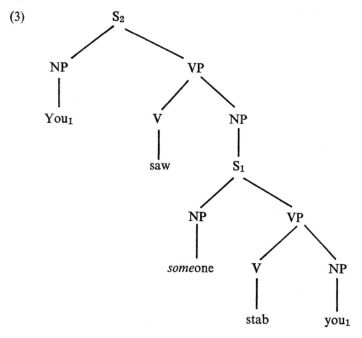

Given these assumptions, REFLEXIVIZATION would not apply either on the S_1 or on the S_2 cycle of 3, and therefore the derivation of 2 would be blocked. If this is correct, Postal continues, the ungrammaticality of 5 should be explainable in the same way:

(4)   Who did you$_1$ see stab you$_1$
(5)   *Who did you$_1$ see stab yourself$_1$

But for this to be possible, he argues, WH-Q-MOVEMENT and REFLEXIVIZATION must be extrinsically ordered as in 6:

(6)   1. REFLEXIVIZATION
        2. WH-Q-MOVEMENT

Postal's reason for this is that, if the structure underlying 4 is 7,

(7)

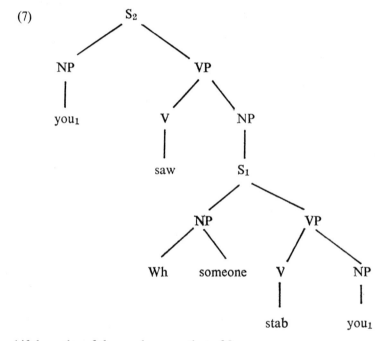

and if the order of these rules were that of 8,

(8)   1. WH-Q-MOVEMENT
        2. REFLEXIVIZATION

moving the subject of the embedded clause *wh someone stab you* by WH-Q-MOVEMENT in P-markers like 7 would result in pruning the S-node over the embedded clause and wrongly predicting reflexivization in all such P-markers. There would therefore be no way to block the derivation

of sentences like 5. In essence, then, PRUNING is crucial to Postal's argument for postulating 6: assuming Ross's pruning convention, 6 guarantees that pruning has not taken place at the time REFLEXIVIZATION
applies, and this, in turn, guarantees that the derivation of sentences like
5 is blocked.

But let us now consider sentences like 9:

(9)   You saw yourself stab Betty.

Clearly, the construction exemplified by 9 is identical to that exemplified
by (1); therefore, if 3 is the correct P-marker for 1, we can assume that 10
is the correct P-marker for 9:

(10)

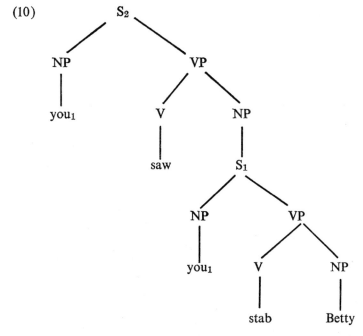

To derive 9, then, we must (a) subject-raise *you* from the embedded
clause into the object position of the main clause, (b) prune the S-node
of the embedded clause, and (c) reflexivize. What is important here is
that SUBJECT-RAISING must apply in the derivation of 9 and, as a consequence, the S-node of the embedded clause is, in accordance with Ross's
pruning convention, pruned.

But now, if SUBJECT-RAISING applies in the derivation of sentences like 9
and if, in addition, Ross's pruning convention is assumed, we are faced
with the paradox that no matter how REFLEXIVIZATION, WH-Q-MOVEMENT,

and SUBJECT-RAISING are assumed to be ordered, the facts in question cannot be accounted for. For example, if SUBJECT-RAISING were to be extrinsically ordered with respect to the way REFLEXIVIZATION and WH-Q-MOVEMENT are ordered by Postal (i.e. with respect to 6), it would have to be ordered in one of the following three ways:

(11)   1. SUBJECT-RAISING
        2. REFLEXIVIZATION
        3. WH-Q-MOVEMENT

(12)   1. REFLEXIVIZATION
        2. SUBJECT-RAISING
        3. WH-Q-MOVEMENT

(13)   1. REFLEXIVIZATION
        2. WH-Q-MOVEMENT
        3. SUBJECT-RAISING

All three of these alternatives for rule ordering must be rejected, however. Alternative 11 must be rejected because, having applied SUBJECT-RAISING, the S-node over the embedded clause is pruned, and REFLEXIVIZATION can no longer be blocked; as a consequence, neither the derivation of sentences like 2 nor that of sentences like 5 would be blocked. Alternatives 12 and 13 must be rejected because, although the derivation of sentences like 2 and 5 would be blocked, there would be no way to derive sentences like 9, i.e. *You saw yourself stab Betty*, since there would be no way to reflexivize either before or after SUBJECT-RAISING has had a chance to apply. That is, as long as REFLEXIVIZATION is extrinsically ordered before SUBJECT-RAISING, REFLEXIVIZATION can never apply to the output of SUBJECT-RAISING because once a rule has been passed in the ordering, it cannot be reapplied within the same cycle. But if REFLEXIVIZATION cannot apply to the output of SUBJECT-RAISING, sentences like 9 cannot be derived.

The fact that alternatives 11-13 must be rejected means that SUBJECT-RAISING cannot be extrinsically ordered with respect to 6. It also means that SUBJECT-RAISING cannot be unordered with respect to 6 either, for if it were, there would be no way to block the derivation of sentences like 2 or of sentences like 5. Thus, as long as Ross's convention of pruning is maintained, there is no way to order SUBJECT-RAISING with respect to 6 so as to account for the facts in question. As a consequence, Postal's argument for 6 collapses. Similar arguments can be given to show that the facts in question cannot be accounted for no matter what the order of application of the three rules in question is said to be.

It has been shown that if Ross's pruning convention is assumed, there is no way to order REFLEXIVIZATION, SUBJECT-RAISING, and WH-Q-MOVEMENT so as to account for the facts in question. If, on the other hand, Ross's pruning convention is not assumed, and the embedded S-nodes are retained in deriving these examples, then these three rules need not be extrinsically ordered to account for the facts that we have observed. Thus, given that there is no pruning convention and that the rules in question are not extrinsically ordered, it is clear that REFLEXIVIZATION cannot apply, for example, either to P-marker 3 or to P-marker 7. But suppose that SUBJECT-RAISING and WH-Q-MOVEMENT have been allowed to apply to 3 and 7 respectively. These rules having been applied, the embedded S-nodes of the resulting P-markers would not be pruned and, as a consequence, REFLEXIVIZATION would not apply to these P-markers either, for they do not meet the structural description of this rule. This results in the correct derivation of sentences 1 and 4 and the exclusion of sentences 2 and 5.

The following conclusions can be reached from this discussion: (1) whether Ross's pruning convention is maintained or not, Postal's argument for extrinsically ordering REFLEXIVIZATION and WH-Q-MOVEMENT is invalid; (2) there is strong evidence that Ross's pruning convention cannot be maintained; and (3) if Ross's pruning convention is not maintained, there is no need to impose extrinsic order on SUBJECT-RAISING, REFLEXIVIZATION, and WH-Q-MOVEMENT. Conclusion (3) supports the following hypothesis regarding rule ordering:

> All restrictions on the relative order of application of grammatical rules are determined by universal rather than language-specific principles.

It follows from this hypothesis that *no grammatical rules are extrinsically ordered* (see Koutsoudas 1971, Koutsoudas, Sanders, and Noll 1971, Lehmann 1971, and Ringen 1971).

University of Wisconsin at Milwaukee

REFERENCES

Koutsoudas, A. 1971. The strict order fallacy. Bloomington: Indiana University Linguistics Club (also in Lg. 48.350-377 [1972].)
Koutsoudas, A., Sanders, G. and Noll, C. 1971. On the application of phonological rules. Bloomington: Indiana University Linguistics Club. [=Lg. 50. 1974. 1-28]
Lehmann, T. 1971. On the ordering of particle movement, extraposition, question,

and extraposition from NP. Bloomington: Indiana University Linguistics Club. (= Some arguments against ordered rules. Lg. 48.541-550 [1972].)

Postal, P. 1971. Cross-over phenomena. New York: Holt, Rinehart and Winston, Inc.

Ringen, C. 1971. On arguments for rule ordering. Bloomington: Indiana University Linguistics Club. (Also in Foundations of language 8.266-273 [1972].)

Ross, J. 1968. Constraints on variables in syntax. Bloomington: Indiana University Linguistics Club.

CHANGES OF EMPHASIS
IN MODERN LINGUISTICS

GIULIO C. LEPSCHY

"Changes of emphasis in Linguistics with particular reference to Paul and Bloomfield" is the title of an article published in 1945 by George Lane, the distinguished comparative philologist of the University of North Carolina. In it Lane traces the defeat of mentalistic linguistics and the victory of the mechanistic method of language study. As a result of this victory, symbolised by Bloomfield's *Language* (1935), concludes Lane, descriptive linguistics, in its independence from the historical and comparative method, "has found its place as a worthy subject of scientific pursuit – a place denied it so long because of the lack of a mechanistic approach" (Lane 1945:483). "A worthy subject of scientific pursuit": these words have the same ring as those which we read at the end of another, more recent, account. The Germanist John T. Waterman concludes his *Perspectives in linguistics* by stating: "At the far end of what we have chosen to call the 'Bloomfieldian era' stands a most rigorous and book-length attempt to organize all of American structuralism into a single body of theory and practice. ... With the publication of *Methods in structural linguistics* American structuralism clearly reached its majority, and could take its place in the world of scholarship as a mature discipline uncompromisingly dedicated to the scientific study of language" (Waterman 1963:98). Today this makes strange reading. Harris's book appears to us not as a step which put American structuralism into the world of scholarship, but rather as the end of the road. As an English linguist put it: "The student who learns linguistics from *Syntactic structures* is, in effect, learning a different subject from the student who learns linguistics from, say, Zellig Harris's *Structural linguistics*" (Thorne 1965:74). The publication of *Syntactic structures*, this slender booklet of 116 pages, is considered today to have been like a bomb shell which acted with cataclysmic consequences on the linguistic scene. If it was a bomb, it was delayed action one; or perhaps some people did not hear it explode. Waterman's book, which was published in 1963, appears in some ways more quaint than Lane's article, which was published in 1945. They are both outmoded today; but Lane was not outmoded in 1945, whereas Waterman was in 1963. Waterman's narrative, to be sure, stops around 1950; but the assumptions on which his 1963 book are based are pre-Chomskian. And Chomsky's work has changed not only linguistic theory, but also many linguists' points of view concerning the history of their subject. There have been changes of emphasis in both fields.

Let us consider the histories of linguistics. A task which has not been performed, and which might be well worth undertaking, would be a comparative examination of recent works in this field (an attempt has been made by Malkiel and Langdon 1969). We find in recent years a flurry of works on the history of linguistics, which in one way or another concern the modern developments which interest us here; some of these works I have quoted in my own book on structural linguistics (Lepschy 1970). Changes of emphasis there undoubtedly are. But they seem to be changes in the sign of plus or minus in front of particular authors and periods, changes in positive or negative judgement, rather than in the real assumptions, changes in appreciation rather than in the factual view of what happened.

The picture seems to be the same: linguistics up to the end of the 18th century; then the foundations of comparative grammar, with the Schlegels and Humboldt; and the progress from Bopp, through Schleicher, to Brugmann, and in our century Meillet and Hirt (to quote just the authors of standard textbooks). But at the beginning of the 20th century we find the seminal teaching of Saussure; and after it the development of different trends of structuralism: the groups of Geneva, of Prague, of Copenhagen; and the American Schools of Sapir and Bloomfield, and their successors, up to Chomsky and the post-Chomskians. This is of course oversimplified; but it is, more or less, the framework on which the traditional expositions are built. We can distinguish a) the conventional comparative philologist's view, according to which scientific linguistics begins with Bopp; what comes before is prehistory; and 20th century structuralist trends are looked at with suspicion and distrust; b) the conventional structuralist view, according to which scientific linguistics really begins with structuralism; when structuralism is made to begin, depends on the particular trend adhered to: it can be 1916, the date of publication of Saussure's *Cours*; or 1928, the date of the first International congress of linguists at The Hague, at which Jakobson, Karcevskij, and Trubeckoj answered the question "Quelles sont les méthodes les mieux appropriées à un exposé complet et pratique de la grammaire d'une langue quelconque?" (this date has the further advantage that it saw the publication of an emblematic programme for a structural treatment of linguistics and poetics by Jakobson and Tynjanov); or 1933, the date of publication of Bloomfield's *Language*; or even 1911, with Boas's *Introduction* to the *Handbook of American Indian languages*. In any case, looking for a particular date is a rather pointless exercise. What is more interesting is the ambiguous attitude of structuralist accounts of the development of linguistics towards traditional comparative philology. On the one hand, they stress the break represented by structuralism; on the other, they point out that what they consider to be good in 19th-century historical linguistics is its systematic side: a bit in the way in which comparative philologists considered what they called prescientific linguistics, from the Renaissance to the end of the 18th century, looking for forerunners, trying to salvage, in the waste land of prescriptive grammar, disputes on the relative pre-eminence of languages, and philosophical speculations, some gems represented by the rare presages of historical comparative method: the occasional correct etymology, or the groping toward the obscure realization of the fact that some languages had certain kinship relationships. But structuralist historians of linguistics looked back (beyond the 19th century, beyond rationalist, Renaissance and Medieval theories, not without some appreciative glances at the Greeks and the Romans) to Indian grammar. This was their Eden, a golden age of linguistic theory. Pāṇini's light had a pallid reflection in the 19th century precursors who rediscovered Sanskrit. The redemption of scientific linguistics was accomplished in 1933. Bloomfield, who was not easily swayed by enthusiasm, and whose prose style was remarkably dry, declares that Pāṇini's grammar "is one of the greatest monuments of human intelligence. It describes, with the minutest detail, every inflection, derivation, and composition, and every syntactic usage of its author's speech. No other language, to this day, has been so perfectly described" (Bloomfield 1935:11). I shall not try to discuss here what the exact meaning can be of describing "with the minutest detail" "every syntactic usage of its author's speech"; but the doubts which this observation inevitably causes lead us naturally to the third view, now also fairly well established: c) the generative transformational one. Here we find that 19th-century comparative linguistics and 20th-century structural linguistics are bracketed together and criticized because they share the same faults: an interest in surface rather than deep structures, and a limitation to classifying rather than an attempt

at explaining linguistic facts. What emerges as a novelty is the rehabi-
litation of 17th- and 18th-century linguistics, with the opposition of a
rationalist to an empiricist position. The former, which Chomsky called
'Cartesian' linguistics, includes Port-Royal, du Marsais, the Encyclo-
pedists, Leibniz, and Humboldt. As for the post-Chomskians, they are
already proposing their own view of modern linguistics. George Lakoff
(1970:627) states baldly: "It has become clear over the past five years
that transformational generative grammar is nowhere near being an
adequate theory of human language."

Generally these views of the history of linguistics are, I think, misleading. They fail to situate the authors and works they discuss in a wider
context of cultural history, and they omit to examine the works that
do not fit into their oversimplified patterns (this has been stressed by
Malkiel and Langdon 1969). They are in fact not so much histories of
linguistics as works of a different kind: a sort of quest for one's own
intellectual ancestors. The traditional historical sketches are so jejune
that they hardly deserve discussion at all; Chomsky's contribution (1966)
has at least the merit of not limiting itself to some stereotype generalizations like the ones I have quoted, and of going back to the original
texts. Certainly not all the texts, and not all in the original. Robin
Lakoff points out quite correctly that some ideas which Chomsky calls
'Cartesian' in Port-Royal in fact go back to the *Minerva* by F. Sánchez,
and she concludes: "Scholars should devote themselves to an examination of the origins of modern linguistic theory: where did Sanctius get his
ideas? Where does transformational grammar really begin?" (Lakoff
1969:364). I am not sure whether she intends to separate or to identify
the two questions. The theory of Sánchez is, I think, interesting, and it
should be studied in its context. We certainly know far too little about
Renaissance and Medieval grammatical theory. *Quod nihil scitur*, the
title of the work by F. Sánchez, the sceptical philosopher contemporary
of the author of the *Minerva*, could almost be adopted as a motto by
historians of linguistics. But the origin of transformational grammar
seems to me a different question, which is more usefully studied in the
works by Chomsky and Harris than in the *Minerva*. In her review R.
Lakoff writes rather cattily: "Sanctius, Chomsky would say, was an
applied linguist, not a theorist. But since the *Minerva* is inaccessible to
anyone who does not read Latin, Chomsky has been forced to rely on
the judgements of writers like Sahlin", who, in her thesis on du Marsais,
does not interpret Sanctius correctly (Lakoff 1969:359). The implication
seems to be that Chomsky cannot read Latin: in which case one hesitates

between shock at the irresponsibility of facing, in such a state of philological nudity, the rigours of 17th- and 18th-century linguistics, and admiration for having succeeded in writing, in such conditions, a book as stimulating, lively, and original as *Cartesian linguistics*. The book has also been violently attacked by Hans Aarsleff, who writes: "I must conclude with the firm belief that I do not see that anything at all useful can be salvaged from Chomsky's version of the history of linguistics. That version is fundamentally false from beginning to end – because the scholarship is poor, because the texts have not been read, because the arguments have not been understood, because the secondary literature that might have been helpful has been left aside or unread, even when referred to" (Aarsleff 1970: 583). Aarsleff's main criticism is that Chomsky ignores the fundamental work of Condillac, denigrates Locke whom he suspects of being a sort of behaviourist, and presents du Marsais as pro-Cartesian while he was, on the contrary, pro-Lockean. However, this is not what I should like to discuss here. I have both great admiration and great reservations regarding *Cartesian linguistics*. What interests me here is the book as a contribution rather to Chomskian than to Cartesian linguistics. What Chomsky found, in his historical research, was a group of illustrious precursors in his defence of mentalism, innatism, universalism, and creativity, and in his fight against behaviourist and empiricist linguistics. And he found that his predecessors were in a way generativists and transformationalists like himself. It seems to me a striking example of how books on the history of linguistics reflect the interests of their authors in the problems of contemporary linguistics. This, in itself, does not make them good or bad history. What I am suggesting is simply that a work on the history of linguistics may be more or less interesting as far as its subject matter is concerned, but is invariably interesting as a document in itself. Modern histories of linguistics discuss changes of emphasis, but even more they reveal other changes of emphasis, in the views which inspired the historians of linguistics who wrote them.

A few words on the theoretical problems which modern linguists have been preoccupied with may help to explain their different attitudes towards the past of their discipline, and to illustrate present-day conditions. It is in a way canonical to start from some of the dichotomies which appear in Saussure's *Cours*. Even now, after the publication of Engler's critical edition and of De Mauro's annotated Italian edition, we are far from being able to deal satisfactorily with the two dichotomies – synchrony vs. diachrony and *langue* vs. *parole*. It is quite obvious that they both have their roots much further back than Saussure, and also that in Saussure they take on a particular value, in the context of 19th-century discussions on historicism on the one hand and on sociology and economics on the other. The illusion of being able to separate clearly the two dichotomies, and each term within the single dichotomies, has directed a lot of work into blind alleys. In much of 20th-century linguistics we find a change of emphasis with respect to previous linguistics: the concentration on synchrony rather than on diachrony, and on *langue* rather than on *parole*, as the proper objects of scientific study. What was a useful, and indeed necessary, distinction of points of view became a damaging separation of different fields of research.

As far as synchrony vs. diachrony is concerned, the School of Prague in the late twenties and in the thirties insisted that it was not a matter of irreconcilable opposition, but of different points of view which had to be integrated. But exactly how they had to be integrated was not made sufficiently clear. In the United States Hockett (1954:211) wrote in a well known article: "if it be said that the English past-tense form *baked* is 'formed' from *bake* by a 'process' of 'suffixation', then no matter what disclaimer of historicity is made, it is impossible not to conclude that some kind of priority is being assigned to *bake*, as against *baked* or the suffix. And if this priority is not historical, what is it?" The advent of transformational theory has not clarified, but further confused this point. Morris Halle (1962:64), defending the introduction of ordered rules in phonology, criticises Hockett's position and states: "Since ordered rules are all but unknown in present day synchronic descriptions, the impression has spread that the imposition of order on statements in a synchronic description is always due to an oversight, to an unjustifiable confusion of synchronic and diachronic. I must therefore stress that, in the preceding examples [from English phonology], order is determined by the simplicity criterion alone and that no historical considerations have entered in establishing it." Chomsky and Halle (1968:251) quote Bloomfield (1939), who had set up (synchronically) basic forms for Menomini which resembled those reconstructed for Proto-Algonquian. But it is not necessary, they insist, that synchronic rules should reflect diachronic laws: "in synchronic grammars one finds numerous rules that cannot be traced directly to any sound change." To my mind this question has not been sufficiently clarified. What is one to make, for instance, of a statement like the following one by Saltarelli (1970:5): "Although the description is strictly synchronic, one can appreciate its diachronic implications by considering, for example, that /čiv+tād+e/ is the underlying representation for *città* 'city' and /dik+t+o/ for *detto* 'said'."?

Another example: Robert A. Hall in his Italian grammar published over twenty years ago followed what were considered at the time Bloomfieldian lines. The presentation was strictly synchronic. The morphology offered a rigid segmentation into morphs even where the result was obviously clumsy and counter-intuitive. All verbal forms had to consist of five segment in the following order: 1) root; 2) thematic vowel; 3) stem-suffix; 4) tense-sign; 5) personal ending. Consequently a form like *so* 'I know' was analysed as follows: 1) root: *sap-*; 2) add the thematic vowel *e*: *sape-*, then change it into zero: *sap-*; 3) add the stem-suffix zero: *sap-*; 4) the vowel or diphthong of the final syllable and all that follows it in the syllable become zero: *s-*; then vowel elision (by now unnecessary as there is no vowel left anyway) and addition of *á* with doubling of the following consonant: *sá^x*; 5) change of *a* into *ɔ*: *sɔ́^{x}* (Hall 1948:25-36). This analysis, it seems to me, speaks for itself and does not require any comment. Hall has recently published in Italian a completely recast version of his grammar ("un totale rifacimento della mia ormai primitiva e superata *Descriptive Italian Grammar* del 1948", Hall 1971: 11); the analysis of *so* is exactly the same (apart from minor changes in notation which do not affect our argument). But in the new edition a footnote is added, which I translate literally: "The fact that /só/ and the other forms of the 1st singular mentioned in this section come from */sáo^x/ etc. as an intermediate stage, is demonstrated by the occurrence of the latter form, not only in the first document of the Italian language (the Capuan formulas of 960) but also, analogically, in the speech of present day children" (Hall 1971:106). Quite apart from the fact that *sao* does not appear as an intermediate stage in Hall's derivation (the change is *sa > so*, and not *sa > sao > so*), and leaving out the question of the doubling of the following consonant which he marks in *sao*, the addition of this footnote, it seems to me, can only be explained by the effect of the new intellectual climate, created by generative transformational grammar, even on such a staunch opponent as Hall. It would, of course, be wrong to use Hall's grammar as a stick with which to beat generative theory. But this attempt to introduce in 1971 a historical and psychological confirmation for an analysis which was produced in 1948 with deliberate disregard for both history and psychology, does seem rather ironic. I think it testifies to a general confusion on the question of how the derivations of generative grammar are related on the one hand to historical changes, and on the other to actual psychological processes.

The dichotomy *langue* vs. *parole* is even more involved. Linguists, both before and after Saussure, had always been interested in *langue*.

If what we have as our raw material, as our data, is a corpus of speech acts (*parole*), linguists had always considered (implicitly or explicitly) that it was their job to provide generalizations which would account for the acts of speech. Saussure apparently attributed a psychological reality to *langue*. But, partly under the influence of neopositivist and behaviourist hypotheses, some structuralists thought that they could do without this psychological reality. Similarly with the description of natural phenomena: some scientists feel that the laws they discover (grammatical description) are not the account of a reality (*langue*) which underlies the data (*parole*), but that they are just theoretical constructs set up to explain the data. It is in a way the old story of the ghost in the machine. I do not intend to deal here with the question of whether there is an evolution of Chomsky's theories from an empiricist to a rationalist view of language. This has been suggested by Lyons (1970:62-3) in his admirable monograph on Chomsky. "In his later publications", – writes Lyons – "Chomsky attaches far less importance to the notion of 'simplicity', and gives correspondingly more weight to the argument that transformational grammar reflects better the 'intuitions' of the native speaker and is semantically more 'revealing' than phrase structure grammar." Then he adds in a footnote: "Chomsky tells me that he is not himself aware of any change in his attitude over the years with respect to the role of simplicity measures and intuitions." The distinction between competence and performance is seen by Chomsky in relation to the distinction between *langue* and *parole* which "Saussure emphasized with such lucidity" (Chomsky 1964:915). I do not recollect it being used in *Syntactic structures*, but we do find there the notion of "understanding a sentence" (Chomsky 1957:86-7). Even before *Syntactic structures* we read that "linguistic theory attempts to explain the ability of a speaker to produce and understand new sentences, and to reject as ungrammatical other new sequences, on the basis of his limited linguistic experience" (Chomsky 1956:113). In other terms, Chomsky's aim seems to have been, from the beginning, to characterize the speaker's knowledge of his language. Hockett (1968:62) in a discussion of Chomsky's theories accuses him of equivocating on the ambiguity of the English verb *know*. Had he been writing in Chinese, Chomsky would have had to choose between *huì* 'to be able to, to know how', and *zhīdào* 'to have knowledge of' in the sense which concerns epistemology. According to Hockett, what one knows about one's language is *huì*, know how to speak it, and not *zhīdào*, have knowledge of it. Similarly a normal man *huì* walk, i.e., knows how to walk; but this does not imply that he *zhīdào* walk, i.e., has knowledge of the physiology of walking. In the first of his John Locke lectures, given in the University of Oxford on April 29, 1969, Chomsky said: "In the past, I have tried to avoid the problem of explicating the notion 'knowledge of language' by using an invented technical term, namely, the term 'competence' in place of 'knowledge' "; what he needs is a notion (and it is irrelevant whether it is normally expressed by a word in English, Chinese, or any other language) which includes conscious knowledge (for instance a speaker of English knows that bachelors are unmarried), unconscious knowledge (for instance of the passive transformation), innate knowledge (for instance of the fact that transformations apply in cyclic ordering. This is universal grammar) (Chomsky 1969). Can the working of the mind "be accommodated within the framework of physical explanation"? Yes, answers Chomsky. But at the same time, it seems to me, he shows that the polemic he is engaged in is that of mentalism vs. behaviourism, rather than of idealism vs. materialism. We can, he writes, "be fairly sure that there will be a physical explanation for the phenomena in question, if they can be explained at all, for an uninteresting terminological reason, namely that the concept of 'physical explanation' will no doubt be extended to incorporate whatever is discovered in this domain, exactly as it was extended to accommodate gravitational and electromagnetic force, massless particles, and numerous other entities and processes that would have offended the common sense of earlier generations" (Chomsky 1968:84). In a forceful polemical essay on the ideology of structuralism, S. Timpanaro (1970: 201-2) quotes this passage as the 'ironic answer' given by Chomsky to the question of a possible physical explanation of innatism. "So science" – comments Timpanaro – "in the course of its development has apparently made no real progress to the detriment of myth and religious faith. It has performed instead a series of verbal tricks: being unable to deny the reality of certain "spiritual" phenomena and not wishing to admit its own defeat, it has found the crafty solution of annexing them by extending its boundaries." I doubt that this is a fair report of the ideological implications of Chomsky's statement (but this does not detract from the many good points in Timpanaro's essay).

Chomsky (1965:3) wants to study "an ideal speaker-listener, in a completely homogeneous speech-community". But, Hockett (1968: 65-6) objects, this is an idealization, and "we must remember what an idealization is. It is not what we are analyzing, not part of our subject-matter; rather, it is part of the terminological apparatus with which we analyze and discuss real objects and systems";

"there is only one 'object of study': specific acts of speech, as historic events."

I should like to end this discussion on a personal note. I had my early training as a linguist in Italy, and I am of course familiar with a tradition which goes back to Benedetto Croce's philosophy of language. From my teachers I learnt that language is the proper object of study not of the natural sciences, nor of logico-mathematical investigations, but of historical research. Croce's thought does not appear to be known to either Hockett or Chomsky, as far as I can see from their published works. If the connexion does not exist, it is, I presume, my own subjective reaction which makes me see in the discussion I have mentioned certain 'changes of emphasis' in relation to Croce's theory. Chomsky stresses that language is creative, and discusses the relationship between the creativity of language and the creativity of art; he sees both in relation to notions like 'freedom' and 'mind'. This could come straight from Croce. But Chomsky is interested in a logico-mathematical characterization of competence which Croce would not have understood and would very likely have rejected. Hockett (1968:75) states that "language is exactly on a par with all other natural phenomena", and that it ought to be studied with the methods of natural sciences, and not of logic and mathematics (Hockett 1968:36). This too Croce would have rejected. But Hockett's statement, quoted above, that "there is only one 'object of study': specific acts of speech as historic events", could also come straight from Croce. Croce's interest was directed towards language as a creative act of the mind, an individual historic event. I do not think that Croce's theories in fact proved to be fruitful for linguistic research. On the contrary, in some cases they proved disastrous. But they contributed to highlighting a problem which is still with us today, after the Saussurean illusion of an autonomous linguistics endowed with a scientific method sui generis. How is language best studied? As a historical phenomenon, with the methods of logic and mathematics, or with the methods of natural sciences?

University of Reading, England

REFERENCES

Aarsleff, Hans. 1970. The history of linguistics and Professor Chomsky. Lg. 46.570-85.
Bloomfield, Leonard. 1935. Language. London: Allen & Unwin.
—. 1939. Menomini morphophonemics. Travaux du Cercle linguistique de Prague 8.105-15.

Chomsky, Noam. 1956. Three models for the description of language. IRE Transactions on information theory, IT-2, 3.113-24.
—. 1957. Syntactic structures. Janua linguarum, 4. The Hague: Mouton.
—. 1964. The logical basis of linguistic theory. Proceedings of the ninth international
congress of linguists, ed. by Horace G. Lunt, 914-78. Janua linguarum, Series
maior, 12. The Hague: Mouton.
—. 1965. Aspects of the theory of syntax. Cambridge, Massachusetts: The MIT Press.
—. 1966. Cartesian linguistics: A chapter in the history of rationalist thought. Studies
in language. New York: Harper & Row.
—. 1968. Language and mind. New York: Harcourt, Brace & World.
—. 1969. Knowledge of language. The Times Literary Supplement, 15 May 1970,
3507.523-4.
Chomsky, Noam, and Halle, Morris. 1968. The sound pattern of English. Studies in
language. New York: Harper & Row.
Hall, Robert A., Jr. 1948. Descriptive Italian grammar. Cornell Romance studies, 2.
Ithaca, New York: Cornell University Press.
—. 1971. La struttura dell'italiano. Roma: Armando.
Halle, Morris. 1962. Phonology in generative grammar. Word 18.54-72.
Hockett, Charles F. 1954. Two models of grammatical description. Word 10.210-34.
—. 1968. The state of the art. Janua linguarum, 73. The Hague: Mouton.
Lakoff, George. 1970. Global rules. Lg. 46.627-39.
Lakoff, Robin. 1969. Review of Grammaire générale et raisonnée, ed. by Herbert E.
Brekle. Lg. 45.343-64.
Lane, George. 1945. Changes of emphasis in linguistics with particular reference to
Paul and Bloomfield. Studies in philology 42.465-83.
Lepschy, Giulio C. 1970. A survey of structural linguistics. Studies in general lin-
guistics. London: Faber and Faber.
Lyons, John. 1970. Chomsky. Fontana Modern Masters. London: Fontana, Collins.
Malkiel, Yakov, and Langdon, Margaret. 1969. History and histories of linguistics.
Romance philology 22.530-74.
Saltarelli, Mario. 1970. A phonology of Italian in a generative grammar. Janua
linguarum. Series practica, 93. The Hague: Mouton.
Thorne, James P. 1965. Review of Constituent structure, by Paul M. Postal. Journal
of Linguistics 1.73-6.
Timpanaro, Sebastiano. 1970. Sul materialismo. Saggi di varia umanità, 12. Pisa:
Nistri-Lischi.
Waterman, John T. 1963. Perspectives in linguistics. Chicago: The University of
Chicago Press.

ON LEARNING A NEW CONTRAST

LEIGH LISKER

Descriptions of the speech behavior of human beings, both their manage-
ment of the vocal tract and their perceptual processing of its audible
output, require data on a wide variety of speakers if we are to separate
the biological and cultural factors which govern speech activity, or,
perhaps more realistically, if we are simply to distinguish between the
features which characterize speech generally and those specific to particular kinds of speech. One obvious way of checking on the degree of
universality of generalizations concerning speech behavior is to compare
speakers of diverse languages. We would suppose, if they manage
phoneme inventories that differ in size and distinctive phonetic properties,
that this is no more to be connected with physical characteristics of the
speech-producing and speech-perceiving mechanisms than are grammatical differences in the languages which their speech 'implements'. Phonetic differences between two languages presumably reflect either different
choices from some general inventory of phonetic dimensions which are,
in principle, equally available to all language users, or different ways of
exploiting the same phonetic dimensions. Thus, for example, the feature
of glottalization may serve to differentiate consonants in one language
and not in another, whose speakers nonetheless might readily distinguish,
if they had to,[1] between glottalized and unglottalized consonants. In
another case, two languages might make use of very much the same
range of vowel sounds, but differ as to just how these are grouped into
categories. Here the problem for the speaker of one language learning
the other would be to adopt new criteria for deciding which sounds were
the same and which different.

In comparing the language behavior of speakers of diverse languages
we may follow certain psycholinguistic testing procedures which involve
speech or speech-like auditory stimuli. Differences in test performance
may in general be taken to reflect differences in the subjects' linguistic
backgrounds, i.e., they represent an effect of learning. What is not quite

clear is exactly what it is that was learned, or the extent to which this
learning may be said to have affected permanently the ability of speakers
of one language to learn to match the performance of speakers of another.
Over the past dozen years researchers at the Haskins Laboratories have
been testing subjects, for the most part speakers of American English,
to determine a relation between their linguistic identification of synthetic
speech stimuli and their ability to detect the acoustic differences between
individual test stimuli. In tests involving the presentation of steady-
state synthetic vowel sounds (Fry, Abramson, Eimas and Liberman 1962,
Stevens, Liberman, Studdert-Kennedy and Öhman 1969) no very close
connection was found between subjects' identification of stimuli with
English vowels and their ability to distinguish them in a conventional
ABX test; items labelled alike were almost as easy to discriminate in this
test as were items labelled differently. On the other hand, for a stimulus
set whose members were distributed among the categories *ba*, *da*, and
ga, it appeared that subjects were able to distinguish only those items
which they assigned to different categories (Liberman, Harris, Hoffman
and Griffith 1957). Thus the results of testing for discrimination of isolated vowel and initial stop appeared to be radically different.[2]

Unfortunately, in the testing program just referred to, no very extensive cross-language data have as yet been collected. However, what
has so far been done in this area does not weaken the notion of a quite
different relationship between labelling and discrimination behavior
for vowels and stop consonants. In one vowel study (Stevens, Liberman,
Studdert-Kennedy and Öhman 1969) American and Swedish subjects
were compared in respect to the labelling and discrimination of certain
vowel-like stimuli that have very different categorial status in English
and Swedish. It was found that linguistic experience, as reflected in
differences in the way in which Swedes and American classified the test
stimuli, had little apparent effect on their ability to discriminate. A cross-
language consonant study (Abramson and Lisker 1970, Lisker and
Abramson 1970), of which the present paper is a continuation, involved
the comparison of several groups of speakers with respect to the dimension of voicing as this serves to distinguish between categories of stops
in synthesized consonant-vowel syllables. Comparison of the labelling
and discrimination behavior of groups of English, Spanish and Thai-
speaking subjects showed differences in the use of voicing as a feature
whereby stop categories in the three languages are phonetically dis-
tinguishable. It will be useful here to review briefly the background and
findings of this study.

In very many of the world's languages distinctive use is made of two, and sometimes three, categories of initial prevocalic stop consonants which differ, among other things, in the extent to which the larynx participates in their production, as this can be measured by determining the time of voice onset relative to that of release of the occlusion. Spectrographic examination of the word-initial stops in a number of languages (Lisker and Abramson 1964) has shown that there are significant differences in voice onset timing ('VOT') from language to language, but that the placement of category boundaries along this dimension is hardly random. Measurement data (Fig. 1) derived from productions of isolated words in a dozen languages suggest that there are three preferred timing relations between voicing onset and stop release: voicing begins almost one hundred milliseconds before release (VOT $\cong$ −90); it begins at or just after the release (VOT $\cong$ +10); or it begins well after the release (VOT $\cong$ +75). These values, we may assume, correspond respectively to the voiced, voiceless unaspirated and voice-

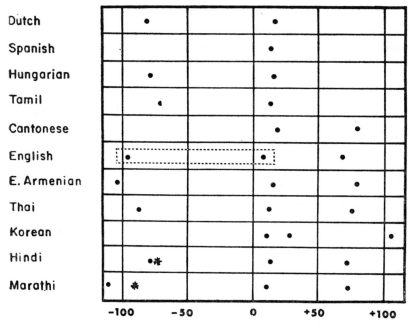

Mean voicing-onset timings for stops in word-initial position (from Lisker and Abramson 1964). Stop release is at O on abscissa, which represents no. of milliseconds by which voicing onset precedes (negative values) or follows (positive values) release. Starred entries are for voiced aspirates.

Fig. 1

less aspirated stops of classical descriptive phonetics. For all but one of the languages in our sample, Korean, it can be said that they differ essentially in the number and selection of stops from this set of phonetic categories. Thus Dutch, Spanish, Tamil and Hungarian each make use of the two categories at VOT $\cong$ -90 and VOT $\cong$ $+10$. Cantonese differs from these languages in that, while it too has two stop categories, they involve VOT values at about $+10$ and $+75$. Languages with three categories along the VOT dimension (Eastern Armenian, Thai, Hindi and Marathi, *but not* Korean) simply select all three of the categories described. Two of the languages examined are anomolous, Korean and English. Korean is a three-category language, but in initial position all of its stops are voiceless, i.e., voicing begins only with or following release, with VOT values at roughly $+10$, $+30$ and $+100$. English is peculiar in being a two-category language that utilizes all three VOT values, but does not distinguish initially between stops with voicing lead and those for which VOT $= +10$. The choice between the two appears to be, for American speakers of English at least, a choice that is partly idiosyncratic (Lisker and Abramson 1964:395) and partly a matter of style (Lisker and Abramson 1967:20-24).

In our comparison of different languages with respect to the timing of voice onset we have been talking as though the only differences among the stop categories being compared are those of voice onset timing. Acoustically, of course, this is| very far from being the truth; the effect of a small change in the timing of voice onset is very different, depending on whether onset precedes, coincides with, or follows the stop release. What we have been calling the VOT continuum is, at best, a continuum only in the articulatory domain, provided we make the no-doubt oversimplifying assumption that a series of syllables such as [ba, ḅa, pa, p'a, pʰa] can be produced by executing an articulatory program that is invariant in respect to those components which effect the supraglottal gestures, and which differs only in respect to those which determine when the laryngeal signal begins. This assumption, which derives from Dudley's well-known model of vocal tract operation (Dudley 1940), is most unlikely to be justifiable in detail. However, it is true enough to be convenient, for it provides the rationale for a relatively simple program for the synthesis of stop-vowel syllables. For a particular syllable in which a fixed spectral pattern determines, for example, that it will be identified as consisting of a labial stop and the vowel [a], the voicing state of the stop is controlled by specifying the time at which the signal 'exciting' the pattern shifts from one of aperiodic to one of periodic type. Thus for each place of stop closure a series of syllables could be generated whose initial consonants ranged from fully voiced (with onset of pulsing well before the burst marking stop release) to heavily aspirated voiceless stops (with pulsing onset considerably after the burst). Spectrograms of sample syllables, produced by means of the Haskins Laboratories' parallel resonance synthesizer under computer control (Mattingly 1968), are illustrated in Fig. 2. The upper pattern illustrates the case in which the spectral pattern is excited from start to finish by a periodic signal. Four successive segments of the pattern may be distinguished: an initial segment characterized by a single very-low-frequency formant with a duration of 150 msecs, which corresponds to the articulatory closure; a burst or transient of about 10 msecs, which corresponds to the release of the stop; an interval of about 50 msecs with three formants of shifting frequencies, which 'transition' corresponds to the interval of articulatory movements from closed stop to open vowel state of the oral cavity; a final segment with three formants at fixed frequencies for 450 msecs, corresponding to the vowel [a] as produced with 'steady-state' articulation. The pattern immediately below represents the case where the periodic excitation begins just after the burst, while the lower pattern shows the synthesizer output where the same excitation begins one hundred milliseconds after the burst. In both of the latter patterns the interval beginning with the burst and ending with the onset of pulsing is excited by an aperiodic signal. Particularly in the lowermost pattern, which listeners identify as a syllable beginning with a heavily aspirated stop [p^h], we can observe the feature of 'first-formant cutback', i.e. complete suppression of the first formant over the interval of noise excitation of the burst and upper formants. This feature must be considered *not independent* of the choice of excitation type (Liberman, Delattre and Cooper 1958). We may suppose that the association between this spectral difference and the voicing dimension arises not only because the larynx is a signal source, but because as a part of the cavity system of the vocal tract its state helps determine the resonance properties of the tract. One might then associate with the absence of pulsing a large attenuation of the first formant, provided a fairly large glottal aperture during the interval between release and voicing onset is assumed.[3] Equally well, perhaps, one might suppose the transmission characteristics of the tract to be essentially identical for periodic and aperiodic source signals, but that the aperiodic source is deficient in intensity over the frequency range below the second formant. In any case, a close relation, both in production and in perception, between the onset of pulsing and the fairly rapid

Three Conditions of Voice Onset Time
Synthetic Labial Stops

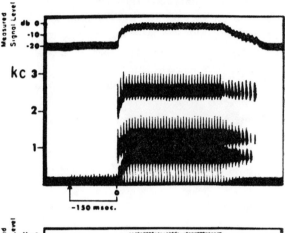

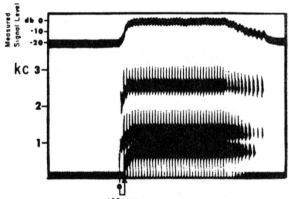

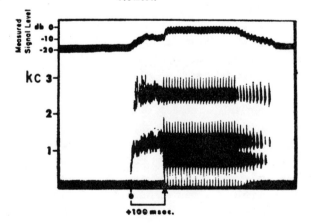

Fig. 2

development of first-formant intensity to a level appropriate to the following vowel was established from spectrographic study of real speech and on the basis of preliminary perception testing of synthetic stop-vowel patterns in which the VOT and first-formant cutback features were independently manipulated. Consequently, in our further discussion of what we have been calling the 'VOT dimension', it is to be understood that the onset of pulsing is regularly accompanied by the simultaneous onset of the first formant.

As part of our cross-language study of stop voicing, three series of synthetic speech patterns of the type illustrated by Fig. 2 were generated, in which VOT was systematically varied over a 300 msec range, from a value of −150 (pulsing onset 150 msec before the burst) to one of +150 (pulsing onset 150 msec after the burst). These stimuli, in various appropriate random orders, were presented to speakers of three of the languages for which we had real-speech VOT measurement data. The languages chosen were English, Spanish and Thai, the first two having two categories of stops each, and the third being representative of 'three-category' languages. Two kinds of data were gathered: labelling responses and something we called 'discrimination' data. The procedure which yielded the labelling data involved asking subjects, native speakers of the languages mentioned, to name the initial stop of a stimulus by identifying it with one or another of the initial stops in their language. The labelling data obtained by presentation of our labial series of stimuli are represented by the curves in Fig. 3. The responses which we took to reflect subjects' ability to discriminate between items of the stimulus set were collected by the following procedure. Stimulus triads were composed of two items that were identical in VOT value and a third differing from these by 20, 30 or 40 msecs along the same dimension. The order of presentation of members was random, with all possible orderings equally represented in the full set of triads submitted to the subjects. The subjects' task was to identify the 'odd ball' as the first, second or third member of the triad. Representative results are given in Fig. 4, which shows discrimination functions for one English-speaking and one Thai-speaking subject.

In the procedure by which labelling responses were obtained as a function of VOT values, the possibility that subjects might recognize more categories than their language possessed was not taken into account. From the discrimination task and the data thereby obtained, it appeared that discriminability is not significantly better than chance for stimulus pairs which are categorially identical, but increases sharply for pairs

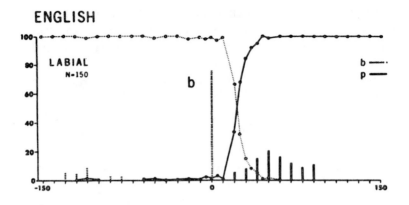

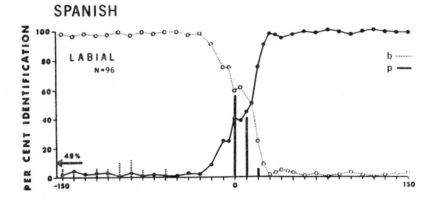

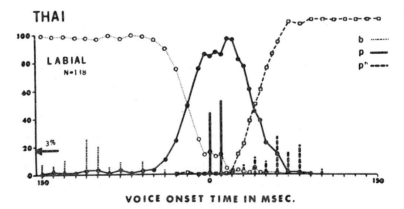

Fig. 3

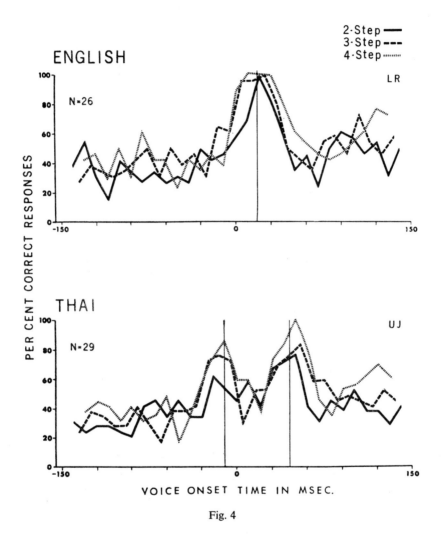

Fig. 4

located near the boundary between categories along the VOT dimension. Insofar as the locations of these discrimination peaks differ for the speakers of different languages, and indeed sometimes for individual subjects, matching thereby the boundaries between linguistic categories established by the labelling tests, it would seem difficult to decide whether the failure to make subcategorial discriminations means that subjects cannot or simply that they did not make such discriminations, given a test in which some comparisons were across a category boundary and others were not. One major purpose of some additional tests carried out at the speech research laboratory of the Pavlov Institute near Leningrad[4] was to learn whether speakers of Russian, a two-category language with voiced and voiceless unaspirated stops, can readily distinguish between stimuli which, for speakers of English, are categorially different, but which for Russians are of the same category. There was, unfortunately, no opportunity to make VOT measurements of spoken Russian stops comparable in quantity with the large body of cross-language data presented in Lisker and Abramson 1964, but a modest quantity of labelling and discrimination data was collected.

In order to obtain VOT labelling data from Russian speakers the same synthetic speech stimuli tested previously with American, Puerto Rican, and Thai subjects were presented to a group of fifteen members of the Pavlov Institute staff. Their responses to these stimuli are given in Fig. 5. Although Russian is a two-category language, with stops resembling those of Spanish and Hungarian, stimuli with VOT values greater

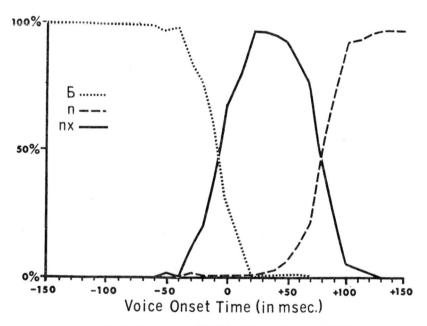

RUSSIAN LABELLING RESPONSES
[N - 75 (15 ss. x 5 tr.)]

Fig. 5

than $+80$ were judged to begin with the cluster *px*, i.e. the voiceless bilabial stop followed by a voiceless velar fricative. The labelling behavior of our Russian-speaking subjects may be compared with the data obtained from speakers of the three other languages previously mentioned (Fig. 3). The differences from language to language are considerable, even if we allow for variations, probably minor, due to the fact that listening conditions could not be rigorously controlled. Presumably the fact that English speakers divide the VOT space into *b* and *p* categories at $+25$, while for Russians the crossover point dividing *b* from *p* is close to -10, is of significance, particularly in view of the fact that this difference is observed in actual speech production as well. At the same time it should be remarked that the match with production data is not always very good, specifically in the Spanish case and in the p-p^h boundary in Thai.

Since English speakers identify stimuli with VOT values in the range $-10 \ldots +25$ with items of lower (i.e. more negative) values, while Russians identify them with items having higher values, the question arises as to whether this difference means that acoustic cues available to both groups are assessed according to different strategies, or whether the cues to which one group attends are simply not available to the other. Is it the case, for example, that Russian listeners are quite capable of distinguishing between items at $+20$ and $+50$, although both are *p* for them, and that Americans can hear the difference between VOT values of -30 and 0, though both are labelled *b*? If one group is able to discriminate between stimuli which are categorially different only for the other, then the implication would be that there is a psychoacoustic basis for the category boundary.

In order to learn whether the boundary at VOT $= +25$ between English *b* and *p* is susceptible of detection by speakers of Russian, the following experiment was carried out. Items having VOT values of $+10$ and $+60$, both of them *p*, were presented to a group of Russian speakers who were trained to assign different labels to them, i.e. to move a toggle switch one way for $+10$ stimuli and the other way for $+60$ stimuli. Subjects' success in learning this task was ascertained by presenting the two stimuli many times in random order, simultaneously registering their responses by means of an electromechanical recording system. It appeared that the test group was able to do significantly better than chance, with a majority of the six subjects tested getting above 90% correct in identifying the $+10$ items. Identification of the $+60$ stimuli was less good, but still better than 75% correct for all but one subject.

Thus it seemed that the subjects as a group could both distinguish the two test stimuli and also apply two different labels to them in a reasonably consistent way.

A second labelling test was next constructed in which was presented a set of stimuli covering the range from $+10$ to $+60$ in steps of 10 msecs. The test subjects' task was to identify each stimulus by judging whether it was more similar to the $+10$ or the $+60$ item. Each stimulus was represented five times in the random order presentation, and the entire set of 30 items was administered to the same group of subjects repeatedly over several days.

The responses of our subjects in the labelling test just described are represented by the solid line in Fig. 6, which shows the percentage of $+60$ identifications as a function of VOT value. This labelling function is to be compared with the two functions representing the behavior of a group of English-speaking subjects tested subsequently in the United States: the dotted line in Fig. 6 gives percentage p judgments derived from tests in which stimuli covering the full $-150 \dots +150$ range were presented, while the dot-and-dash line in the same figure gives responses to the restricted set ranging from $+10$ to $+60$ along the VOT dimension. (The dashed line, representing the Russians' p labellings for the full VOT range, is included in Fig. 6 for ease of comparison.) It is apparent that the Russian and the American English data do not closely match, and one is tempted to believe that, by and large, the Russian listeners were making continuous rather than categorical judgments, i.e., that they were estimating the magnitude of the difference between a given stimulus and each of the standard stimuli rather than deciding whether or not it shared some feature with one of the standards. The Americans' judgments were very much the same in the two labelling tests; whether they were dividing the full VOT range into b and p categories or the restricted range by matching with the $+10$ as against the $+60$ stimuli, their judgments were evenly divided at about $+20$. The Russian judgments, by contrast, show a crossover somewhere between $+30$ and $+40$, i.e. at about the midpoint of the $+10 \dots +60$ range; within this same range, of course, the curve representing the partition of the full VOT range into b and p categories does not approach the 50% value on the ordinate. When we look at the behavior of individual subjects, moreover, we find a marked difference in the degree of variability for the two groups; the American subjects are noticeably more alike in their division of the restricted range of stimuli than are the Russians (Fig. 7), who place their boundaries anywhere between $+20$ and $+50$. It may possibly be true that

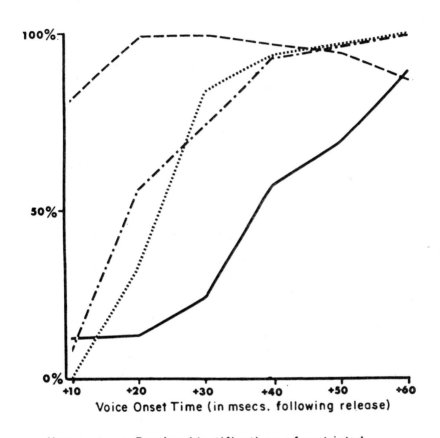

Comparison of Russian and American Labelling of
Full and Restricted Ranges Along
the VOT Dimension

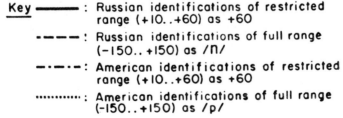

Key ————— : Russian identifications of restricted
range (+10..+60) as +60

— — — : Russian identifications of full range
(−150..+150) as /п/

— · — · — : American identifications of restricted
range (+10..+60) as +60

············ : American identifications of full range
(−150..+150) as /p/

Fig. 6

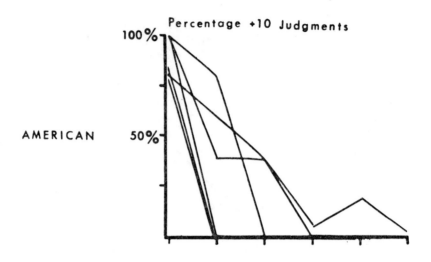

AMERICAN

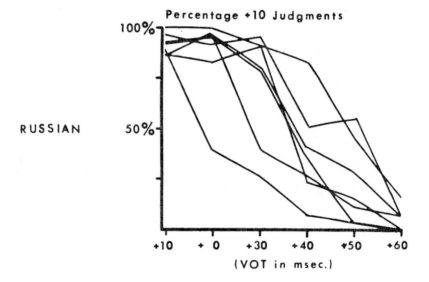

RUSSIAN

Individual Variation in
Identification of Stimuli
with +10 as against +60

Fig. 7

the single Russian listener who observed a crossover value near +20 was following the Americans' strategy, but the Russians as a group were certainly not attending to the same cues as the latter. On the other hand, it is possibly only accidental that the Russian crossover near +40 is very nearly at the midpoint of the +10 ... +60 range, so that we cannot be certain that they were estimating difference magnitudes rather than responding categorically to some acoustic cue. There is the possibility, moreover, that this crossover value near +40 is to be related to one of the crossover values determined for our Thai subjects in the full-range labelling test (Fig. 3). What we can be reasonably certain of, on the basis of our present data, is that our Russian listeners did *not* generally observe the boundary which served the American subjects in both labelling tasks. It would be appropriate to determine Russian crossover values for several additional VOT ranges, e.g. +20 ... +70 and +30 ... +80, that fall within the *p* category, in order to learn whether the crossover values remain fixed or tend to move with the range boundaries. In the first event we should be in a position to assert that the Russian listeners were evaluating the stimuli, in categorical fashion, according to acoustic criteria other than those motivating the American listeners; in the second event we should have to suppose that a continuous kind of perception and comparison was being practiced.

University of Pennsylvania

NOTES

[1] As in a phonetic or psycholinguistic exercise, for example. If subjects discriminate between items they call 'the same' so far as differentiating words of their language, then this counters the view that linguistic coding always intervenes between the peripheral processing of the acoustic signal and the execution of the discrimination task.

[2] Whether these differences can be taken as evidence for the motor theory of speech perception may be regarded as doubtful, since the acoustic variables involved in the vowel and consonant studies differ markedly. Nor can one readily assume that conclusions based on tests using steady-state vowel patterns will be valid for the perception of vowels in running speech.

[3] Current work involving motion picture photography of the glottis via fiberoptics indicates that this is regularly the case during production of voiceless aspirated stops, at least for English.

[4] These tests were conducted by the writer as a guest researcher at the speech laboratory of the Pavlov Institute of Physiology, which he visited under the auspices of the cultural exchange program of the National Academy of Sciences of the U. S. and the Academy of Sciences of the U.S.S.R. The work reported here could not have been accomplished without the generous cooperation of Dr. L. A. Chistovich and her colleagues of the Pavlov Institute.

REFERENCES

Abramson, A. S., and Lisker, L. 1970. Discriminability along the voicing continuum: cross-language tests. Proceedings of the 6th International Congress of Phonetic Sciences, Prague, 1967.

Dudley, H. 1940. The carrier nature of speech. Bell System Technical Journal 19:495-515.

Fry, D. B., Abramson, A. S., Eimas, P. and Liberman, A. M. 1962. The identification and discrimination of synthetic vowels. Language and Speech 5:171-189.

Liberman, A. M., Harris, K. S., Hoffman, H. S. and Griffith, B. C. 1957. The discrimination of speech sounds within and across phoneme boundaries. J. Exp. Psych. 54, No. 5:358-368.

Liberman, A. M., Delattre, P. C. and Cooper, F. S. 1958. Some cues for the distinction between voiced and voiceless stops in initial position. Language and Speech 1:153-167.

Lisker, L. and Abramson, A. S. 1964. A cross-language study of voicing in initial stops: acoustical measurements. Word 20:384-422.

—. 1967. Some effects of context on voice onset time in English stops. Language and Speech 10:1-28.

—. 1970. The voicing dimension: some experiments in comparative phonetics. Proceedings of the 6th Congress of Phonetic Sciences, Prague, 1967, 563-567.

Mattingly, I. G. 1968. Experimental methods for speech synthesis by rule. IEEE Transactions. Audio 16:198-202.

Stevens, K. N., Liberman, A. M., Studdert-Kennedy, M. and Öhman, S. E. G. 1969. Crosslanguage study of vowel perception. Language and Speech 12, Pt. 1:1-23.

SEMANTIC RELATIONS
BETWEEN NUCLEAR STRUCTURES

EUGENE A. NIDA

While a number of linguists have been interested in the semantic relations
within nuclear structures, that is, the relations between an event word
and its 'case' satellites, for example, agent, goal, instrument, location,
and benefactive (Anderson 1969, Fillmore 1967, Halliday 1968, Lyons
1966, and Robinson 1968), relatively few have concerned themselves
with the semantic relations between nuclear structures or groupings of
nuclear structures. Staal (1967) made an important beginning and Fuller
(1968) showed the application of certain internuclear semantic relations
to the problems of interpretation and translation, but, with the exception
of his emphasis upon larger discourse units, Fuller's approach is not
significantly different from traditional descriptions of syntactic relations
found in standard language texts such as Smyth's (1916). What has been
needed is a systematic analysis of all the meaningful relations between
nuclear structures and an application of these relations to the various
levels of discourse. The following paper, which sets forth certain aspects
of the problem, is one attempt to fill an increasingly felt need. A more
complete analysis is found in a book entitled *Exploring semantic
structures*.

RELATION OF SEMANTIC STRUCTURES TO SYNTACTIC STRUCTURES

As long as semantics was viewed primarily as a system for putting
convenient labels on syntactic structures, it was inevitable that little
or no real progress could be made in establishing a solid theoretical
base for semantics. Only the recognition that semantics has to be treated
as a structure in its own right produced the necessary basis for the required
formulations. Chafe 1970 has been particularly important in helping to
establish the autonomy of semantic structure.

Any analysis of the relations between semantic and syntactic structures must not, however, be limited to some narrow or restricted segment of syntactic structure. Theoretically, one should expect that the meaningful relations between any two event expressions would also hold for the relations between groups of events. That is to say, the reason-result relation between two nuclear structures in 1:

(1)   Because the volcano erupted, the people fled from the region.

should also be applicable to more extended structures which include embedded nuclear structures, as in 2:

(2)   Because the explosion destroyed the factory, the people decided that they would have to migrate to another region where work was available.

That is precisely what does happen. In fact, the reason-result relations may be applicable to entire sections of a discourse. One part of an article may state the reason for some activity, while the second part may describe the result.

In analyzing relations between nuclear structures, it is often necessary to back-transform to a somewhat deeper level than is frequently the case when kernel structures are discussed. For example, in 3:

(3)   The explosion destroyed the factory.

there are two nuclear structures. *Explosion* is itself an event expression and implies that (*something*) *exploded*. This first nuclear structure is the cause of the second, the destruction of the factory.

In attempting to determine the relations between nuclear structures one cannot be guided solely by syntactic forms. For example, in the relation of setting to event, one would assume that in a single complex sentence the setting would always be in the dependent clause and the characterized event in the independent clause, as in 4:

(4)   After the guns had fired, the band played the national anthem.

In some instances, however, the setting is expressed in an independent clause, while the focal event is in the dependent clause, as in 5:

(5)   He was walking into town, when suddenly he collapsed beside the road.

Dependence upon syntactic forms can also be misleading, since there is often a considerable degree of ambivalence or ambiguity. In 6:

(6)   Seeing is believing.

one may describe the semantic relations between the two events as means-result (by seeing one believes), condition-result (if one sees, one believes), or cause-effect (seeing causes one to believe). Similarly, in 7:

(7)   His resignation produced anxiety among his colleagues.

his resignation (equivalent to the nuclear structure *he resigned*) is related to the rest of the sentence (equivalent to the nuclear structure, [*X*] *caused his colleagues to be anxious*) either as cause-effect, reason-result, or means-result. Lack of preciseness in the relations between nuclear structures should not, however, worry the analyst. A certain degree of ambivalence in such relations is typical of the higher levels of structure and by no means absent from lower levels. If a source wishes to be completely precise about semantic relations, he can be; but complete preciseness is neither required nor perhaps even desirable in many discourses.

CLASSIFICATION OF SEMANTIC RELATIONS
BETWEEN NUCLEAR STRUCTURES

The following outline of semantic relations makes a primary distinction between coordinate and subordinate relations. The coordinate relations are divided between 'additive' and 'dyadic', while the subordinate relations are divided between 'qualificational', which might also be called 'specificational', and 'logical'.

    I. Coordinate
       A. Additive
          1. Equivalent
          2. Different, in parallel structures or 'unfolding'
       B. Dyadic
          1. Alternative (*or*)
          2. Contrastive (*but*)
          3. Comparative (*than, as, like*)
   II. Subordinate
       A. Qualificational
          1. Substance
             a. Content
             b. Generic-specific
          2. Character
             a. Characterization, of whole or of part
             b. Manner
             c. Setting
                i. Time
               ii. Place
              iii. Circumstance

B. Logical relations
   1. Cause-effect
   2. Reason-result
   3. Means-result
   4. Means-purpose
   5. Condition-result
   6. Ground-implication
   7. Concession-result

ADDITIVE RELATIONS

Additive-equivalent relations involve two expressions which are essentially identical with one another:

(8)   He's so stupid; he's so dumb!
(9)   He didn't stay; he left.

In both 8 and 9 the semantic relation between the two parts is equivalence. Both parts say the same thing, but in slightly different forms. One expression is merely added to another for the sake of emphasis.

   Additive-different relations are much more complex. They may involve (a) parallel structures, as in 10 and 11, with either the same or different participants,

(10)   He laid aside the magazine and picked up a book.
(11)   She was chatting on the phone and he was working in the basement.

or (b) unfolding structures, in the sense that a nonfocal element in one expression becomes the focal element in the next, as in 12 and 13:

(12).   He came suddenly upon the buffaloes and one of them charged him.
(13)   She slapped Michael and he knifed her.

In 13 there is certainly the implication of reason-result. One may say, therefore, that in 13 the overt relation is additive-different: two events are added to each other and they are different. But the covert relation is reason-result. Whether the overt or the covert relation is the principal one can only be determined from the entire context in which such a sentence occurs. In certain styles the real intent is often masked somewhat by intentionally imprecise overt markings.

   In all additive relations there must always be some situational connection between the parts. Normal speech simply does not contain such sentences as 14 and 15:

(14)   *I want to go home tomorrow and the doctor is my friend.
(15)   *He went for a walk in the woods and I want to work in the factory.

although these are quite common types of sentences of mentally deranged persons.

DYADIC RELATIONS

In dyadic relations there is a measure of reciprocal interaction or interference. Alternative relations may, of course, take a number of different forms, depending upon the element or elements of the respective clauses which function as alternatives, for example, subject, event, goal, setting, etc.: 16, 17, and 18:

(16)   I will come or Bill will.
(17)   I will speak with him or write him a letter.
(18)   Either I will send you the package, or Jim will send it to you tomorrow.

Contrastive relations are signaled in English by such conjunctive expressions as *but, however, nevertheless, on the contrary* (for example, *He came but the party was over*); and comparative relations are normally marked in English by the distinctive particles *than, as,* and *like* (for example, *He is much stronger than Bill*).

QUALIFICATIONAL RELATIONS

Relations of content include what are traditionally classified as predicate complements 19, 20, and 21:

(19)   He wanted to go.
(20)   We heard that he was coming.
(21)   He felt that he had been slighted.

Generic-specific relations do not occur so frequently between the parts of a single sentence, though this is the relation in 22:

(22)   His father was stingy; he would never spend a dime for a soft drink.

in which the second paratactically combined clause gives a specific instance of the generic statement in the first clause. Generic-specific relations are, however, quite frequent on higher levels of discourse, and in fact constitute the principal feature of expository discourse. Many textbooks are organized on this principle: the first chapter introduces the principal concept, and the following chapters provide specific instances or aspects of the generic declaration.

Characterization may be of the whole or of a part. For example, in 23:

(23)   Working for John was terrible.

was terrible is a characterization of the subject, which is a nuclear structure, (*someone*) *worked for John*. But characterization may relate to only a part of a nuclear structure, as in 24:

(24)   We shot the bear which had mauled the child.

in which only *bear* is characterized by the final relative clause.

The relation of manner consists of the characterization of one event by another, as in 25:

(25)   He came into town riding in a maroon Rolls-Royce.

in which *riding in a maroon Rolls-Royce* characterizes the manner in which the person *came into town*. Relations of setting often parallel closely those of manner, but they should be distinguished carefully from the former. In 26:

(26)   Yesterday he worked three hours.

the introductory expression *yesterday* is one of temporal setting, while *three hours* is a temporal satellite of the verb *worked*, since it designates the extent of the working, not the temporal setting of the working. Similarly, in 27:

(27)   At camp Jim ran three miles.

at camp is an expression of place setting, while *three miles* is a spatial satellite to the verb nucleus. Settings of time and place are best analyzed as consisting of truncated nuclear structures.

Circumstantial setting is much less frequent than temporal or spatial setting, since circumstantial setting is much more likely to be expressed in terms of some logical relation between nuclear structures. In 28 and 29, however,

(28)   The wind was already at hurricane speed when Jim set sail.

(29)   The fire engine came careening down the street just as Maude backed out of the driveway.

the first clause in each instance states the circumstances relating to the event specified in the second clause.

LOGICAL RELATIONS

Logical relations, whether real or presumed, have been classified in a number of different ways by logicians and philologists, but they can be conveniently reduced to seven basic relations: cause-effect, reason-result, means-result, means-purpose, condition-result, ground-implication and concession-result. Though many combinations of nuclear structures may be semantically ambiguous (since preciseness in expressing semantic relations is not required in all utterances), it is nevertheless possible to mark related events in such a way as to indicate more or less clearly which of the logical relations is involved. In the following series the same events are related in seven different ways so as to illustrate the diverse logical relations:

(30)   John's going to New York caused him to meet Mary.
        (cause-effect)
(31)   Because John wanted to meet Mary, he went to New York.
        (reason-result)
(32)   By going to New York, John met Mary.
        (means-result)
(33)   John went to New York in order to meet Mary.
        (means-purpose)
(34)   If John had gone to New York, he would have met Mary.
        (condition-result)
(35)   Since John went to New York, he must have met Mary.
        (ground-implication)
(36)   Although John went to New York, he did not meet Mary.
        (concession-result)

IMPLICATIONS OF THE ANALYSIS OF INTERNUCLEAR RELATIONS

As the result of employing this system of nineteen semantic relations in the analysis of extensive texts and in the elicitation of these nineteen different semantic relations in a number of languages, several important conclusions may be drawn.

First, these nineteen relations seem to be applicable to any and all structures of all languages. There has been no instance in which any one of these relations could not be expressed in other languages, and these languages included some which have been traditionally regarded as completely different from the more usual types of languages (e.g. Kung Bushman of Southwest Africa and Enga of New Guinea). Furthermore, no structures in discourses have failed to be classifiable in terms of this series of relations.

Second, though the manner in which the semantic relations are expressed differs widely from one language to another (e.g. comparison may be marked by a verb meaning 'to surpass' rather than by a conjunction such as *than* or *as*), there is no doubt about the semantic structures which underlie the various formal devices.

Third, languages differ markedly in the extent to which they normally make the relations explicit. For example, they may be like literary Classical Greek which employed conjunctions between almost every clause and sentence, or they may be like biblical Hebrew which employed considerable parataxis. On the other hand, they may be somewhat in between the two extremes, as in the case of modern English and most other European languages.

Fourth, when semantic relations are not specifically marked, there may be several different interpretations, but in an actual discourse the possibilities of interpretation are usually contextually well restricted. However, a single nuclear structure may have one relation to a preceding nuclear structure, another relation to one which follows, and several different relations to different structures at different structural levels. The semantic relations of a series of nuclear structures seldom, if ever, resemble a chain; they appear to be much more like a somewhat irregular spider's web with several points of attachment. In fact, the complete analysis of a complex expository structure reveals a number of intersecting semantic relations on several different planes and levels, one of the most complex structures in the entire realm of language.

Fifth, the same semantic relations which may exist between two nuclear structures are also applicable to the meaningful relations between any set of units on any level of discourse structure: sentences, paragraphs, sections, chapters, and even related volumes.

The application of semantics to this area of discourse structure appears to be one of the most productive and challenging of any which have been explored up to this time.

REFERENCES

Anderson, John. 1969. Adjectives, datives, and ergativization. Foundations of Language 5.301-323.

Chafe, Wallace L. 1970. Meaning and the structure of language. Chicago: University of Chicago Press.

Fillmore, C. J. 1967. The case for case, in E. Bach and R. Harms (eds.), Proceedings of the 1967 Texas conference on language universals. New York: Holt, Rinehart and Winston.

Fuller, Daniel P. 1968. Delimiting and interpreting the larger literary units. Notes on Translation 28.1-12.

Halliday, M. A. K. 1968. Notes on transitivity and theme in English, part 3. Journal of Linguistics 4.179-215.

Lyons, John. 1966. Toward a 'notional' theory of the 'parts of speech'. Journal of Linguistics 2.209-236.

Nida, Eugene A. 1975. Exploring semantic structures München: Fink.

Robinson, Jane J. 1968. Case, category, and configuration. PEGS paper no. 64.

Smyth, Herbert Weir. 1916. A Greek grammar. New York: American Book Company.

Staal, J. F. 1967. Some semantic relations between sentoids. Foundations of Language 3.66-88.

SOME ASPECTS OF
BAUDOUIN DE COURTENAY
AS BOOK-REVIEWER

D. L. OLMSTED

The reviews that flow from a scholar's pen in the course of a long career are not the best index of his interests and accomplishments; extraneous factors may play a role. For one thing, the books offered him for review are chosen in accordance with his interests and skills as seen by editors, not necessarily as seen by himself. The choice items of his youth may go to riper men, while he cuts his teeth on lesser works. And, as his interests change and broaden, editors' knowledge of such permutations is likely to lag several years behind their actual dates. For another, the decision to review a book, if offered, may not have much to do with the extent to which one is interested in it or makes use of it. As Macaulay wrote, refusing to review Dickens' book on the United States: "I cannot praise it" (because it is "at once frivolous and dull") "and I will not cut it up" (because Dickens was a good and talented man who "hates slavery as heartily as I do") (Trevelyan 1908:424). However, since scholars are seldom forced to review books, the positive decision to do so has some meaning, even if the converse is not the case.

The book reviews of a figure such as Baudouin de Courtenay are of particular interest. One of the great progenitors of modern linguistics, he has been shamefully neglected in the West, as Professor Keith Percival (1967) has pointed out. Moreover, his long and varied career was marked by frequent changes of locale, gnarled by political persecution, and stifled by the long distances, bad communications and general inefficiency of Tsarist Russia. In such circumstances, the books he read and reviewed are valuable guideposts along the road of his professional development; their value is enhanced by the melancholy fact that much material that would have been of value to the biographer did not survive the catastrophe that Warsaw suffered under the heels of foreign armies during World War II.

Jan Niecisław Baudouin de Courtenay (known in the Russian literature as Ivan Alexandrovich Boduen de Kurtene) was thoroughly Polish, despite his surname.[1] Born in 1845 near Warsaw, he was educated at home, under conditions of Poland's partition. In the portion of the country under Russian rule, the use of the Polish language on any official occasion was proscribed. The very porters in the railroad stations were fined for speaking anything but Russian (Pares 1939:64). After finishing the Realgymnasium, where he distinguished himself in mathematics and by his zeal for Latin, he entered the Preparatory Course for the Szkoła Główna, subsequently passing into the latter institution. The Szkoła Główna was founded and organized by Poles as a substitute for the University of Warsaw, which had been taken over by the occupying power to be used as an instrument of Russification. The Szkoła Główna was permitted by the Tsarist authorities for a scant eight years. In the meantime, although not having the name of university, it gave baccalaureate degrees to a phalanx of Polish intellectual leaders, many of whom distinguished themselves in the struggle to keep the national culture alive in hopes of the reconstitution of Poland. Baudouin graduated in 1866, having specialized in Slavic philology.

In 1867, he left to study abroad, on a scholarship from the Russian government. It was apparently understood that he would return to Warsaw University as Professor of Linguistics, but, after a year spent in Prague, Jena, and Berlin, he returned to find that Russian policy forbade appointment of any Pole to the faculty at Warsaw. He was informed that the terms of his scholarship required him to serve in some other Russian university, so he accepted a Fellowship at St. Petersburg, where he began work on Old Polish. In 1870 he went to Leipzig, where he was given a doctorate on the basis of his famous paper on analogy in the Polish declination. The next year, his work on Old Polish gained him a Master's degree from St. Petersburg, and the same institution granted him a doctorate in 1874. His career continued to be dogged by politics: an offer to him from Kiev University was countermanded by the authorities, who decided that "as a Pole, he would be dangerous in Kiev" (Ułaszyn 1934:14). Worse still, the chair of comparative Slavic philology fell vacant at Cracow, and, though it was offered to him, Baudouin de Courtenay could not accept, since he was still bound by the terms of his scholarship. Naturally, the Russians would not release him to accept a position in Austria-Hungary at the one institution of higher learning where Polish was the medium of instruction – the source of nationalist light during the long darkness of partition. Instead, he went to Kazan – as close to Siberia as one could get in the Russian university system of the time – as docent in comparative Indo-European. There he remained until 1883, rising to full professor. From 1883 to 1893 he occupied the chair of comparative Slavic linguistics at the University of Dorpat. At that point, his twenty-five years of obligated service to Russia having ended, he retired and went to Cracow. There, however, he received only a temporary appointment as Contract Professor, since he was a foreigner in the eyes of the Austrians. Moreover, his outspokenness and independence, combined with the belief of the authorities that comparative Slavic studies were politically dangerous in the context of the Dual Monarchy, rendered him persona non grata to the administration; in 1899 his contract was not renewed.

Baudouin de Courtenay therefore returned to St. Petersburg as Professor of Comparative Linguistics and Sanskrit and remained there until the reconstitution of Poland in 1918. Then he removed to Warsaw, where, as Honorary Professor, he spent his remaining years, departing this life in 1929. This brief sketch of his career as student, scholar, and pedagog may serve as base-map in which to place the details of his activity as book-reviewer.

It appears from Szober's (1930) bibliography that 82 book reviews issued from Baudouin's pen. Not all are easily accessible today, since the vehicles which carried them range from well-known linguistic journals, such as the *Archiv für slavische Philologie*, *Prace Filologiczne*, and the *Indogermanische Forschungen*, to short-lived Polish magazines and Slovene newspapers. Though some of the latter reviews cannot so far be located, it is possible to judge from their titles that they are duplicates or near-duplicates of other reviews of the same works published by Baudouin de Courtenay in either Russian or German. Apparently he contributed toward the continuity of Polish intellectual life by reviewing, in Polish, works for which reviews had been sought by (and delivered to) more widely-distributed linguistic journals. Whether the difference of audience induced simplification or other changes in his treatment cannot be discovered without comparing the texts. However, we do know that Baudouin de Courtenay was indefatigable in his work with groups of laymen interested in keeping Polish alive and he was never 'above' suiting his discourse to his readership. Since many of the works treated to dual reviews concern the Polish language, one may imagine that his review was addressed to an audience of educated native-speakers, rather than linguistic specialists.

Two of the reviews date from his student years at the Szkoła Główna. Of the rest, all but eleven were published or in press by the time Baudouin de Courtenay left Kazan. Those eleven were scattered thinly over the next forty-five years. Thus the bulk of his activity as book-reviewer, represented by 69 reviews, was concentrated between the years 1870 and 1884. Ten were published before he left St. Petersburg and 14 appeared in the first Kazan year (1874). During the next ten years he averaged nearly five reviews a year. Upon moving to Dorpat, he virtually abandoned reviewing books; only one such production came from his study in the next decade.

Thus, Baudouin's book reviews were a part of his early maturity as a scholar, when he was making his reputation as scholar and administrator, assembling and instructing the group of younger linguists who were to become known as the 'Kazan School'; those years of Baudouin's activity have left a profound and enduring impression on linguistics in Russia. The languages in which the reviews were written (or – at any rate – appeared) tend to support this hypothesis. Fully fifty of the 82 were written in Russian, 18 were written in Polish, 13 appeared in German, and one in Slovene. The fifty reviews in Russian may be viewed as a partial repayment on his scholarship from the Russian government; they served well their purpose of analyzing, for the Russian reader, the latest achievements in the various fields of linguistics. The 18 written in Polish were part of Baudouin de Courtenay's contribution to the perpetuation of Polish intellectual life during partition and, as such, must have been repugnant to the Russifying authorities. (Unlike Przewalski (Kropotkin 1971) and many other Poles resident in Russia, Baudouin never allowed depolonization of himself or his family, though he resided in Russian-speaking territory for more than forty years.) The German ones served to keep Baudouin's name before the Western scholarly world and to maintain his connections with his former teachers and peers in Germany. This must have seemed particularly important to the young man immured in distant Kazan, particularly insofar as he entertained hopes of moving to some more desirable post.

When we turn to the languages in which the reviewed books were published, a somewhat different picture emerges: 28 were in Russian, 22 each in Polish and German, 3 each in Serbian, Latin and Czech, and one in French. The subjects of the books reviewed may be roughly classified as follows: the Polish language 21, Comparative Slavic and Proto-Slavic 10, Slavic dialects 10, General linguistics 7, Slavic folklore and literature 5, the Russian language 5, philology and historical linguistics 4, Comparative Indo-European 3, the Czech language 3, the Serbocroatian language 3, phonetics 2, the Greek language 2, the Sanskrit language 2, child language 1, and the Lithuanian, Latvian, and English languages one each. Thus, though Baudouin spent most of his life as a professor of Sanskrit and Comparative Indo-European and made his greatest impact upon the development of the discipline in the realm of general linguistics, particularly descriptive analysis, both those fields are poorly represented among his reviewing chores. His reviews mark him over-whelmingly as a Slavist, and preeminently as a student of Polish in all its aspects.

Of his 22 reviews of books written in Polish, fully 15 had the Polish language as the subject. In this way, though he could not personally go to Cracow and teach, he could keep his hand on the tiller of Polish linguistics even from distant Kazan. Of the other Polish books, two deal with general linguistics, while the subjects of the others are scattered among philology, Slavic dialects, Russian, Lithuanian, and English.

The books written in Russian show a more diverse set of interests: eight of them deal with Comparative Slavistics, five with the Russian language, four with Polish, four with Slavic dialects, two with general linguistics, and the others are scattered among phonetics, Greek, Sanskrit and child language. Possibly the generalized interest in non-Russian Slavs is to be related to the Panslavic movement in the Russia of the time, whereas the Poles (who were even left out of the Panslavic family by some Russian thinkers) were less concerned with emphasizing their Slavhood than with establishing their political independence.

The works in German reflect the furious linguistic activity of the late nineteenth century in the German-speaking world: 5 concerned Slavic dialects, 4 dealt with Slavic folklore and literature, three were on general linguistics, three on Comparative Indo-European, two had Polish as subject, two concerned Comparative Slavic, and the others were scattered among phonetics, philology, and Latvian.

The three Serbian works all concerned Serbocroatian, while the three Czech works concerned Czech; two of the Latin books concerned historical linguistics and the other had Greek as its subject. The one French work reviewed by Baudouin dealt with Slavic folklore.

In summary, it may be said that Baudouin served as a vital link between the scholarship of Germany and the readership of Russia in linguistics. He was the first to see clearly the limitations of a purely historical approach to language, and his reviews of the work coming out of Germany ensured that the nascent linguistic tradition in Russia would start from a better vantage-point. In a series of masterful articles, Jakobson (1971b, c, d, e) has outlined the relations between Baudouin and his pupil and collaborator Kruszewski in the formation of what Jakobson has felicitously named the 'Kazan School of Polish linguistics'. Their momentous cooperation, so fruitful for modern linguistics, ended after only a few years when Kruszewski was gripped with mortal illness and, after his untimely death, Baudouin left Kazan for Dorpat. In the years that followed, his scientific work took, according to Jakobson, new directions. For some time, he did not persevere in the development of a general analytical theory based upon the findings of the 'Kazan School' and, among other things, threw himself into the struggles for an independent Polish intellectual life in his years at Cracow. It is hard to escape the conclusion that the end of his interest in book reviewing was connected with such sharp turns in his intellectual and personal[2] life.

University of California, Davis

NOTES

[1] His ancestors derived from Louis VI of France, by way of Baldwin of Flanders; the family reached Poland at the beginning of the 18th Century. Cf. H. Ułaszyn 1934.
[2] To the decade of the eighties also belonged the tragic death of Baudouin's first wife, his remarriage, and the foundation of his family.

REFERENCES

Jakobson, Roman. 1971a. Selected writings. Vol. 2. The Hague: Mouton.
—. 1971b. Jan Baudouin de Courtenay. In Jakobson 1971a, 389-393.
—. 1971c. The Kazan school of linguistics and its place in the international development of phonology. In Jakobson 1971a, 394-428.
—. 1971d. Polish-Russian cooperation in the science of language. In Jakobson 1971a, 451-455.
—. 1971e. Značeniye Kruševskogo v razvitii nauki o jazyke. In Jakobson 1971a, 425-450.
Kropotkin, Peter. 1971. Memoirs of a revolutionist. New York: Dover.
Pares, Bernard. 1939. The fall of the Russian monarchy. Vintage Books.
Perceval, Keith. 1967. Review of I. A. Boduen de Kurtene, Izbrannye trudy po obščemu jazykozaniju. Glossa 1.82-85.
Szober, Stanislaw. 1930. Bibliografja prac naukowych Prof. J. Baudouina de Courtenay. Prace Filologiczne 15.xxiv-liv. Warsaw.
Trevelyan, George Otto. 1908. Life and letters of Lord Macaulay. London: Longmans, Green and Co. Silver Library Edition.
Ułaszyn, H. 1934. Jan Baudouin de Courtenay. Poznań: Gebethner and Wolff.

A POEM ON
DISCONNECTING FORM AND MEANING

KENNETH L. PIKE

In a small volume on the Gospel of Mark I attempted to illustrate each part of the narrative with interwoven poems and comments.[1] In retrospect, I find one scene (pp. 115-16) which I feel I did not capture very well. This was the point when, dying, Christ cried out "My God, my God, why hast thou forsaken me?". The problems were substantial, because of the extensive contrasts: (1) He had been portrayed as the Light of the world, but a strange darkness was over the land at this moment.[2] (2) He had been portrayed as existing from eternity, but here was death. (3) He had been described as a link from eternal personal Spirit to incarnate body, but here was the reversal, splitting of soul from flesh. In the accompanying poem I have tried to capture and concentrate these clashes.

But the problem is related, it seems to me, to a basic issue in linguistics, since it is related to deeper characteristics of man: Can form be separated from meaning? Just as there seems to me to be a perennial Greek-like attempt to treat the body as evil, and to treat it as separable from spirit, so there appears to me to be an attempt to treat form as abstractable from meaning, in one of two several ways: (1) Some scholars would feel that *first* one should study form, and then later study the meanings which may be conveyed by it. (2) Others would feel that one should first see an underlying meaning structure, and then and only then relate the meanings to form, either by a generative process or by a relational mapping. Both seem to me to point eventually to the death of linguistic discovery and recognition:

(1) Linguistic communicative reality, I would rather affirm, is discoverable only by keeping a form-meaning composite in view at every stage. The attempt to *find* significant form with no regard to meaning (using, as a minimum meaning, differential meaning) leads to an infinite regress to physical detail; with no semantic check for thresholds of relevance, acoustic details become endless, and grammatical variability within a formal unit uncontrollable.

(2) Similarly, the attempt to *recognize* a unit, and to understand its relation to structure, is ultimately dependent upon one's ability to see its relevance to the larger structural context of communication – including its relation to the structure of specific discourses. The alternative, which surrounds us, is the discussion of grammaticality in a discourse vacuum – in a climate in which sentences are supposed to be meaningful, but are treated as detached from the very encounter of man with man which can alone provide the test for impact and meaning.

Perhaps, then, it is worth stopping for a moment to see an emotional situation in which richer analogues of meaning and form are being divorced via divorce of soul from body:

DEATH THE ABSTRACTOR

Mark 15:34

Hurt revulsion
  sees naked spirit
    stripped from body
    in Gnostic split
  abstracting Son-of-Man
    from AM-ALL.

Point of view inverts
  God-perspective
    ("Well pleased, Son,
    linked into Eternity of Light")
  to man-perspective
    ("Why disconnect me –
    broken, dark?").

LIFE concretes
  Light
    in resurrected flesh.

University of Michigan

NOTES

[1]   *Mark My Words*, Grand Rapids, Eerdman's, 1971. See pages 115-16.
[2]   Compare the alternative narration of the same event in Matthew 27:45-46, which includes this datum.

'PHONEMIC OVERLAPPING AND REPULSION' REVISITED

REBECCA POSNER

Why should I be 'revisiting' these phenomena at this point of time? It is not, I think, that I have changed my mind about the subject since it came to my attention as a graduate student tussling with that so-'random' sound change process 'dissimilation' (Posner 1961). What, helped then to crystallize my views was an elegant and lucid article of Archibald Hill's (Hill 1936, already at that time some 25 yeard old but for me, timeless). So my reconsideration of the problem is prbmpted by the opportunity to pay hommage to a scholar to whom I owed enlightenment, even though, for me, he remained 'disembodied' for many years. Even if I misunderstood his position, or if he has changed' it l must express my gratitude to him for guiding my thoughts about the contribution of phoneme theory to consideration of sound change.

Recent furore concerning the phoneme (particularly Chomsky 1964, Vachek 1964, Householder 1965, Chomsky and Halle 1965, Postal 1968, Sampson 1970, Schane 1971) leaves many of us wondering what all the song and dance is about. Is the issue that segmentation is invalid – an idea familiar to British linguists versed in Firthian theory (cf. Palmer 1970) – but apparently denied by Postal's 'Naturalness Condition'? Or is it that distinctive features do not come in 'readipaks' – 'bundles' in Trubetzkoyan terminology – or that phonemes are not 'real' (in whatever sense)? Sampson 1970 demonstrates that tendency towards symmetry hints that contrastive phonological units – however 'superficial' – have some degree of autonomy; Schane 1971 does the same for historical processes. What it all seems to come down to, then, is the (surely) metalinguistic question of whether in a Chomskyan grammar the phonemic level is superfluous, in that it does not aid formulation of certain 'significant generalizations'. If morphophonological variiaton is accorded the importance it has in such a grammar, then 'autonomous phonemics' does indeed seem out of place. The clever polemics of Chomsky and Halle 1965, putting the burden of proof on to the defenders of the phoneme, obviously threw these into disarray: the issue has remained so confused that even when the phoneme is reinstated (albeit as a 'bastard', to quote Schane 1971:520) no-one knows quite what to use it for.

Chomsky's most cogent attacks on 'phonemics' ('taxonomic' as he calls it) deride the procedural principles he claims underly the theory: one of these is 'invariance' – implying that the 'same sound' will always be interpreted as a member of the same phoneme. Thereby can be precluded 'complete overlapping' as defined by Bloch 1941 (quoted with apparent approval by Hill 1955, whose clear formulation makes him a target for Postal's jibes[1]). However, insistence on 'invariance' (and indeed on 'linearity' and 'biuniqueness'[2]) is an extreme position avoided by many phonemicists: 'archiphonemic' (Prague-school) phonemics, of course, accepts overlapping as an essential feature of the sound system.[3] Even within 'classical' phonemics, some degree of confusion (perhaps via Hockett's (1965) 'random drift', or socio-dialectal contacts) is usually regarded as inevitable in practice. Chomsky and Halle 1965:131 may sneer at Vachek's (1964:417) appeal to a 'state of flux' but language as she is spoke (mere performance?) is always in such a state (cf. Hill 1958:59-61).

Hill 1936, in discussing the doublet *porridge/pottage*, envisaged a 'state of flux' in which overlapping of the intervocalic allophones of the /r/ and /t/ phonemes threatened; but reaction led to withdrawal towards a central 'target' area of the phoneme. Such 'phonemic repulsion' suggests that the 'target' has some sort of reality (mental?) and that distinctions accidentally lost can be recovered and emphasized in certain conditions.[4] Hill 1936:21-2 speaks of "selection by speakers of variants which offer less overlapping and so tend to increase the distance between the phonemes rather than to lessen or eradicate it"; and goes on to say:

The selection of those phones within a given phoneme which offer least likelihood of confusion may often spring from a necessity for clearness which has too often been ruled out of court by students of language.

Doublets like *porridge/pottage* are often indicative of such conflicts at some time in the past. I wish here to discuss two well-known examples from French both dating from the 'transitional' period known often as Middle French; the first is exemplified by the suffixes of *chinois* 'Chinese', and *japonais* 'Japanese', both derived from Latin suffix *-ēnse*; the second by *chaire* 'professorial, etc. chair' and *chaise* 'chair' (for sitting on), both derived from Graeco-Latin *cathedra*.

1) *-ais/-ois*: [e] or [ɛ]/[wa]

By the 15th century in Parisian French, there were probably only two complex vowel nuclei (former diphthongs *ue* and *eu*, for example, having been reduced to [ø]). These were [je] *ie* (principally from Latin tonic free *ĕ*) and [we] *oi* (principally from Latin tonic free *ē*). In most positions these were in contrast with [e] (from OFr. diphthong *ai*, Latin tonic blocked *ĕ* and *ē*, Latin tonic free *a* etc.), with which, by this period, they can rhyme (Villon *remiré* : *mueray*; *telles*: *toiles*; *chiere*: *machouere*; cf. Pope 1934:186-7, 192). Examples in which the contrast is used include *père/pierre/poire* (but see below for the *r/rr* contrast), *mette/miette*, etc. However, after a palatal consonant there appears to have been overlapping of /je/ and /e/ by this period (Pope 1934:192-3); after a labial there was also a tendency for /we/ and /e/ to overlap.[5] Moreover neither [we] nor [je] seems to have occurred before [ʎ] or [ɲ],[6] and sequences [jwe] and [wje] were avoided, where not impossible (Fouché 1958:276). The distribution of /je/ and /we/ thus suggests that the palatal and labial element may have been more like a Firthian prosodic feature than a segment: certainly the partial complementarity of both with each other and with /e/ points to neutralisable oppositions involving the features ⟨± palatal⟩ and ⟨± labial⟩.

In most of northern France outside the Parisian area /we/ and /e/ were regularly merged as /e/ before this period (Fouché 1958:274-5): indeed the West had probably never known the distinction[7] (Fouché 1958:271). By the 16th century the merger had affected popular Parisian speech, to the general disgust of grammarians, who often attributed the 'lax' pronunciation to the influence of detested Italian courtiers (Pope 1934: 196). Whether it was the pressure exerted by the arbiters of correctness, or the fear of excessive homonymy that was responsible for the inconsistent[8] reimposition of the [we] pronunciation is impossible to tell: probably both worked together. The *-ois/-ais* doublet cited above is a left-over from the period of hesitation[9].

When /we/ was reimposed, popular speech probably favoured a variant [wɑ], attested already at the end of the 13th century and widespread in the 15th (Fouché 1958:272); confusion with /e/ became thus less likely, and the phoneme was drawn into the /ɑ/ orbit, where there was probably less risk of homonymic confusion.[10] The socially superior pronunciation remained [wɛ]/[we] till the Revolution when [wa]/[wɑ] became accepted.[11]

2) *chaire/chaise*[12]: [R]/[z]

Old French knew no distinction between geminate and single ('long' vs. 'short', or 'strong' vs. 'weak') consonants, except apparently in the case of *rr* vs. *r* in intervocalic position. The few reflexes of Latin *-rr-* (e.g. *terre*) were supplemented by continuators of VLat intervocalic clusters *-tr-, -dr-* (> [ðr] > [rr]); though in conditions that are not wholly clear. [rr] seems to have simplified to [r]. Indeed *rr* and *r* from these sources may have been in complementary distribution, with the length of the preceding vowel determining the choice of phone in Old French:[13]

V:		V		*père*	*verra*
ei	} r	ie	} rr	*creire*	*pierre*
ai		ue		*gaire*	*fuerre*
				(mod. *guère*)	

We may assume that in Old French the 'strong' vs. 'weak' *rr/r* distinction was realized phonetically as rolled vs. flapped articulation. In non-intervocalic positions the distinction was neutralized, with the 'strong' form used in initial-of-word position and the 'weak' elsewhere (as in Castilian today). From the 12th century onwards we have evidence of confusion of *rr* and *r* even in intervocalic position (Fouché 1966:862-3): 16th century grammarians bewailed the fact that the distinction was no longer being made and sought to impose it in 'correct' usage. Nevertheless by the end of the 17th century complete merger appears to have won the day: even Boileau rhymes *terre* with *chaire*.

In vulgar Parisian speech of the 15th century, however, the distinction must still have been alive, for intervocalic single *r*, but not *rr*, is often represented graphically as *z* or *s* (*Pazys* or *Pasys* for *Paris*, etc.). The fricative pronunciation, much ridiculed by socially superior speakers, was probably apico-alveolar and possibly was not confined to intervocalic position.[24] The margin between the apico-alveolar allophone of /r/ and the dorso-alveolar fricative /z/[15] was so slight as to allow 'phonemic attraction'. The number of words permanently affected was small: besides *chaise, bésicles* and *nasiller* are usually cited, in the development of which dissimilation may have played some part.[16] Some morphophonological use is also made of the [r]/[z] distinction: cf. *menteur/menteuse, vendeur/vendeuse*, in which, after assimilation to the *heureux/heureuse* type of alternation, the delinquescent final *-r* of the masculine forms was reimposed on correct usage.

The dismay of the grammarians at the threatened [r] > [z] change possibly played some part in determining speakers' reaction against a process that would have resulted in a large new batch of homonyms. The reaction would very likely take the form of emphasizing 'r-like' features of the threatened phones, resulting eventually in confusion with strong *rr* (less dangerous as the 'functional load'[17] of the *r/rr* distinction was comparatively small).

What is particularly interesting is that with the 'strengthening' of *r* a new pronunciation made its appearance among the Parisian bourgeoisie: characterized as *'grasseyé'*, implying palatal articulation, during the 17th century, it became the uvular [R] that was eventually accepted as correct after the Revolution. Elsewhere in Romance – notably in Occitan and Brazilian Portuguese – a non-apical *r* can be a reflex of older *rr*, contrasting with *r* in intervocalic position:

> Arles *sero* [seːro] 'evening' / *serro* [sɛːRo] 'saw';
> Brazil *caro* [kaɾu] 'dear' / *carro* [kaʁu] 'cart'.[18]

Thus it seems not unlikely that a (doomed) attempt to maintain the *rr/r* distinction was accompanied by emphasized differentiation of pronunciation, in certain types of speech. A palato-velar dorsal pronunciation of the 'strong' member of the pair may have been encouraged by the existence, at the time, of two other similar pairs – /ʎ/ v. /l/ and /ɲ/ v. /n/ – which might be characterized as 'strong' vs. 'weak' (note that, in Castilian, Latin geminates -*ll*- and -*nn*- > [ʎ] and [ɲ]). So for a brief period the pair '*r grasseyé*' vs. 'apical *r*' may have formed part of the same micro-system. However, by the end of the 17th century, the Parisian bourgeoisie had ceased to use [ʎ] (> [j], a change not accepted as correct until after the Revolution), as well as apical *r*, leaving /ɲ/ v. /n/ (*agneau* v. *anneau*, etc.) as an isolated contrast.[19]

The examples of 'phonemic repulsion' I have discussed illustrate the contention, pugnaciously argued by Postal 1968, but many years before advanced by Hill 1936, that some types of sound-change are 'mentalistic' not 'mechanical', 'sudden' not 'gradual' in their operation – but also that sociolinguistic factors may sometimes over-ride internal linguistic processes. I am drawn towards the conclusion that 'phonemes' – 'bundles' of features – have some sort of reality for speakers (especially literate ones?) who are able in a few cases to react against 'drift', in Hockett's sense, by emphasizing the central characteristics of the 'bundle', even at the expense of some peripheral features. But perhaps here I am flogging a dead horse: disagreement on the 'phoneme' question may be more terminological and methodological than substantial – whether we

describe our 'bundles' as 'phonemes', or 'local frequency maxima'
(Hockett 1965:194-5) or as 'elements of the discrete code of articulatory
instructions transmitted from the nervous system to the articulatory
apparatus' (Postal 1968:292) or as 'sets'.[20]

University of York

NOTES

[1]   Postal 1968:224 quotes the article as reprinted in Allen 1958. Professor Hill could
himself tell us if his sympathetic mention of Bloch's compelling argument implied
that he himself agreed with it: certainly a few years later (Hill 1958:51-3) he suggests
that some degree of overlapping is inevitable, though he states as a procedural principle "the statement of phonemic patterning should in rigorous method involve a
minimum of overlapping rather than a maximum". Hill's undogmatic attitude is
exemplified by his recognition that "there is no uniquely right answer in scientific
analysis" and by his references (Hill 1958:59-61) to the sort of 'irregularities' in
language that allow for change.
[2]   Literal 'biuniqueness', Chomsky seems to admit, was almost never a requirement,
except perhaps in the weaker form Chomsky calls 'local determinacy'.
[3]   The attitude of generative phonologists to 'archiphonemic' phonology is not clear
to me, though Schane 1971 refers to some unpublished works by younger generativists
which appear to be sympathetic. Postal 1968:226 calls complete overlapping 'neutralization', but this is possibly different from the Trubetzkoyan variety. When I once
suggested (CA review 1968:132) that Chomsky's objections to phonemics might be in
some way met by Trubetzkoyan neutralization, he retorted (CA review 1968:167)
that the concept had 'no relevance' and that he had discussed it in detail in Chomsky
1964:196, Section IV. I can find no such reference there, however: it is possible he is
referring to the pagination (96-7) of the version of his work printed in Fodor and
Katz 1964, where he cites an example from the *Grungdzüge* [sic]. The page reference
to the Cantineau translation (46) is obviously wrong: on p. 64 of that work (Troubetskoy 1949) the example Chomsky gives is discussed, but it has to do not with 'neutralization', but with 'linearity'. Incidentally, even among adherents of Prague school
phonology there is some measure of disagreement about the scope of neutralization.
Vachek 1964:425, for instance, suggests that in Bloch's 'partial overlapping' example
throw/Betty the phonetic identity of *r* and *tt* as [D] cannot be explained in terms of
neutralization because it is not only "contrary to the laws of the phonological structure
of English (there is no positive phonematic basis common to the two phonemes) but
also to the laws of its morphology and morphonology (there is no morphological
alternation in English of the type [θ D]:[θ Vt] and the like). Thus the phonic identity
of the [D] sounds in *throw* and *writer*, *Betty*, etc. must necessarily appear as overlapping
of the phonemes /t/ and /r/." I do not follow Vachek's argument: in Trubetzkoyan
terms the opposition /r/ v. /t/ may not be '*neutralisable*' in that it is not bilateral
(Troubetskoy 1949:80-1), but where (as in Hill's dialect: Hill 1958:46) the /t/ vs.
/d/ opposition – e.g. in *latter/ladder* – is one of 'time' not 'voice' or 'tenseness', either
/t/ or /d/ might be in bilateral, privative opposition with /r/ ($<\pm$ occlusion$>$?).
Martinet 1960:71 covers such cases by referring to 'partial complementarity', as
a help towards specifying distinctive features. I know of nothing in Vachek's own
work which would go counter to this, though Vachek 1960 quotes Trnka as distinguish-

ing 'apparent neutralization' from 'simple non-existence': perhaps it is that /t/ simply doesn't exist after /θ/?

4 It is well known that English speakers who never normally use a rolled *r* will sometimes do so for emphasis, especially in response to questions like 'Did you say *reap* or *leap*?' or '... *correct* or *collect*?'.

5 The very frequent change of *e* to [we] following a labial consonant (e.g. *aboie* for *abaie, armoire* for *armaire, poêle* for both *paile* < *pallium* and *paele* < *patella* etc. Cf. Fouché 1958:376-7) suggests overlapping in this position. Perhaps the unexplained OFr. *aller* forms, *vois* and *voise* (replaced in the 16th century by *vais and aille*), owe something to the same process [vwe] < [ve] < [vai] < *vadeo*; the dual outcome of [we] allowed differentiation of *je vais* 'I go' and *je vois* 'I see', after the Middle French period.

6 The *-oign-* sequences of modern French were pronounced [oɲ] before the 17th century (cf. Pope 1934:178 on *éloigner* etc.) Today *oignon* 'onion' is still pronounced [ɔɲɔ̃] in correct usage.

7 In the West [ei] > [e] not [oi]; in the same region [ie] was reduced to [e] from the 12th century on (Fouché 1958:267).

8 In the imperfect endings of the verbs, of course, [e]/[ɛ] remained correct (the spelling *-ais, -ait* etc. being accepted on Voltaire's recommendation): possibly the influence of verbs with stems terminating in [j] – like *voyait* etc. – was responsible. In a large number of other cases (cf. Fouché 1958:274) no single explanation can be found for the retention of [e], though individual cases can be explained in terms of analogy and so on. Some of the [e] forms accepted by grammarians did not survive (notably some in which [e] was preceded by a labial consonant: *moisson, poilu, poirier, voiture, voie*). A few doublets survived for some time as stylistic variants: of these *roide* and *harnois* remain as archaisms for *raide* and *harnais*.

9 A possible explanation of the distribution of *-ois* and *-ais* might be that [we] was reduced in more frequently used forms (with e.g. *japonais* modelled on *lyonnais* etc. and modern forms like *sénégalais* formed when the alternation was no longer active). For discussion of names of inhabitants of regions within France see Fouché 1958:278.

10 The timbre of the second element of /wɑ/ varies in much the same way as that of *a*: however, the /ɑ/ vs. /a/ (or /a:/ vs. /a/) distinction (*pâte/patte*) of certain conservative types of speech is apparently not reflected in /wɑ/, which today is most frequently pronounced [wa] (though sometimes *croit, boit* [wa] are distinguished from *croix, bois* [wɑ]). We might plausibly suggest the 16th century pronunciation was nearer [wɑ:] – possibly even with a labialized back *a* used in popular Parisian today. Contemporary attempts at orthography (e.g. *oâ*) support the suggestion. Since the 16th century, vowel length, and tense vs. lax character, is largely determined by phonetic environment, in Parisian French.

11 Pairs like *moi/ma, toi/ta, soi/sa* may be seen to be morphologically determined (but see also *mais, taie* [OFr. *toie*], *ses*). Otherwise we may note *pare/poire* (also *père*), *moite* (for earlier *moide*) / *mate* (also *mette*); *poisse* (in substandard usage) / *passe*. Note also such pronunciations as [mwal] for *moelle*, earlier *meolle*, and popular Parisian, now obsolete, [fwɑ] for *fouet*.

12 Martinet 1962 brilliantly sketched an explanation of this double development in terms of phonemic repulsion. Here I develop his argument, with some modifications and additions.

13 The interaction of our two chosen examples can be seen in the early reduction of [we] to [e] with consequent doubling of *rr* in *veire* > *verre, tonneire* > *tonnerre, eire* > *erre*. It is to be noted that some types of speech today differentiate the vowel, [ɑ] v. [a], of *mari/marri, parage/parrage*.

14 The 'weakness' of *r* in preconsonantal implosive position is well-documented, and *s* was sometimes substituted for it in orthography (and vice-versa: Fouché 1966:862-3).

[15] Martinet 1969:141 assumes that [z] was dorsoalveolar as for most French speakers today. Although the similar English sound is described as dorso-alveolar by most phoneticians, some dialects (including my own) use an apico-alveolar. I have also detected a similar pronunciation among French (admittedly non-Parisian) speakers.
[16] The r of OFr. *beril* and *nariller* may have been dissimilated by the following lateral. It is suggested that the single r of reflexes of *cathedra* also results from dissimilation at the stage [ʃaðeðrə] > [ʃaðerə]: conceivably *chaire* could continue undissimilated [ʃaerrə] while *chaise* represents [ʃaerə]. However, I am dubious about the possibility of dissimilation of this sort.
[17] I remain unconvinced by the attack on the concept of 'functional load' in King 1967; cf. also Meyerstein 1970.
[18] For distribution of [ʁ] and [ɾ] in Brazilian Portuguese cf. Brasington 1971:156.
[19] In certain types of speech [ɲ] is pronounced as [nj]; unit phonemic status of /ɲ/ may consequently be lost.
[20] Chomsky and Halle 1965:136: "the speaker's set is largely a matter of his knowledge of the language and this may (in fact surely does) lead him to make perceptual judgments that are not simply related to physical fact."

REFERENCES

Allen, Harold B., ed. 1958. Readings in applied English linguistics. New York: Appleton Century-Crofts.
Bloch, Bernard. 1941. Phonemic overlapping. American Speech 16.278-84.
Brasington, R. W. P. 1971. Noun pluralization in Brazilian Portuguese. JLi. 7.151-77.
CA review. 1968. Review of Current trends in linguistics, Vol. iii: Theoretical Foundations, ed. by T. A. Sebeok. Current Anthropology 9.125-79.
Chomsky, Noam A. 1964. Current issues in linguistic theory. The Hague: Mouton.
Chomsky, Noam A., and Halle, Morris. 1965. Some controversial questions in phonological theory. JLi. 2.97-138.
Fodor, Jerry A., and Katz, Jerrold J., eds. 1964. The structure of language. Englewood Cliffs, N. J.: Prentice-Hall, Inc.
Fouché, Pierre. 1958. Phonétique historique du français, Vol. 2: Les voyelles. Paris: Klincksieck.
—. 1966. Phonétique historique du français, Vol. 3: Les consonnes. 2nd ed. Paris: Klincksieck.
Hill, Archibald A. 1936. Phonetic and phonemic change. Lg. 12.15-22.
—. 1955. Linguistics since Bloomfield. Quarterly Journal of Speech 41.253-60. Reprinted in Allen 1958.14-27.
—. 1958. Introduction to linguistic structures. New York: Harcourt, Brace and Co.
Hockett, Charles F. 1965. Sound Change. Lg. 41.185-205.
Householder, Fred W. 1965. On some recent claims in phonological theory. JLi. 1.13-34.
King, Robert D. 1967. Functional load and sound change. Lg. 43.831-52.
Martinet, André. 1960. Éléments de linguistique générale. Paris: Colin.
—. 1962. R du Latin au français d'aujourd'hui'. Phonetica 8.193-202. Reprinted in Martinet 1969.
—. 1969. Le français sans fard. Paris: P. U. F.
Meyerstein, R. S. 1970. Functional load. The Hague: Mouton.
Palmer, F. R., ed. 1970. Prosodic analysis. Oxford: University Press.
Pope, Mildred. 1934. From Latin to modern French. Manchester: University Press.
Posner, Rebecca. 1961. Consonantal dissimilation in the Romance languages. Oxford: Blackwell.

Postal, Paul. 1970. Aspects of phonological theory. New York: Harper and Row.
Sampson, Geoffrey. 1970. On the need for a phonological base. Lg. 46.586-626.
Schane, Sandford A. 1971. The phoneme revisited. Lg. 47.503-21.
Troubetskoy, Nicolas S. 1949. Principles de phonologie, tr. by J. Cantineau. Paris:
    Klincksieck.
Vachek, J. 1960. Dictionnaire de linguistique de l'École de Prague. Utrecht-Anvers:
    Spectrum.
—. 1964. On some basic principles of 'classical' phonology. Z. für Phon. 17.409-31.

AN EXCLUDED GENERALIZATION

GARY D. PRIDEAUX

It has been argued by Chomsky (1964:62, 1965:27) and others that a generative grammar for a particular language should be constructed so that it captures the linguistically significant generalizations of the language and thereby characterizes the competence of the native speaker. The notion of linguistic competence has been subjected to critical examination by several scholars (e.g. Fodor and Garrett 1966, Gleitman and Gleitman 1970, Derwing 1973), while the issue of just what constitutes the significant generalizations of a language has been addressed by Garcia (1967) and Leech (1968). In a recent paper (Prideaux 1971), I have discussed the methodological criteria by which linguists seem to judge whether or not a particular analysis has captured linguistically significant generalizations. The three criteria which must be satisfied by such an analysis are (i) that observational adequacy is met, (ii) that the rules must be conflatable by some generally accepted notational conventions, and (iii) that (at least some of) the rules must be independently motivated. It was further argued that the criteria are formal rather than empirical.[1] Consequently when such an analysis is formulated, there is no justification for the claim that it is a description of the native speaker's competence (in the sense of Chomsky 1965), and not simply a neat, compact statement of the combinatorial possibilities in the utterance types under consideration.

In the present paper we will examine a particular problem from Japanese, outlining three alternative formulations for the description of the adjective. First we will review two familiar analyses, and then we will propose a third formulation which can be shown to capture a linguistically significant generalization in terms of the criteria mentioned above – a generalization not captured by the first two analyses. Arguments will then be presented to the effect that such an analysis, while perhaps reflecting some part of the historical development of the adjective, must be excluded from a synchronic grammar of Japanese.

1. In modern colloquial Japanese both the verb and the adjective are generally treated as inflected categories since both are marked for tense as well as for several other grammatical properties. We have the following (partial) paradigm for the verb (for complete verb and adjective paradigms see Jordan 1963, Part 2:364-6):

(1)   Stem   (a) *tabe-*'eat'   (b) *kak-*'write'
       Present   *taberu*   *kaku*
       Past   *tabeta*   *kaita*
       Tentative   *tabeyoo*   *kakoo*

       (c) *mat-*'wait'   (d) *ar-*'be'
           matu   *aru*
           matta   *atta*
           matoo   *aroo*

In this paradigm there is no adverbial form of the verb. For the adjective we have:

(2)   Stem   (a) *taka-*'tall'   (b) *samu-*'cold' (c) *ooki-*'big'
       Present   *takai*   *samui*   *ookii*
       Past   *takakatta*   *samukatta*   *ookikatta*
       Adverbial   *takaku*   *samuku*   *ookiku*
       Tentative   *takakaroo*   *samukaroo*   *ookikaroo*

Jordan (1963, Part 1:18) treats the adjectives and the verbs as two distinct lexical categories. However, since verbs and adjectives participate in almost identical paradigms and since there are no other inflected forms in the language, it is tempting to claim that the verb and the adjective are best treated as subclasses of the same lexical category. Thus we have the two rather common analyses: (i) verbs and adjectives constitute distinct lexical categories, and (ii) verbs and adjectives are subclasses of the same lexical category. In order to decide which is the better analysis, it is relevant to notice just how verbs and adjectives are alike and how they differ. They are alike in the following ways: (a) Both are inflected for tense as well as for other grammatical properties. (b) Both have similar selectional restrictions such that, for example, only certain nouns are acceptable as subjects for certain verbs and adjectives. Thus we may have *inu wa tabeta* 'the dog ate' (literally, 'dog subject-marker (SM) ate'), and *teñki wa samui* 'the weather is cold' (weather SM cold'), but not *isi wa tabeta '*the rock ate' ('rock SM ate') or *siñri wa samui '*the truth is cold' ('truth SM cold'). (c) Both adjectives and verbs occupy the same syntactic positions in sentences (sentence-final position), and both function alike within relative clauses. For example we have *kare ga tabeta gohañ* 'the rice which he ate' ('he SM ate rice') and *samui otya* 'tea which is cold' ('cold tea'). (d) Although the adjective can be used in sentences without the support of the copula, both adjectives and verbs can be made polite in sentence-final position by the addition of a politeness morpheme, which for the adjective is the polite form of the copula *desu*. For example, we can have polite expressions containing an adjective, such as *teñki wa samui desu* 'the weather is cold' as well as polite expressions containing a verb (see Rule 8 below for examples).

The verb and the adjective differ in the following ways: (a) The phonological shapes of the suffixes are different. For the verb the present-tense suffix is *-ru* (or *-u* after a consonantal stem) and the past-tense suffix is *-ta*. For the adjective the present-tense suffix is *-i* and the past-tense suffix is *-katta*. (b) The verb may enter into aspectual, causative, and passive formations, while the adjective cannot. Thus we can have *kaite iru* 'is writing', *kakaseru* 'cause to write', and *kakareru* 'be written'. On the other hand, only the adjective may exist in the adverbial form, such as *samuku* 'coldly'.

In light of the great overlapping in the two paradigms and in light of the similarities outlined above, it would appear that the preferred solution would be to treat the verb and the adjective as subclasses of a single lexical category and state the selectional restrictions, tense assignment, etc. only once. The phonological differences in the shape of suffixes and the restrictions on participation in certain constructions would then have to be stated in terms of subclass memberships. The decision to treat verbs and adjectives as sublcasses of a single lexical category is then made in terms of overall economy of description.[2]

2. However, a third analysis is possible, and within this analysis we shall find a potential explanation for some of the pecularities of the adjective-suffix shapes. In the adjective paradigm one thing which stands out is the reappearance of *-k* in the suffixes for the past tense (*-katta*), adverbial (*-ku*) and tentative (*-karoo*). Only in the present tense is the *k* absent. In both of the formulations outlined above, the stem of the adjective is taken to be the present-tense form minus the final *-i*. Thus the stem for 'cold' is usually established as *samu-*. Japanese is, however, interesting in that no word may end with a consonant other than the syllabic nasal *ñ*. Thus we can have *hoñ* 'book' but not **samuk*. A general rule can be proposed which adds *i* to consonant-final words:

(3)　　$\emptyset \rightarrow i \mid C\underline{}\#$ (where $C \neq \bar{n}$)

This rule is probably best treated as part of a more general one which inserts i not only in word-final position but also in stem-final position before certain suffixes. For example, the stem for 'write' is *kak-* and the past-tense morpheme shape is *-ta*. Thus the underlying representation for 'wrote' is *kak+ta*. The i insertion rule may be formulated as:

(4)　　$\emptyset \rightarrow i \mid \begin{bmatrix} C \\ -\text{nas} \end{bmatrix} \underline{} + C$ (where the two C's are different).

Clearly 3 and 4 can be conflated into a single rule as:

(5)　　$\emptyset \rightarrow i \mid C \underline{} \begin{Bmatrix} \# \\ +C \end{Bmatrix}$ (with appropriate conditions on the C's).

However, in all verb stems with a final velar, the velar is deleted in certain cases in which the i has been added. The velar deletion rule may be formulated as:

(6)　　$\begin{Bmatrix} k \\ g \end{Bmatrix} \rightarrow \emptyset \mid \underline{} i) + $
　　　　　　　　　　　　stem

Thus the derivation for 'wrote' is *kak+ta* › (by 5) *kak+ta* → (by 6) *kai+ta* = /kaita/.

Rules 5 and 6 are needed within the grammar in order to handle the verb morphology. It is consequently tempting to look again at the adjective situation. Suppose that the k of all the adjective suffixes is really a part of the stem and not of the suffixes. That is, suppose that the stem form of adjectives is not vowel-final but rather k-final, and that the k is analyzed as the adjective marker. If we make this assumption, we immediately notice that the present-tense form of the adjective can be handled directly. The underlying form of the stem for 'cold' is now *samuk-* and there is no present tense suffix at all. If we then apply Rules 5 and 6 to *samuk-* we obtain the following derivation: *samuk* → (by 5) *samuki* → (by 6) *samui* = /samui/. The claim made by the analysis is that the present-tense form of the adjective really has no tense marker at all, and the final i is phonologically introduced via independently-motivated rules.

If we now turn to the other forms of the adjectives and treat the k as part of the stem we have the following parsings:

(7)　　Past　　　　　　*samuk + atta*
　　　　Adverbial　　　*samuk + u*
　　　　Tentative　　　*samuk + aroo*

Immediately we notice that *atta* is identical to the past-tense form of the existential verb *ar-* 'be', and the *aroo* is identical to the tentative form of *ar-*. The *u* of the adverbial has no analogue in the verb paradigm simply because verbs may not exist in such a form. With the exception of the adverbial form, we may conclude that the various forms of the adjective are really instances of the adjective stem with final *k* plus inflected forms of *ar-*. We are then led to the underlying form of the past tense of 'cold' as *samuk + ar + ta* (with the general and independently-motivated rule for geminating the *r* to the following *t*). The unmarked present tense of the adjective also involves the deletion of *aru* when an adjective precedes.

There is historical evidence that the adjective in the present-tense form did at one time have a stem-final *k*, and in fact it still does in the literary form.[3] The historical evidence is discussed by Sansom (1928:90, also in Chapter IV). Chamberlain (1907:121ff.) notes that the form with stem-final *k* was a historical stage through which the language passed.

The above analysis does indeed capture a linguistically significant generalization in terms of the criteria outlined above since (i) it provides observational adequacy; (ii) certain of the rules (the *i* epenthesis rules) can be conflated; and (iii) all of the rules used in the adjective derivations are independently motivated. In addition, the analysis claims that verbs and adjectives are in fact not members of the same category, and that rather only the true verbs are inflected (including the verb *ar-*).

3. While the analysis presented above satisfies the formal criteria for capturing a linguistically significant generalization, it must nevertheless be excluded from a synchronic grammar of Japanese. Challanges to the plausibility of the analysis and reasons for its exclusion are presented below.

3.1 The strongest argument that could be raised against the analysis is that it simply does not work. However, almost any analysis can be salvaged by clever manipulation of various rules. We will see that while the analysis, in a slightly modified form, does indeed work, it must be rather tightly constrained. In particular, the viability of Rule 6 must be called into question. This rule implies that stem-final velars are deleted when followed by *i* and a morpheme or word boundary. While the rule works for the adjective, there is ample evidence that it must be further constrained, since within the language, even within the verb forms, we do have retention of the final velar in certain instances. For example,

in addition to the forms cited in 1 we have the polite forms of the verbs
as follows:

(8)   Stem   *tabe-*   *kak-*   *mat-*   *ar-*
       Present Polite   *tabemasu* *kakimasu* *matimasu* *arimasu*
       Past Polite   *tabemasita* *kakimasita* *matimasita* *arimasita*

These forms may be analyzed as stem + *(i)mas* + tense, where *(i)mas*
is the phonological spelling of the politeness morpheme. Regardless
of whether the initial *i* of the politeness morpheme is present in the
underlying representation or whether it is introduced by a rule such as
5, our current formulation of 6 would indicate that for velar-final stems
such as *kak-* we would expect **kaimasu* instead of *kakimasu*. Since this
is not the case, we must further limit 6 so that it does not operate across
all morpheme boundaries, but only across the boundary between a stem
and a tense suffix (as in *kaki* + *ta*), or between a stem and the phonologically added *i* (as in *samuki*). However, even this is not good enough,
since in Japanese we find nouns with a final velar plus *i*, as in *ki* 'tree'
and *kaki* 'persimmon'. We also find verbs within the honorific paradigm without deletion of the velar, as in *okaki ni narimasu* 'write'. It can
be argued that within such honorific forms we really have a paraphrastic
construction containing a nominalization of the verb (*okaki* in this
instance). If so, Rule 6 can be modified as:

(9) $\begin{Bmatrix} k \\ g \end{Bmatrix} \rightarrow \emptyset \ / \ \underset{V, A}{\_\_\_} \ i) \ \begin{Bmatrix} + ta) \\ \text{tense} \\ \# \end{Bmatrix}$

Thus by positing a stem-final *k* in the adjectives, the adjective derivation
catches a free ride (in the sense of Zwicky 1970) on Rules 5 and 9.
But for the ride to be truly free, 9 must be limited as described above.
Furthermore, Rule 9 now allows velar deletion in two kinds of environments, one paradigmatic and the other phonological. There is nothing
within the abbreviatory conventions which prevents the conflation of
rules with different functions into a single rule.[4]

The analysis can be saved, but in its modified form much of its initial
plausibility and appeal vanishes, especially in light of the general im-
plausibility of the free-ride principle, as pointed out by Zwicky (1970).
With such a loss the claim that a significant generalization has been
captured is open to serious question.

3.2 A second objection to the analysis can be formulated in terms of the
disparity between the purported underlying form of the adjective with
a final *k* and the surface canonical patterns of Japanese which do not

allow such word-final consonants. Hale (1973), in exploring problems dealing with differences between deep and surface canonical forms, suggested, then withdrew as being too strong, a general constraint which disallows any such disparity. However, he argues that, in general, there appears to be a tendency to minimize "the necessity to postulate underlying phonological representations of morphemes which violate the universal surface canonical patterns of the language". He concludes that "it would be incorrect to impose a completely general constraint disallowing deep-surface canonical disparities. ... If such a constraint exists, it must be limited in ways which are not yet clear." If we adopted the strong form of the constraint, we could not have underlying representations of morphemes with final consonants. This would mean that such verb stems as *mat-*, *kak-*, etc., would be disallowed along with the adjective stems such as *samuk-*. Perhaps one kind of limitation that Hale is seeking might be along the following lines. In order for an underlying representation which violates a surface canonical pattern to be postulated, there must be surface alternations such that at least one of the alternates contains the underlying form non-ambiguously.[5] In the case of the consonant-final verb stems, there are many instances in which the stem form is either present or uniquely recoverable. In the forms listed in 1c, for example, *mat-* always represents the stem, while *-u* and *-ta* are the present and past suffixes. To see that this is the case, we need only parse *matu* as *ma+tu* and do likewise for all the consonant-final stems. We would then be faced with a host of allomorphs for the present tense morpheme (e.g. *-tu*, *-ku*, *-ru*, *-bu*, *-mu*, *-nu*, etc.) each of which would be associated with a specific class of verbs. This would be an extreme example of what Hale calls the 'conjugation analysis'. If we took such a step we would find that the other suffixes would exhibit a similar proliferation of allomorphs. The tentative suffix, for example, would have the allomorphs *-too*, *-koo*, *-roo*, *-boo*, *-moo*, *-noo*, etc. The important point is that the allomorphs from a variety of different morphemes, all with the same initial consonant, would cooccur with exactly the same verb classes. That is, *-tu* and *-too* would be associated with the class containing *ma-*, while *-ku* and *-koo* would go with the class containing *ka-*, etc. Following Hale's arguments, one result of such an analysis, were it correct, would be that successive generations of Japanese speakers would tend to lose the linkage between the particular verb classes and the appropriate allomorphs. That is, we might expect to hear **mabu* for *matu*, etc. But nothing of the sort has occurred in Japanese as it appears to have in Hale's Maori passive examples. In the Japanese case, the presence of the same consonant in a host of instances within the same paradigm tends to strengthen the analysis in which the final consonant is part of the verb stem.

For the adjectives, however, the situation is not the same. In the colloquial language the final *k* never appears in the present form of the adjective. If we posit a stem-final *k* for all adjectives it must always be deleted in the present-tense forms. If, on the other hand, we allow the surface canonical patterns to determine the shape of the adjective stems, we are left with just those stems as cited in 2. Furthermore, such stems appear overtly in every instance of the paradigm. In such an analysis the overt *k* within the past tense, adverbial, and tentative forms is assigned to the suffixes and not to the stem. However, nothing at all is lost by such an assignment since only one segment *k* is involved and it appears in specific places in the paradigm of all adjectives. There is, in the adjective situation, no proliferation of allomorphs as was the case in the conjugation analysis which we examined and rejected for the verbs. Furthermore, if we establish the stems as in 2, rather than as in 7, we do not need to exploit the independently-motivated rule of velar deletion at all – it is only excess baggage since the suffixes for the adjectives contain the velar in just those places where it appears on the surface.

3.3 A third objection which can be raised against the analysis which purports to capture a linguistically significant generalization hinges on native speakers' judgments as to the intuitively correct parsing of adjectives. My informants have insisted that the *-i*, *-katta*, *-karoo*, etc., are not morphologically complex, but that *-i* is the present-tense suffix, *-katta* the past-tense suffix, and *-karoo* the tentative suffix for adjectives. Furthermore, the native speakers with whom I have discussed the matter, including one who is not linguistically naive, refuse to equate the *-i* suffix on the adjective with the (morphologically empty) *i* added by a general phonological rule to words with a final consonant. It would then appear that the analysis outlined above is not consistent with the native speakers' intuition and it does not characterize his competence (in spite of Chomsky 1965:27). One might of course claim that the competence characterized by the analysis we are rejecting is somehow deep and remote – inaccessible to investigation. However, such a notion of competence would then be simply a designation given to an unknown and unknowable state of affairs and as such is empty it can serve to explain nothing, nor can it be dealt with empirically.

The objection might be raised that the reason the native speaker rejects the analysis which purports to capture a linguistically significant generalization is due to his heavy reliance on his own traditional grammar. This is definitely not the case, however, since the traditional Japanese grammatical formulation of the adjective paradigm is far more complicated than any of the analyses cited above. In fact, within traditional Japanese school grammar each adjective is treated as having a host of allomorphs plus auxiliaries as suffixes. For example, the forms cited in 2a are parsed within the traditional grammar as follows:

(10) *taka* + *i* $\begin{cases} \textit{(rentaikei} \text{ 'prenominal form' and} \\ \textit{(syuusikei} \text{ 'terminal form')} \end{cases}$

   $\begin{matrix} \textit{takakat} + \textit{ta} \\ \textit{takaku} + \textit{naru} \end{matrix} \Big\}$ *(renyookei* 'adverbial form')

   takakaro + *o*   *mizenkei* 'incomplete form')

Within traditional grammar the adjective is treated as having several distinct stems with particular endings associated with each. It might be noted that these forms are also not in accord with the native speaker's judgments as to how adjectives should be parsed.

4. We can conclude, then, that even though a rather elegant analysis can be constructed for the adjective – an analysis which appears to capture a linguistically significant generalization in terms of formal criteria – such an analysis is open to serious objections and thus must be excluded from a grammar of the language. The analysis which native speakers seem to recognize as intuitively correct is really a very superficial one involving a parsing of the sort suggested by both Jordan (1963), a structuralist, and Inoue (1969), a transformationalist and a native speaker of the language. As a historical note, we might observe that while the analysis treating adjectives as having a stem-final k seems to reflect the diachronic development of the adjective paradigm, at some point it appears that speakers of the language reanalyzed the forms simply as stems with a final vowel plus specific suffixes, much along the lines that Hale (1973) suggests would be expected.

   Just because an analysis satisfies the formal criteria for the capturing of a linguistically significant generalization, we can have no assurance that it is in fact the correct description of the native speaker's knowledge of his language. Empirical evidence external to the notational system must also be brought to bear on the question of the correctness of the description.

The University of Alberta

NOTES

[1] The first criterion is obviously empirical, but only in the weakest sense: any proposed analysis must meet it simply to qualify as a candidate for the correct description.
It is obvious that linguists have always, implicitly or explicitly, assumed such a requirement for their analyses.
[2] This is the choice made in Prideaux 1970.
[3] I am indebted to Mr. Norio Hosoi for this observation.
[4] Schane (1971) has noted that rules such as 9, which include syntactic information,
serve a morphophonemic function, while rules such as 5 are essentially phonetic.
Within generative grammar, phonological rules have generally been considered as a
single list of ordered rules, but it would appear that the different functions served by
such rules call for some sort of partitioning. In particular, morphophonemic rules
tend to have paradigmatic functions, and so are highly limited in their applicability,
while phonetic rules have a far wider application in discussing the questions of explanation and naturalness in phonology. Derwing (1973) treats these problems in considerable detail.
[5] The issue of limitation on underlying representations is treated in Derwing (forthcoming, especially Chapter 4). He explores various proposals for constraints on underlying forms, and selects as most viable the one which in effect requires that the underlying forms be uniquely recoverable from the surface forms.

REFERENCES

Chamberlain, Basil Hall. 1907. A handbook of colloquial Japanese. 4th ed., revised.
    London: Crosby Lockwood and Son.
Chomsky, Noam. 1964. Current issues in linguistic theory. The structure of language,
    ed. by Jerry A. Fodor and Jerrold J. Katz, 50-118. Englewood Cliffs, N. J.:
    Prentice-Hall.
—. 1965. Aspects of the theory of syntax. Cambridge, Mass.: MIT Press.
Derwing, Bruce L. 1973. Transformational grammar as a theory of language acquisition.
    Cambridge: University Press.
Fodor, J., and M. Garrett. Some reflections on competence and performance. Psycho-
    linguistic papers, ed. by J. Lyons and R. J. Wales, 135-54. Edinburgh: University
    Press.
García, Erica C. 1967. Auxilaries and the criterion of simplicity. Lg. 43.853-70.
Gleitman, Lila R., and Henry Gleitman. 1970. Phrase and paraphrase. New York:
    W. W. Norton.
Hale, Kenneth. 1973. Deep-surface canonical disparities in relation to analysis and
    change: An Australian example. Current trends in linguistics 11.401-58.
Inoue, Kazuko. 1969. A study of Japanese syntax. The Hague: Mouton.
Jordan, Eleanor Harz. 1963. Beginning Japanese, 2 Parts. New Haven: Yale University
    Press.
Leech, Geoffrey N. 1968. Some assumptions in the metatheory of linguistics. Lin-
    guistics 39.87-102.
Prideaux, Gary D. 1970. The syntax of Japanese honorifics. The Hague: Mouton.
—. 1971. On the notion 'linguistically significant generalization'. Lingua 26.337-47.
Sansom, George. 1928. An historical grammar of Japanese. London: Oxford Universi-
    ty Press.
Schane, Sanford A. 1971. The phoneme revisited. Lg. 47.503-21.

Zwicky, Arnold M. 1970. The free-ride principle and two rules of complete assimilation in English. Papers from the 6th regional meeting, Chicago Linguistic Society, 579-88.

LINGUISTIC SPECULATIONS
OF EDWARD BREREWOOD (1566-1613)

JOHN A. REA

Edward Brerewood, identified by the *Dictionary of National Biography* as an "antiquary and mathematician", was Professor of Astronomy at Gresham College, London, from 1596 until his death.[1] His book *Enquiries Touching the Diversity of Language and Religion through the Chief Parts of the World*, published posthumously in 1614,[2] contains conclusions by Brerewood on the nature and causes of linguistic change which are quite unexpected for the period, and which the author indicates run counter to those of the authorities with whom he was familiar.

The Preface points out that the book was written, not just as idle speculation, but in answer to certain questions that Brerewood had been asked, including the geographical extent of Greek in ancient times, whether Latin had been the common language of the Western Empire during the period of the early Church and whether it was the source for the modern languages of that same area, whether the Scriptures were originally read publicly in Hebrew or in Syriac, and, finally, the location of Christians throughout the world, their organization, and their differences from the Roman Church.

It will readily be noted that the emphasis in Brerewood's book is in fact more on religious matters, including the languages of the liturgy, than on linguistic topics in general. In addition he includes a fascinating range of subsidiary topics and outright digressions, as may be seen by the following list of a few of the many subjects he treats: The Ancient Largeness of the Greek Tongue; Of the Beginning of the Italian, French and Spanish Languages; The Beginning and Change of the Syriack Tongue; The Weak State of Christianity in Africk; Muhametanism Why so Mightily Increased; The Vast Extendment of Idolatry in America; State of the Jews in Europe, Asia, and Africk; The People of America are the Progeny of the Tartars; the Dimensions of the Elephant and the Whale; the Depth of the Sea is More Than the Height of the Mountains; The Great Vastness of the Antarctique Continent; of the Nestorians; Patriarch of Jerusalem his Great Jurisdiction; The Pestilent Strain of Eutiches his Heresie; Of the Several Languages wherein the Liturgies of Christians in Several Parts of the World are Celebrated.

Brerewood's other works show similar evidence of the wide range of his curiosity and also emphasize his historico-religious interests, but regrettably seem not to include any further material dealing with linguistics. His other books include: *De ponderibus et pretiis veterum nummorum; Elementa Logicae; Tractatus quidam logici de praedicabilibus et praedicamentis; Tractatus duo : quorum primus est de meteoris, secundus de oculo; A Treatise of the Sabbath; Commentarii in Ethica Aristotelis;* and, *A Declaration of the Patriarchal Government of the Ancient Church.*

What interests us is the material on linguistic diversity in the *Enquiries* ..., especially the sections on Latin and the origin of the Romance Languages (15-54), and to a lesser extent the discussion, "Of the Decaying of the Greek tongue, and of the Present Vulgar Greek" (10-15). In these passages Brerewood is led to speculate on the causes of linguistic diversity, and specifically on the general causes of language change and of the reasons for the development of the Romance Languages from Latin. His theories depart from those generally accepted in his day, and are surprisingly like those held currently by many modern scholars of diachronic Romance linguistics. He reminds us that the general assumption in his time was rather like a shallow version of the superstratum theory, wherein everything was vaguely blamed on the disruptive incursions of barbarians into Latin-speaking territory.

The common opinion ... is that the mixture of the Northerne barbarous nations among the ancient Inhabitants, was the cause of changing the Latine tongue, into the languages which they now speak, the languages becomming mingled, as the nations themselves were. Who, while they were inforced to attempt and frame their speech, one to the understanding of another, for else they could not mutually express their mindes ... they degenerated both, and so came to this medley wherein now we find them (30).

Brerewood, however, feels strongly that this picture is much oversimplified, and he suggests two other sources of the linguistic changes which led to the evolution and diversification of the Romance languages.

But to deliver plainly my opinion, having searched as farre as I could, into the originals of these languages, and having pondered what in my reading, and in my reason I found touching them, I am of another minde ... namely that all those tongues are more aunicent, and have not sprung from the corruption of the Latin tongue, by the inundation and mixture of barbarous people in these provinces, but from the first unperfect impression and receaving of it, in those forraine countries. Which unperfectness ... had, as I take it beginning from the evil framing of forraine tongues to the right pronouncing of Latine. ... So that, I rather thinke the barbarous people to have been a cause of increasing corruption, and of further alteration and departure of those languages from Romane, then of beginning them (36-36).

Thus does Edward Brerewood, already by 1613, propose the substratum theory, combined indeed with a superstratum as a principal factor in causing linguistic change, especially as regards phonological change, and as a basis for the differentiation among the Romance languages. Now the notion of 'substratum' as a cause of change in the Romance language family is commonly attributed to Diez 1854, over two centuries after Brerewood, although credit for coining the term itself is given to Ascoli 1881. The term 'superstratum' is attributed to von Wartburg 1936, who has been a leader in studies intended to show the effects of both superstratum and substratum languages on Romance, although the notion that the migrating German tribes were a primary factor in the evolution of the Neo-Latin languages is of course a venerable one, as pointed out above.

But Brerewood's conclusions on the origin of the Romance languages are still not complete with these two postulated sources of change and differentiation. For he has noted that the Greek language, among others, has become greatly changed like Latin through the centuries in circumstances where neither a substratum nor a superstratum can safely be presumed as a significant cause of linguistic change:

But as I said, the Greeke tongue is ... also much degnerated and impaired as touching the pureness of speech. ... But yet not without some rellish of the ancient elegancie ... which corruption yet, certainly hath not befallen that tongue through any inundation of barbarous people, as is supposed to have altered the Latine tongue, for although I know *Greece* to have been overrunne and wasted, by the Gothes, yet I find not in histories any remembrance of their habitation or long continuance in *Greece* and of their coalition into one people with the *Grecians*, without which, I conceave not, how the tongue could be greatly altered by them. And yet certaine it is, that long before the Turkes came among them, their language was growne to the corruption wherein now it is. ... Insomuch that the learned Grecians themselves, acknowledge it to bee very ancient, and are utterly ignorant when it began in their language: which is to me a certaine argument that it had no violent nor sodaine beginning by the mixture of other forrain nations among them, but hath gotten into their language by the ordinarie change, which time and many occasions that attend on time are wont to bring to all languages in the world, for which reason, the corruption of speech growing upon them, little and little, the change hath been unsensible (9-10).

Here, then, is a third casual factor for linguistic change, which in recent times has been referred to as drift, so that in addition to the *external* influences of substratum and superstratum languages, Brerewood has now postulated an *internal* mechanism, one inherent in language itself, and therewith the evolutionary notion that languages, *all* languages, are subject to change even without disruptive outside factors. This, indeed, is his most modern-sounding notion, combined as it is with some emphasis on the gradualness and imperceptibility of linguistic change, which latter view is only just now coming into serious discussion. In fact it is interesting to compare the above passage with two statements by Hockett 1958: "Gradual change in the design of living language is part of its life and inexorable" (368), and further the claim that sound change is "gradual change in habits of articulation and hearing taking place constantly, but so slowly that no single individual would ever be aware" (439).

It might be well before we go on to point out that the word *corruption* used throughout by Brerewood did not necessarily carry in earlier times such strong pejorative connotations as it now does, as may be seen from the following two early eighteenth century citations from the OED: "When a thing is destroyed or ceases to be what it was before, we call it corruption," and, "We say an egg is corrupted when we see the Egg no longer, but a chicken in its place."

Brerewood presents then his evidence for the assertions made in the previous excerpt:

There is no language which of ordinary course is not subject to change, although there were no forraine occasion at all ... which may be wel proved by observations and instances of former changes, in the very tongue (the latine) whereof I now dispute. For Quintilian recordeth, that the verses of the Salij which were said to be composed by Numa could hardly be understood of their priests in the latter time of the commonwealth. ... And yet to add one instance more, of a shorter duration of time, and a clearer evidence of the change that the Roman tongue was subject to, and that, when no forraine cause thereof can be alleadged: there remaineth at this day in the Capital at Rome ... a piller (they call it Columnam rostratam). ... Where you may see in many words, *e* for *i*, *c* for *g*, *o* for *u*, and sometimes *e*, and *d* superfluously added to the end of many words. But, (to let forraine tongues passe) of the great alteration that time is wont to worke in languges, our owne tongue may afford us examples evident enough (42-43).

Having discussed three causes of change in language, those causes today termed superstratum, substratum, and drift, Brerewood sums up his view of the development of the Romance languages as a result of these:

So that methinkes, I have observed three degrees of corruption in the Roman tongue, by the degeneration whereof, these languages are supposed to have their beginning. The first of them was in Rome itselfe ... insomuch that, Tertullian in his time, when as yet none of the barbarous nations had by invasion touched Italie ... chargeth the Romans to have renounced the language of their fathers. The Second steppe was the unperfect impression ... made of the Romaine tongue in the forraine provinces among strangers, whose tongues could not perfectly frame to speake it aright. ... And the Third, was that mixture of manie barbarous people (to which others attribute the beginnings of the languages in question) which made the Latine, that was before unperfect, yet more corrupt then they found it, both for words and for pronouncing (39).

These reasons perhaps ... may perswade you as they have done mee, that the barbarous nations of the north, were not the first corruption of the latine tongue, in the provinces subject to Rome, nor the beginners of the Italian, French and Spanish tongues (40).

Having demonstrated three and a half centuries ago that the linguistic changes attributable to drift and to substratum predated those brought about by superstratum influences from the barbarian incursions, Brerewood is faced with the problem that there is in fact no attestation for such changes prior to these incursions. He must ask himself, "How falleth it if these vulgar tongues be so ancient, that nothing is found written in any of them of great antiquity?" Why is there not, in other words, evidence during Imperial times of the changes which must already have taken place in Latin, especially in the provinces? His answer to this question not only faces the problem of the lack of such early documentation in a way accepted by many modern scholars, by pointing out that those educated enough to write at all would write in an educated style, but his answer seems also to contain something of the appreciation we now have of the differences between written and spoken styles of the same language. "Learned men", he explains in reply to his own question, "would rather write in the learned and grammatical than in the vulgar and provincial" (42).

In closing it is interesting to note that two modern commentators on Brerewood have not noted these conclusions of his on linguistic change. Bonfante 1955 discusses Brerewood's survey of the languages spoken in Europe, comparing it with those spoken today, pointing out one or two errors, but does not deal with the matter of linguistic change. Borst 1960:1237, commenting on various details of languages mentioned by Brerewood, mistakenly claims that Brerewood, "erwähnte, daß die Völkerwanderung das Latein verdorben habe".

University of Kentucky

NOTES

[1]   An earlier version of this paper was presented to the annual meeting of the International Linguistic Association in New York on 15 March 1970.

[2]   Pagination varies considerably in the various editions. Besides the 1614 edition, printed in London by John Bill, others appeared in 1622, 1625, 1635, and 1674. Translations into French appeared in 1640, 1662 and 1663; translations into Latin in 1650, 1659 and 1679.

REFERENCES

Ascoli, G. I. 1881. Lettere glottologiche. Rivista di filologia e d'istruzione classica 10:1-71.

Bonfante, Giuliano. 1955. Una descrizione linguistica d'Europa de 1614. Paideia 10:224-7.

Borst, Arno. 1960. Der Turmbau von Babel. Stuttgart: Anton Hiersemann.

Dictionary of national biography, Vol 2, 1917. Ed. by Leslie Stephen and Sidney Lee. Oxford: Oxford University Press.

Diez, Friedrich. 1854. Etymologisches Wörterbuch der romanischen Sprachen. Bonn.

Hockett, Charles F. 1958. A course in modern linguistics. New York: Macmillan.

OED = A new English dictionary on historical principles. 1903. Ed. by James A. H. Murray. Oxford: Oxford University Press.

von Wartburg, Walter. 1936. Die Ausgliederung der romanischen Sprachräume. ZRPh 56:1-48.

TO HAVE HAVE
AND TO NOT HAVE HAVE

JOHN ROBERT ROSS

In this note,* I will suggest, largely on the basis of facts pointed out to me by colleagues, that the immediate source of 1 is one of the sentences in 2:

(1)   I wanted a bagel.

(2)   I wanted to $\begin{Bmatrix} \text{have} \\ \text{get} \end{Bmatrix}$ a bagel.

Such a rule is semantically justified, for 1 and 2 are synonymous. Since I assume the remote structure of 2, which I will schematically represent as in 3,[1]

(3)

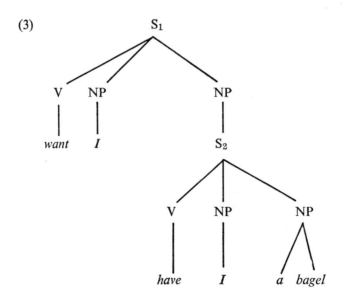

is almost identical to semantic representation (that is, that *want* is semantically a two-place predicate, relating an animate experiencer and the proposition in S_2), the alternative to a syntactic rule of HAVE DELETION would be a semantic rule which would convert the single-clause syntactic structure which would underlie 1 into the semantically necessary bi-propositional structure which would parallel 3. That is, there can be no choice on grounds of simplicity between a syntactic rule of HAVE DELETION and an interpretive semantic rule of proposition building, for the operations are essentially inverses of one another.

There are, however, several reasons for preferring the syntactic solution, which I will refer to as 'the deletion analysis', contrasting it with a possible interpretive analysis.

First, if there is a rule of HAVE DELETION, the selections for *want* can be simplified. Without such a rule, *want* would have to be allowed to occur in remote structure either before NP, or before $[S_{subj}]$,[2] for virtually all non-complement NP's occur following *want*, as the sentences in 4 show:

(4)
$$
I \text{ want} \begin{Bmatrix} \text{a cold} \\ \text{a sister} \\ \text{freedom} \\ \text{a driveway} \\ \text{*sentencehood} \end{Bmatrix}.
$$

The fact that nouns like *sentencehood* cannot follow *want* is accounted for by an analysis incorporating the rule of HAVE DELETION, because such nouns cannot occur as the object of *have*, as 5 shows:

(5)
$$
I \text{ have} \begin{Bmatrix} \text{a cold} \\ \text{a sister} \\ \text{freedom} \\ \text{a driveway} \\ \text{*sentencehood} \end{Bmatrix}.
$$

Secondly, note that such strings as *Teddy to play with* can occur after *have*, but not in general after all transitive verbs:

(6)
$$
I \begin{Bmatrix} \text{have} \\ \text{*kicked} \\ \text{*bit} \\ \text{*tricked} \\ \text{*teased} \end{Bmatrix} \text{Teddy to play with.}
$$

While the source of such sentences is unclear, the fact that this same object type occurs, at least in some cases, after *want*, as in 7:

(7)   I wanted Teddy to play with.

also supports the deletion analysis, for in an interpretive analysis, both *have* and *want* would have to be marked in such a way that they, in contrast to the other verbs in 6, could exhibit whatever remote structure strings turn out to underlie such superficial strings as *Teddy to play with*. In the deletion analysis, this configuration can be restricted to occur only after the verb *have*, thus simplifying the lexical representation of *want*.

Thirdly, as Masaru Kajita has called to my attention,[3] such future-time adverbs as *by tomorrow* can follow the past tense of *want*, while this is not a property of most past tense verbs:

(8) a.   I wanted a bagel by tomorrow.

b.   *I $\begin{Bmatrix} \text{ate} \\ \text{described} \\ \text{drooled over} \\ \text{got sick from} \\ \text{thought about} \end{Bmatrix}$ a bagel by tomorrow.

Semantically, it is clear that the phrase *by tomorrow* in 8a does not modify *wanted*, but rather the semantically necessary predicate, *have*, which is the main predicate of the proposition which constitutes the semantic object of *want*. That is, Kajita has rightly observed that the phrase *by tomorrow* is a syntactic relic area in 8a – it and the NP *a bagel* are the only traces of the clause S_2, which was present in the remote structure 3. Once again, the deletion analysis accounts naturally for Kajita's observation, while an interpretive solution would have to postulate some *ad hoc* feature on *want* which would allow it, but not the verbs of 8b, to occur with future-time adverbs like *by tomorrow*.

Fourthly, as David Perlmutter has pointed out to me,[4] certain abstract nouns, such as *help, cooperation, sympathy*, etc., cannot follow *have* if the possessive pronoun modifying them is coreferential with the subject of *have*.

(9)

a.   I had $\begin{Bmatrix} \text{*my} \\ \text{your} \\ \text{his} \\ \text{their} \\ \text{Ed's} \end{Bmatrix}$ cooperation.

b.   You have $\begin{Bmatrix} \text{my} \\ *\text{your} \\ \text{his} \\ \text{Ed's} \end{Bmatrix}$ sympathy.

c. Ed_i had $\begin{Bmatrix} \text{my} \\ \text{your} \\ \text{her} \\ *\text{his}_i \end{Bmatrix}$ help.

The fact that the same spectrum of grammatical and ungrammatical sentences is preserved if *want* is substituted for *have* in 9 thus provides strong evidence for the deletion analysis, for it is not in general true that such nouns as those in the objects of 9 cannot occur in object position when preceded by a possessive pronoun which is coreferential to the subject of the sentence, as 10 shows:

(10) $\text{They}_i \begin{Bmatrix} \text{mentioned} \\ \text{boasted about} \\ \text{described} \\ \text{played up} \\ \text{regretted} \\ \text{etc.} \end{Bmatrix} \text{their}_i \begin{Bmatrix} \text{help} \\ \text{cooperation} \\ \text{sympathy} \end{Bmatrix}.$

Within the deletion analysis, it appears likely that all restrictions pertaining to the coreferentiality of possessive pronouns and subjects can be reduced to the restrictions which show up in sentences like 9. The rule of HAVE DELETION will then explain why the same facts should show up in the object of *want*.

Of course, the rule of HAVE DELETION will not be restricted to operate only after *want*. The same phenomena which motivate postulating it for such sentences as 1 also suggest that it applies after the verbs of 11:

(11) $\text{I} \begin{Bmatrix} \text{needed} \\ \text{expected} \\ \text{required} \\ \text{demanded} \\ \text{would like} \\ \text{sought} \\ \begin{Bmatrix} \text{hoped} \\ \text{begged} \\ \text{pleaded} \\ \text{etc.} \end{Bmatrix} \text{for} \end{Bmatrix} \begin{Bmatrix} \text{a bagel} \\ \text{a cold} \\ \text{freedom} \\ \text{a driveway} \\ *\text{sentencehood} \\ ?\text{Teddy to play with} \\ \begin{Bmatrix} *\text{my} \\ \text{your} \\ \text{Ed's} \end{Bmatrix} \begin{Bmatrix} \text{help} \\ \text{cooperation} \\ \text{sympathy} \end{Bmatrix} \end{Bmatrix} \text{(by tomorrow)}$

Obviously, the verbs which can undergo HAVE DELETION share semantic properties, but my understanding of their semantic commonality is not sufficient to allow the prediction of the applicability of this rule. In particular, what explains the contrast in 12?

(12)
$$I \begin{Bmatrix} \text{wanted} \\ \text{desired} \\ \text{would} \begin{Bmatrix} \text{have liked} \\ \text{like} \end{Bmatrix} \\ *\text{liked} \\ *\text{preferred} \end{Bmatrix} \text{a bagel by tomorrow.}$$

At present, I can do no better than claim that HAVE DELETION only works in the objects of some desiderative and 'future' verbs.[5] (See also immediately below.)

One final note: as Ray Dougherty has pointed out to me,[6] the rule of HAVE DELETION appears to be applicable after *give* and certain other double object verbs.

(13)
$$I \begin{Bmatrix} \text{gave} \\ \text{loaned} \\ \text{sent} \\ \text{mailed} \\ \text{etc.} \end{Bmatrix} \text{Ted my keys until tomorrow.}$$

Just like the adverb *by tomorrow*, the adverb *until tomorrow* does not generally occur in past tense sentences:

(14)
$$*I \begin{Bmatrix} \text{sang her an ode} \\ \text{painted the house} \\ \text{called Winky a sod} \end{Bmatrix} \text{until tomorrow.}$$

Moreover, as David Perlmutter has noted,[7] sentences with *give* parallel sentences with *have* with respect to the class of nouns like *cooperation*, *sympathy*, etc.:

(15)
$$\text{I gave Peter}_i \begin{Bmatrix} \text{my} \\ *\text{your}^8 \\ *\text{Ed's}^8 \\ *\text{his}_i \end{Bmatrix} \begin{Bmatrix} \text{cooperation} \\ \text{sympathy} \end{Bmatrix}.$$

This suggests that 16a be derived from some structure like 16b:

(16) a.   I gave the madame my Bankamericard.

   b.

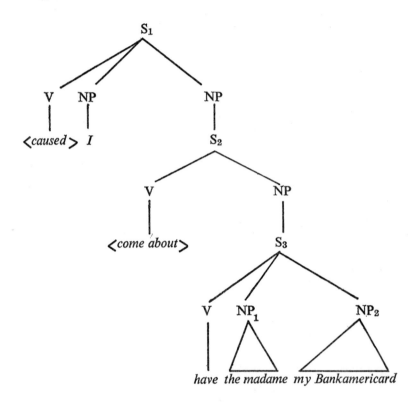

have the madame my Bankamericard

an analysis which would accord well with at least the assertion part of the semantics of *give*. If 16b is in fact an approximately correct remote structure for 16a, then it may be unnecessary to postulate a separate rule of DATIVE to account for the relationship between 16a and 17,

(17)   I gave my Bankamericard to the madame.

for the rule which interchanges NP_1 and NP_2 in relating these two sentences might apply at the level of S_3. This rule is largely invisible in English,[9] but it seems to appear in the grammars of many languages. Thus 20b may have *20a as a source, which would (obligatorily, in English) undergo a rule interchanging the two NPs of the sentence, paralleling the facts of French 18 and German 19.

(18) a. $\begin{Bmatrix} \text{Ce} \\ \text{*Un} \end{Bmatrix}$ livre est a moi.

$*\begin{Bmatrix} \text{This} \\ \text{A} \end{Bmatrix}$ book is to me.

b.   J'ai $\begin{Bmatrix} \text{ce} \\ \text{un} \end{Bmatrix}$ livre.

    I have $\begin{Bmatrix} \text{this} \\ \text{a} \end{Bmatrix}$ book.

(19) a. $\begin{Bmatrix} \text{Dieses} \\ \text{*Ein} \end{Bmatrix}$ Buch ist mir (dial.).

    $*\begin{Bmatrix} \text{This} \\ \text{A} \end{Bmatrix}$ book is to me.

b.   Ich habe $\begin{Bmatrix} \text{dieses} \\ \text{ein} \end{Bmatrix}$ Buch.

    I have $\begin{Bmatrix} \text{this} \\ \text{a} \end{Bmatrix}$ book.

(20) a. $\begin{Bmatrix} \text{?The} \\ \text{*A} \end{Bmatrix}$ top is to this table.

b.   This table has $\begin{Bmatrix} \text{*the} \\ \text{a} \end{Bmatrix}$ top (to it).

If these unsupported speculations can be made to stand up, then the fact that the rule of HAVE DELETION can play a role in getting rid of the rule of DATIVE will constitute further evidence for the correctness of the deletion analysis.[10]

Massachusetts Institute of Technology and
The Language Research Foundation

NOTES

  *   The research on which this paper was based was supported in part by a grant from the National Institute of Mental Health (Number 5-PO1-MH 13390-05) and by a grant from the National Science Foundation (Number GS-3202). I would like to thank George and Robin Lakoff, Paul Postal, and especially David Perlmutter for much discussion and for many helpful ideas.

[1]   Cf. McCawley 1970 for justification of the claim that English exhibits VSO order in underlying representations.

[2]   The symbol S_{subj} is intended to stand as a mnemonic for the type of tenseless *that*-clauses which such verbs and adjectives as *desire, require, mandatory, obligatory,* etc., cooccur with:

$$\left\{ \begin{matrix} \text{Tom desires} \\ \text{We require} \\ \text{It is} \left\{ \begin{matrix} \text{mandatory} \\ \text{obligatory} \end{matrix} \right\} \end{matrix} \right\} \text{ that the ice cream } \left\{ \begin{matrix} \text{be} \\ *\text{is} \end{matrix} \right\} \text{ stewed.}$$

For some reason, *want* allows S_{subj} in remote structure (cf. *What I want is that the ice cream be stewed*), but must convert it to an infinitival clause, if immediately after *want*.

3   Personal communication.
4   Personal communication.
5   By 'future' verbs, I mean such verbs as *expect, anticipate, predict*, which require

semantically future tenses in their complements (cf. *I predicted that he* $\left\{ \begin{matrix} \textit{would leave} \\ *\textit{(had) left} \end{matrix} \right\}$.).

The verb *expect* appears to delete a wider range of verbs than is possible for *want* or other 'future' verbs, however:

$$\text{I} \left\{ \begin{matrix} \text{expected} \\ *\text{wanted} \\ *\text{anticipated} \end{matrix} \right\} \text{John from New York by tomorrow.}$$

$$\text{I} \left\{ \begin{matrix} \text{predicted} \\ \text{expected} \\ \text{anticipated} \end{matrix} \right\} \left\{ \begin{matrix} \text{a party} \\ \text{a hurricane} \\ \text{an investigation} \end{matrix} \right\}.$$

6   Personal communication.
7   Personal communication.
8   Since the sentences.

$$\text{Peter has } \left\{ \begin{matrix} \text{your} \\ \text{Ed's} \end{matrix} \right\} \left\{ \begin{matrix} \text{cooperation} \\ \text{sympathy} \end{matrix} \right\}$$

are perfectly well-formed, it is obvious that some ancillary restrictions pertaining to *give* must be relied on to reject the second and third versions of 15.
9   Unless it should turn out to be identical to the rule of *Psych Movement* (cf. Postal 1970).
10   For a much more detailed study of HAVE DELETION see McCawley (1973) which sharpens greatly the analysis I have presented, clears up a number of inadequacies, and extends it to a wider class of cases.

REFERENCES

McCawley, James D. 1970. English as a VSO language. Lg. 46.86-93.
—. 1973. On identifying the remains of deceased clauses. Language research 9:2. 73-83. (Language Research Institute, Seoul National University, Seoul, Korea).
Postal, Paul M. 1970. Crossover phenomena: A study in the grammar of coreference. New York: Holt, Rinehart and Winston.

ON DEEP AND SURFACE STRUCTURES
IN ONOMASTICS

J. B. RUDNYCKYJ

The recent growing literature on generative-transformational linguistics seems to be topically restricted to appellative material only. So far transformationalists have avoided discussion of topo- and anthroponymic structures in light of their theory. Onomastics exemplifies a fairly sharp distinction between the two levels of structure: a basic deep and a resulting surface structure. For it is the name that in its primary function of individualizing identification of someone or something displays a complex system of interrelated elements which depend on each other not only in the contextual but also in consituational respect. The latter aspect is very important in onomastics. The fact, e.g., that *St. Andrews* church was built (and consequently was located) *on the Red* River in Manitoba was decisive for naming it: *St. Andrews on the Red*. Moreover, due to external consituational factors, this toponym began to designate not only the church itself but also the settlement around it. All this, perceived on the deep level, found its expression on the surface level in an oversimplified syntactical name *St. Andrews on the Red*.

There are very many examples for both levels in onomastics. To mention only one from anthroponymy: the surname *Johns*. As a patronymic it derives, no doubt, from the full name *John/s/son*: 'son of John'. Again the deep level of this onomastic structure represents a syntactic unit: '(this is) the son of John', or something similar; on the surface level, however, it is *John/s/son* or simply *Johns*.

The latter example leads us to the consideration of an important fact, namely, the existence of more than one surface level in onomastics. If we consider *John/s/son* the primary and *Johns* the secondary structure, then the two surface manifestations (S_1 and S_2) differ considerably from each other. The basic process here is the ellipsis of the 'full name' – dropping of the element *son*. There is no doubt that this ellipsis has a syntactic background, which might be presented in the following series of evolution: *son of John* – *John's son* – *John/s/son*, the latter being only an 'orthographical' compound.

The process of ellipsis of primary and secondary onomastic surface structures is well documented in historical sources. My investigations of some toponyms in Eastern Europe confirm *non plus ultra* the transformation of S_1 into S_2 structures. Thus, e.g., the name of the West Ukrainian capital *L'viv* (Polish *Lwów*, Russian *L'vov*) was still known in the 13th century as *horodъ Lvovъ* 'Leo's City', corresponding to the Latin designation of this city: *Ciutat de Leo* (1375) or *Leopolis* (1422), and German *Leonburg* (1387), later *Lemburg* (1552) and *Lemberg* (1403, cf. Rudnyckyj 1958:33-34). The generic *horod* is used still today on solemn occasions in high-style expressions: *L'viv horod*. The deep structure underlying both forms of this toponym might be formulated as 'the city founded in 1250 by King Danylo and named after his son Leo'. It is clear that the transformational process from this deep structure to the original surface structure was *L'vovъ horodъ*, which was transformed in to a simplified final *L'vov* or *L'viv*.

There are many examples for this kind of toponymic ellipsis in Europe, and elsewhere. On the American continent such names might be mentioned as:

> *Wolf*, Alberta from *Wolf Branch* (in 1959)
> *Wolverine*, Alberta from *Wolverine Point* (in 1814)
> *Westhall*, Alberta from *Bedford West Hall*, a.o. (Rudnyckyj 1958:15)

Yet ellipsis is not the only transformational process in onomastics. Very close to it is the non-morphological mechanical abbreviation found in anthroponymy in connection with adjustment of 'foreign' names to the English-speaking majority milieu. Thus, such names as *Pry* from *Prygrodzki* (Klymasz 1961:57), *Smerch* from *Smerechanski* (*ibid*.: 59), *Stem* from *Stempkowski* (*ibid*.: 61), etc., whatever their deep structures may be, attest the changes from original surface formation to the secondary one. The latter form may lead to new structures of the kind *Transcona* from the deep structure: 'place where the transcontinental railway crosses' (Rudnyckyj 1958:11), and further to the compound abbreviations of the type:

> *Winnitoba* = *Winni*peg – Mani*toba*
> *Saskoba* = *Sask*atchewan – Mani*toba*
> *Meleb*   = *Mel*nyk – *Leib*man
> *Krydor* = *Kry*sak – Theo*dor*

$Ukalta$ = Ukraina – $Alta$ (= Alberta), etc. (Rudnyckyj
1958:15)

Surface transformation in some names can influence deep structures
(D_1, D_2) and *vice versa*. An analogous switch from D_1 to D_2 emerges.
The best illustrations of this process are onomastic folk-etymologies.
Thus, the name *Clear Lake* in Manitoba was transformed in the language
of the Ukrainian pioneers into *Krilyk* 'Rabbit' and consequently the
change of meaning from D_1 – *Clear Lake* to D_2 – 'Rabbit' occurred.
Similarly:

> *Egg Lake*, Alberta – *Iglyky* 'Needle People'
> *Stuartburn*, Manitoba – *Shtombury* 'Stumps"
> *Beausejour*, Manitoba – *Boži Dziury* 'God's Holes'
> *Cooks Creek*, Manitoba – *Kustryky* 'Bush'
> *Regina*, Saskatchewan – *Urozhayna* 'Fertile'
> *Arbakka*, Manitoba – *Harbata* 'Tea' (Rudynckyj 1958:15)

To these may be added

> *Missouri*, USA – *Mazury* 'Mazurians'.

It is quite evident that such changes occur only in bilingual (or multilingual) situations as a result of 'languages' or rather 'names in contact'.

In summing up our considerations of deep and surface structures in
onomastics we might state in general that:

1) The main transformation of deep structures in names results
in the elliptization of generics.

2) Abbreviations and/or compound abbreviations are also evident in
the onomastic material.

3) Both surface and deep structures are transformed in consequence
of the so called folk-etymology.

Further research in onomastics in this respect is badly needed and
highly recommended.

University of Manitoba

REFERENCES

Klymasz, R. B. 1961. A classified dictionary of Slavic surname changes in Canada.
Onomastica UVAN 22. Winnipeg.
Rudnyckyj, J. B. 1958. Studies in onomastics, II: Toponymy. Onomastica UVAN
15. Winnipeg.

UTTERANCE IMITATION
BY HEBREW-SPEAKING CHILDREN

ROBERT J. SCHOLES AND PAMELA FRYDMAN GROSSMAN

INTRODUCTION

In earlier research using English-speaking children (Scholes 1969 and 1970) the senior author investigated the criteria which children of various ages use to distinguish well-formed from ill-formed utterances (that is, sentences from non-sentences) and the strategies which may be applied in distinguishing between content and function words – the strategy which yields the typical TELEGRAPHIC speech of young children. During an extended visit at Tel Aviv University in Israel, the hypotheses posited by the earlier findings were investigated, using Hebrew-speaking children.

In the report which follows, the notions of sentencehood and of the content/function word dichotomy will be discussed in terms of the deletion errors made by the Israeli subjects. Some discussion of other topics and other types of errors will be found in Grossman and Scholes 1971.

METHOD

Materials

Well-formed Hebrew sentences (WF) were constructed utilizing words observed to occur in children's spontaneous speech. There were six such sentences: two, four words long each, two, six words long, and two, eight words long. Using the WF strings as a basis, six anomalous word strings were constructed, i.e., two each of four-, six-, and eight-word length. The words of the WF strings were then scrambled to construct six ill-formed word strings varying, as the others, in length. The anomalous and ill-formed strings are abbreviated as AN and IF, respectively. The WF and AN strings are presented in Latin script and translation in the Appendix. The IF strings are not given here since various randomizations of the words were used.

Subjects

Twenty-eight Hebrew-speaking children were tested. The results and discussion in this paper are based on sixteen of these subjects (Ss) for whom we have reasonably complete data. Some additional observations based on the full set of Ss can be found in Grossman and Scholes 1971. The sixteen Ss ranged in age from 29 to 60 months (average is just over 46 months) and were equally divided between boys and girls. They all attended preschool nursery schools in and around Tel Aviv. All Ss were native speakers of Hebrew, but typically came from homes in which one or more additional languages are spoken – it is difficult to find monolinguals in Israel.

Procedure

Each S was asked to repeat the E's production of one of the 18 utterances described above presented with normal sentential intonation or with a citation-form, word-by-word intonation.[1] Thus, each word string was presented to each S twice; once as a sentence, once as a word list. Each S was also tested on short-term memory using random strings of number names. Strings of number names ranged from two to seven names. This testing was stopped as soon as the S failed to negotiate all three of any n-length strings. E's presentation and S's imitation of all stimuli were tape recorded. Analyses of S's errors were based on both the taped recordings and E's on-the-spot notes.

RESULTS

The data considered here are deletion errors. Specifically, these are cases where the S attempted to repeat the stimulus, left some word or words out in his repetition, and the omitted portion was not replaced by some other words. In other words, a case where no portion of the stimulus utterance is repeated doesn't count in the analysis; nor do cases where a word is not found in the imitation, but where a word is substituted for the original word.

Length of utterance.

Deletion errors are clearly related to how many words there are in the stimulus. Practically no errors occur for the fourword strings of any type: consequently, these strings are not considered in the other analyses which follow. For six-word strings 12.6% of the attempted words were deleted; and for eight-word strings the deletion rate was 36.8%.

Age and STM Effects

Ss were divided into two groups on the basis of both age and STM. Deletions for these two groupings are shown in Table 1. The errors shown are the average total word deletions per S for two six-word and two eight-word utterances, there being thus 28 possible per cell.

TABLE 1

Average Number of Deletions per S for Two Groupings

			+Intonation			−Intonation		
Group	Age	N	WF	AN	IF	WF	AN	IF
I	39.5	8	5.9	7.9	10.4	6.9	7.1	9.0
II	53.5	8	4.4	4.4	9.0	5.0	3.7	11.9

A. By age

Group	STM	N	WF	AN	IF	WF	AN	IF
I	3.25	8	6.1	7.5	11.0	6.6	6.0	11.5
II	4.42	8	4.1	4.7	8.4	5.2	4.6	9.4

B. By short-term-memory

These two ways of looking at the data show interesting aspects of the effects of age and STM on these kinds of tasks and stimuli. They show the expected relation in that as age increases, deletion rate decreases overall, but not for -Intonation, IF stimuli. This latter fact no doubt indicates the child's increasing awareness of the strangeness of such material. On the other hand, using STM we do find a decrease in errors for the better STM in the IF cases, which are, of course, most like the material (unordered strings of terms) on which STM is based.

This analysis confirms the earlier finding (Scholes 1969) that, in the absence of intonational cues, the distinction between well- and ill-formed strings increases with age. In the present case, the younger children make 1.3 times as many errors with IF as with WF strings in the -Intonation condition, while the ratio is 2.4 for the older children. In the 1969 study using English-speaking children, the ages and ratios were: 43

months, equal; 49 months, 1.5; 53 months, 1.7; 56 months, 2.0. The comparison suggests that the Hebrew-speaking children are slightly ahead of their English-speaking counterparts in attaining an internalized criterion for sentencehood, but this must be highly speculative at this point in research. Although the same distinction increases with age when intonational cues are present, the increase is not as great: 1.7 to 2.0.

Over all Ss and string types, the presence or absence of sentential intonation makes little difference, there being 353 errors for the +Intonation condition and 359 for the —Intonation. In the word-by-word analysis which follows, we pool these data.

Deletions and the Function/Content Dichotomy

Total deletions for each word or part of word across Ss and conditions are shown in Table 2.

TABLE 2

Total deletions (out of 32 attempts) for each item in the WF and AN utterances. WF = 1, 2, 5, 6: AN = 3, 4, 7, 8.

1. *ha-ganenet shel-nu bah kol boker l-gan*
     0   3   1   6   4   1
2. *ha-xatul shoteh et ha-halav shel ha-kelev*
     3   0   0   0   2   2   0
3. *ha-ganenet shel ha-kelev bah b-boker l-gan*
     1   1   6   6   1   4   1
4. *ha-xatul shoteh et kol ha-ganenet shel-nu*
     1   1   2   1 3   0   2
5. *hayom tsiyarti tsiyur shel bayit im ets gadol*
     9   5   14   27   11   2 4   1
6. *b-kayits ani halaxti l-brexah v- shaxakti b-mayim im ha-kadur*
     13   19   9   11   7   4   13   5   5
7. *hayom shaxakti b-kayits gadol im ets shel brexah*
     4   1   16   13   9 7 14   4
8. *b-kayits ani halaxti l-tsiyur v- tsiyarti b-mayim im ha-kadur*
      8   21   11   21   5   8   11   4 2   2

The WF and AN strings are presented together in Table 2 since there is no motivation for treating them distinctly. The children appear to be unruffled by our notions of what constitutes a strange sentence.

The most startling aspect of these data is the extremely low number of deletions for what we think of as function words – article, prepositions, etc. Hebrew prepositions may be either bound or free morphemes. The bound forms, *l*- 'to', and *b*- 'in', are never deleted without deleting the whole word of which they are a part. The free form *im* 'with' is generally deleted only as part of a whole constituent deletion, but shows a few autonomous deletions. The preposition *shel* 'of' or *shelnu* 'of us' = 'our' (the -*nu* is never deleted separately) is deleted often, particularly in 3, 5, and 7. In these cases, however, the *shel* deletions can largely be accounted for by constituent phrase deletions; i.e. the phrase *shel ha-kelev* 'of the dog' in 3, *tsiyur shel* 'a drawing of' (which results in 'I drew a house ...') or *shel bayit* 'of a house' (which results in 'I drew ... with a big pen' – assuming *ets* 'tree' is interpreted as *et* 'pen' by some children) in 5, and *ets shel* 'tree of' (resulting in '... with a pool') or *shel brexah* 'of a pool' in 7.

The function word par excellence is the accusative particle *et*. It has no external reference at all, its function being to indicate the existence of a following direct object. It is deleted just once out of 64 attempts. The definite article *ha*- (a bound form) is deleted only in subject position (in 2, 3, and 4) and in the prepositional phrase *im-ha-kadur* 'with the ball' in 8. There are a total of seven *ha*- deletions out of 320 possible, hardly the kind of figure we would expect for FUNCTION WORD deletions.

Two words in these sentences are entirely redundant – *ani* 'I' in 6 and 8, and *tsiyur* 'a drawing' in 5 (but not in 8). *ani* is redundant both syntactically and semantically since the past tense of Hebrew verbs obligatorily indicates number and person; thus, the high deletions for this word are expected and are presumed to indicate redundancy effects. *tsiyur* is semantically redundant in 5 (*tsiyarti tsiyur* 'I drew a drawing') but not syntactically redundant since we might need to express what was drawn; it is nonetheless often deleted. In 8 *tsiyur* is head of a prepositional phrase 'to a drawing' which is largely nonsensical in the context.

Another bound form found in these stimuli is *v*- 'and'. This form is always prefixed to the second of conjoined elements. In the cases here, it conjoins two entirely separable clauses and can easily be dropped without causing any syntactic or semantic problems.

As for major lexical items, deletions can be accounted for by reference to constituent deletions resulting in shorter but still well-formed utterances. Thus we tend to get the following child versions of the utterances indicated:

1. *ha-ganenet bah l-gan*   'The teacher comes to school'.
2. as is
3. *ha-ganenet bah l-gan*   as above
4. *ha-xatul shoteh et ha-ganenet*   'The cat drinks the teacher'.
5. *tsiyarti im et gadol*   'I drew with a big pen'.
6. *shaxakti im ha-kadur*   'I played with the ball'.
7. *hayom shaxakti im ets/brexah*   'Today I played with a tree/pool'.
8. *b-kayits tsiyarti im ha-kadur*   'In the summer I drew with the ball'.

A comparison of the data for the WF and AN strings with the deletions for IF cases show that the constituent-deletion strategy posited for the WF and AN cases is strongly influenced by position in the utterance. When, for example, prepositional phrases such as *b-mayim* and *l-brexah* occur more remotely from utterance-final position, they are deleted more often. The redundancy effect is also seen in that *tsiyur* is not deleted as often in the IF cases where the redundancy does not obtain. Otherwise, little change is seen in IF as compared to WF or AN material.

DISCUSSION AND CONCLUSION

The results of our research on imitation of utterances by Hebrew-speaking children appear to partially confirm an hypothesis that children progress from an earlier acoustically oriented criterion for sentencehood to a later grammatical one. The notion of a clear distinction between content and function words is complicated by these data. The deletion strategies of these Israeli children appear to follow two general rules: (1) Delete whole constituents if in so doing a shorter but still well-formed sentence results. (2) If a number of contituents can be deleted under the conditions stated in 1, retain the right-most – that is, the most recent.

NOTE

[1]   Rina Gal, Robyn Gottesdienner, Rivka Krzepicki, and Sara Simchoni were the Es in this work. We gratefully acknowledge their considerable skill and energy in getting the children to contribute to our confusion concerning language acquisition.

APPENDIX

LITERAL TRANSLATIONS OF THE WF AND AN UTTERANCES SHOWN IN TABLE 1.

1. *ha-ganenet shel-nu bah kol boker l-gan*
   the nursery school teacher of ours comes every morning to the nursery school
2. *ha-xatul shoteh et ha-halav shel ha-kelev*
   the cat drinks (accusative particle) the milk of the dog
3. *ha-ganenet shel ha-kelev bah b-boker l-gan*
   the nursery school teacher of the dog comes in the morning to the nursery school
4. *ha-xatul shoteh et kol ha-ganenet shel-nu*
   the cat drinks (accusative particle) all the nursery school teacher of ours
5. *hayom tsiyarti tsiyur shel bayit im ets gadol*
   today I drew a drawing of a house with a big tree
6. *b-kayits ani halaxti l-brexah v- shaxakti b-mayim im ha-kadur*
   in the summer I I walk to the pool and I play in the water with the ball
7. *hayom shaxakti b-kayits gadol im ets shel brexah*
   today I played in the summer big with a tree of a pool
8. *b-kayits ani halaxti l-tsiyur v- tsiyarti b-mayim im ha-kadur*
   in the summer I I walked to the drawing and I drew in the water with the ball

REFERENCES

Grossman, Pamela Frydman, and Scholes, Robert J. 1971. The role of grammaticality and intonation in imitations of word strings by Hebrew-speaking ,children. Communication Sciences Laboratory Quarterly Progress Reports.

Scholes, Robert J. 1969. The role of grammaticality in the imitation of word strings by children and adults. Journal of Verbal Learning and Verbal Behavior 8.225-29.

—. 1970. On functors and contentives in children's imitations of word strings. Journal of Verbal Learning and Verbal Behavior 9.167-70.

'SEMIOTICS' AND ITS CONGENERS

THOMAS A. SEBEOK

> "... a long-standing result of linguistic study, of whatever period or school, is the denial of the existence of perfect synonyms. ... Synonyms are the most probable substitutes, in any given situation – but in one situation only, which is an important limitation" (Hill 1958:412).

A theory of signs was variously developed on the part of the Epicureans, and especially the Stoics, as a way of proceeding by inference from what is immediately given to the unperceived, and was thus analogous to a doctrine of evidence, particularly medical. Bodily motions were interpreted as a sign of the soul, blushing as a sign of shame, and fever as a sign, viz. symptom – later considered as an 'unintended index' – of a disease. Since none of the many works of the Stoic logicians and semanticists, those of Chrysippos (c. 280-206 B.C.) included, nor a full account of their Epicurean critics, is extant – their ideas are known to us largely through such surviving sources as Sextus Empiricus and Diogenes Laërtius, that postdate by nearly half a millennium their greatest period of efflorescence – the detailed nature of their philosophy of language remains "the most tantalizing problem in the history of semantics" (Kretzmann 1967:363; the fullest relevant exposition is Weltring's 1910 dissertation). In any event, the Greek doctrine of signification, with strong medical overtones (in special reference to Galen), acquired the designation *semeiotikē*, from *sêma* 'sign', *sēmeiōtikós* 'observant of signs'.

At the end of the 17th century, the Greek word *semeiotikē* was injected into the mainstream of English philosophical discourse by John Locke (1632-1704). Locke declared the 'doctrine of signs' to be that branch of his tripartite division of all sciences – namely, logic, physics, and ethics – "the business whereof is to consider the nature of signs, the mind makes use of for the understanding of things, or conveying its knowledge to others" (1690, Bk. IV, Ch. XXI, §4). Specialists like Aaron (1955:309) find Locke's use of *semeiotiké* for that part of philosophy which is logic rather perplexing, because the Gassendists seemingly made no use of the term, and because there is no evidence, either, that Locke, who was a physician by profession, came across the word in his medical studies and converted it to his own uses (he certainly does not explicitly connect it with symptomatology). Russell (1939), however, has convincingly argued that Locke adapted *semeiotiké* from neither logical nor medical writings, but from writings on Greek music. His immediate source was probably John Wallis' 1682 edition of Ptolemy's *Harmonics* (although Russell doesn't mention this, the fact that the word doesn't occur in Locke's first draft of the *Essay*, in 1671, strengthens his argument). Wallis, Locke's friend and former mathematics professor in Oxford, appears, in turn, to attribute the term *semeiotiké*, as the art of musical notation, to Marcus Meibomius, with two references to the latter's *Antiquae musicae auctores septem* (1652).

The English word, and some of its congeners, first appear, nearly two centuries later, in the works of C. S. Peirce (1839-1914), as *semeiotic* (1.444), rarely *semeotic* (8.377), but most commonly as *semiotic* (never, however, as far as I have been able to determine, as *semiotics*). Moreover, he also uses *semeiosy*, "or action of a sign" (5.473), and, of course, *semiosis*, pluralized as *semioses* (5.490) (he claims that its variant, *semeiosis*, "in Greek of the Roman period, as early as Cicero's time, if I remember rightly, meant the action of almost any kind of sign" [5.484]). Peirce undoubtedly took the term *"semiotic (semeiotiké)"* over, with its attendant definition as the "quasi-necessary, or formal, doctrine of signs" (2.227), directly from the usage of Locke, of whose work he had written elsewhere: "The celebrated *Essay Concerning Humane Understanding* contains many passages which ... make the first steps in profound analyses which are not further developed" (2.649). In a famous remark, Peirce viewed himself as "a pioneer, or rather a backwoodsman, in the work of clearing and opening up what I call *semiotic*, that is, the doctrine of the essential nature and fundamental varieties of possible semiosis ..." (5.488).

Although Peirce makes repeated references (e.g., in 4.353) to J. H. Lambert (1728-1777), he seems, puzzlingly enough, not to have explicitly mentioned the latter's ten masterful chapters on "Semiotik oder Lehre von der Bezeichnung der Gedanken und Dinge" (Lambert 1764:5-214), where the cardinal principles of communication and signification are

well grasped and lucidly set forth in a consistently semiotic frame
(cf. Söder 1964), prefiguring his own opus in several important respects,
including his very use of the term *semiotic*.[1] In fact, as was pointed out
by Resnikow (1968:189), despite Lambert's interesting contributions,
"beeinflussten seine Arbeiten die Entwicklung der logisch-semiotischen
Probleme kaum". In common German usage, until lately, *Semiotik*
continued to mean symptomatology. To cite only one example, Rudolf
Kleinpaul, the author of one of the first and most comprehensive books
on non-verbal communication, employed the term with its conventional
meaning: "Die Mediziner haben eine Wissenschaft, die sie *Semiotik*
nennen, die Lehre von den *Kennzeichen* der Krankheiten oder, wie wir
gewöhnlich sagen, den Symptomen ..." (Kleinpaul 1888:103), although,
he quickly added, "Es wäre nun wohl schön, wenn ... auch die Gesund-
heit ihre *Semiotik* hätte" (106). Husserl, on the other hand, equated
Semiotik with "Logik der Zeichen", as spelled out in his important essay
on the subject written in 1890 (Husserl 1970:340-73). The usage of
Hermes (1938), who meant by *Semiotik* pure general syntax, in contra-
distinction to descriptive syntax, seems highly idiosyncratic. Nowadays,
the impact of American Pragmatism, especially of Peirce, and of quasi-
behavioristic social science, namely, semiotic, particularly as represented
by Morris, is such in Germany that *Semiotik* has come to be equated
overwhelmingly and, it would seem, conclusively, with the "Allgemeine
Theorie der Zeichen" (cf., e.g., Bense 1967).

Meanwhile, back in America, *semiotic* became a commonplace in
philosophical usage, and beyond, through the incentive and persuasive
stimulation provided by Charles Morris in a series of publications dealing
with various aspects of the general theory of signs, particularly his now
classic 1938 monograph, *Foundations of the theory of signs*, and his
more elaborate 1946 book, *Signs, language, and behavior* (both included,
among others, in Morris 1971). According to Read (1948:85), neither
semiotic nor *semeiotic* had appeared in print during Peirce's lifetime,
but, of course, he did use variants of the term, ca. 1908, in his correspondence with Lady Victoria Welby (a part of which was first published in
Ogden and Richards 1925:281f.; cf. Peirce 8.342). Read cites a Polish
mathematician, Leon Chwistek, as having actually used *semeiotics*,
rendering in English his German *Semantik*, in 1924; but *semiotic* was
not truly launched in printed English until its appearance in the work of
Morris.

Morris told his readers that "'Semantics' is perhaps the most widely
accepted name for the discipline which studies signs. 'Semiotic', the

term here chosen, was used by the Stoics, John Locke, and Charles Peirce. Linguists and logicians restrict 'semantics' to a part of the whole field, namely the part which deals with the significata of signs. Hence we use 'semiotic' as a general term; 'semantics' will be employed for that part of semiotic which deals with significata" (Morris 1971:106). Morris's terminology was immediately and prestigiously propagated by Carnap (1942:9), who assigned "The whole science of language", consisting of syntax, semantics, and pragmatics, a tripartite distinction previously introduced by Morris, to *semiotic*.

Leaving aside here a detailed treatment of the entangled historical interplay of *sem(e)iotic* with *semantics*, and most of their multifarious rivals – some of the lexicographical aspects are expertly discussed by Read (1948) – it does seem worthwhile to enumerate, in this connection, at least those that can be traced back to Greek *sēmeîon*: *sem(e)iology*, the only terms in the set I return to below; Reisig's *Semasiologie* (1839-), in English, *semasiology* (1877-); Benjamin H. Smart's *sematology* (1831-), and the perhaps independent coinage of Bühler, *Sematologie* (1934:34f.), which, employed by the latter with a meaning very close to that of *semiotic*, have both more or less disappeared now; and Noreen's *semology* (cf. Lotz 1966:58, 61f.), currently popular in certain American linguistic circles (e.g., Joos 1958 or Lamb 1966:31f.). One should also mention, in passing, Lady Welby's *sensifics* (1896), and her much better known *significs*, that, in 1917, became the rallying cry of a group of Dutch scientists calling themselves the *significi* (Mannoury 1969).

Then there is the curious case of *semiotics*, which belongs to the form class of '*-ics* words' that once preoccupied Hill, who demurred that "at least a part of the confusion which learners experience in handling the *-ics* words ... is caused by the fact that no dictionary makes clear that the final *-s* in these words, no matter what its origin, is not identical with the familiar plural morpheme of nouns which happens to be homonymous with it" (1948:11). As I have already observed, Peirce never used *semiotics* at all, and neither does Morris, who, in fact, requested the editor of the *Approaches to semiotics* series, in which his collected writings were recently republished, to add a special "Terminological note" to his book to account for the divergence between his usage and that of the series (Morris 1971:9-10). Almost every true *semiotician* – another Morris coinage (1971:81), to label a practitioner of the art – working in the Peirce tradition, notably, the philosophers clustering around the Charles S. Peirce Society (see the eleven volumes of their *Transactions* 1965-), as well as such prominent linguist partisans and promoters of Peirce as Roman Jakobson (1971, *passim*), assiduously shun *semiotics*, which they tend to regard as a barbarism. Nevertheless, the term has cropped up in print all along, including in some peculiar ghastly manifestations: thus, in the Index of Subjects to the 5th volume of the Peirce papers (p. 425), there is an entry "Semiotics", but in the paragraph referred to (488) this form does not occur; perhaps the same gremlin is responsible for the identical entry in the Index of Subjects to Bocheński's monograph (1968:134), but the sole variant that I have been able to locate in his text is *semiotic* (30ff.). Each of the sporadic occurrences of *semiotics*, since the 1940's, must be presumed to have been impelled by an identical mechanism of analogical recreation on the model of what Hill has called the *-ics* words of English, most probably *semantics* (Michel Bréal's late 19th century coinage of which was itself anticipated, in 17th century English, by *semantick*). Its eventual diffusion and, since the mid-1960's, its increasing acceptance, or as Hermann Paul might have put it, the summation of repetitive shifts in idiolects culminating in a novel Language Custom, must surely be ascribed to the forceful intervention of one individual, Margaret Mead, who, on May 19, 1962, in the final moments of the first American conference ever held on aspects of the emerging field, announced: "It would be very nice if we could go away from here with at least a preliminary agreement on the use of some phrase that we could apply to this whole field. ... If we had a word for patterned communications in all modalities, it would be useful. I am not enough of a specialist in this field to know what words to use, but many people here, who have looked as if they were on opposite sides of the fence, have used the word 'semiotics'. It seems to me the one word, in some form or other, that has been used by people who are arguing from quite different positions" (Sebeok 1964:275). I then wrote in the editorial Preface: "Implying the identification of a single body of subject matter, this summative word was incorporated, overburdened as it is, and not without remonstrations from several quarters, into the main title of our work," that is, *Approaches to semiotics* (Sebeok 1964:5). This same phrase was later selected to serve as the over-all title of a series designed to accommodate book-length contributions to the theory of signs (Sebeok 1969b). On the other hand, at the formative meeting, on January 21, 1969, of what was to become the International Association for Semiotic Studies (IASS), the issue what to call the Association's journal was hotly debated, in part because of its intended bilingual character, but in part also because the by then very real rivalry of the synonyms *semiotic/semiotics* had become acute. The matter was ingeniously resolved by naming our fledgling journal *Semiotica* (Sebeok 1969a). My impression of the present state of affairs is that *semiotics* has made irreversible inroads over its competitor, and is likely to entirely replace *semiotic* within a decade or so, in spite of a residue of strong, variously rationalized, scholarly predilections in this regard. Furthermore, a minute holdout dismisses both, in favor of *semeiotics*, on the argument that "The spelling is better etymology than semiotics, and it avoids the ambiguity of semi-. Semi-otics would be nonsense" (Count 1969:76n.).

In broad strokes, then, it can be recorded that the family of labels that has become attached to the theory of signs is *sem(e)iotic(s)*. In the Soviet Union, where the discipline flourishes with unmatched concentration and distinction (Meletinsky and Segal 1971), and where the first colloquium devoted to its foundations was held in 1962 – almost coincidentally with our own initiatory efforts – the favored terms are likewise *semiotic(s)*. It is interesting to note, however, that the famed center of semiotic studies, established about 1964 at the University of Tartu, where lectures and summer courses on the structural study of secondary systems giving rise to models are offered at regular intervals, publishes its Proceedings under the revivalistic banner *Semeiotiké* (subsequently echoed in the title of Kristeva 1969), subtitled, in Russian, "Works on systems of signs", which is then explicitly rendered, both in English and Estonian, on the verso of the half-title page, as "Works on semiotics – Tööd semiootika alalt" (Lotman 1964-). In Poland, a country which has contributed heavily to the advancement of the theory of signs, and where the impetus for the IASS actually germinated, a clear preference is shown for *semiotics*; cf. the name of the International Conference on Semiotics (convened in Poland, in September, 1966), and M. R. Mayenowa's report about "Semiotics today" (reprinted in Kristeva 1971:57-62), or the usage of Polish logicians, as reflected, e.g., in the studies of Pelc (1971, *passim*) and his associates. The situation is much the same throughout the rest of the Slavic world; and the word used in Hungarian is likewise *szemiotika* (cf. Voigt 1969:377f.).

In contrast to what might be called the 'Locke-Peirce-Morris pattern', outlined so far, that prevails generally in America, as it does, too, in both Northern and Eastern Europe, there exists quite another tradition, widespread throughout the Romance areas, but not confined to them, since reflexes of it occur in English, particularly British. This tradition, that I shall refer to as the 'Saussure pattern', actually has two different sources: originally, Greek medicine; then, superimposed much later, the direct heritage of Ferdinand de Saussure (1857-1913). Synchronically, we are dealing here with the simultaneous multilingual interplay of polynymy (involving several similar forms) and polysemy (involving several connected meanings). Let French serve as the Romance prototype (data from Robert 1967:1633): there are two forms, a) *sémiologie* and b) *séméiologie*, both with two definitions, 1. "Partie de la médecine qui étudie les signes des maladies", and 2. "'Science qui étudie la vie des signes au sein de la vie sociale'", or "Science étudiant les systèmes de signes (langues, codes, signalisations, etc.)", in brief, 1) meaning symptomatology, dated 1752 (*Dictionnaire de Trévoux*), and 2) meaning the general theory of signs, illustrated by a quotation from Saussure, dated about 1910. This information can be displayed as a simple matrix:

Forms	a.	b.
Meanings	1.	2.

There are also two additional forms, dated 1555, c) *sémiotique* (Ambroise Paré, livre XX bis, 23), and d) *sémeiotique*, both with essentially the same two definitions, 1. "Sémiologie", and 2. "Théorie générale des signes", or reconverted into an expanded matrix:

Forms	a.	b.	c.	d.
Meanings	1.		2.	

The situation is, *mutatis mutandis*, the same in the other Romance languages: in Italian, however, forms c) and d) are polarized in respect to meanings 1. and 2.; that is, *semiotica* has come to refer to the theory of signs, whereas *semeiotica* continues to be confined to the medical context; in Romanian, on the other hand, *semiologie* means only "parte a medicinii care se ocupă cu diagnosticarea bolilor după simptomele lor", whereas a Romanian form c) is used for a meaning 2. (e.g., Golopenția-Eretescu 1971; on increasing activity in this field in Romania, cf. also Pop 1972); in Brazilian Portuguese, the preferred term is *semiótica*, with an awareness that "Na Europa, a Semiótica é chamada de Semiologia ..." (Pignatari 1971:27).

Meaning 1. need not detain us (cf. Barthes 1972); our prime concern is with *sémiologie* in the secondary sense, which, as every linguist knows, was launched by Saussure. In one variant, the key citation read:

La langue est un système de signes exprimant des idées, et par là, comparable à l'écriture, à l'alphabet des sourds-muets, aux rites symboliques, aux formes de politesse, aux signaux militaires, etc., etc. Elle est simplement le plus important de ces systèmes.

On peut donc concevoir *une science qui étudie la vie des signes au sein de la vie sociale*: elle formerait une partie de la psychologie générale: nous la nommerons *sémiologie* (du grec *sēmeîon* 'signe'). Elle nous apprendrait en quoi consistent les signes, quelles lois les régissent. Puisqu'elle n'existe pas encore, on ne peut dire ce qu'elle sera: mais elle a droit à l'existence, sa place est déterminée d'avance. La linguistique n'est qu'une partie de cette science générale, les lois que découvrira la sémiologie seront applicables à la linguistique, et celle-ci se trouvera ainsi rattachée a un domaine bien défini dans l'ensemble des faits humains. (Saussure 1967:46-49.)

After the word *sémiologie*, the *Cours* has a footnote reference to a book by Naville (1901:104), who recorded this early version of his Geneva colleague's views on the subject: Saussure insists on the importance "d'une science très générale, qu'il appelle *sémiologie*, et dont l'objet serait les lois de la creation et de la transformation des signes et de leur sens. La sémiologie est une partie essentielle de la sociologie. Comme le plus important des systèmes de signes c'est le langage conventionnel des hommes, la science sémiologique la plus avancée c'est la *linguistique* ou science des lois de la vie du language" (cf. Godel 1957:181). The notion, and its designation as *sémiologie*, appear to have been first recorded in a note of Saussure's, dated November, 1894 (Godel 1957: 275). Beginning 1916, and especially after the monographic treatment of the subject by Buyssens (1943), the word spread throughout French scientific, viz., linguistic discourse, and is now featured in such standard texts as those by Barthes (1964), Mounin (1970), and Guiraud (1971). However, this seemingly straightforward story has recently become considerably muddled by a double crossover: while *sémiologie* has come across the English Channel, in the guise of *semiology*, meaning 'semiotic', *semiotic* has travelled in the opposite direction, returning across the Atlantic, by a zigzag track, to revitalize *sémiotique*, meaning 'sémiologie'. Thus Barthes' influential essay, *Éléments de sémiologie*, was published in England (and subsequently distributed in America as well) under the title, *Elements of semiology*, and this is the term that, reinforced by the prestige of Parisian intellectual life, now turns up regularly in British newspapers and magazines, such as *The Times Literary Supplement*, and in an outpouring of volumes on the most diverse verbal and non-verbal arts, ranging from architecture ("Semiology of architecture", Part I. of Jencks and Baird 1969; in a comparable context, see Spanish *semiología*, in Gandelsonas 1970) to cinematography: a nice illustration of the latter emerges from the contrast of an English chapter, on "The semiology of the cinema" (Wollen 1969:116-62), with an American essay, published simultaneously, on "The development of a semiotic of film" (Worth 1969). At the same time, *sémiotique* occurs with such frequency in French (e.g., cf. Kristeva 1971), that one scholar has even issued a prescriptive caution: for *semiotics*, "La meilleure traduction française reste: sémiologie. Le terme *sémiotique* a pénétré en français ... pour désigner la sémiologie en général – usage à déconseiller ..." (Mounin 1970:57n.)! Summarizing once more: in British English, the form *semiology* seems to be firmly established, whereas its success in American English, in competition with *semiotic(s)*, appears negligible; in French, *sémiologie* now has a rival in *sémiotique*, with the eventual outcome of the competition still in doubt.

Even in the narrow sense, excluding, that is, their medical uses, *semiotic, semiotics, semiology*, to mention only the three most common English congeners, are by no means wholly interchangeable. While every contributor to *Semiotica* – to stick with a parochial illustration – may indulge his personal taste when attaching a label to the theory of signs, his terminology within the same piece of discourse will not oscillate ad libitum, for his initial selection will have signaled to his sophisticated readership whether he has chosen to align himself with the Locke-Peirce-Morris tradition, the Mead variation, or the Saussurean pattern of thought and action. And while these words may – though they need not, of course – all share the same denotatum, the intellectual ambiance evoked by each is so different that Hill's dictum about synonymy, featured in the epigraph to this article, is reconfirmed once again.

A few scholars have deliberately kept the denotatum of *semiotic* distinguished from that of *semiology*. Such was the eventual English practice, notably, of Hjelmslev, who provided these formal definitions: for *semiotic* (Danish *semiotik*) – "hierarchy, any of whose segments admits of a further division into classes defined by mutual relation, so that any of these classes admits of a division into derivatives defined by mutual mutation"; and for *semiology* (Danish *semiologi*), "meta-semiotic whose object semiotic is a non-scientific semiotic" (Hjelmslev 1953:85, 87). Hjelmslev, moreover, used *semiotics* as well, although casually and informally (1953:69), and was responsible for the introduction, with formalization, of *metasemiotic* (vs. *object semiotic*) and *metasemiology*. His select followers seek to perpetuate the cleavage: "The independent science that is sought turns out to be rather an immanent semiology – the science that studies semiotics [*sic*], or sign systems in general" (Francis Whitfield, in Hill 1969:258); and, sporadically, others: "It may be useful," a social anthropologist pleads, "to retain *semiology* to describe the study of *semiotics*, used as the plural [!] of *semiotic*. In its turn, a *semiotic* is a sign system" (Ardener 1971: lxxxvi, n. 16). In French, the denotata of *sémiotique* and *sémiologie* are variously distinguished from one another, for instance, by Kristeva (1969, 1970) and by Mounin, who, as already mentioned, objects to the designation of "la sémiologie en général" by the term *sémiotique*, although he would appear to be content if the employment of it were restricted "pour désigner un système de communication non linguistique particulier: le code de la route est une sémiotique, la peinture en est peut-être une autre, etc." (Mounin 1970:57n.). In Italian, the meaning of *semiologia* on the one hand is sharply differentiated from that of *semiotiche* on the other, by the author of the most interesting textbook on the subject so far, not at all on the basis of existing usage, but, so to say, *ex cathedra*, in order to establish a convention – how viable this will be remains to be seen – intended to clarify ensuing discussion (Eco 1968:384).

In conclusion, I should like to adjoin, very briefly, two sets of observations:

1. In 1963, I set afloat a new compound, *zoosemiotics*. Since its first appearance in *Language*, I tried to keep track of its passage from a linguistic context to all sorts of other scientific texts and, eventually, to fiction and comic strip, as well as of its transmutation from English into other Indo-European and Finno-Ugric languages, and Japanese. My accounts of these events (Sebeok 1968, 1970) can be regarded as companion pieces to this article.

2. A comment on another related term, *asemasia*: Jackson, in his paper on affections of speech, expressed reservations about the term aphasia, on the cogent grounds that "there is, at least in many cases, more than loss of *speech*; pantomime is impaired; there is often a loss of defect in symbolising relations of things in any way", and went on to say that "Dr. Hamilton proposes the term Asemasia, which seems a good one" (Jackson 1932:159). His somewhat recondite reference is to Allan McLane Hamilton, a prominent neurologist who practiced in New York City, and who had written a book on nervous diseases, wherein he remarked: "It has occurred to me that the word 'aphasia', as at present used, has too restricted a meaning to express the various forms of trouble of this nature, which not only consist of speech defects, but loss of gesticulating power, singing, reading, writing, and other functions by which the individual is enabled to put himself in communication with his fellows. I would, therefore, suggest 'asemasia' as a substitute for

'aphasia'" (Hamilton 1878:161n.). It is possible, as Jakobson claims (1971:289), that Hamilton not only proposed but actually coined this term as a cover for the general deficit of semiotic activities beyond the merely verbal; but, if so, he was anticipated by Steinthal, who had recognized, at least by 1871, that "die Aphasie ... erweitert sich ... zum allgemeinen Mangel an Erkenntniss von Zeichen, Asemie" (Steinthal 1881:458).[3]

Indiana University

NOTES

[1] Peirce (in 5.178, but unindexed) does refer to Lambert's "large book in two volumes" on logic ("and a pretty superficial affair it is"), clearly meaning the *Neues Organon*, in whose second volume the *Semiotik* appeared; Peirce's set is still at The Johns Hopkins, although there are no annotations in it (Max H. Fisch, personal communication).

[2] Besides its medical use, French *sémiotique* was also used, towards the middle of the 19th century, in a military context: "Art de faire manoeuvrer les troupes en leur indiquant les mouvements par signes ..." (Alain Rey, personal communication), a sense for which sometimes *sémantique* was also used (Rey 1969:6).

[3] This article was submitted to the editors on December 22, 1971. It is now superseded, in a number of important respects, by a series of the author's publications which have appeared in the intervening four years.

REFERENCES

Aaron, R. I. 1955² [1937¹]. John Locke. London: Oxford University Press.
Ardener, E., ed. 1971. Social anthropology and language. London: Tavistock Publications.
Barthes, R. 1964. Éléments de sémiologie. Paris: Seuil. [In English, 1967: Elements of semiology. London: Jonathan Cape Ltd.]
—. 1972. Sémiologie et médecine. In: R. Bastide, ed., Les sciences de la folie 37-46. Paris: Mouton.
Bense, M. 1967. Semiotik. Allgemeine Theorie der Zeichen. Baden-Baden: Ägis-Vlg.
Bocheński, J. M. 1968² [1965¹]. The methods of contemporary thought. New York: Harper & Row.
Bühler, K. 1965² [1934¹]. Sprachtheorie. Die Darstellungsfunktion der Sprache. Stuttgart: Gustav Fischer Vlg.
Buyssens, E. 1943. Les langages et le discours. Essai de linguistique fonctionnelle dans le cadre de la sémiologie. Brussels: Office de Publicité.
Carnap, R. 1942. Introduction to semantics. Cambridge, Mass.: Harvard University Press.
Count, E. W. 1969. Animal communication in man-science: An essay in perspective. In: T. A. Sebeok and A. Ramsay, eds., Approaches to animal communication 71-130. The Hague: Mouton.

Eco, U. 1968. La struttura assente: Introduzione alla ricerca semiologica. Milan: Bompiani.

Gandelsonas, M., et al. 1970. Semiología arquitectonica. Summa 32.69-82.

Godel, R. 1957. Les sources manuscrites du Cours de linguistique générale de F. de Saussure. Geneva: E. Droz.

Golopenția-Eretescu, S. 1971. Explorări semiotice. Studii și cercetări linguistice 22.283-91.

Guiraud, P. 1971. La sémiologie. Paris: Presses Universitaires de France.

Hamilton, A. MC. 1878. Nervous diseases: Their description and treatment. Philadelphia: Henry C. Lea.

Hermes, H. 1938. Semiotik: Eine Theorie der Zeichengestalten als Grundlage für Untersuchungen von formalisierten Sprachen. Forschungen zur Logik und zur Grundlegung der exakten Wissenschaften 5. Leipzig: S. Hirzel.

Hill, A. A. 1948. The use of dictionaries in language teaching. Language learning 1.9-13.

—. 1958. Introduction to linguistic structures: From sound to sentence in English. New York: Harcourt, Brace.

—, ed. 1969. Linguistics today. New York: Basic Books.

Hjelmslev, L. 1953 [1961², 1963³; Danish original, 1943]. Prolegomena to a theory of language. Baltimore: Indiana University Publications in Anthropology and Linguistics.

Husserl, E. 1970. Philosophie der Arithmetik, ed. L. Eley. The Hague: Martinus Nijhoff.

Jackson, J. H. 1932. On affections of speech from disease of the brain. In: Selected writings of John Hughlings Jackson 2.155-70. London: Hodder and Staughton.

Jakobson, R. 1971. Word and language. Selected writings 2. The Hague: Mouton.

Jencks, C. and Baird, G. 1969. Meaning in architecture. London: Barrie & Jenkins.

Joos, M. 1958. Semology: A linguistic theory of meaning. Studies in linguistics 13.53-70.

Kleinpaul, R. 1888. Sprache ohne Worte. Idee einer allgemeinen Wissenschaft der Sprache. Leipzig: Vlg. Wilhelm Friedrich.

Kretzmann, N. 1967. History of semantics. The encyclopedia of philosophy 7.358-406.

Kristeva, J. 1969. Semeiotiké. Recherches pour une sémanalyse. Paris: Seuil.

—. 1970. La mutation sémiotique. Annales économies, sociétés, civilisations 25.1497-522.

—, et al., eds. 1971. Essays in semiotics – Essais de sémiotique. The Hague: Mouton.

Lamb, S. M. 1966. Outline of stratificational grammar. Washington, D.C.: Georgetown University Press.

Lambert, J. H. 1764. Neues Organon oder Gedanken über die Erforschung und Bezeichnung des Wahren und dessen Unterscheidung vom Irrthum und Schein, 2. Band. Leipzig: Johann Wendler.

Locke, J. 1690. Essay concerning humane understanding. London: Thomas Basset.

Lotman, J. M., ed. 1964 –. Semeiotiké: Trudy po znakovym systemam 1 –. Tartu: Transactions of the Tartu State University.

Lotz, J. 1966 [1954]. Plan and publication of Noreen's Vårt Språk. In: T. A. Sebeok, ed., Portraits of linguists 2.56-65. Bloomington: Indiana University Press.

Mannoury, G. 1969. A concise history of significs. Methodology and science 2.171-80.

Meletinsky, E., and Segal, D. 1971. Structuralism and semiotics in the USSR. Diogenes 73.88-115.

Morris, C. S. 1971. Writings on the general theory of signs. The Hague: Mouton.

Mounin, G. 1970. Introduction à la sémiologie. Paris: Les Editions de Minuit.

Naville, A. 1901². Nouvelle classification des sciences. Paris: Felix Alcan.

Ogden, C. K., and Richards, I. A. 1925. The meaning of meaning. London: Kegan Paul, Trench, Trubner.

Peirce, C. S. 1965-1966. Collected papers of Charles Sanders Peirce. Cambridge, Mass.: Harvard University Press. [References are to volumes and paragraphs, not pages.]

Pelc, J. 1971. Studies in functional logical semiotics of natural languages. The Hague: Mouton.

Pignatari, D. 1971[5]. Informação. Linguagem. Comunicação. São Paulo: Editôra Perspectiva.

Pop, M. 1972. Le laboratoire de sémiotique de l'université de Bucarest, Roumanie. Semiotica 5.301-02.

Read, A. W. 1948. An account of the word semantics. Word 4.78-97.

Resnikow, L. O. 1968. Erkenntistheoretische Fragen der Semiotik. Berlin: VEB Deutscher Vlg. der Wissenschaften. [Enlarged edition, translated from the Russian 1964: Gnoseologičeskie voprosy semiotiki. Leningrad: University.]

Rey, A. 1969. Remarques sémantiques. Langue française 4.5-29.

Robert, P. 1967. Dictionnaire alphabétique & analogique de la langue française. Paris: Société du Nouveau Littré, Le Robert.

Russell, L. J. 1939. Note on the term *semeiotike* in Locke. Mind 64.405-06.

Saussure, F. de. 1967-[1916[1]]. Cours de linguistique générale. Wiesbaden: Otto Harrassowitz.

Sebeok, T. A. 1968. "Zoosemiotics". American speech 43.142-44.

—. 1970. The word "Zoosemiotics". Language sciences 10.36-37.

—, ed. 1969a –. Semiotica: Journal of the International Association for Semiotic Studies 1 –. The Hague: Mouton.

—, ed. 1969b –. Approaches to semiotics 1 –. The Hague: Mouton.

—, et al., eds. 1964. Approaches to semiotics. The Hague: Mouton.

Söder, K. 1964. Beiträge J. H. Lamberts zur formalen Logik und Semiotik. Greifswald.

Steinthal, H. 1881[2] [1871[1]]. Einleitung in die Psychologie und Sprachwissenschaft. Berlin: Ferd. Dümmlers Vlg.

Transactions of the Charles S. Peirce Society. 1965 –. A quarterly journal in American philosophy, ed. R. Robin.

Voigt, V. 1969. Modellálás a folklorisztikában. Studia ethnographica 5.347-430.

Weltring, G. 1910. Das *Semeion* in der aristotelischen, stoischen, epikureischen und skeptischen Philosophie: Ein Beitrag zur Geschichte der antiken Methodenlehre. Bonn: Hauptmann'sche Buchdruckerei.

Wollen, P. 1969. Signs and meaning in the cinema. Bloomington: Indiana University Press.

Worth, S. 1969. The development of a semiotic of film. Semiotica 1.282-321.

LEST THE WHEEL
BE TOO OFT RE-INVENTED:
TOWARDS A REASSESSMENT
OF THE INTELLECTUAL HISTORY
OF LINGUISTICS[1]

RUDOLPH C. TROIKE

> "Those who do not know history are doomed to repeat it." (Santayana)

In 1958 Archibald Hill first published a description of the relative order of prenominal modifiers in English,[2] in his well-known summation of the aims and methods of structural linguistics as applied to English, *Introduction to linguistic structures: From sound to sentence in English*. His famous example (1958:176)

All the ten fine old stone houses

illustrating the order

Pre-det-Determiner-Number-Description-Age-Material-Noun

became virtually a cliché in linguistics circles during the decade of the 1950's.

Interest in this subject and much of what it represented was largely buried in the revolution touched off in 1957 by the publication of another book, *Syntactic structures*, by Noam Chomsky.[3] The enormous amount of work in linguistic theory generated by this book almost completely transformed the field in a few short years, as fermenting intellects, leaving 'mere' surface structure as described by Hill far behind, probed further and further into the depths of syntactic structure, until some of them broke through the bottom and discovered semantics and logic, and found that the formalisms already developed by logicians made much of the linguistic work of the preceding decade seem relatively trivial.[4]

Recent work in linguistic theory has also developed along another path, exploring the power and limitations of various formal devices employed in Chomskyan models of linguistic description. In a couple of carefully-reasoned papers, Lakoff (1968) and Perlmutter (1970) have convincingly shown that deep structure conditions and transformational rules are unable to account for such facts as those described by Hill,[5] and that no constraints or devices formulable within traditional generative grammar are able to do so either. As a result, they propose that a concept of 'surface structure constraints' be incorporated into linguistic theory to accomodate such fàcts.

This demonstration of the inadequacy of transformational grammar to account for facts which had previously been dismissed as uninteresting, and the incorporation of positional slots into the model, is seen as a major advance in the explanatory adequacy of linguistic theory. To those familiar with the work of pre-Chomskyan structural linguists, it must seem that the prediction of Santayana has indeed come true, and that the history of scientific revolutions is repeating its usual cycle.

A careful reading of work in the description of English grammar over the past several centuries reveals that this is not a new situation, however, and that American linguists throughout this century have been equally guilty of re-inventing the wheel, even as they disparaged or failed to acknowledge the work of their predecessors.[6]

The influence of Charles C. Fries and Leonard Bloomfield was largely responsible for creating in the United States a 'devil image' of traditional grammarians, which has to the present time essentially prevented an objective assessment of their work. In an antitraditional work first published in 1927, entitled *What is good English*, Fries wrote as follows:

Most of the grammars published from 1586, the date of the first English grammar, to the end of the seventeenth century were of two kinds. They were either directed to foreigners who wished to learn English and for this purpose were often written in Latin or in French; or they were quite frankly introductions to the study of Latin, and aimed simply to take advantage of the use of the pupil's native language in order to facilitate his mastery of Latin grammar. The grammars of the eighteenth century, however, were usually English grammars for English people. They aimed to teach English people correct English. ... The rules furnished in the grammars were generally either carried over from Latin syntax or the new creations of a so-called 'rational grammar' and thus based upon 'reason' or the 'laws of thought' (1927:10, 17).

Leonard Bloomfield, in his book *Language*, which is regarded by many as the virtual charter of modern linguistics, echoed this as follows:

The background of our popular ideas about language is the fanciful doctrine of the eighteenth-century 'grammarians'. This doctrine, still prevalent in our schools, brands all manner of forms as 'incorrect', regardless of fact. ... It would not have been possible for 'grammarians' to bluff a large part of our speech-community, and they would not have undertaken to do so, if the public had not been ready for the deception. ... All of this, moreover, is set in a background of pseudo-grammatical doctrine, which defines the categories of the English language as philosophical truths and in philosophical terms ("a noun is the name of a person, place, or thing", "the subject is that talked about", and so on) (1933:496, 497, 500).

In *The structure of English*, undoubtedly his most influential work, Fries compared traditional grammar with Ptolemaic astronomy and concluded that it "cannot be expected to provide any satisfactory insight into the mechanisms of our language or any grasp of the processes by which language functions" (1952:277). This view of traditional grammar has assumed the status of a myth in modern linguistics, and is still to be found in more recent writings. It has come to be transmitted as part of the folklore of the discipline, and, as with most myths, its validity has rarely been questioned. While Fries knew the work of the early grammarians at first hand, most linguists have been willing to repeat his evaluation without examining the original sources. Where they have done so, their tendency has been to view the material selectively, with an eye to finding evidence in support of their preconceptions. As a result, the authoritarianism of earlier grammarians has been overemphasized at the expense of a recognition of their positive contributions.

Even where contradictory evidence has been offered, it has usually been ignored. In his doctoral dissertation, Fries studied the use of *shall* and *will* in a number of plays dating from 1557 to 1915, and concluded that the statements by grammarians that *shall* is used with the first person and *will* with the second and third persons to denote simple futurity,

... did not arise from any attempt to describe the practice of the language as it actually was either before the eighteenth century or at the time the grammar was written in which these rules first appeared ... (1940:153).

The distinction was first stated by John Wallis, in his *Grammatica Linguae Anglicanae* (1653); the linguist Robert A. Hall, Jr., has described the situation somewhat dramatically as follows:

A seventeenth-century English grammarian, one John Wallis, sitting in his study, dreamed the rule up, manufactured it out of whole cloth, and put it in his book; and later grammarians have copied and re-copied it, each from his predecessor (1960:24).

J. R. Hulbert (1947), however, has presented important counter-evidence to Fries' thesis, showing that the distinction correctly represented educated written usage from at least 1650 on. Inasmuch as Fries' figures were based on plays, it is likely that they represent less educated usage and less formal conversational style. Although Hulbert's findings should have served as an immediate corrective to Fries' work, information about his findings almost totally failed to penetrate the profession, and linguists have continued to the present time to 'copy and recopy' Fries' conclusions without modification.

The discovery by structural linguists, which has been adopted into the formulations of generative grammarians, that English verbs have only two 'structural' tenses, *past* and *nonpast*, has often been made a major point of emphasis in vaunting the superiority of a linguistic approach to the analysis of English grammar. Traditional grammarians have in particular been criticized for distorting English into a Latinate or philosophical mold by describing the language as containing a 'future tense'. Yet John Wallis, one of the most anathematized of the traditional grammarians, almost three centuries before Fries, declared that tense was a matter of form, and that English therefore had only two tenses.

On perhaps no other point have traditional grammarians been more bitterly denounced than that of their treatment of cases in the noun. The familiar school-grammar distinction of subjective and objective case has been held up to ridicule by showing that nouns in English show no change of form corresponding to these two supposed cases (while despite their espousal of substitutions as a method for defining class membership, structuralists failed to note or see as requiring explanation the correlated differences in the form of pronoun substitutes). From a 'scientific' point of view, nouns were demonstrated to have only two cases, the general and the possessive or genitive.

Yet virtually all of the major grammarians from Ben Jonson (1635) to Lindley Murray (1795), including Samuel Johnson (1755) and Bishop Lowth (1762), listed only two cases for the noun, and it was not until after 1800, when Murray introduced the objective case in his grammar, that school grammars came to recognize three cases. Thus structural linguists, in criticizing recent traditional grammarians for supposedly forcing English grammar on a Procrustean bed of Latin grammar, were in fact merely returning to a position held by traditional grammarians themselves two centuries earlier. On this point Wallis, who was a rigorous formalist, out-structuralized the structuralists by declaring that English had *no* case in nouns, since, as he rightly pointed out, the genitive is an adjective and not a noun.

Transformationalists, despite their avowed respect for history, have not fared much better. As any freshman composition handbook will point out, passive sentences in English are 'weaker', 'less forceful', 'more static' than active sentences, and students are encouraged to avoid their use. Yet in most of the early transformational literature, it was assumed that actives and passives had essentially the same meaning. Not until recently have the semantic differences been recognized, and as yet there is no fully satisfactory accounting of these differences in generative terms.

Chomsky's 'predeterminer' analysis of such strings as *some of the boys, many of the boys*, which treated *some of, many of*, as a constituent (1965), not only departed from traditional analyses, which treated the preposition as belonging with the following NP in a prepositional phrase, but was also unable to account for the verb agreement in a sentence such as *One of the boys is here*. More recent work has returned in part to the traditional view, but no definitive analysis has yet been reached.[7]

Finally, one of the most significant departures in post-Chomskyan generative grammars has been Charles Fillmore's (1968) proposal for a 'case grammar' model (which, despite his own disavowal of it, has become the most widely used and viable of recent models). An essential feature of Fillmore's theory was the recognition that prepositions in English serve as markers of case, parallel to the use of suffixes in Latin, Finnish, or Quechua. The view that prepositions were the 'signs of cases' was widely held by English grammarians in the seventeenth century, including writers such as John Wallis.[8] This 'sign theory' of prepositions did not disappear entirely from English grammars until the close of the eighteenth century, after which prepositions were simply listed in grammars with no explanation of their function. Thus, in giving recognition to the case-marking function of prepositions, Fillmore was in part returning to a view generally accepted three centuries ago, but forgotten in the intervening period. Santayana's warning indeed must make us wonder what rediscovery will be tomorrow's great new breakthrough in linguistics, and how much is really new under the linguistic sun.

University of Texas at Austin

NOTES

[1]   I am indebted to Raven I. McDavid, Jr. for the first part of this title. It is a pleasure to be able to dedicate this paper to A. A. Hill, from whom I received my first introduction to the relative order of adjectives in English, during the time when his book was still being written.

[2] This was an expanded version of the pattern worked out earlier in a doctoral dissertation done under his supervision by C. Westbrook Barritt in 1952.

[3] The subject has been pursued further in another dissertation done under Hill's direction by Donald M. Lance 1968.

[4] Cf., e.g., Gilbert Harmon 1971. In particular, formal language philosophers have developed rules for semantic interpretation of their formalisms along with the formalisms themselves, whereas until recently linguists have largely ignored this question.

[5] One relatively unsuccessful prior attempt was that by Sandra S. Annear 1964.

[6] This wilful ignorance of history has been true of other areas of linguistics as well, notably psycholinguistics, as attested by a recent study by David Ingram 1971, in which he concludes, "The argument for sentential treatment of one-word utterances is not a new one, but rather a fact suggested in 1890, in an era of great findings in child language. That modern students of child language have, by and large, ignored this period, along with its valuable insights, has been costly."

[7] See Jackendoff 1968.

[8] Emma Vorlat 1964.

REFERENCES

Annear, Sandra S. 1964. The ordering of pre-nominal modifiers in English. Project on linguistic analysis, report No. 8.95-121. Ohio State University.

Bloomfield, Leonard. 1933. Language. New York: Holt.

Barritt, C. Westbrook. 1952. The order classes of English modifiers. Doctoral dissertation, University of Virginia.

Chomsky, Noam. 1957. Syntactic structures. The Hague: Mouton.

—. 1965. Aspects of the theory of syntax. Cambridge, Mass.: MIT Press.

Fillmore, Charles J. 1968. The case for case. Universals in linguistic theory, ed. by Emmon Bach and Robert T. Harms, 1-88. New York: Holt, Rinehart and Winston.

Fries, Charles C. 1927. What is good English? Ann Arbor, Mich.: George Wahr.

—. 1940. American English grammar. New York: Appleton-Century-Crofts.

—. 1952. The structure of English. New York: Harcourt, Brace & World.

Hall, Robert A., Jr. 1960. Linguistics and your language. Garden City, N. Y.: Doubleday & Company.

Harmon, Gilbert. 1971. Deep structure and logical form. Unpublished paper, Princeton.

Hill, Archibald A. 1958. Introduction to linguistic structures. New York: Harcourt, Brace & World.

Hulbert, J. R. 1947. On the origin of the grammarians' rules for the use of 'shall' and 'will'. PMLA 62.1178-82.

Ingram, David. 1971. Transitivity in child language. Language 47.888-910.

Jackendoff, Ray. 1968. Quantifiers in English. Foundations of Language 4.422-42.

Johnson, Samuel. 1755. A grammar of the English tongue.

Jonson, Ben. 1635. The English grammar.

Lakoff, George. 1968. Pronouns and reference. Bloomington: Indiana University Linguistics Club.

Lance, Donald M. 1968. Sequential ordering in pronominal modifiers in English: A critical review. Doctoral dissertation, University of Texas at Austin.

Lowth, Robert. 1762. A short introduction to English grammar.

Murray, Lindley. 1795. English grammar.

Perlmutter, David M. 1970. Surface structure constraints in syntax. Linguistic Inquiry 1.187-255.
Vorlat, Emma. 1964. Progress in English grammar, 1585-1735. Luxembourg: Ed. A. Peiffer.
Wallis, John. 1653. Grammatica linguae Anglicanae. Oxford.

EMBEDDING AND AMBIGUITY

AKIKO UEDA

1. EMBEDDING IN ENGLISH AND THE JAPANESE EQUIVALENT

Sentence 1 below, which is given by Postal (1968:269), brings up a question: why is the English sentence "barely understandable when written, but when spoken ... beyond comprehensibility" as he tells us, while the Japanese equivalent 2 is readily comprehended?

(1)   The rat which the cat which the dog chased ate was black.

(2)   *Inu ga otta neko ga tabeta nezumi wa kurokatta.*
        'dog (Subj) chased cat (Subj) ate rat (Top) was black'.[1]

Sentence 1 and 2 are generated similarly through two applications of the relative clause transformation in English and Japanese respectively from:

The rat was black.	*Nezumi ga kurokatta.*
The cat ate the rat.	*Neko ga nezumi o tabeta.*
The dog chased the cat.	*Inu ga neko o otta.*

A sentence similar to 1 is given by Jacobs and Rosenbaum (1971:116).

(3)   This house in which the malt that the rat that the cat killed ate
        lay was built by Jack.

Jacobs and Rosenbaum consider this sentence "vastly indigestible", ascribing its indigestibility to the complexity on the left of the sentence in contrast with the following sentence, which is readily understood, with the complexity on the right (Jacobs and Rosenbaum 1971:116):

(4)   This is the cat that killed the rat that ate the malt that lay in the
        house that Jack built.

Sentence 4 means the same as sentence 3, but is vastly more digestible, according to Jacobs and Rosenbaum, since "for some not well understood reason complexity on the right of a sentence is more easily understood than complexity on the left" (Jacobs & Rosenbaum 1971:115-6).

Though it is true that 4 is much easier to understand than 3, it is not

because of the position of the complexity on the right of a sentence.
Compare 4 with 5 below:

(5)   The cat that killed the rat that ate the malt that lay in the house
       that Jack built was not a big one.

This is not less digestible than 4, though the complexity is on the left.
The difficulty in understanding 3 comes from the fact that multiple
nesting of relative clauses is built up in the center of embedding sentences
whose subjects and verbs are separated by the intervening relative clauses,
and thus a juxtaposition of subjects with some relatives in-between is
produced in the beginning and one of verb phrases at the end of the
sentence.

For simpler explanation, let us look at 1 again and compare it with the
following:

(6)   The dog chased the cat which ate the rat which was black.

Sentence 6, which is readily understood, though somewhat clumsy,
is generated from the same set of three sentences which produce 1,
and conveys the same information. In the simplified tree diagrams, the
surface structures of 1 and 6 are shown as below:

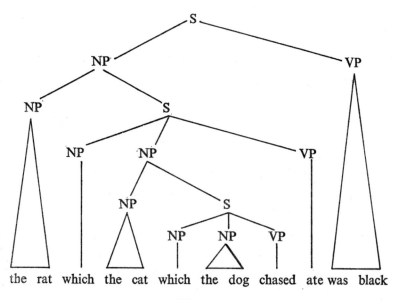

the rat which the cat which the dog chased ate was black

Diagram 1

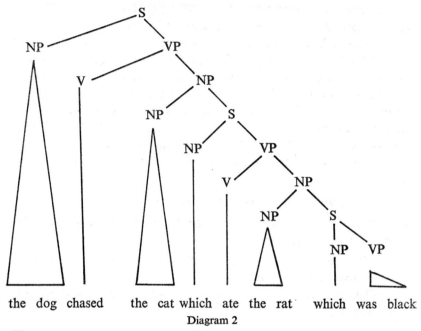

the dog chased the cat which ate the rat which was black

Diagram 2

The Japanese sentence in 2 is similar in form to the English sentence in 6, with the relative clauses added in the reverse direction.

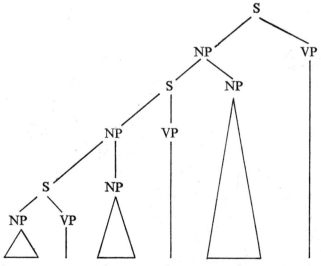

inu ga otta neko ga tabeta nezumi wa kurokatta
'dog (Subj) chased cat (Subj) ate rat (Top) was black'

Diagram 3

The same sort of tree diagram can be drawn for sentences 3 and 4; for 3 the branches are added to the center of the tree as in 1, and for 4 they extend to the right as in 6. In Japanese the relative clauses are added to the left of the noun phrases. Whether added to the right or to the left, as long as the branches are added in one direction, and toward the outside of a tree, the addition of relative clauses does not interfere with comprehensibility of a sentence. Jacobs and Rosenbaum's sentence 3 is incomprehensible not because the complexity is on the left of the sentence but because it is built up in the center of the sentence. Though this is very common in the relative clause formation with just one relative clause as in:

> The rat which the cat ate was black

the addition of one more relative clause in the center would make this sentence incomprehensible.

(7)   *Otokonoko wa otokonoko ga attakoto no nai ojisan ga okutte kureta mari o nageta.*
        The boy threw the ball which his uncle whom he had not met sent him.

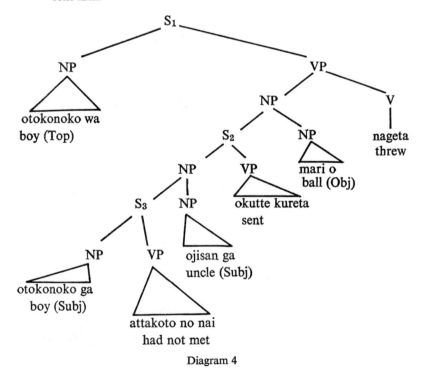

Diagram 4

Japanese, which adds relative clauses to the left of a noun phrase, is not completely free from multiple nesting of relative clauses in the center of a sentence. However, so long as we do not consider the noun phrases in adverbial phrases, it is only the subject noun phrase of the first (most outside) sentence that gets separated, as in 7. Relative clauses do not separate verbs from the other noun phrases either in the embedded or embedding sentences.

In 7, another point comes up. Since the deepest embedded S_3 modifies *ojisan* 'uncle' in S_2, *ojisan* in S_3 has been deleted in relativizing, but the subject of S_2 *otokonoko ga* 'boy (Subj)' remains, following the subject of the most outside embedding S_1 *otokonoko wa* 'boy (Top)'. The second *otokonoko ga* is deleted later by the identical-noun-phrase-deletion transformation.[2] In this case no ambiguity results, but there are cases in which the application of the transformation results in ambiguity. This phenomenon is perhaps peculiar to Japanese in which two successive noun phrases with the same form and referent can be found in the deep structure. We will come back to this matter later, in section 3.

2. TWO RELATIVE CLAUSES MODIFYING A NOUN PHRASE

In Japanese as well as in English, a noun phrase can be modified by two separate relative clauses. In such a case, if there is some other noun phrase in the surface structure of the embedded sentence which comes next to the modified noun phrase, the outer relative clause may be understood to refer to the noun phrase in the embedded sentence. The same applies to the noun phrases in adverbials.

In most cases, the reference is made clear with the help of other devices. In 8, though there is a noun phrase *New York* in the inner embedded sentence, the outer relative clause with *who* at the beginning cannot refer to *New York* as the antecedent. The same is true of 9, and in 10 the plural verb form in the relative clause indicates that it cannot refer to *Japan.*

(8) John met a man who was from New York who had never been to the top of the Empire State Building (Smith 1964:42).

(9) I met many Americans in Japan who could speak Japanese fluently.

(10) There are many social arrangements and habits of life in Japan which have close parallels even in the primitive tribes of the Pacific islands (Benedict 1946:8).

(11)   We visited many shrines in Japan which had a long history.

In 11, however, the relative clause can refer either to *Japan* or to *shrines*. If it refers to *shrines*, the adverbial phrase *in Japan* can be moved up to the beginning of the sentence, but if it refers to *Japan*, the phrase has to stay where it is, still leaving the possibility of its referring to *shrines* as well.

    In Japanese we find a similar phenomenon in the following passage:

(12)   *korehodo hanahadashiku kotonatta kōdō to shisō no shūkan o* ...
         'to this extent very different acting and thinking of habit (Obj)'
         (Hasegawa 1967:5)

The original in English is the following:

(13)   such exceedingly different habits of acting and thinking ...
         (Benedict 1946:1)

Different clearly modifies *habits* in English, but in the Japanese translation, *kotonatta* 'different' is more likely to be interpreted as modifying *kōdō to shisō* 'acting and thinking' which comes next to it, rather than *shūkan* 'habits'. In this sentence, *korehodo... kotonatta* can be moved to the position in front of *shūkan*, preventing the incorrect reference. However, if two relative clauses modifying the same noun phrase have in each a noun phrase, there is no use of shifting the two relative clauses around for clarity.

(14)   *Kare wa zōkin de yoku huita kyōshitsu no kokuban ni e o kaita.*

'He (Top) $\begin{Bmatrix} \text{a piece} \\ \text{of cloth} \end{Bmatrix}$ with well wiped classroom of blackboard

on picture (Obj) drew'

He drew a picture on the blackboard in the classroom which someone wiped well with a piece of cloth.

In 14, *zōkin de yoku huita* 'wiped well with a piece of cloth' can refer either to *kyōshitsu* 'classroom' or *kokuban* 'blackboard', and if we move this relative clause to the position before *kokuban*, producing *kyōshitsu no zōkin de yoku huita kokuban*, then *kyōshitsu no* may refer either to *zōkin* or *kokuban*.

    In English as well as in Japanese there are cases from which ambiguity cannot be removed when two relative clauses modify the same noun phrase.

3. 'SOMEONE' DELETION AND IDENTICAL NOUN PHRASE DELETION IN JAPANESE

From a Japanese sentence, especially from an embedded sentence, an unidentified-subject noun phrase is often deleted optionally, in most cases without causing any difficulty in understanding, just as *by someone* is deleted from a passive sentence in English. The deletion of such noun phrases is called 'someone' deletion.

(15)   *Neko wa hoshita zabuton no ue de nete iru.*

'cat (Top) $\begin{Bmatrix} \text{placed in} \\ \text{the sun} \end{Bmatrix}$ cushion on top of sleeping is'

A cat is sleeping on a cushion (someone) placed in the sun.

Hoshita 'placed in the sun' is not a passive form of the verb *hosu*, and so there must be someone who placed the cushion in the sun. Since it does not matter who did it, 'someone' is the subject which is deleted by the 'someone' deletion to produce the surface structure in 15.

In some cases, however, the 'someone' deletion transformation causes ambiguity, when the same surface structure is generated either through this transformation or through the identical-noun-phrase-deletion transformation.

As for the identical-noun-phrase-deletion transformation, the following serves as an example:

(16)   *Itō san wa sannenkakatte kaita hon o shuppanshita.*

'Mr. Ito (Top) $\begin{Bmatrix} \text{taking three} \\ \text{years} \end{Bmatrix}$ wrote book (Obj) published'

Mr. Ito published a book which took him three years to write.

Before the application of the identical-noun-phrase-deletion transformation, *Itō san wa* 'Mr. Ito (Top)' was followed directly by *Itō san ga* 'Mr. Ito (Subj)', which was consequently deleted. In this sentence also there is no ambiguity.

(17)   *Pianisto wa chōritsushita piano o hiki hajimeta.*
        'pianist (Top) tuned piano (Obj) play started'
        The pianist started to play the piano which someone (or, he) had tuned.'

In 17, the subject of the verb *chōritsushita* 'tuned' can be *pianisto* 'pianist' which was deleted by the identical-noun-phrase-deletion transformation, or 'someone' deleted by the 'someone'-deletion transformation, as indicated in the English translation.

Let me give another example:

(18)   *Otokonoko wa kinō e ni kaita kaigan de takibi o shita.*
        'boy (Top) yesterday picture in drew beach on bonfire (Obj) made'

> The boy made a bonfire on the beach which he had drawn in a picture the day before.

Sentence 18 is odd at least, because *enikaita kaigan* 'the beach drawn in the picture' could come from a Japanese sequence meaning 'the beach someone had drawn in the picture' with the implication that it is the beach in the picture rather than the real beach where the boy made the bonfire. On the other hand, the sentence could come through the identical-noun-phrase-deletion transformation, deleting the second noun phrase *otokonoko ga* 'boy (Subj)'. If the second noun phrase is pronominalized, the oddness of the surface structure as well as the ambiguity is removed. The same is true with 17. To what extent this pronominalization is necessary remains yet to be determined, for in many more cases the deletion of the second identical noun phrase is sufficient.

Another problem in this connection presents itself in a translation:

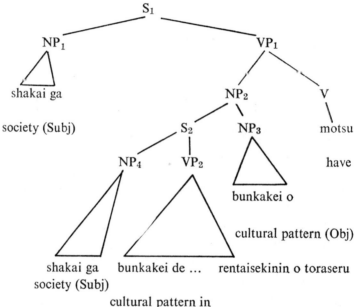

Diagram 5

(19)   ... *rentaisekinin o toraseru bunkakei o motsu shakai* ... (Shimizu & Inugai 1952:93)

'joint responsibility (Obj) let take $\begin{Bmatrix} \text{cultural} \\ \text{pattern} \end{Bmatrix}$ (Obj) have society'

At first glance, one may take that it is *bunkakei* 'cultural pattern' which imposes or lets take *rentaisekinin* 'joint responsibility', but on second thought, he will see it is odd for the cultural pattern to impose joint responsibility. In 20, the original English sentence is given and the italicized part is the section whose translation is shown in 19:

(20)   Lastly in *societies which have patterns of joint responsibility* for the acts of any family member ... (Linton 1945:71)

20 is generated from the deep structure shown in diagram 5.

In embedding S_2, it is *bunkakei de* 'in the patterns' that is deleted, and NP_4 remains. Since NP_4 is identical to NP_1, NP_4 is deleted, thus creating the undesired outcome. That is, in the absence of NP_4, NP_3 is taken to have been the subject noun phrase of S_2.

4. OBSERVATION

When we compare embedding in English with the Japanese equivalent, an interesting difference comes up. In the cases where the normal relativizing process results in difficulty in understanding, there is in English a juxtaposition of verbs at the end of a sentence separated from their respective subjects or objects by the existence of more than one intervening relative clause. In Japanese, it is the juxtaposition of noun phrases in the beginning of a sentence which triggers the identical-noun-phrase-deletion transformation and 'someone'-deletion transformation to operate, and thus creates the chances for misunderstanding or at least ambiguity.

In the transformational process of relativization proper, both languages operate in the same way, but the difference in the direction of attaching relative clauses brings out different sorts of surface structures with different kinds of ambiguities and difficulties in understanding.

Tsuda College

NOTES

[1] (Subj), (Top), and (Obj) stand for the functions of noun phrases in which the postpositions *ga*, *wa*, and *o* are included: subject, topic, and object respectively. For the difference between (Subj) and (Top), see Note 2. Under Japanese sentences, word for word translation is given first, and then the English equivalent where necessary.

[2] The postposition *wa* is a marker for 'topic'. A noun phrase can be topicalized when the original postposition in the noun phrase is replaced by *wa*. In such a case, the whole noun phrase is usually brought to the beginning of a sentence.

At the same time *wa* is a marker for the subject of an embedding sentence. When two noun phrases identical in form and reference (except in postpositions) occur in the beginning of a sentence, it is the second noun phrase, the subject of the embedded sentence, that is deleted. The first noun phrase remains with the postposition *wa* as the marker. This fact is proved by embedding the sentence in a larger frame. If we embed 7 in the following, the outcome is perfectly grammatical:

> *Otokonoko wa sora o miageta.*
> The boy looked up at the sky.
> *Attakoto no nai ojisan kara moratta mari o nageta otokonoko wa sora o miageta.*
> The boy who threw the ball which his uncle whom he had not met sent him looked up at the sky.

If *otokonoko wa* is the subject of an embedded sentence, the outcome should be, and is, ungrammatical, as shown easily by embedding a sentence with two different noun phrases from an embedding sentence and an embedded one in the beginning of a sentence.

REFERENCES

Benedict, Ruth. 1946. The Chrysanthemum and the sword. Tokyo: Tuttle.

Hasegawa, Matsuji. 1967. Kiku to katana, trans. of The chrysanthemum and the sword by Ruth Benedict. Tokyo: Shakaishisōsha.

Jacobs, Roderick A., and Peter S. Rosenbaum. 1971. Transformations, style, and meaning. Waltham, Mass.: Xerox College Publishing.

Linton, Ralph. 1945. The cultural background of personality. New York: Appleton-Century-Crofts.

Postal, Paul M. 1968. 'Epilogue' in Roderick A. Jacobs and Peter S. Rosenbaum, English transformational grammar. Waltham, Mass.: Blaisdell.

Shimizu, Ikutaro, and Yasuhiko Inugai. 1952. Bunka-jinruigakunyūmon, trans. of The cultural background of personality by Ralph Linton. Tokyo: Tokyo-sōgensha.

Smith, Carlota S. 1964. Determiners and relative clauses in a generative grammar of English, Lg. 40.37-52.

DEVOICING AND ELISION
OF SOME VOWELS
IN JAPANESE AND ENGLISH

MINORU UEDA

It is a well-known fact that the high front vowel [i] and the high back unrounded [ɯ] in Modern Standard Japanese are devoiced or even elided under certain clearly definable conditions. On the other hand, the devocalization and deletion of the mid central vowel [ə] and the high front lax vowel [ɪ] in certain phonetic environments in English seem to have drawn very little attention. It may therefore be of some value to investigate these phenomena and compare the conditions under which they occur with those for the voiceless or elided Japanese vowels.

In Modern Standard Japanese, [i] and [ɯ] are normally pronounced voiceless, when they are preceded by voiceless stops such as [p], [k],[1] and followed by voiceless consonants. Consequently, we have instances like *pikapika*[2] [pi̥kàpi̥kà] 'brightly', *kusí* [kɯ̥ʃi] 'comb', *kutu* [kɯ̥tsɯ́] 'shoe', etc.. The formula for this is:

$$(1) \quad \begin{bmatrix} + \text{ voc} \\ - \text{ cons} \\ + \text{ high} \\ \alpha \text{ back} \end{bmatrix} \rightarrow \begin{bmatrix} - \text{ voice} \\ \alpha \text{ back} \end{bmatrix} / \begin{bmatrix} - \text{ voc} \\ + \text{ cons} \\ - \text{ voice} \\ - \text{ nasal} \\ - \text{ cont} \end{bmatrix} - \begin{bmatrix} - \text{ voc} \\ + \text{ cons} \\ - \text{ voice} \\ - \text{ nasal} \end{bmatrix}^3 .$$

Furthermore, [i] and [ɯ] normally disappear between a preceding voiceless continuant consonant and a following voiceless consonant. This may be formulated as:

$$(2) \quad \begin{bmatrix} + \text{ voc} \\ - \text{ cons} \\ + \text{ high} \end{bmatrix} \rightarrow \emptyset / \begin{bmatrix} - \text{ voc} \\ + \text{ cons} \\ - \text{ voice} \\ - \text{ nasal} \\ + \text{ cont} \end{bmatrix} - \begin{bmatrix} - \text{ voc} \\ + \text{ cons} \\ - \text{ voice} \\ - \text{ nasal} \end{bmatrix}$$

Words like *Misisíppi* 'Mississippi', *tukusi* 'horsetail' are thus pronounced [miʃʃppi], [tskɯ̥ʃi̥].[4] When, however, the high front or low back vowel with a tonal nucleus preceded by a voiceless consonant is immediately followed by the sequence *si, su, ti* or *tu* occurring before a pause or before a voiceless consonant, it is this sequence whose vowel is lost, while the vowel with a nucleus remains fully voiced. Examples are: *susu (to)* [súس (tò)] 'soot (and)', *súsi (to)* [súʃ (tò)] 'sushi (and)', *Kísi* [kíʃ]' Kishi (a personal name)' (cf. *kisí* [ki̥ʃí] 'shore'), *kísu (si)* [ki̥ʃʃ] 'kiss(ing)', *kisú* [ki̥sú] 'sillago', *kisú to* [ki̥stò] 'sillago and', *kúsu* [kúس][5] 'camphor tree', *kútu* [kúts] 'to rot (archaic)', *kúti* [kútʃ] 'rot (verb) and'.

Rules (1) and (2) must then be modified as follows:

(1)′

$$
\begin{bmatrix} + \text{voc} \\ - \text{cons} \\ + \text{high} \\ \alpha \text{ back} \end{bmatrix} \rightarrow \begin{bmatrix} - \text{voice} \\ \alpha \text{ back} \end{bmatrix} / \begin{bmatrix} - \text{voc} \\ + \text{cons} \\ - \text{voice} \\ - \text{cont} \end{bmatrix} - \begin{bmatrix} - \text{voc} \\ + \text{cons} \\ - \text{voice} \\ - \text{nasal} \\ \alpha \text{ cont} \end{bmatrix}
$$

$$
\begin{bmatrix} + \text{voc} \\ - \text{cons} \\ \begin{bmatrix} - \alpha \text{high} \\ - \alpha \text{back} \\ \left\{ \begin{matrix} - \alpha \text{high tone} \\ + \alpha \text{high tone} \end{matrix} \right\} \end{bmatrix} \end{bmatrix}^{6}
$$

(2)′

$$
\begin{bmatrix} + \text{voc} \\ + \text{high} \end{bmatrix} \rightarrow \emptyset / \begin{bmatrix} + \text{cons} \\ - \text{voice} \\ - \text{nasal} \\ + \text{cont} \end{bmatrix} - \begin{bmatrix} + \text{cons} \\ - \text{voice} \\ - \text{nasal} \\ \alpha \text{ cont} \end{bmatrix} \begin{bmatrix} + \text{voc} \\ - \text{cons} \\ \begin{bmatrix} - \alpha \text{high} \\ - \alpha \text{back} \\ \left\{ \begin{matrix} - \alpha \text{high tone} \\ + \alpha \text{high tone} \end{matrix} \right\} \end{bmatrix} \end{bmatrix}
$$

We have just given a brief sketch of the Japanese devoicing and elision system. Let us now turn our attention to the devoicing of French vowels. Otto Jespersen (1913:90) discusses this showing such examples as *ce n'est pas beaucoup* [s nɛ pɑ ⌈bo⌉ ku̥], *n'y pensons plus* [ni pã ⌈sɔ̃⌉ plу̥], *c'est ici* [sɛ ⌈ti⌉ si̥]. And he explains the frequent devoicing of high vowels before pauses by arguing that the voiceless high vowels tend to acquire a greater degree of audibility because of their norrow strictures which increase the audible friction of air stream in the oral cavity.[7] Furthermore, Jespersen gives some examples where devoicing occurs even in mid or low French vowels: *le barometre est monté* [l(ə) barɔmɛtr ɛ ⌈mɔ̃⌉te̥], *tu ne l'auras pas* [ty n lɔ ⌈ra⌉ pɑ̥].

Now in Modern English, such devocalization often results in a total obliteration of the devoiced vowel, especially under conditions similar to rule (2)′ in Japanese, so that this phenomenon tends to be treated simply as elision or omission in English phonetics (Gimson 1965:231-2, Heffner 1950:178-80). Here, however, the vowel that is devoiced or elided is in most cases an unaccented, mid central schwa [ə] (including [ɚ]) normally occurring right before the primary stress in the next syllable. Such examples are numerous: (a) *potential* [pə̥tɛ́nʃəl], *particular*, [pɚ̥tíkjələ], *to take* [tə̥ ték], *perform* [pɚ̥fɔ́frm], *perhaps* [pɚ̥hǽps], *secretary* [sɛ́kə̥tɛ̀rɪ];[8] (b) *society* [ssáɪətɪ], *suppose* [spouz], *photography* [ftágrəfɪ]. In group (a), the devocalized schwa seems to remain between a preceding voiceless stop and a following voiceless consonant in order, perhaps, to facilitate the release of the former consonant, whereas in group (b) the preceding voiceless continuant takes over the syllabicity of the schwa, thus replacing it completely. This accounts for the total disappearance of the vowel [ə] here. The rules for (a) and (b) then will be:

$$(3) \quad \begin{bmatrix} + \text{ voc} \\ - \text{ high} \\ - \text{ low} \\ - \text{ front} \\ - \text{ back} \end{bmatrix} \rightarrow [- \text{ voice}] / \begin{bmatrix} - \text{ voc} \\ + \text{ cons} \\ - \text{ voice} \\ - \text{ cont} \\ - \text{ nasal} \end{bmatrix} - \begin{bmatrix} - \text{ voc} \\ + \text{ cons} \\ - \text{ voice} \\ - \text{ nasal} \end{bmatrix} \begin{bmatrix} + \text{ voc} \\ - \text{ cons} \\ + \text{ stress} \end{bmatrix}$$

$$(4) \quad \begin{bmatrix} + \text{ voc} \\ - \text{ high} \\ - \text{ low} \\ - \text{ front} \\ - \text{ back} \end{bmatrix} \rightarrow \emptyset / \begin{bmatrix} - \text{ voc} \\ + \text{ cons} \\ - \text{ voice} \\ + \text{ cont} \\ - \text{ nasal} \end{bmatrix} - \begin{bmatrix} - \text{ voc} \\ + \text{ cons} \\ - \text{ voice} \\ - \text{ nasal} \end{bmatrix} \begin{bmatrix} + \text{ voc} \\ - \text{ cons} \\ + \text{ stress} \end{bmatrix}.$$

The similarity of rules (3) and (4) in English to rules (1)′ and (2)′ in Japanese is apparent, and the elision derived from rule (4) should perhaps be kept distinct from the other types of elision such as in *police* [plís], *believe* [blív], *delightful* [dláɪtful] *ferocious* [fróʃəs], *saloon* [slún], and so on, since in the former type of elision the process of devoicing is involved.

The schwa which devoiced or deleted by rule (3) or (4) may best be represented as a higher mid-central vowel akin to Daniel Jones' [əɪ] (Jones 1957:92), since a high front vowel like [ɪ] also tends to be elided under similar conditions. The commonest example of this is *university* [jùnɪvɛ́ˑstɪ], where [ɪ] is elided between [s] and [t]. Similarly [ɪ] is found elided after [f] in [práftəb]] (Heffner 1950:179). On the other hand, the devoiced [ɪ̥] is observed in such examples as *peculiar* [pɪ̥kjúljɚ], *orchestra* [ɔ́rkɹ̩strə]. In all these examples, the rules governing their devocalization and deletion look similar to rules (3) and (4) above.

Sporadic devoicing of [ɪ] is not restricted to the conditions given above, and in fact the author himself has witnessed such an extreme case as *U. S. B-52 bombers* [jú és bi f(ɹ)ftɹ̩ tu bámɚz] (*have staged three raids* ...) (from the Far East Network News, June 1971). A repeated tape replay seems to indicate that here the devoiced [ɹ̩] is absent, leaving the preceding [f] palatalized and syllabic. Curiously enough, however, the [ɹ̩] after [t] remains voiced in this example. As an interesting example of the [ɪ] Heffner (1950:200) mentions under 'haplology' the case where the word *substitute* is pronounced *substute*, which may be interpreted as a result of the process: [sʌ́bstɪtjùt] > [sʌ́bstɪ̩tjùt] > [sʌ́bsttjùt] > [sʌ́bstyùt].

It will be some time before any coherent system of devoicing and deletion rules for [ə] and [ɪ] in English becomes available. For so much depends on the detailed investigation of widely collected speech materials, since, after all, the aforesaid linguistic phenomena are mostly unconscious activities, forbidding any conscious retrospection on the part of their speaker.

Waseda University

NOTES

[1] The sequence *ti* and *tu* are pronounced [tʃi] and [tsɯ] respectively, so that there is no instance where [i] or [ɯ] is preceded by [t].

[2] An acute accent in our orthography represents a tone accent or nucleus, indicating a high tone which is always followed by a low tone in the next syllable, provided that a given accented vowel is voiced. When the accented vowel is voiceless, the presence of the tonal nucleus is recognized by a low tone in the next syllable (indicated by a grave accent): *kíta* [kítà] 'came'. Since the nucleus must always be followed by a low tone, its occurrence in the final syllable ismply indicates the possible occurrence of a particle with a low tone: *kutú* (*ga*) [kɯtsɯ́ (ŋà)] 'shoe (nominative)'. The same acute accent used in the phonetic transcription, however, stands for a high tone regardless of whether this high tone is immediately followed by a low tone or not. Examples are: *hasí to* [hàʃtò] 'bridge and', *hasi to* [hàʃtó] 'edge and', *skiyaki* [skíyákí] 'sukiyaki', *sayonára* [sayónárà] 'sayonara'. The rule here is that when a nucleus does not occur in a polysyllabic word (including the particle that follows it), such a word (together with the accompanying particle) will have successive high tones except for its initial syllable, which has a low tone. Moreover, if there is an extra intervening syllable between the initial low tone syllable and the syllable carrying a nucleus, such a syllable or syllables will also have high tones.

[3] Here we generally follow the practice in Noam Chomsky and Morris Halle 1968.

[4] The symbol [ʃ] used here represents a palatalized *s* akin to the Russian *s'* as in *zd'es'* 'here'. The dot in [ʃ̩] indicates syllabicity.

[5] Needless to say, when a word like *kúsu* is followed by a particle beginning with a voiced sound, the (word-) final syllable restores its vocality, thus giving a sequence like: *kúsu o tukau* [kʊ̥sʉ̀ ó tʂkáʉ́] 'to use camphor tree (as material)'.

[6] The symbols '+ high tone' indicate that when the preceding consonant is a voiceless (nonnasal) continuant, the vowel, if it is of a high front or high back variety, must carry a high tone in order that the high front or high back vowel in the preceding syllable be devocalizaed. The presence of a high tone does not always mean that the vowel in question has a tonal nucleus, unless this high tone is immediately followed by a low tone. Compare note 2.

[7] "Da es nun nach der Natur der Sache am leichtesten ist, einen stimmlosen Vokal hörbar zu machen, wenn die Luft einen eingeengten Mund zu passieren hat, so tritt diese Erscheinung am leichtesten bei den hohen Vokalen [i. u, y] ein, ..." (Jespersen 1913:90).

[8] This devoiced form comes from the dissimilated form [sékətèrɪ] of [sékrətèrɪ].

[9] Though Chomsky and Halle classify [ʌ] as + back, the schwa used here is treated as central, that is, – front, – back.

REFERENCES

Chomsky, Noam, and Halle, Morris. 1968. The sound pattern of English. New York: Harper & Row.

Gimson, A. C. 1964. An introduction to the pronunciation of English. London: Edward Arnold.

Heffner, R.-M. S. 1950. General phonetics. Madison: University of Wisconsin Press.

Jespersen, Otto. 1913. Lehrbuch der Phonetik. Zweite Auflage. Leipzig: Teubner.

Jones, Daniel. 1957. An outline of English phonetics. 8th ed. Cambridge: W. Heffer & Sons.

—. 1967. Everyman's English pronouncing dictionary. 13th ed. by A. C. Gimson. London: J. M. Dent & Sons.

Kenyon, John., and Knott, Thomas A. 1951. A pronouncing dictionary of American English. 2nd ed. Springfield, Mass.: G. & C. Merriam.

THE OBJECTIVIST POSITION

BJARNE ULVESTAD

In retrospect, it is difficult to escape the impression that the leading proponents of generative transformational syntax have, openly or tacitly, abandoned virtually all the spectacular claims and promises made during the late fifties and early sixties. Hundreds of theoretical and practical studies have been written over the past 14 years, in addition to dozens of more or less elementary introductions, but as yet there seems to be little common ground except for the prevailing disdainful attitude toward the theories and methods of the so-called 'prescientific' structuralists et al. A number of presumably fundamental concepts (e.g. deep structure, competence, performance, ideal speaker, grammaticality, insight, explanatory adequacy, rule power, revealing formalization) are still, in spite of, or because of, embarrassing definitional questions posed by A. A. Hill and other outstanding objectivists,[1] too nebulous to be amenable to really satisfactory and progressive critical evaluation. What remains to-day, apart from representational, especially graphic, formalism (formulaism), appears to be a deep conviction that TG mentalism is nevertheless the superior brand of scientific credo. This appears to be a group-consolidating view that is in part bolstered by recurrent general statements to the effect that most objectivist critiques are simply due to "misunderstanding, ignorance, and prejudice", to quote from one of the more revealing recent introductory handbooks.[2] However, the ease and relative frequency with which allegibly intuition-right and structure-revealing TG rules have been discarded as in reality counterintuitive and nonrevealing, and then either replaced by others or provisionally dropped (pending further research), would seem to indicate a goodly measure of basal theoretical deficiency. In addition, it is worth noticing that even militant latter-day champions of TG tend to regard much of the TG description published so far as ad hoc and of ephemeral interest, cf. Hovdhaugen's interesting statement (1969:186): "Personally, I believe that very few of the practical results that one has achieved so far, will survive."

This state of affairs, with respect to the development of theoretical foundations as well as to practical achievements, will, in my opinion, continue and grow even more serious in the years to come. One of the main reasons for this lies, in my view, at least partly in the increasingly intricate problems that each TG rule falsification normally entails with respect to implementation. As this may a priori seem a bit counterintuitive, some explanation is in order.

In the early days of TG discussion, rule questioners and rule falsifiers like myself were often smilingly disarmed with a variant of the following statement: "There will of course be a little rule to take care of this", e.g., regarding the fact that the sentence *all the men were drowned*, in one of its meanings, it not a transform of an active sentence. But, almost invariably, the 'little rule' turned out to be enormously complicated in comparison with the rule which it was intended to amend. To objectivists, i.e. linguists who do not look upon corpus analysis and correlative description as reprehensible, there is a solid though rarely stated empirical reason for this situation: The sizes of the relative portions of related data covered by a set of rules are inversely proportional to the complexity of the respective rules. If we prefer to talk about the relative number of rules rather than about rule complexity (rule- and-sub-rule systems), the statement runs as follows: More rules are ordinarily required to take care of the smaller subgroups of empirical data than of the larger.[3] Thus in an exhaustive description of the German *der*-relatives (D) with regard to the distance from their reference nouns (N), based on a large number of empirical data (4785 relative clauses taken from printed modern prose), the relationships are found to be:

> Rule 1: ND (D immediately following N, e.g., *der Mann, der*), covers 72% of the material.
> Rules 2–9: NED (one element between N and D, e.g., *den Mann zu sehen, der*), cover 23% of the material.

The remainder of the empirical material, 5% (two or more elements between N and D, e.g., *der Mann war nicht mehr im Hause zu finden, der*), would require more than one hundred rules, and it is this set of rules whose formulation and number are hardest to state and to estimate in a beyond-the-corpus grammar.

It also seems to be an empirical fact that most of the TG rules that have been described in the past, apart from some simple recursive rules, (corpus-typologically) correspond to Rules 1–9 above, i.e., intuition regularly 'generates' sentences belonging to what we may conveniently call the .9-grammar (or 90%-grammar). That may be the chief reason why it is so easy to propose rather elegant TG rules based on native intuition.[4] It may also be the reason why almost all TG rules published so far can be falsified the moment they are fully understood by a critical (objectivist) reader who knows the language described, or as soon as they are confronted with a corpus. In my opinion, a corpus-related description, of a given syntactic phenomenon, a description (e.g. a .9-grammatical description) in which proper account is taken of statistical primacies, is both possible and desirable, and, to judge from most extant descriptions, it is the .9-grammar that yields the most important insight into the structure of a given language. The .9-grammar also, because of its relative simplicity, furnishes a sound basis for pedagogical grammar work (including foreign-language instruction).

TG is still antagonistic to considerations of probabilistic approaches to syntax. The present scholarly conflict between mentalists and objectivists would be far less severe if corpus and even frequency relations were paid more attention to on the part of the mentalists, for the two groups differ far less in basic descriptive approaches than in the ways in which they emphasize different aspects of their theoretical postulates, as I hope to show in the following.

Leaving aside the question of corpus analysis culminating in general .9-grammatical rules of generative power, we now turn to one rule system that both mentalists and objectivist make abundant use of, namely the rigid Aristotelian type, for which statistics presumably does not enter into the picture. Out of a large number of illustrative examples taken from TG descriptions of modern German, I shall select two, the recording of which will occupy little space on the page. Both will serve to lay bare some important practical differences between mentalist and objectivist rule problem solutions.

In a pioneering work that has already, and deservedly, become a classic in German linguistics, Bierwisch (1963:113f.) states a rule that both in its informal wording and in its formalization excludes the following two dependent clauses as deviating or ungrammatical: (1) *weil wir ihn die Partie haben singen gehört*, (2) *weil wir ihn haben kommen gesehen*, whereas (3) *weil wir ihn die Partie haben singen hören* and (4) *weil wir ihn haben kommen sehen* are correct or grammatical. The conditioning factor is allegedly the position of the finite verb *haben* (correct is: (5) *weil wir ihn die Partie singen gehört haben*). However, on closer inspection of relevant corpus material, one must conclude that the empirical facts simply do not support this rule.[5] Sentences (1) and (2) must be regarded as no less grammatical than (3), (4). The possible statistical corpus relationships between (1), (2) and (3), (4) do not concern us here, since numerical relationships are extraneous to TG rule systematics.

The next example is more interesting, as it refers to a much more general TG rule. In an article by a group of linguists referring to themselves as the Frankfort Circle (*Frankfurter Kreis*), what purports to be a revealing illustration of TG rule-making as compared to traditionalist practice is given, with reference to the use of the so-called preliminary *es* in German declarative main clauses. The rule is first informally worded as follows (Frankfurter Kreis 1970:64): "Any declarative sentence whose subject is not a personal pronoun or *man* can be transformed into an *es*-clause", and then formalized thus: XVY → *es*VXY (V = finite verb). The following comments can be made about this rule: In its informal wording, the rule is old and relatively well known, at least in European schools. Thus I find it in the old Norwegian grammar of German that I used as a student 25 years ago: "With personal pronouns and *man*, one cannot use *es* [as preliminary subject]" (Falk and Selmer 1934:71). The two worded rules seem practically identical, but there is a difference: The Frankfort Circle rule claims exhaustive validity,[6] whereas its Norwegian counterpart merely states (important) constraints. The German rule is explicit enough for immediate falsification by anyone interested in testing it. The Norwegian rule is basically right in its description of constraints (note, however, that one can say, with stressed personal pronoun: (6) *es kam auch er*); the German rule fails precisely where it goes beyond the statement of constraints and claims exhaustive validity for the remaining domain. The TG rule above would for instance generate also these ungrammatical sentences: (7) **Es hat Mutter recht*, (8) **es macht Liebe blind*, (9) **es war Schwester Rose entzückt*, (10) **es sah zertreut Hans ihnen zu*.[7] It would fail to generate grammatical sentences like (11) *es weinte auch sie*, (12) *es irrt auch er*, (13) *ja, es war sie*.[8] There can be no doubt that a really exhaustive rule or rule complex governing preliminary *es* usage would be vastly more complicated than the one envisaged by the young German TG enthusiasts.[9]

Both examples adduced here would seem to be characteristic of TG research, of a scientific approach that is more concerned with setting up explicit and thus falsifiable hypotheses than with the relevant material basis for such hypotheses. They are instances of what objectivists term premature generalization. One reason why objectivists publish relatively less on syntax than do mentalists, would seem to be the fact that tradition has looked upon the kind of rule formulation described here as reprehensible practice, to quote Martinet (1949:35): "Linguists should never forget that it is not for a language to meet the requirements of a descriptive method, but for the method to adapt itself to the whims of linguistic reality." Now, premature generalization is not found only in TG work. Objectivist tradition admittedly includes numerous instances of vacuous description, as do of course pedagogical grammars. Still, the objectivist position has on the whole been that spurious, easily falsifiable syntactic rules are of ultimately questionable linguistic value, whereas mentalists seem to be much more tolerant on this point.

In the field of foreign language instruction, rules such as those exemplified above may often do more harm than good. A telling illustration from a modern grammar of German will be given here; it is closely related to Bierwisch' rule (above), and runs as follows: "The simple infinitive stands for a past participle [with verbs such as] *sehen, hören.* ... In the Umgangssprache the past participle may ... also be used" (Schulz and Griesbach 1970:83). One of the examples given is: (14) *Wir haben die Vögel im Wald singen hören.* Bierwisch (1963:108) on the other hand, permits the I[nfinitive] as well as the P[article] in such sentences, thus also (15) *Wir haben die Vögel singen gehört,* which Schulz-Griesbach surprisingly enough relegates to be substandard *Umgangssprache.* The rule as stated is general and explicit, i.e. testable, and it has recently been tested by means of a questionnaire with randomized test sentences submitted to ten German informants.[10] The results are presented here (acceptable [in Hochsprache] = 1, impossible = −1, uncertain = 0). Each questionnaire frame was tested both with I (*hören*) and with P (*gehört*), and the evaluation figures (e.g., 10/5) indicate that the sentence with I scored 10 points (all informants found it grammatical), and the one with P scored 5 points. Only the relevant portions of the test frames are included here.[11]

(16)   er hat es kommen *hören/gehört* (10/5)
(17)   kommen *hören/gehört* hat er es (8/8)
(18)   kommen hat er es nicht *hören/gehört* (2/10)
(19)   er wird es kommen *hören/gehört* haben (−2/10)
(20)   er würde es kommen *hören/gehört* haben (−6/10)
(21)   hat er es kommen *hören/gehört?* (10/8)
(22)   er kann es haben kommen *hören/gehört* (10/2)
(23)   er will es kommen *hören/gehört* haben (−2/10)
(24)   es kommen *hören/gehört* zu haben (−2/10)
(25)   wer hat es nicht kommen *hören/gehört?* (10/6)
(26)   dass er es hat kommen *hören/gehört* (10/4)

(27) dass er es kommen *hören/gehört* hat (−10/10)
(28) um es kommen *hören/gehört* zu haben (−6/10)

Only the particular frames (16), (22), (25), and (26) would seem not to contradict the general rule cited above, the all-round result being:

1. P (*gehört*) has a higher score than I (*hören*) in 7 frames out of 13.
2. P has no negative score.
3. I has a higher score than P in 5 frames out of 13.
4. I has a negative score in 6 frames.
5. I is found to be ungrammatical by all informants in one frame (27).
6. Score sum for P: 103, for I: 32.

If a choice has to be made between I an P, e.g. for pedagogical reasons, the better choice would clearly be P, not I, which amounts to stating that the validity of the general rule stated above has not been confirmed, but on the contrary falsified.

It is obvious that material-based elaboration of syntactical rules, whether the material is derived through elicitation or through corpus analysis, entails much painstaking work. However, if one wishes to avoid operating within a competence framework that is basically a projection of one's own or one's informants' limited idiolectal intuition, one should not try to "... arrive at a grammar by intuition, guess-work, all sorts of partial methodological hints, reliance on past experience etc." (Chomsky 1957:56). In other words, the problem regarding discovery procedures (corpus analysis is one such procedure) is not a trivial one. E.g., the testing of particular syntagmatic types in various frames or sentence transforms is one of the most powerful discovery procedures known, something that has been known to grammarians for centuries.

Especially the TG predilection for premature rules stating the impossibility of various syntactic sequences has on several occasions in the past provoked objectivist disapproval, and justly so. When for instance the attributive adverb *links* in (29) *der Schornstein links* and similar noun phrases is said to be obligatorily placed to the right of the noun (Clément 1969:29ff.), the ensuing 'rule' can be easily falsified, even with reference to current standard grammars.[12] The construction type is not very frequent, but I have found it in more than 70 modern German proseworks, and it is, on the basis of my material, possible to state a rule of 95.5% validity (a .9-grammatical rule): Locative adverbs (*links, dort, unten, drinnen* etc.) and prepositional locative adverbials whose prepositions are those that govern the accusative or the dative (*an, auf, hinter, in* etc.) can occur either to the left or to the right of the nominal nucleus in noun phrases, thus: (30) *links der Schornstein*, (31) *dort die Russen*, (32) *hier das*, (33) *im Garten die Kinder*, (34) *hinter dem Haus die Bäume*, (35) *in seinen Armen das Kind*, etc.[13]

Numerous typologically related spurious impossibility rules could of course be easily adduced, but enough has been said to permit of a few general considerations regarding the two competing approaches to syntactic description.

There is in reality no basic difference between the mentalist and the objectivist position. As stated above, the difference is rather one of relative emphasis regarding certain aspects of the practical derivation of rules.[14] Both groups obviously agree that syntactical rules should be based on observations of linguistic data, and it goes without saying that both groups agree that the syntax of a particular historical language is largely rule-governed. And both agree that the rules must generate particular constructions that are not in the data observed. Where, then, lies the difference? It pertains, in my opinion, chiefly to the relative observation-processing stage at which the jump is made from the particular to the general, from the data to the generalizations or rules. The objectivists want to propose their rules as basically 'true', though naturally subject to falsification, i.e., they ideally present their rules together with whatever evidence they can muster, including a description of the data-analytic procedure employed. The mentalists do not wait as long before they generalize. The objectivists aim for longer-lasting results and therefore ordinarily test their hypotheses carefully before publishing them, whereas the mentalists are content to propose quick hypotheses for falsification by others. The objectivists are Baconian in scientific outlook, the mentalists are Cartesian. It does, in fact, make good sense to talk about B[aconian] vs. C[artesian] linguists. So far, it seems that the B-linguists haved erred less, or relatively less frequently, than the C-linguists. In my opinion, the famous 19th Baconian Aphorism can be used for a reasonably fitting characterization of the two types: The C-linguist "... flies from the senses and particulars to the most general axioms, and from these principles ... proceeds to judgement and to the discovery of middle axioms." The B-linguist, on the other hand, "... derives axioms from the senses and particulars, rising by gradual and unbroken ascent, so that [he] arrives at the most general axioms last of all."[15] For 'axioms' and 'principles', one may read 'rules'.

The B-linguist, whose primary concern is the generalization of masses of observed data, does not, or cannot, permit grammaticality decisions about linguistic usage on the basis of a fixed theory. He is theoretically unbiased in this respect, whereas the C-linguist is more apt to set theory above data. What does not fit into the theory, is too often rejected. An illustrative example of this is the following:

Both in English and in German one finds noun phrases of the type (36) *that man yesterday*, (37) *der Mann gestern*. They are structurally related to the constructions (30)-(35) above, but the temporal adverbials occur, it seems, only to the right of the nouns. These syntagmatic constructions have proved very troublesome to a number of TG scholars. The first derivation suggested was from (38) *der Mann, der gestern kam* (Motsch 1968:115),[16] but it soon became clear that this TG solution could not be accepted. Renate Steinitz, though frankly admitting that the construction is "umgangssprachlich",[17] finally decided to supply it with an asterisk. The reason is, of course, clearly related to the current TG theory of unique abstract deep structures for determining the semantic inter- pretations of a given construction: "... beliebig viele Möglichkeiten der Rekonstruktion des eliminierten Teilsatzes [are] denkbar", is the ex- planation given (Steinitz 1969:116).[18] Since such uniqueness clearly cannot be established in this case, Steinitz introduces what Bacon aptly calls a "frivolous distinction",[19] by simply deciding to regard the con- struction as ungrammatical in the *Hochsprache* (but it must reasonably also be considered ungrammatical in the *Umgangssprache*, so the problem is only postponed).

I do not know whether this example may be as serious for TG as the recalcitrant problem of discontinuous elements is supposed to be for the so-called structural syntax, but the B-linguist position can only be that the noun phrases (36) and (37) are to be considered genuinely grammatical if they belong to the regular recurrent patterns of the language. They do. Thus for the reader of one particular German novel, the following sentence is both grammatical and meaningful: (39) "Trotz- dem hatte Jan ... ein böses Gewissen wegen der sonderbaren Seesäcke gestern",[20] ('... because of those strange duffel-bags yesterday'). The reader of the novel will know that the reference is to the duffel-bags that smugglers had taken from the ship to the launch. There must be a large number of different relative clauses that could be equally well used for the standard TG derivation of the temporal attribute *gestern* in (39). That, however, is a problem for the C-linguists. To the B-linguists, the description of the German or English noun phrase consisting of a noun with postpositive temporal attribute has never been a matter of great theoretical concern.

University of Bergen

NOTES

[1] For a succinct discussion regarding linguistic problems from the point of view of mentalism vs. objectivism, see Hill 1970.

[2] Hovdhaugen 1969:166. Similar assessment of objectivist criticism can be found in most introductions to transformational grammar.

[3] This one will find verified in dozens of TG articles as well as in (larger) traditional grammars. But one may note that sometimes rule modification may actually lead to simplified description, as in the case of removal of unwarranted constraints. Thus erasing the asterisk in front of perfectly normal constructions like *im Augenblick, als er eintrat, *im Jahre, als ich in Heidelberg studierte, would help simplify J. McKay's rules (1968:25ff.).

[4] It seems to make little difference whether we discuss this data: rule relationship on the basis of running text or with reference to rules vs. portions of rule systems. Regarding the rules for the strong verb conjugation in German, for instance, it has been established that one quarter of the rules generate 7/10 of the rule aggregate. The English verb system evinces a largely identical set of relationships of this type, cf. Ulvestad 1970.

[5] The data are of two kinds: 1) questionnaire-elicited data gathered by Gerda Moter Erichsen and myself (ten informants in all), and 2) a number of examples taken from 20th-century German prose, starting with the G. Hauptmann sentence: "... dass es wahrscheinlich die Frau eines Glasbläsers sei, die ich ... nachts hatte singen gehört" (1903, in Jahresring 62/63 [Stuttgart: Deutsche Verlags-Anstalt, 1967], 14), and ending with the following sentence in H. Habe, Off Limits (Bergisch-Gladbach: Bastei-Verlag, 1969), 210: "... obwohl er sie nie zuvor hatte rauchen gesehen". Not one of my German friends and colleagues has found sentences such as these ungrammatical. Curiously enough, sentence (1) is, in a statistical sense, clearly more acceptable than (2).

[6] "One must demand of a rule that it is valid for all cases, i.e., one must be able to prove [bescheinigen] its exhaustivity," Frankfurter Kreis, 64.

[7] The kernel sentences for these examples can easily be reconstructed by the reader, e.g. Mutter hat recht → *es hat Mutter recht, etc.

[8] Cf. Sanders 1883:54ff., and Curme 1952:461.

[9] A research program involving also the present-day use of es has been started in the Department of German, University of Bergen: "Corpus analysis vs. intuition in syntactic rule elaboration".

[10] Cf. fn. 5, above.

[11] Thus, e.g., sequence (24) runs, in its questionnaire representations: Er behauptet, es kommen hören zu haben; er behauptet, es kommen gehört zu haben. The two sentence do not occur contiguously on the test sheet, of course.

[12] There are, for instance, eleven such 'impossible' prepositive attributive adverbials to be found as rule examples in the standard Swedish grammar of German (Lide and Magnusson 1970:341f.), including: Rechts die grosse Kahlfläche scheint mir geeigneter (v. Lehndorff).

[13] An article discussing this rule will be published in the Forschungs-Berichte des Instituts für deutsche Sprache (Mannheim). The rule is admittedly slightly more complicated than in this formulation, since certain reservations drawn from the 4.5% residual material must be made, e.g., to avoid such deviating noun phrases as für den Winter das Holz (deviating from a statistical point of view).

[14] I look upon the purely formalistic aspects of rule construction as of little consequence, theoretically speaking. Transparent formalization is naturally always to be prefered to longwinded verbalization of rules, which often precludes useful or interesting insight. Even the question whether the concept of deep structure vs. surface structure is useful or necessary for stringent description may turn out to be less crucial

than it seems to be at present. Multiple meaning need not be any more problematic in syntactic constructions than in word forms. E.g. the semantic ambiguity of certain genitive constructions (*genitivus subjectivus/objectivus*) must be considered part of our inventarized grammar.

[15] Cited from S. Hampshire. *The Age of Reason* (New York: Mentor Books, 1956), 25.

[16] Motsch considers the phrase grammatical. So do all my native German informants who are not TG linguists.

[17] It may be noted that the phrase construction under discussion is perfectly acceptable also in the *Hochsprache* and written standard, to judge from several examples found in German literary prose works.

[18] Cf. H. Whitaker's criticism of J. Deese, whose description of the TG concept of deep structure "... fails to point out clearly that an ambiguous sentence must be represented by as many different deep structures as there are different meanings". Whitaker's statement (1970:993) reflects current TG theory; at least there seems to be no deviating view so far made public in print.

[19] Hampshire, 26.

[20] H. Leip, *Jan Himp und die kleine Brise* (Hamburg: Chr. Wegener Verlag, 1949), 73.

REFERENCES

Bierwisch, M. 1963. Grammatik des deutschen Verbs. Berlin: Akademie-Verlag.

Chomsky, Noam. 1957. Syntactic structures. The Hague: Mouton.

Clément, Danièle. 1969. La structure des groupes nominaux en allemand moderne. Stuttgart: Lehrstuhl für Linguistik. Papier Nr. 10.

Curme, G. O. 1952. A grammar of the German language. 2nd ed., 7th printing. New York: Frederick Unger.

Falk, H., and Selmer, E. W. 1934. Tysk grammatikk for studerende og lærere. Oslo: Aschehoug.

Hill, A. A. 1970. The hypotheses of deep structure. Studia linguistica 24:1-16.

Hovdhaugen, E. 1969. Transformasjonell generativ grammatikk. Oslo: Universitetsforlaget.

Lide, S., and Magnusson, R. 1970. Tysk grammatik. Stockholm-Göteborg-Lund: Läromedelsförlagen.

Martinet, André. 1949. About structural sketches. Word 5.13-35.

McKay, John. 1968. Some generative rules for German time adverbials. Language 44.25-50.

Motsch, W. 1968. Syntax des deutschen Adjektivs. 5th ed. Berlin: Akademie-Verlag.

Sanders, D. 1883. Satzbau und Wortfolge in der deutschen Sprache. Berlin: Abenheimische Verlagsbuchhandlung.

Schulz, Dora, and Griesbach, H. 1970. Grammatik der deutschen Sprache. 8th ed. München: Max Hueber.

Steinitz, Renate. 1969. Adverbial-Syntax. Berlin: Akademie-Verlag.

Ulvestad, Bjarne. 1970. Das Konjugationssystem der starken Verba im Deutschen. Vorschläge für eine strukturale Grammatik des Deutschen, ed. H. Steger, 332-348. Darmstadt: Wissenschaftliche Buchgesellschaft.

Whitaker, H. 1970. Review of Psycholinguistics, by J. Deese. Language 46.991-97.

*** (Frankfurter Kreis). 1970. Zum Beispiel: Reflexion über Sprache. Linguistik und Didaktik 1.56-71.

ON STATIC AND DYNAMIC SYNCHRONY

JOSEF VACHEK

In his well-known synthesis of descriptivist approaches to language, Professor A. A. Hill (1958) surveyed, among other controversial issues, also the notorious problem of the phonemic interpretation of the ModE [h]-sound. In principle, he accepts the familiar Trager-Bloch interpretation of [h] as the 'third semi-vowel' although, in Hill's own words, this interpretation called forth a 'violent' controversy. Hill, with his typical clearness of argument and exactness of reasoning, states the cause of that interpretation as one that indeed logically follows from the premises of the Yale descriptivist and distributionist approach to the facts of language. As such, the interpretation may be qualified as a remarkable achievement. Still, if the analyst starts from a different conception of language and thus draws his conclusions from different premises, he may throw some light on the given problem from an angle not covered by the Yale approach. The comparison of the results obtained by two different approaches, e.g. that of Yale and that of Prague, may be fruitful, as it is only by the mutual exchange of views that one can come closer to definitive solutions of such complex problems as are constituted by what has been aptly called the 'moot points' of language structure.

We would like to take up the problem of the ModE [h] here again for another reason also. This issue is particularly fit to disclose the differences of the two approaches, viz. those of the Yale and Prague groups, as exemplified by the differences that underlie the divergent interpretations of ModE [h] as presented by Hill and by ourselves.

It will be easily seen that the most fundamental premise of the two approaches is virtually identical: in both cases one has to do with a structuralist approach, rightly stressing that no element of language can be duly grasped and correctly evaluated unless its relation is established to other elements coexisting with it in the given language system. On the other hand, the approaches differ very widely in a number of features superimposed on this common fundamental premise. Perhaps the most obvious of these features is the functionalist conception of language in the Prague theory as against the neopositivist gnoseological basis of the Yale approach, which has hardly ever examined speech phenomena with regard to the functions they perform in their language communities. In the present context, however, we are mainly interested in another difference: while the analysis of the Yale group can be, at least roughly, regarded as a specimen of what F. W. Householder has aptly termed 'a hocus-pocus approach', the analysis of the Prague group is closer to his 'God's truth approach'. The latter analysis is effected with the presupposition that structural relations do exist in a language and that the analyst's task is to discover and to formulate them. The Yale approach, on the other hand, is often characterized by an effort to organize the ascertained phenomena into a pattern which is as simple and as economically built up as possible, even if some phenomena subjected to this organization must be more or less 'adapted' in order to fit into that pattern. This is exactly the case with the Yale interpretation of ModE [h] where, as Hill puts it, "the pattern is the sole important reason for the final classification of the sound" (p. 39); further, Hill asserts that "a different classification of /h/ would largely destroy the pattern" (*ibid.*).

The Prague approach, on the other hand, does not want to squeeze into the pattern all language phenomena and to pay for this by over-looking those features in the pattern which do not very well conform to it. The analysis done according to Prague principles is able to respect these seemingly nonsystemic phenomena because it is prepared to discover that such phenomena do occur in language systems. This expectation is the natural consequence of the Prague thesis that language constitutes not a closed but an open system and that its character is not static but dynamic. In other words, one must expect to find in any system of language a number of 'moot points' which are either relics of older stages ('leftovers', in Hill's conception) or else which point out the way in which the system is likely to shift, in the given point, at the next stage of its development.

As a matter of fact, the conception of language constituting an open, dynamic system appears to be the only one that can account satisfactorily for the very fact of language development. As R. Jakobson (1929) duly pointed out, many changes of language should be regarded as therapeutic, i.e. as endowed with the task of restoring the jeopardized balance of the system of language (where by balance is meant the adequacy of the language means to the functions they are called upon to perform). This, of course, by no means denies some participation of external factors in influencing language development, though naturally the main part is played by the internal, systemic motivation of changes (cf. Vachek 1962). It appears that this area of problems has hardly ever been considered by the Yale approach. In our opinion, it is particularly the problem of the interpretation of the ModE [h]-sound that can serve as a testcase revealing the different treatments of the same problem, and at the same time disclosing the benefit that can be drawn in solving that problem from the application of the idea of the open, dynamic, non-static system to it.

In a detailed analysis of the problem which we presented, for the first time, some twenty years ago (Vachek 1952, 1964), we pointed out that throughout the history of English the original Old English /h-χ/-phoneme was being gradually discarded, with the result that in present-day English it has been left only in a single word-position, i.e. at the beginning of a stem morpheme before a vowel (this covers also the instances of word-initial [hj]- because the ModE sound [j] constitutes an allophone of the phoneme /i/; cf. Vachek 1964). Thus /h/ must be quali-fied as a phoneme with a slight functional load, which is thus apt to be discarded from the phonological system of language.

Clearly, there has been in ModE a tendency at work directed at the dropping of /h/ from the ModE phonological system. But this tendency cannot be consistently brought to an end in the standard language be-cause a large number of sociolinguistic factors (such as the influence of school, radio and TV, of all sorts of lectures, of the theatre and sermons, etc., and, above all, the social prestige of the standard form of ModE, enforced by all these institutions) work against it and thus considerably delay its effective operation. It is, however, most remark-able that in a large majority of the local dialects of England, in which the above-mentioned delaying factors do not assert themselves, this last remaining stronghold of the [h]-sound has been given up (see a map prepared by the English Department of Leeds University and publish-ed in *The Reader's Digest complete atlas of the British Isles*, London, s.d., p. 122).

Particularly interesting is the situation in the London Cockney, with its familiar 'dropping of one's *h*'s' (and, a fact which is usually not stated but just as important, its inserting of *h*'s where they are etymologically unjustified). A closer analysis of the matter reveals that the situation in Cockney represents the final stage of the whole long discarding process (which started in OldE by contractions like *fōhan > fōn). The interesting point is that Cockney did not solve the problem by simply dropping the [h]-sound but by re-evaluating it from a phoneme to a kind of stylistic signal marking emphasis, so that, e.g., the sequence [ɔt] implements the stylistically unmarked (i.e., purely communicative, non-emotional) form, while the sequence [hɔt] signals the emotive, stylistically marked one. In other words, the phonetic combination '[h] + vowel' constitutes what the Prague terminology calls the combinatory stylistic variant of the vowel phoneme. (In Trubetzkoy's terminology, the Cockney [h]-sound is no longer a matter of phonology, but rather of phonostylistics; cf. Trubetzkoy 1939:17ff.)

It should also be noted that the exceptional expressions in which [h] is found to stand in the middle of words and which are quoted by Hill on p. 38 (such as *aha, teehee, youhou*) are emotively strongly marked, so that they cannot be used as arguments against our phonological interpretation. The three words rather confirm this interpretation, because in them the occurrence of [h] in positions in which it is otherwise unknown functions as a signal of emotional approach. (In the fourth item adduced by Hill, *behest*, one finds the morphemic limit before the [h]-sound; besides, the word clearly ranks as archaic and is thus again strongly marked from the stylistic viewpoint.)

One might object to our interpretation by pointing out that the ModE /h/-phoneme does not have so slight a functional load as we assert, because it is also found in phonemic combinations like /ah/, /oh/, etc. (which, according to the American descriptivists, are interpreted, respectively, as [ɑ:], [ɔ:] — see also instances like /fahðər/, and /bɔht/ quoted by Hill on p. 63). However, as demonstrated already by N. S. Trubetzkoy (and accepted by R. Jakobson and M. Halle 1956), the relation of the so-called 'short' and 'long' vowels in ModE represents what may be classified phonologically as an opposition of contact (i.e. of checked *vs.* unchecked vowel phonemes, the 'short' vowel implementing the marked, checked member and the 'long' one the non-checked, unmarked member of the opposed pair). (For a more detailed discussion on this point, see Vachek 1963).

The slight functional load of the ModE [h] is remarkably coupled with its unsatisfactory integration in the pattern of ModE consonant phonemes (in the sense of A. Martinet 1955). This unsatisfactory integration, also duly noted by Hill, should of course not urge the analyst to integrate it at any cost (as is done in the descriptivist interpretation of [h] as the 'third semivowel'); it rather qualifies this phoneme as a kind of marginal component in the system, a component whose position in the pattern has become palpably weakened.

The case of ModE /h/ is, of course, only one specimen of the application of the most fruitful methodological conception of the open, dynamic (i.e. non-static) system of language. We discussed it in some detail, on a more general level, some five years ago (Vachek 1967), and a year later demonstrated its usefulness on the basis of copious materials taken from present day Standard Czech (Vachek 1968). It can hardly be doubted that an application of this conception to other language materials is bound to reveal more interesting facts which will make the descriptions of languages more realistic by pointing out more vividly, as in a relief map, a number of features that remain hidden to the purely static approach of the descriptivist analysis.

Prague

REFERENCES

Hill, Archibald A. 1958. Introduction to linguistic structures. New York: Harcourt, Brace & Co.

Jakobson, Roman. 1929. Remarques sur l'évolution phonologique du russe comparée à celle des autres langues slaves. TCLP 2. Prague. Reprinted in Jakobson's Selected Writings, vol. 1, 7-116. The Hague: Mouton.

Jakobson, Roman, and Halle, Morris. 1956. Fundamentals of language. The Hague: Mouton. Reprinted in Jakobson, Selected writings 1, 464-504.

Martinet, André. 1955. Économie des changements phonétiques. Bern: Francke.

Trubetzkoy, N. S. 1939. Grundzüge der Phonetik. TCLP 7. (The English translation by Chr. A. M. Baltaxe was published under the title Principles of phonology. Berkeley and Los Angeles: University of California Press, 1969.)

Vachek, Josef. 1952. Foném h/x ve vývoji angličtiny. Sborník prací filosofické fakulty brněnské university A 1, 121-35. The enlarged English version of the paper forms Chap. II of Vachek 1964.

—. 1962. On the interplay of external and internal factors in the development of language. Lingua 11. 433-48.

—. 1963. The phonematic status of Modern English long vowels and diphthongs. Philologica Pragensia 6.59-71.

—. 1964. On peripheral phonemes of Modern English. Brno Studies in English 4.7-109.

—. 1967. The non-static aspect of the synchronically studied phonological system. Phonologie der Gegenwart = Wiener Slavistisches Jahrbuch VI. 79-87. Graz-Wien-Köln: Böhlaus Nachf.

—. 1968. Dynamika fonologického systému současné spisovné češtiny. Praha: Academia.

VOWEL ALTERNATIONS IN ENGLISH, GERMAN, AND GOTHIC: REMARKS ON REALISM IN PHONOLOGY

I. ON PHONOLOGICAL THEORY

It is generally known that transformational-generative (TG) syntax has failed to develop into a theory which provides principled unique solutions to linguistic problems (cf. Partee 1971 for a recent survey of the various schools of thought within this model). It is somewhat less widely recognized that TG phonology has likewise failed. What was once intended to be a theory of the phonological knowledge of an ideal native speaker has degenerated into a catalog of ambiguous routines for the description of phonological structures, augmented by a list of ad-hoc amendments to be applied in case the basic catalog does not provide a solution to a given problem. The desolate state of this model is admirably characterized by one of the theoreticians of TG phonology (Lightner 1971:574):

Each time they [the TG phonologists] find a difficult problem in some language, they will propose a new addition to the theory to take care of THAT PARTICULAR PROBLEM. Another difficulty causes them to propose another addition; thus, we have *global rules, left-to-right iteration, neighborhood conventions, left and right linear rules, conspiracies* and so on. This is not the right way to handle things. ... Clearly it's wrong to propose amendments to the theory each time a new problem arises. Something basic has to be done; I don't know what.

The difficulties alluded to in the quotation have arisen from a wide-spread confusion, viz. the erroneous assumption that a descriptive system, if properly adjusted to accommodate newly discovered problems, automatically develops into a theory, or, more simply, that a descriptive system is a theory. TG phonology, although intended to be a theory by its original authors (Chomsky and Halle 1968, Postal 1968), has been designed and 'amended' as a descriptive system rather than a theory (Foley 1970). This can be seen from the all-pervading preoccupation with the details of formalization, where exactly what is to be formalized is often unclear. The expectation is that the formalism, once its rudiments are set up, will automatically develop into a guide to further insights: The formalism creates hypotheses which the linguist is invited to test.

I believe that the correct procedure for the construction of a theory is the opposite. First, one should study the nature of the object which the theory is to be a theory of. The hypotheses contained in this theory can be tested with a minimum of descriptive apparatus. When a sufficiently rich body of hypotheses is assembled and organized, formalization of the theory MAY begin (but need not: a theory does not become more of a theory by formalization).

In phonology, the most basic things are still a matter of dispute: What exactly is the set of phonological features? What is a phonological rule? Are phonological rules ordered? Are there two sets of phonological rules, one in the lexicon (morpheme structure conditions or lexical redundancy rules) and one in the 'phonological component', or is there only one set? Is there a systematic difference between morphophonemic rules and phonological rules proper? What are the constraints on the relationship between lexical and phonetic representation? Thus, phonologists should be concerned with settling these basic issues, rather than with formalization, because formalization at this point can only be formalization of what we do not know: The most fundamental constraints on phonological structure, though perhaps intuited by some phonologists, are for the most part unknown, as everyone with more than a superficial knowledge of the subject will readily admit.

This paper, especially the following section, is concerned with one aspect of phonological theory about which little is known: the relationship between the phonetic and lexical representation. This section was written and distributed at UCLA in 1969, but was not published because I felt that it departed too radically from the then dominant model to be paid any attention in the linguistic community. (I could see later that my suspicion was well-founded when a dissertation, Krohn 1969, which proposes lexical vowels for English similar to those given below, attracted no attention.) Since then the climate has changed. The sentiment reflected in the quotation from Lightner 1971 above is not that of just one man but that of many linguists. I think the time is now ripe for a fresh investigation into some of the unsolved questions raised above. Some discussion of hypotheses concerning morphophonological structure and morphophonological change can be found in Vennemann 1971a, b, 1972 a-d; cf. also Vennemann and Ladefoged 1971. I feel that the present early expression of my misgivings with TG phonology may now make a contribution to the further development of phonology, and I present them here with only a minimum of corrections. I interpret these suggestions in the framework of the theory of natural generative phonology in the third section.

II. VOWEL ALTERNATIONS IN ENGLISH, GERMAN, AND GOTHIC

1. There are, to my knowledge, no generative phonologists who believe in a principle popularly summarized as 'once a phoneme, always a phoneme'.[1]

From the fact that the vowels in English *mice* and *nice* are identical in a systematic phonetic description a generative phonologist would not conclude that they must be identical at all other levels of the grammar. Rather he would appreciate the secondary status of the [ay] in the plural *mice*, which he must relate to the vowel of the singular *mouse*, while no such connection needs to be captured in the case of the adjective *nice*, or the singular noun *rice*.

The stressed vowels in the German plural nouns *Gäste* 'guests' and *Reste* 'remainders' are identical phonetically. However, the generative phonologist would take into account the fact that the vowels of the corresponding singulars, *Gast* and *Rest*, are different.

The vowels in the Gothic nouns *dragk* [draŋk] 'drink' and *þank* [θaŋk] 'thank' are assumed to be phonetically identical by all scholars, but the generative phonologist would express in his description the fact that *dragk* is a derivative of *drigkan* 'to drink', while *þank* is a basic noun not so derived.

2. There seems to be an interpretation of the above proverb, however, which most generative phonologists would find agreeable with their own phonological theory and practice. In *The sound pattern of English*, Chomsky and Halle have presented a phonology of English without diphthongs in lexical items (1968:236). The phonetic diphthongs of English are all derived from monophthongs by phonological rules. For example, the diphthong [ay] in *divine* is represented in the lexicon as a tense monophthong /ī/. The argument for this abstract reconstruction is persuasive. It is based on the facts that the [ay] in *divine* alternates with [i] in *divinity* and that this alternation and comparable ones, such as [iy : e] in *serene : serenity*, [ey : æ] in *sane : sanity*, also [aw : ʌ] in *profound : profundity*, [ow : a] in *cone : conic* call for a systematic

treatment. There are, of course, English words in which [ay] does not
alternate with [i], e.g., *nice, kite, ripe*. But since the mechanism for
deriving [ay] from /ī/ has been established on the basis of the alternating
words, the non-alternating words too are represented with the monophthong /ī/, and the same is true of words with all the other diphthongs
that do not undergo alternation.

Similarly, Vennemann (1968:308-77) develops a rule system that a) derives German umlaut vowels, including [oy], from the corresponding non-
umlauted vowels followed by an /i/ in the next syllable, b) reduces
unstressed /i/ to /ə/, c) apocopates /ə/ after sonorants and voiceless
obstruents in certain grammatical categories. Each of these steps is well
motivated: a) by such alternations as *Haus* 'house' : *häuslich* 'domestic',
b) by the observation that [ə] is the only completely unstressed vowel
in German, c) by the suggestive distribution of final [ə] and zero in the
class of neuter collectives of the type *Gebirge* (*Berg* 'mountain') : *Gebälk*
(*Balk*+*en* 'beam'), *Gewürm* (*Wurm* 'worm'). However, combined they
allow the derivation of the 'umlaut vowels' [ü ü: ö ö: ä: oy] from back
vowels in *all* German words containing them, so that these six vowels can
be dispensed with in the lexicon.

Buckalew (1964:15) likewise adheres to the motto 'once a systematic
phoneme, always a systematic phoneme', as is clear from the following
quote: "Although *ai* and *au* may be regarded as always representing
monophthongs on the resultant level, the fact that they alternate with *aj*
and *aw* respectively under regular conditions makes it desirable to consider them diphthongs everywhere on the underlying level."

3. I will now consider in some detail the case of Gothic. I will illustrate
the kind of descriptive and interpretive difficulties into which adherence
to the above saying concerning systematic phonemic representations
can lead, and will suggest a principle to avoid them. The treatment of
Gothic is meant to serve as a model for English, German, and other
languages with similar alternation problems.

I assume the following phonetic vowel system for biblical Gothic:[2]

(1)   Phonetic vowels of Gothic.[3]

	Short vowels		Long vowels		Diphthong[4]
i		u	ī		ū	iw
			ē		ō	
ε	a	ɔ	ɛ̄	ā	ɔ̄	

The Latinized graphic representations of these vowels are:

for [i u ɛ ɔ a]: *i u ai au a*; for [ī ū ē ō ɛ̄ ɔ̄ ā]: *ei u e o ai au a*; for [iw] : *iu*.

The question is: What is the lexical vowel system of Gothic? The following are some of the facts which must be considered in the analysis.

3.1 ABLAUT. Gothic shows an alternation of [i] in the present tense with [a] in the indicative past tense singular of a large number of so-called ablauting verbs, e.g. *binda : band* 'I bind/bound', *nima : nam* 'I take/ took', *mita : mat* 'I measure(d)'.[5] Since the present is the unmarked tense, these verbs are represented lexically with an /i/. The forms with [a] result from application of rule (2).

(2)   Abtönung.

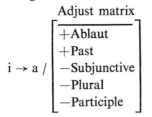

Ablauting verbs in [iw] show an alternation not with *[aw], but with [ɔ̄] under otherwise identical conditions, e.g., *-biuda : bauþ* 'I offer(ed)', *tiuha : tauh* 'I pull(ed)'. We can nevertheless use an analysis by rule (2) if we add a rule aw → ɔ̄.

Ablauting verbs in [ī] show an alternation with [ɛ̄] in the category mentioned, e.g., *greipa : graip* 'I seize(d)', *gateiha : gataih* 'I indicate(d)'. While in the [iw : ɔ̄] alternation there is at least one member of the abtönung alternation phonetically present, here neither one is overt. However, the monophthongization rule for /aw/ would appear more systematic if [ɛ̄] were derived from an /ay/ just as [ɔ̄] is from an /aw/. One will therefore analyse [ɛ̄] here as /ay/ and posit rule (3) which is known from many languages.

(3)   Monophthongization of /ay aw/.

$$\begin{bmatrix} V \\ +low \end{bmatrix} \begin{bmatrix} -vocalic \\ -consonantal \\ +high \\ \alpha back \\ \alpha round \end{bmatrix} \rightarrow \begin{bmatrix} 1 \\ \alpha back \\ \alpha round \\ +long \end{bmatrix}, \begin{bmatrix} 2 \\ \emptyset \end{bmatrix}$$

However, the analysis of [ɛ̄] as /ay/ makes sense only if we can derive the /a/ from an /i/ by rule (2), i.e., if we analyze [ī] as /iy/ and add rule (4).

(4)   Monophthongization of /iy/.

$$
\begin{bmatrix} V \\ +\text{high} \\ -\text{back} \\ \\ 1 \end{bmatrix}
\begin{bmatrix} -\text{vocalic} \\ -\text{consonantal} \\ +\text{high} \\ -\text{back} \\ \\ 2 \end{bmatrix}
\rightarrow
\begin{bmatrix} 1 \\ +\text{long} \end{bmatrix},
\begin{bmatrix} 2 \\ \emptyset \end{bmatrix}
$$

3.2 GRAPHIC ALTERNATION OF *ai, au* WITH *aj, aw*. As mentioned in the quotation from Buckalew in §2 above, [ɛ̄] and [ɔ̄] alternate with [ay] and [aw], respectively, in a small number of words, the monophthongs occurring in final position, the vowel plus glide sequences before vowels, e.g. *bai* : *bajoþs*, both meaning 'both', *maujos* : *mawi* 'girl (gen./nom.)'. There would, of course, be nothing wrong with an analysis which introduces a homorganic glide after a mid vowel before a vowel, with subsequent lowering and merging of the mid vowels into [a] before high glides. A more elegant description, however, is gained if [ɛ̄] and [ɔ̄] are represented as /ay/ and /aw/, a solution which converges with that given for ablaut in 3.1. Under this assumption, the only descriptive complication is the introduction of an environment in rule (3).

3.3 ALTERNATION OF LONG AND SHORT VOWELS. We find in root-final position alternations of *ei* and *i(j)*, *e* and *ai*, *o* and *au*.[6] Examples: for *ei* : *i(j)*, i.e. [ī : i(j)]: a root /frī/ appears in *frij+on* (also *fri+on*) 'to love', in *fri+aþwa* (also *frij+aþwa*) 'love'; for *e* : *ai*, i.e. [ē : ɛ]: *se+þs* 'seed', *sai+an* 'to sow'; for *o* : *au*, i.e. [ō : ɔ]: *sto+jan* 'to judge', *stau+ida* 'I judged', *stau+a* 'judge'. The long vowels of each pair occur everywhere except before vowels, the short vowels only before vowels.

(5)   Pre-vocalic laxing.

$$V \rightarrow [-\text{long}] / \underline{\quad} V$$

The optional *j* seems to capture a low-level phonetic fact, the transition between [i] and a back vowel.

3.4 LOWERING. [i] and [u] do not occur before [r h hʷ]. Where we would expect [i] or [u] before these consonants on morphological grounds, we find [ɛ] or [ɔ] instead. For example, the past tense forms not subsumed by rule (2), and the past participle, of ablauting verbs in [iw] normally have [u], and those in [ī] have [i], e.g. *-budum* 'we offered', *budans* 'offered', *gripum* 'we seized', *gripans* 'seized'. This suggests a rule (6) ordered after (2).[7]

(6)   Abstufung.

$$i \rightarrow \emptyset / \begin{bmatrix} +\text{Abl} \\ +\text{Past} \end{bmatrix} \quad [+\text{sonorant}]$$

When the /i/ in /iy iw/ is lost through (6), the remaining glides become vowels, /i u/, by a universal principle. However, in *gataihum* 'we indicated', *gataihans* 'indicated', *tauhum* 'we pulled', *tauhans* 'pulled' we find instead [ε] and [ɔ]. Similarly, the verb *wairpan* 'to throw' is exactly like *bindan* above, except that it has [ε] and [ɔ] wherever the latter has [i] and [u], and the same is true of *bairan* 'to carry' as compared with *niman*, and of *saiƕan* [sεhʷan] 'to see' as compared with *mitan*. Therefore, we need rule (7).[8]

(7)   Lowering.

$$
\begin{bmatrix} V \\ -\text{long} \\ +\text{stress} \end{bmatrix} \rightarrow [+\text{low}] \ / \ \underline{} \begin{bmatrix} C \\ +\text{low} \end{bmatrix}
$$

4. The analyses given in §§ 3.1-4, which many generative phonologists would easily arrive at or at least readily accept upon presentation, raise nevertheless a number of grave descriptive problems.

4.1 If [ī] in ablauting words derives from /iy/ by rule (4), does non-alternating [ī], e.g. in *eisarn* 'iron', *leiþu* 'fruit wine', have to be represented as /iy/, too?

4.2 If the answer to §4.1 is negative, does this suggest that a lexical opposition /iy : ī/, coupled with the morphological feature Ablaut, should be permitted, although a purely phonological contrast of this sort does not exist in any known language?

4.3 If the answer to §4.1 is positive, does this imply that [ū] too must be analyzed as /uw/ (and perhaps [ē] as /ey/ and [ō] as /ow/ and [ā] as /aə/), despite the fact that [ū] does not alternate with anything?[9]

4.4 If [ε̄ ɔ̄] derive from /ay aw/ by rule (3) and ultimately from /iy iw/ in §3.1 (and perhaps from basic /ay aw/ in §3.2), what is the lexical representation of the numerous instances of [ε̄ ɔ̄] that are not the result of Abtönung and/or monophthongization, such as *ains* 'one', *hlaifs* 'bread', *aukan* 'increase', *haubiþ* 'head'?

4.5 If [ε ɔ] derive from /i u/ by rule (7) in §3.4, where the presence of these /i u/ can be demonstrated morphologically, what about the numerous instances of [ε ɔ] that do not stand in a relationship to any other vowel, such as in *airþa* 'earth', *faihu* 'money', *haurn* 'horn', *dauhtar* 'daughter'?

5. The questions in §§4.1-3 may seem rather trivial because [iy] and [ī] are very close phonetically and occur in some languages, e.g. English,

as free, conditioned, or dialectal variants of the same phoneme. In a feature-counting phonological description, however, the difference becomes more significant, because instead of carrying specification for length, all phonetically long vowels of Gothic, or at least all long high vowels, or at least all [ī]'s, or at least all ablauting [ī]'s must be represented phonologically with an additional segment to be specified as a) a glide, b) different from /w/. Depending on the degree to which diphthongal representation is posited for the various long monophthongs including ablauting and non-ablauting [ī], one arrives at lexicons of different values in a feature-counting evaluation metric. Even if we limit diphthongal representation to [ī], or to ablauting [ī], we have a certain amount of lexical complication. In addition, of course, we have a situation, embarrassing from the point of view of systematicality, in which a set of long vowels /ū ē ō ā/ (with or without /ɛ̄ ɔ̄/) is complemented by a diphthong /iy/, or a diphthong /iy/ and /ī/ in morphological complementary distribution.

While the problem may appear to be rather abstract in the present case because of the obvious phonetic similarity of [iy] and [ī], quite parallel situations arise in other languages where the phonetic similarity is less direct. For example, in those Germanic languages where /e/ and /i/ did not merge into /i/ as in Gothic, e.g. in the reconstructed ancestral language of Gothic, Proto-Germanic, and in Old and Middle High German, it is /e/ that ablauts with /a/ and zero, not /i/. Ablauting [ī] must therefore be represented as /ey/ in the grammars of those languages if the regularity in the ablaut system (corresponding to rules (2) and (6) above) is to be revealed. Old and Middle High German have a phonological vowel system in which [ī] fills two holes, as it were, indicated by * in (8).

(8)   Lexical vowels of Old and Middle High German (disregarding 'umlaut vowels').

	i		u		*		ū		*		ew
	e		(o)			ē		ō			
	a						ā			ay	aw

If we posit only an /ey/, the set of tense vowels will remain strangely incomplete.[10] If we posit both /ī/ and /ey/, as Motsch (1967:127) does for Proto-Germanic,[11] we have the strange correlation of /ī/ with [−Ablaut] and of /ey/ with [+Ablaut] mentioned above.[12]

While no further considerations apply in the case of §4.4, two additional problems arise in the case of §4.5. The reduplicative prefix in the Past

Tense of certain verbs takes the form [C₀ɛ-], irrespective of the root-initial consonantism, i.e. not only in cases like *-rairoþ* [rɛ-rōθ] 'predestinated', *haihait* [hɛ-hɛ̄t] 'named', *hvaihvop* [hʷɛ-hʷōp] 'boasted', but also in cases such as *lailot* [lɛ-lōt] 'let', *faifah* [fɛ-fāh] 'caught', *taitok* [tɛ-tōk] 'touched', *-aiaik* [ɛ-ɛ̄k] 'denied', *-aiauk* [ɛ-ɔ̄k] 'augmented'. How are these [ɛ]'s to be represented phonologically? The same question arises in the case of foreign words, in which both [ɛ] and [ɔ] occur freely before all consonants and vowels: *aikklesjo* [ɛk̃lēsjō] 'church', *Gainnesaraiþ* [gɛñēsarɛθ], *Baiailzaibul* [bɛɛlzɛbul] or [-būl], *apaustaulus* [apɔstɔlus].

6. All these problems dissolve if we assume for Gothic lexical representations no /iy ay aw/ at all[13] but /ī ɛ̄ ɔ̄/, and /ɛ ɔ/ in addition to /i u/. For the purposes of ablaut, /ī/ is reanalyzed 'as if' it were a diphthong, /iy/. Therefore, instead of a monophthongization rule for an /iy/, we posit an interpretive rule (9).

(9)   'As if' analysis of /ī/.

$$
\begin{bmatrix} V \\ +\text{high} \\ -\text{back} \\ +\text{long} \\ +\text{Ablaut} \\ +\text{Past} \\ 1 \end{bmatrix} \Rightarrow \begin{bmatrix} 1 \\ -\text{long} \end{bmatrix} \begin{bmatrix} 1 \\ -\text{vocalic} \end{bmatrix}
$$

This rule makes the past participle and all past tense forms available for the ablaut rules (2) and (6). The present tense forms will never change their /ī/. A monophthongization rule (4), of which (9) is a highly restricted inverse, is not needed. Rules (2), (3), (5), (6), (7) remain the same.

In all words where [ɛ̄ ɔ̄] are not demonstrably derived from /ī iw/ by rules (2) and (3), with principle (9), they are lexically precisely what they are phonetically, /ɛ̄ ɔ̄/. Similarly, where [ɛ ɔ] are not demonstrably derived from /i u/ by rule (7), and perhaps further from /ī iw/ by (6) with principle (9), they are lexically what they are phonetically, /ɛ ɔ/.[14] In the case of foreign words, this is simply the minimal assumption. But also in the case of non-foreign material, where [ɛ ɔ] occur only before /r h hʷ/ and do not contrast with [i u], this is the most direct representation of the phonetic facts and leads to no descriptive difficulties: Rule (7) is as natural a lexical constraint as it is a phonological rule.[15]

7. The answer to the question asked above in §3 after (1) is now obvious:

The lexical vowel system of Gothic is identical with the phonetic system (1).

It should be clear that this aspect of my analysis of the Gothic vowels makes a lot of sense in terms of language learning theory: A child, discovering an abstract phonetic vowel system (1) in his language data, which is in perfect agreement with his innate knowledge about possible vowel systems, will consider this as the lexical system as long as his growing knowledge of the rule system of his language does not call for a reanalysis—which never happens in Gothic, although it does, of course, happen in other languages. When the child learns the ablaut system, he will develop an economical, productive, and predictive rule system that captures these regularities, and in order to make this system work he must treat /ī/ 'as if' it were a diphthong, /iy/. But he will do so only in the case of actual change, i.e., only if he is really going to apply one of the ablaut rules (2) and (6). In all other cases an /ī/ remains the same abstract entity as which it has been originally internalized. Analogous considerations apply in the case of [ɛ̄ ɔ̄] and [ɛ ɔ].

I propose the following constraint (10) on phonological descriptions:

(10)   'As if' principle.

The phonetic representation of a segment is at the same time its lexical representation, except where the system of morphophonological rules of the language requires a different representation. To make possible those generalizations which cannot be based on the lexical representations of segments directly, such segments can be treated 'as if' they were something different, but only in forms that actually participate in alternations described by such generalizations.

8. Applying this principle to German umlaut, we find that the umlaut vowels are part of the lexical system of German. Words like *Rüde* 'male dog', *spät* 'late', *grün* 'green', *müde* 'tired', *heute* [hoytə] 'today' are learned and committed to the lexicon with their phonetic vowels unchanged, and there never arises any necessity to modify this lexical representation. In words like *böse* 'evil', *häuslich* [hoysliç] 'domestic', *Häute* [hoytə] 'skins' the vowels will be represented as back vowels because of alternation with *Bosheit* 'malice', *Haus* 'house', and *Haut* 'skin'.[16] Clearly we need a fronting rule, operating partly in a phonetci environment (before suffixal /i/, as in *häuslich*), partly in predictabel grammatical environments, as in collective neuters of the type *Gebüsch*

'bushes' and in plurals formed with /ər/, partly in a morphological environment [+Umlaut], as in the case of masculine plurals in /ə/ which may or may not have umlaut.[17] Principle (10) does not permit a reanalysis of umlaut type vowels as back vowels in non-alternating words, although the descriptive apparatus to derive them from back vowels followed by an /i/ in all cases is in the grammar of German. This is obvious in the case of [e] which must always be represented as /e/ unless it demonstrably derives from an /a/. But also in all other cases principle (10) seems to insure an analysis in closer agreement with our intuition about the learning process.

9   The case of the English vowel alternations is somewhat more complex than the preceding ones, yet I believe that it should be and can be treated on the basis of principle (10), too.

A system of lexical vowels proposed for Contemporary American English is given in (11).[18]

(11)   Lexical vowels of American English according to Chomsky and Halle 1968.

Lax vowels		Tense vowels		Diphthongs
i	u	ī	ū	(none)
e	o	ē	ō	
æ	ɔ	ǣ œ̄ ā ɔ̄		

A word like *divine* is assigned by Chomsky and Halle's system the lexical representation /dVvīn/. If in a laxing environment, this form becomes /dVvin/; this is the case before the suffix -*ity* in *divinity*. If not in a laxing environment, the /ī/ adds a homorganic glide and shifts to [a], as in the basic adjective itself, [dəvayn]. Since the apparatus for the derivation of [ay] from /ī/ is thus established in the grammar, *all* words in [ay] are assumed to derive from underlying forms with /ī/, e.g. *nice, kite, bye, I*. This assumption is illegitimate if principle (10) is accepted.

While the front unround tense vowels of Chomsky and Halle occur in a substantial number of alternating roots and suffixes, so that an analysis with an underlying tense vowel also in non-alternating words does at least not lack plausibility altogether, the extension of this analysis to the back vowels is motivated only by a desire for systematicality. The number of alternating pairs with back vowels is so small as to lend very little independent justification to this approach. In addition, the parallel is in part broken by further modifications not matched in the front series.

Thus there are a few pairs like *pronounce* : *pronunciation*, but they show an alternation [aw : ʌ] rather than [aw : u] as suggested by the [ay : i] of *divine* : *divinity*. The same is true of *cone* : *conic*, where instead of [ow : ɔ], paralleling the [ey : æ] of *sane* : *sanity*, we find [ow : a].

The weakest point in (11) is, of course, the tense low front round vowel /œ̄/. If a phonological system is supposed to be a possible phonetic system, then system (11) must be rejected because it would be a rare language that distinguishes roundness in front low vowels without at the same time distinguishing it in front non-low vowels. Phonetically, front round vowels do, of course, not occur at all in the contemporary language. So in order to posit an /œ̄/ one would have to be compelled by an over-powering wealth of structural evidence, such as numerous alternating pairs with no other vowel left to represent one of the alternants. There is no such structural evidence. The phonetic reality which the posited /œ̄/ is to represent at the phonological level is [ɔy]. [ɔy] is a reasonable diphthong beautifully fitting into the set of genuine diphthongs of American English, [ay aw ɔy], a frequent set in the languages of the world.[19] [ɔy] does not alternate with anything.[20] Thus the only 'evidence' Chomsky and Halle propose is the weakest possible argument in phono-logical description: a gap-in-the-pattern argument, where in addition the alleged gap, /œ̄/, is in reality a left-over: It does not fit in (11) at all because of universal constraints on vowel systems.

The different dialects of Contemporary American English have in part different underlying vowel systems. A dialect which has the same systematic phonetic vowel [a] in the words *cot, caught, bother, father, bomb, balm, soft, long, maudlin*, will naturally have only one low back systematic phoneme, /a/. Where differences are made, the number of underlying low back vowels is greater. For example, *cot* and *caught* may have /a/ and /ɔ/, respectively, and *bother* and *father* may be distinguished by /a/ vs. /ā/. Thus one possible system of lexical (and systematic phone-mic) vowels could be (12).

(12)   Lexical vowels of (one dialect of) American English.

Lax vowels		*Tense vowels*		*Diphthongs*
i	u	ī	ū	ay ɔy aw
e	ʌ	ē	ō	
æ	a		ā ɔ̄	

Examples (following columns from left to right):
Lax vowels: *pit, pet, hat, putt, pot (bother)*, *put* (*root, roof*
                    for those who have a lax vowel here).

Tense vowels: *neat, hate, father, loot (root, roof), boat, wrought.*
Diphthongs: *tight, boy, out.*

In unstressed syllables, a further vowel, [ə] or [ɨ], occurs. It may be lexical, as in *giraffe* /jəræf/, *crocodile* /krakədayl/, etc., but also derive from any other vowel if it is completely unstressed.

/ē/ and /ō/ are regularly diphthongized, [ey ow]. Also /ī/ and /ū/ appear as diphthongs, at least in certain environments.

(13)   Glide insertion.

$$\begin{bmatrix} V \\ +\text{tense} \\ -\text{low} \\ \alpha\text{back} \\ \alpha\text{round} \\ 1 \end{bmatrix} \rightarrow \begin{bmatrix} 1 \\ -\text{tense} \end{bmatrix} \begin{bmatrix} 1 \\ -\text{vocalic} \end{bmatrix}$$

A glide [y] is also frequently found before /ū/. This is in part an idiosyncratic matter and must in this case be specified in the lexicon. For example, all dialects distinguish *coo* [kuw] /kū/ and *cue* [kyuw] /kyū/. There is a lot of dialect variation on this matter. Thus some dialects distinguish between *due* and *do*, others do not. There are also certain redundancies. For example, the dialects that have [y] in *due* have it redundantly in that part of the vocabulary which Chomsky and Halle call Derivational, e.g. in *produce*. Such redundancies must be captured by a grammar of these dialects. But it would be illegitimate to posit two underlying vowel phonemes, e.g. /ū/ and /ǖ/ (or /ɨ/) — or /ō/ and /ū/, in which case the /ō/ of (12) would have to be /ɔ/, the /ɔ/ to be something different still, as in Chomsky and Halle 1968 — to account for the difference between *coo* and *cue*, because no generalization would be gained by this circular procedure.

The Vowel Shift presents a certain problem because this change works in both directions, so to speak: /i e æ a/ in alternating pairs become /ay ī ē ō/ in a tensing environment, /ay aw ī ē ō/ become /i ʌ e æ a/ in a laxing environment.[21] Take for example *vary* : *variety*. The /i/ of /væri/ becomes tense before a vowel, /værī+iti/. It then undergoes glide insertion, vowel shift and backness adjustment, ī → īy → ēy → ǣy → āy. In order to apply laxing in /dVvayn+iti/, however, we must first reconstruct a tense /ī/ from the /ay/, i.e., apply the named changes backwards, so to speak; subsequently laxing will yield the correct [dəvinəti]. It was this apparent duplication of changes which motivated Chomsky and Halle to postulate underlying tense vowels /ī ū ē ǣ ɔ̄/ for phonetic [ay aw iy ey ow]. Laxing and unrounding now yield [i ʌ e æ a], and both underlying /ī/ and /ĭ/ deriving from /i/ by tensing yield [ay] by the rules named above, and similarly with the other vowels. This analysis was then extended to non-alternating words in order to avoid duplication of all the underlying segments: /ī ∼ ay/, /ū ∼ aw/, /ē ∼ iy/, /ǣ ∼ ey/, /ɔ̄ ∼ ow/.

Principle (10) tells us that this ingenious solution to the problem is illegitimate. The underlying final vowel of *vary* is /i/, that of *divine* is /ay/. Therefore we need a rule system that leads from /i/ to [ay] (in *variety*) as well as from /ay/ to [i] (in *divinity*). Chomsky and Halle's rules can do the work for us if we allow them to operate in both directions: A tensing environment would introduce a feature specification that would trigger application of the set of rules in one order, a laxing environment would specify a form for application of the same set of rules in the opposite order. (By being run through the shifting apparatus the superficial diphthongs would thus be treated 'as if' they were tense monophthongs for the purpose of laxing.) I believe that this is indeed the correct description, but since the notion of a reversible rule block is probably somewhat unfamiliar, and since I do not want to create the impression that the basic correctness of principle (10) hinges on this notion, I will give an alternative description along more familiar lines. (As should be clear from the discussion, I do not assume any reality for this description, and the hurried reader is invited to skip these unappetizing 'rules'.)

In what Chomsky and Halle define as a laxing environment, the nuclei of /ay aw/ are dropped. Of the resulting vowels, the back one is at the same time unrounded and lowered, so that [i] and [ʌ] result. /ī/, /ē/, and /ō/ are, in addition to being laxed, specified as undergoing vowel shift, [+ VS]. Nucleus loss and specification for vowel shift occur, of course, only in alternating vocabulary, because in non-alternating words we would not start out with a vowel that requires a quality change.

(14)   Laxing.

$$
\begin{bmatrix} V \\ \alpha\text{tense} \\ \langle+\text{Alter}\rangle \end{bmatrix}
\begin{bmatrix} -\ \alpha\text{segment} \\ -\text{vocalic} \\ -\text{consonantal} \\ +\text{high} \\ \beta\text{back} \end{bmatrix}
\rightarrow
\begin{bmatrix} 1 \\ -\text{tense} \\ -\text{round} \\ \alpha\text{segment} \\ \langle+\text{VS}\rangle \end{bmatrix},
\begin{bmatrix} 2 \\ +\text{vocalic} \\ -\text{round} \\ -\ \beta\text{high} \end{bmatrix}
$$

           1   2

in a laxing environment.

In what Chomsky and Halle define as a tensing environment, the lax vowel /i/ becomes a diphthong, [ay], and /e æ a/ are tensed and specified as undergoing vowel shift. Again the qualitative changes apply to alternating vocabulary only.[22]

(15)   Tensing.

$$
\begin{bmatrix} V \\ \langle \begin{smallmatrix} \alpha high \\ +Alter \end{smallmatrix} \rangle \\ 1 \end{bmatrix} \rightarrow \langle \begin{bmatrix} 1 \\ +low \\ +back \\ \alpha segment \end{bmatrix} \rangle \begin{bmatrix} 1 \\ +tense \\ \langle \begin{smallmatrix} -\alpha vocalic \\ -\alpha VS \end{smallmatrix} \rangle \end{bmatrix}
$$

in a tensing environment.

We have now two sets of vowels both specified as [+ VS], laxed vowels, /i e ʌ/, from /ī ē ō/, must be lowered to /e æ a/, respectively: tensed vowels, /ē æ ā/, from /e æ a/, must be raised (and rounded) to /ī ē ō/, respectively, if characterized as [+ VS].

(16)   Vowel Shift.

$$
\begin{bmatrix} V \\ \beta high \\ \gamma low \\ \langle \begin{smallmatrix} +back \\ +tense \end{smallmatrix} \rangle \end{bmatrix} \rightarrow \begin{bmatrix} -\gamma\alpha high \\ \beta\alpha low \\ \langle +round \rangle \end{bmatrix} / \begin{bmatrix} \overline{} \\ \alpha tense \\ + VS \end{bmatrix}
$$

This schema abbreviates the following subschemata (considering that rounding applies only to raised /ā/):

(16) (a) $\alpha = +$ (ē, æ, ā), therefore $\beta = -$.

$$
\begin{bmatrix} V \\ -high \\ \gamma low \\ \langle +back \rangle \end{bmatrix} \rightarrow \begin{bmatrix} -\gamma high \\ -low \\ \langle +round \rangle \end{bmatrix} / \begin{bmatrix} \overline{} \\ +tense \\ + VS \end{bmatrix}
$$

(16) (b) $\alpha = -$ (i, e, ʌ), therefore $\gamma = -$.

$$
\begin{bmatrix} V \\ \beta high \\ -low \end{bmatrix} \rightarrow \begin{bmatrix} -high \\ -\beta low \end{bmatrix} / \begin{bmatrix} \overline{} \\ -tense \\ + VS \end{bmatrix}
$$

(16a) changes /ē/ to /ī/ for $\gamma = -$, and /æ/ to /ē/ and /ā/ to /ō/ for $\gamma = +$.
(16b) changes /e ʌ/ to /æ a/ for $\beta = -$, and /i/ to /e/ for $\beta = +$.

10. As in the case of Gothic, principle (10) guarantees the close correspondence between the systematic phonetic and the lexical

vowel system of English. Again this is in agreement with what I would consider the learning process regarding these vowels: A child will consider his abstract phonetic representation [bɔy bay baw biy buw bey bow pit pet] etc. as his lexical representations, except for certain modifications owing to the phonological rules of English. One such rule is the glide insertion rule (13) which he formulates on the evidence that non-low tense vowels and diphthongs with a non-low nucleus never form an opposition. With this rule the words become /bɔy bay baw bī bū bē bō pit pet/ etc. With this as well as other vowel rules not mentioned here he thus arrives at the lexical system (12). This is a perfectly natural system which gives him no cause to reanalyze /bɔy/ as /bœ̄/. Also when he learns the word pairs in which his vowel phonemes alternate, he will formulate the rules accounting for the alternations, e.g. /ay : i/, on the basis of this system rather than change at one point the underlying vowel phonemes of a sizeable portion of his vocabulary on no other evidence than a comparatively small number of alternating pairs. Thus *divine* and *nice* are lexicalized with /ay/, and extrasystemic factors determine whether the corresponding -*ity* noun will be subject to laxing, [dəvinəti], or not, [naysəti]. Likewise a new word like *prestige* will be lexicalized with an /ī/. If asked to derive an adjective from this noun he may say [prestiyžəs] or [prestiyjəs] or [prestijəs], but hardly *[prestejəs] which he would if his lexical form had been with an /ē/, as in the Chomsky-Hallean system. Laxing, tensing, and vowel shift are thus far from being inescapable rules which a speaker of English cannot help applying whenever certain conditions are met. They are rather on, and perhaps beyond, the borderline to becoming morphological rules, whose status in a psychological grammar aiming at a representation of the speaker's knowledge of his language must be very different from the purely phonological rules. The credibility gap in Chomsky and Halle's description of the English vowels ([bɔy] = /bœ̄/, and [haws] = /hūs/ because of [prəfawnd : prəfʌndəti]); the absurdity of deriving German [grün] from /grūni/ for no other reason than that the rule apparatus for doing so is available; the descriptive difficulties resulting from an overly abstract representation of the Gothic vowels — these are only some of numerous examples suitable to remind us that our goal in phonology is a representation of the speaker's knowledge rather than formal elegance based on some unwarranted notion of simplicity.

III. THE VOWEL ALTERNATIONS IN
NATURAL GENERATIVE PHONOLOGY

The descriptions proposed in the preceding section were arrived at with arguments from linguistic typology and language learning, supported perhaps by plausibility and common sense. Essentially the same descriptions are, however, forced by general principles of natural generative (NG) grammar.[23]

The central principle of this theory is that rules of grammar cannot be ordered but have to be formulated in such a way that correct derivations result if each rule applies whenever its structural description is met.[24] The consequences of this principle are far-reaching. For example, there cannot be a systematic difference between morpheme-structure conditions (or lexical redundancy rules) and phonological rules:[25] Morphophonological rules, like all rules of grammar, apply as soon as their structural description is met, which may occur in the lexicon. For example, the Lowering Rule (7) of Gothic applies to *tauhum* [tɔhum] 'we pulled' like a TG 'P-rule', namely after the 'readjustment rules' and other 'P-rules' have changed /tiwh/ plus morpho-syntactic information into /tuh+um/. But it applies to *dauhtar* [dɔhtar] 'daughter' in the lexicon, in the sense that it makes the lowness of the back vowel before /h/ redundant. The lexical representation is thus /dɔhtar/. Note that it is POSSIBLE to posit a still more abstract representation /duhtar/, but it is also completely meaningless. It is meaningless because it remains without any consequence: Rule (7) immediately changes the form to /dɔhtar/.[26] NG grammar, therefore, contains a principle ruling out such more abstract representations (the Naturalness Condition of NG phonology): In the absence of rule-governed alternations, the phonetic representation of a linguistic form, including all its phonetic detail, is its lexical representation.[27] The redundancies of the representation, i.e. the systematic lessening of the informational value and the resulting facilitation of acquisition by the language learner, is expressed by the rules of the language. Thus, the fact that Gothic /dɔhtar/ cannot contrast with a hypothetical */duhtar/ is adequately expressed by including rule (7) in the grammar of this language. A representation of /dɔhtar/ as a more abstract /duhtar/ adds nothing to the expression of this redundancy.[28]

Similar considerations apply to all the other vowels of Gothic considered above. The vowel system (1), to the extent that it is indeed the phonetic system of Gothic, is at the same time the lexical system in a NG grammar of this language.

Turning now to the 'umlaut' vowels of German, we find that the Naturalness Condition of NG grammar requires that non-alternating [ü ǖ ö ȫ ä oy] are represented in the lexicon as such.[29] Where these vowels are demonstrably derived from back vowels, as in plurals, certain verb forms, comparatives, etc., i.e. in case of alternation, the lexical representation does contain the corresponding back vowels.

The analysis of English vowels given in section II is likewise the one forced by NG grammar, with the exception that the 'vowel shift' is not even a generative rule in a NG grammar of English, but merely a lexical correspondence (or 'via rule', Vennemann 197zc).

Chomsky and Halle (1968) were the first to propose that English possesses a residue of the historic Great Vowel Shift as a synchronic generative rule. They propose a systematic-phonemic vowel system which reflects to a high degree the Middle English phonetic vowel system, and a rule designed to derive the actual phonetic vowels from them. In order to be able to formulate the vowel shift as one schema, they propose a convention never heard of before and designed strictly ad hoc to the 'problem' at hand: the convention that parts of rules may be 'conjunctively ordered'. They promptly proceed to introduce a formalism for this convention, curly braces,[30] and study the consequences of the introduction of this formalism. This is the kind of methodology which I think is misguided, in linguistics as in any other science. As long as we do not know with certainty what the nature of lexical representation is, and what is and what is not a rule of grammar, there is no point in discussing details of formalization. Thus, since it is at best unclear if the vowel shift is a rule of English, it is pointless to formalize it and to propose conventions in the process which have no justification independently of the problem under study.[31]

Transformational-generative grammar, as a descriptive system lacking constraints which would make it qualify as a theory, allows alternative solutions of the problems discussed in section II of this paper. It thus creates pseudo-problems of abstractness, just as it creates pseudo-problems of 'absolute neutralization', 'non-uniqueness', etc. in the analysis of other language data. Natural generative grammar, which is being developed as a theory rather than a formal system for the description of languages, forces in each case a unique interpretation of the data discussed. Problems such as the 'inventory' problem illustrated, the 'degree of abstractness' problem, as well as the related 'absolute neutralization' and 'non-uniqueness' problems, are prevented from arising by the most fundamental principles of this theory. Since these problems are entirely fictitious, completely devoid of a foundation in empirical evidence,[32] and are thus pseudo-problems created by insufficiently constrained models of language, I consider their non-existence in natural generative grammar as evidence in favor of this approach to language.[33]

Universität München

NOTES

[1] Cf. Chomsky (1964:80-2 et passim) for criticism of the biuniqueness condition.
[2] The discussion of Gothic vowels has been updated so as to be in accordance with Vennemann 1971e.
[3] The vowels [ü] and [ṻ], which occur only in foreign words, are omitted.
[4] It is possible that Gothic had a long monophthong [m] or [ɨ] rather than a diphthong [iw].
[5] All examples are taken from Braune 1966.
[6] No examples are recorded for an alternation of [ū] with a lax vowel. However, external (comparative) evidence shows that /ū/ became [ɔ] before a vowel: Old High German *būan* 'dwell', *trūan* 'trust' attest to an older /ū/ in Gothic *bauan, trauan* (Braune 1966: §26). Synchronically, these words must probably be grouped with those that have alternation, i.e. they must be represented with /ō/. – No examples exist with /ā/ before a vowel.
[7] The reason for adding the resonant in the environment is the following. Ablauting verbs with /i/ followed by either a root-final resonant or an obstruent have [ē] in the past tense forms not covered by (2). Therefore, we need a rule (D) ordered between (2) and (6).

(D) Dehnstufe.

$$i \rightarrow \bar{e} \; / \left[\begin{array}{c} \overline{} \\ +\text{Ablaut} \\ +\text{Past} \end{array} \right] \left\{ \begin{array}{c} \left[\begin{array}{c} +\text{sonorant} \\ +\text{consonantal} \end{array} \right] + \\ \left[-\text{sonorant} \right] \end{array} \right\}$$

All ablaut past participles of /i/-verbs have zero (with anaptyctic /u/ before the syllabified resonant), except those with only obstruents after the radical /i/, which keep the /i/ unchanged. This is captured by rule (6).
[8] The glottal glides [h] and [hʷ] are clearly [+low], so that lowering of /i/ before these is an assimilatory process: The tongue is lowered for the production of short /i u/ in anticipation of the tongue position in the glide. Older Germanic /r/ is a postdental trill. There is no reason to assume that the same was not true of Gothic /r/. A trill cannot be produced easily with the body of the tongue raised. Therefore, Gothic /r/ is distinctively non-high compared, for instance, with /l/. I group it as low together with [h] and [hʷ] to show the phonetic identity of the assimilation processes involved. – Notice that long /ī ū/ are not affected by this lowering rule. This is no surprise: "Tense sounds are produced with a deliberate, accurate, maximally distinct gesture that involves considerable muscular effort; non-tense sounds are produced rapidly and somewhat indistinctly" (Chomsky and Halle 1968:324). The latter should therefore be more susceptible to regressive tongue height assimilation. (Cf. now Vennemann 1971a for a discussion of vowel-consonant assimilation.)

[9] The same problem exists in Old and Middle High German where [ī] alternates with [ay] and [i], and richly documented [ū] with nothing at all. See below.

[10] Likewise, if only /ī/ is posited, the set of diphthongs has a hole, although this is a less conspicuous gap: Exhaustive sets of diphthongs are as rare as symmetrical sets of monophthongs are frequent. Notice that /uy/ and /iw/ (and /oy/ and /ow/) are absent from (8) anyway.

[11] He also assumes (1967:132-3) both /ī/ and /iy/ for Gothic, if I understand him correctly.

[12] The diphthong, /ey/, would occur only in ablauting roots, the monophthong, /ī/, only in non-ablauting roots. Therefore, this approach requires the addition of a redundancy rule to the grammar: /ey/ → [+Ablaut]. Otherwise, one would be storing redundant information, [ey, + Ablaut] : [ī, -Ablaut], in the lexicon.

[13] Lexical representations with /ay aw/ may still have to be posited where *ai, au* alternate with *aj, aw*, as in *aiw* [ɛ̄w] 'time': *ajukduþ* [ajukdūθ] 'eternity' from /ayw/, *mauja* [mɔ̄ja] 'girl (acc)': *mawi* [mawi] 'girl (nom.)' from /mawj/. Similarly in the case of *iu* vs. *iw* as in *þiujos: þiwi* 'female servant (gen. : nom.)' from /θiwj/, if *iu* represents [ǖ] or [ɨ] rather than simply [iw] (cf. note 4 above).

[14] The reduplicative vowel [ɛ] is not in the lexicon anyway but is introduced by rule – we may assume: as [ɛ].

[15] If markedness theory demands that in cases of neutralization like this, /i u/, as less marked than /ɛ ɔ/, have to be used in the lexicon, this would not change the picture in any significant way. We would simply have a redundancy rule restricting non-central vowels to high before /r h hʷ/ in non-Foreign roots. I doubt, however, that a reasonable theory of naturalness in phonology would force us to have such an absurd redundancy rule, the exact opposite of what was the real constraint in Gothic, namely (7).

[16] The secondary status of the umlaut vowels in the case of alternation is established by the facts that 1) in the vast majority of alternants the unumlauted form is morphologically or syntactically basic, such as in singulars as opposed to plurals, positives as opposed to comparatives, neutral nouns as opposed to diminutives; 2) the umlaut vowels [ü ü: ö ö: ä:] are more highly marked than their unumlauted counterparts. This leads to a representation also of *böse* with an unumlauted vowel, although it is basic and *Bosheit* is derived. (A different view is taken for the *böse: Bosheit* alternation in Vennemann 1972c.)

[17] Formally one may have a readjustment rule like:

$$V \rightarrow [+\text{Umlaut}] / \text{———} C_o \left\{ \begin{array}{l} i \\ \left[\begin{array}{l} \text{ər} \\ +\text{Plural} \end{array}\right] \\ [+\text{Diminutive}] \\ \left[\begin{array}{l} +\text{Collective} \\ +\text{Neuter} \end{array}\right] \\ \cdot \\ \cdot \\ \cdot \end{array} \right\}$$

and a simple morphophonemic rule:

$$V \rightarrow [-\text{back}] / [+\overline{\text{Umlaut}}]$$

[18] Chomsky and Halle 1968:187, 192, 203, 206, et passim.

[19] There is some dialectal variation, such as [ᵃʸ ᵃʷ] for [ay aw], [æw] for [aw], [ɔy] for [ɔy]. This is irrelevant to the discussion because it can be accounted for by low-level phonological rules.

[20] Some linguists have facetiously suggested pairs like *point : punctual, join : junction, ointment : unction.*

[21] Which member of a pair of alternating vowels is the lexical one is determined on the grounds of stress assignment and vowel reduction.

[22] It is understood that a glide will be non-tense.

[23] Certain details are not supported. For example, what is said about ordering of the morphophonemic rules of Gothic is inapplicable in NG grammar, because of the general non-orderability of rules in this theory (see below); and the vowel shift of English is not a synchronic rule of this language (see below). Also, the 'as if' aspects of the Gothic morphophonemics in II strike me as an artifact of a model in which shortness of representation ('simplicity') is still considered a value in itself. I see no obstacle to a morphophonology in which ī → ɛ, iw → ɔ, and i → a under certain morpho-syntactic conditions, rather than just i → a where then a group of supporting rules and unsupported principles are needed. The surface-oriented ī → ɛ, iw → ɔ, i → a, etc. analysis predicts that these processes can change and obsolesce independently, which is, of course, exactly what has happened in the Germanic languages.

[24] The basic principles of NG grammar are stated in Vennemann 1972 b, d. The concept of extrinsic rule ordering has been criticized independently within TG grammar by Koutsoudas, cf. Koutsoudas 1972, Koutsoudas et al. 1974.

[25] NG phonology shares this property with Stampe's "Natural phonology", cf. Stampe 1969.

[26] It has never been established that more 'abstract' representations than are warranted by actual rule-governed alternation have any REAL consequence, where REAL means a consequence for linguistic behavior such as language acquisition, language use, language change, rather than purely descriptive consequences such as symmetry or shortness ('simplicity') of 'phoneme inventories'.

[27] This principle is contained in the 'as if' principle (10) of section II above. It is the NG analog of Postal's (1968) Naturalness Condition. It is a stronger requirement than what has since become known as the Alternation Condition (Kiparsky 1968a), because the Alternation Condition requires only that non-alternating forms be entered in the lexicon in 'roughly their autonomous phonemic representation', i.e., abstracting away from 'low-level, automatic phonetic processes' such as 'the vowel shift of English, or the loss of final /g/ in *sing*'. The Naturalness Condition of NG grammar requires that a non-alternating form is entered in the lexicon *exactly* in its *phonetic* representation, with all the 'low-level' redundancies already introduced. (It is, of course, questionable if the rules mentioned by Kiparsky are 'low-level, automatic phonetic rules'. This question is answered negatively for the vowel shift below; the answer is likewise negative in the case of /g/–deletion.)

[28] It will be noted that the concept of a 'phoneme' becomes completely meaningless in this system: The only real objects in this phonology are fully specified representations and rules, where, as mentioned, the term 'rule' is used synonymously with 'constraint' i.e. a general condition of a grammar which may simply state a redundancy (the TG morpheme structure condition), or bring about actual change (the TG P-rule), or both (the situation in which a TG grammar requires a morpheme structure condition plus an identical P-rule). I consider this consequence of my theory, the 'reality of the allophone', as desirable: The 'phoneme' has always presented nothing but problems to theoreticians. I consider the problem of the phoneme as a pseudo-problem created by insufficiently constrained models of grammar, just like the 'abstractness' problem and the 'absolute neutralization' problem. NG grammar draws support from the fact that these pseudo-problems do not arise in it, see below.

[29] Morphophonological changes in certain German dialects support the untenability of the view that such vowels are synchronically derived from back vowels, as is shown in Kiparsky 1968b.

[30] They propose this formalism even though curly braces have been traditionally used for dis unctive ordering, both in syntax and phonology.

³¹ The only other place in Chomsky and Halle 1968 where the principle of conjunctive ordering is used is in the formulation of the stress rules, which is even more questionable than their vowel description. Conjunctive ordering of parts of rules must be prohibited by a general principle.

³² I agree with Crothers (1970) that the only kind of evidence crucial to demonstrating a need for 'abstract' phonology, empirical evidence of the kind characterized above in note 26, has not yet been found.

³³ I am grateful to Laryy M. Hyman and Robert P. Stockwell for valuable comments on this paper.

REFERENCES

Braune, Wilhelm. 1966. Gotische Grammatik. First published 1880. 17th edition by Ernst A. Ebbinghaus, Tübingen: Niemeyer.

Buckalew, Ronald E. 1964. A generative grammar of Gothic morphology. Diss. University of Illinois, Urbana. Ann Arbor, Michigan: University Microfilms.

Chomsky, Noam. 1964. Current issues in linguistic theory. 2nd printing, 1966. The Hague: Mouton.

Chomsky, Noam, and Morris Halle. 1968. The sound pattern of English. New York: Harper and Row.

Crothers, John. 1970. A note on the abstractness controversy. Monthly Internal Memorandum, Nov. 1970, Phonology Laboratory, POLA, University of California, Berkeley.

Dingwall, William Orr, ed. 1971. A survey of linguistic science. College Park, Maryland: Linguistics Program, University of Maryland.

Foley, James. 1970. Goals of phonological theory. Lecture given at the University of Southern California.

Kiparsky, Paul. 1968a. How abstract is phonology? Cambridge: Massachusetts Institute of Technology, MS.

—. 1968b. Linguistic universals and linguistic change. Universals in linguistic theory, ed. by Emmon Bach and Robert T. Harms, 170-202. New York: Holt, Rinehart and Winston.

Koutsoudas, Andreas. 1972. The strict order fallacy. Language 48.88-96.

Koutsoudas, Andreas, Gerald Sanders, and Craig Noll. 1974. On the application of phonological rules. Language 50.1-28.

Krohn, Robert K. 1969. English vowels. Diss. University of Michigan.

Lightner, Theodore M. 1971. Generative phonology. In Dingwall 1971: 498-564, with Discussion 565-74.

Motsch, Wolfgang. 1967. Zum Ablaut der Verben in der Frühperiode germanischer Sprachen. Studia Grammatica VI: Phonologische Studien, 119-144. Berlin: Akademie Verlag.

Partee, Barbara Hall. 1971. Linguistic metatheory. In Dingwall 1971: 650-80.

Postal, Paul M. 1968. Aspects of phonological theory. New York: Harper and Row.

Stampe, David. 1969. The acquisition of phonetic representation. Papers from the Fifth Regional Meeting of the Chicago Linguistic Society, ed. by Robert I. Binnick et al., 443-54. Chicago: Department of Linguistics, University of Chicago.

Vennemann, Theo. 1968. German phonology. Diss. University of California, Los Angeles. Ann Arbor, Michigan: University Microfilms.

—. 1971a. The interpretation of phonological features in assimilation rules. Working papers in phonetics, UCLA, 19.62-68. [Cf. Vennemann 1972e.]

—. 1971b. Natural generative phonology. Paper read at the Annual Meeting of the Linguistic Society of America, St. Louis, Mo.

—. 1971c. The phonology of Gothic vowels. Language 47.90-132.
—. 1972a. Phonetic analogy and conceptual analogy. In Theo Vennemann and Terence H. Wilbur, Schuchardt, the Neogrammarians, and the transformational theory of phonological change: Four essays (Frankfurt/Main: Athenäum) 181-204.
—. 1972b. Phonological uniqueness in natural generative grammar. Glossa 6.105-116.
—. 1972c. Rule inversion. Lingua 29.209-242.
—. 1972d. On the theory of syllabic phonology. Linguistische Berichte 18.1-18.
—. 1972e. Phonetic detail in assimilation: Problems in Germanic phonology. Language 48.863-892. [Extended version of Vennemann 1971a.]
Vennemann, Theo, and Peter Ladefoged. 1971. Phonetic features and phonological features. Working papers in phonetics, UCLA 21.13-24. [Also: Lingua 32 (1973) 61-74.]

Note added in proof: After proofreading this paper, more than four years after its submission, I feel that a few remarks should be added in the interest of clarity.

1) The theory of phonology implicit in the preceding criticisms and descriptions has been developed further especially in the following works of myself and others: 'Phonological concreteness in natural generative grammar', in R. W. Shuy – C.-J. N. Bailey (eds.), *Towards tomorrow's linguistics* (Washington, D.C.: Georgetown U. P., 1974) 202-219; 'Restructuring', *Lingua* 33 (1974) 137-156; 'Words and syllables in natural generative grammar', in A. Bruck et al. (eds.), *Papers from the parasession on natural phonology* (Chicago: Chicago Linguistic Society, 1975) 346-374; Joan B. Hooper, *Aspects of natural generative phonology* [Diss., UCLA, 1973] (Ann Arbor, Mich.: University Microfilms; Bloomington: Indiana University Linguistics Club); Grover M. Hudson, Suppletion in the representation of alternations [Diss., UCLA, 1975] (Ann Arbor, Mich.: University Microfilms).

(2) Gothic post-sonorant *h, ʾ* are interpreted above (fn. 8 et passim) as glottal and, as such, as [+ low], following Chomsky and Halle 1968: 307. They are identified as lax uvular spirants in Vennemann 1972e: 878.

ON NOUMENALIZATION

JOHN W. M. VERHAAR, S. J.

By way of an apology for the cumbrous title, and name for the topic, of this paper, let me approach that topic obliquely, for easier digestibility.*

All linguists are familiar with the logical mention/use distinction. *I* in *I believe you* is used,[1] *I* in *I is a pronoun* is mentioned. The distinction is also relevant linguistically, for *I is* [...] is ungrammatical unless *I* is mentioned, not used. De Groot has invented a term for such cases from the linguist's point of view: self-naming function (*zelfnoemfunctie*; de Groot 1949:78). I propose to call it, simply, self-reference.

What is problematic about self-reference is the fairly large number of aspects of the "self". The "self" of what? In this case, of a word. But the word "word" is problematic in terms of identity, and may be considered under the aspects of its sounds, spelling, meaning, and a number of others determined by grammar. This appears clearly from sentences such as *Book has four letters, Book has three phonemes, Book ends in a stop, Book means what my dictionary says it does, Book may occur in Subject and Object positions, Book is a Noun*, etc. In all these cases *book* is mentioned, not used.

Now, one thing coming in in what I shall call "noumenalization" is a substitution of the "noumenal" for something that the noumenal is not. The noumenal is always something semantic (though not necessarily inversely), so meaning replaces something-not-meaning; that something-not-meaning is, in the present case (but not always) the referent. Therefore, in *Book means* [...] the speaker refers not to a book, but to the meaning of *book*; or, the use of *book* in this sentence is a case of noumenalization. Note that, as in noumenalization it has to be the *meaning* that substitutes for whatever it happens to be that the meaning is not, not all cases of mention *vs* use come under noumenalization; for example, *book* in *Book ends in a stop* does not. This obliges us to drop mention *vs* use as a workable concept in the present paper. There is another (terminological) reason for doing this: all mention itself is also a form of use. For "use" is here conceived as referring to something; that once in a while what is being referred to is (under the aspect of meaning) the same as that which does the referring does not make use cease to be used. With this, the mention/use distinction has left the stage. What do we put in its place?

For one thing, we will retain the term "use". For the moment it is something belonging to words as lexical items (though not all words). Words as such may be considered as dictionary entries, in which case they are items of *langue*. Dictionary entries, it is true, do not refer, which is what they may sometimes look like doing, seeing that dictionary definitions, paraphrastic as they often are, may look like descriptions of referents, at least with quite many words. Words with referential capacity are actually referential only in *parole*; or, in the unit of *parole*, the sentence. We may further consider use, in the case of words whose meaning has referential capacity, as the *application* of the meaning to the referent (Reichling 1967:319ff.). In noumenalization the referent is that meaning itself. Note that even words not normally referential (such as *of*, or *or*, in English) become so when noumenalized: *Or means* [...], *Of means* [...], etc.

Now word meaning is a notorious problem.[2] Even if one considers meaning and reference to be distinct (as most linguists and philosophers do), there is the question if referentiality enters meaning. As words may be classified according to whether they refer or not, along lines which practically constitute super-categories along word class lines (for example: Nominals and Verbals are referential): it may be thought that that matter is grammatical and not lexical. However, it seems to me that such a super-categorization, though no doubt grammatically semantic (*cf.* the *categoremantica vs* the *syncategoremantica* of medieval philosophy of language), cannot be considered altogether detached from lexical semantics (their grammatical nature consisting largely in their "filling" capacity as "fillers" for the grammatical functions as "slots"). Let us therefore say that, though reference does not enter meaning, referential capacity does. This entails that *book* in *Book is a noun* is used self-referentially in a manner involving *also* meaning; to that extent, then, *book* in that sentence is *also* a case of noumenalization.

Although "hypostatization" as a term is scarcely less terrifying than "noumenalization," it may be asked if "hypostatization," which is at least better known, is not a better term for the problem discussed here.[3] I submit that it is not. For also cases of self-reference *not* involving meaning are cases of hypostatization. To say a word or two more on that

term, however, has its advantages: for it shows that not only the "concrete" (in the sense in which sounds, or letters, are "concrete"), but also
the "abstract" (in the sense in which meanings are "abstract") are subject
to isolation and objectification. This is well enough known in learned
terminology; a technical term may be considered as a hypostatized
meaning, or a concept, which can be manipulated more precisely than
can meanings of words in natural language (see Verhaar 1963:126-34).
My point now is that this hypostatization may be found also in natural
language, in part no doubt because many a scientific or philosophical
term has found its way into natural language, especially in cultures with a
highly developed education, but yet not confined to such cases alone.
As already noted, such hypostatization has even grammatical consequences. — Now, does noumenalization entail more than the examples
just given and similar ones? To go into this, a few more reasons for
tackling these problems must first be briefly discussed.

Why not simply say that words, or even parts of words under some
principle of their division, or segments more extensive than words,
may be used self-referentially, that such use may make the word's
meaning the referent, and have done with it? I have selected noumenalization as a basic concept here, not only because of potential results which
may have consequences for language typology, but also on the more
generally theoretical ground that it is possible to consider language —
natural language — as a particular way of thinking. Speech is a mental
activity of great sophistication, even for the illiterate. When we talk about
thinking we apparently have the irrepressible urge to plunge into all
kinds of epistemologies; this is an honorable occupation, so long as we
remember that natural language embodies thinking as much as, though
differently from, the kind of thinking attained through the accumulation
of academic credits. I now suggest that what is semantic in natural
language (lexical and grammatical) is, identically, some form of thinking;
and the point of recognizing this is something important not only to the
philosopher but also to the linguist: that language is specifically and
uniquely human. Now, if language, from the point of view of semantics,
is also thinking, and if thought contents may be hypostatized, it makes
sense to ask whether the hypostatization may take forms on which also
the linguist may put his finger. The kind of self-reference involving a
word's meaning as referent is a clear example of this. The question is if
there is more.

Consider the sentence *One may obtain these articles from market ven-
dors, who in turn buy them from the farmers,* and specifically the meaning

of *in turn*. This phrase relates, not to the actual order in which the articles move from producer to consumer, but to the "noumenal" order in which the speaker traces them to their origin. No dictionary is likely to specify this phrase as indicating a link in a regressive order; in fact, if we hyposta- tize the cognitive order, it *is* not in that sense regressive. This is a clear case of noumenalization, while yet is it not a case of self-reference. Note that to think that *in turn* "means" here something that would include that feature of regressiveness would be to confuse objective information with semantic content. Here follows a similar example. Consider the two sentences *I am primarily concerned with politics in this job*, and *I am ultimately concerned with politics in this job*. One would tend to think that *primarily* and *ultimately* are interchangeable, or at least could be, without making any difference. This would be true on the level of information, but not semantically. Whatever the semantic description of these words would be, at any rate with *primarily* a feature 'first' and with *ultimately* a feature 'last' would have to come in. How then can the information be the same, especially seeing that semantically there is not only difference but even antonymy. Scholastic philosophy has, non-linguistically, long known the answer: *quod primum in intentione ultimum in executione*; the "intention" here belongs to the cognitive order, the "execution" does not. Therefore the *primarily* sentence, but not the one containing *ultimately*, presents a case of noumenalization. I do not know if there are many cases of such apparent synonymy, but one more is the pair *formal(ly)* and *material(ly)*. It may be remarked that forms like these are terms rather than words, and belong therefore on a level different from that of natural language. I am far from denying the technical (specifically philosophical) importance of such analyses, but it happens that this particular pair not only does turn up in natural language sometimes, but is also highly relevant to the terminology of linguistic theory, which is also of professional importance for the lin- guist. "Formal" and "form" are central concepts in linguistic theory, and though this is not necessarily true of "material," the notion of substance which de Saussure and Hjelmslev said language was not, defining language as form rather than substance, is so close to the formal-material distinction that the problem just mentioned cannot legitimately be ignored. I may add that the *suppositio formalis* and *suppositio materialis* in medieval language philosophy have also been used in one another's sense, but if anyone says that at least is not necessarily the linguist's business, I will not quarrel.

Consider another example again: *Nowadays many people are in quest of a personal God.* The assumption is that all of those people are mono-theists. Then what is *a* doing in the sentence, for *a* is used only if there are more of the same. However, whoever believes that there is only one God may yet feel one may have different kinds of experience of God; some are what one is in quest of; others are not. Owing to the presence of *a*, the phrase *a personal God* is a case of noumenalization. Again consider the sentence *A wall three feet high is not high.* There has to be some collocational explanation (collocational it has to be, because I object to the grammaticalization of the lexicon as obtaining in "selec-tional restrictions") of why the wall is supposed to be both *high* and *not high*. *High* in its first occurrence is not antonymical to *low*, but stands for any vertical measure, here duly specified by *three feet*; the second occurrence of *high* is antonymical to *low*. The second does not entail any noumenalization, but the first, being a mathematical ab-straction, does, through the process which I have elsewhere called "neutralization;" in this case what it "neutralizes" is precisely antonymy (Verhaar 1970 and 1972).

Yet another case of noumenalization takes grammatically the form of derivation, in the Graeco-Latin mode which has become international. We speak about *psychological problems, theological questions, linguistic issues, sociological features*, meaning not problems, questions, etc. of the disciplines of psychology, theology, etc., but emotional problems, questions of religious faith, issues of language, features of society. It is true, of course, that these problems, questions, etc. may be treated on a technical disciplinary level, on an "ideal" level, in the disciplines con-cerned, but psychology is not emotional balance, theology not the faith, etc. What the *-logical* derivation does is noumenalize the referent of the word following the form ending in *-logical*, out of prejudice in favor of a discipline perhaps, and perhaps ultimately out of cultural bias in favor of idealization; and in many cases thoughtlessly. In some way such as this we have to account for *abnormal psychology*, in which what is abnormal is not psychology, but only one of its objects.

A curious case is one already known to quite a different approach in linguistics, and well exemplified in a sentence like *One cannot elapse a book*, of which a paraphrase would be something like 'Elapse is not a word that can take *book* as an object'. Here, however, it may be asked if we have a true case of noumenalization, for it might be said that seman-tic and/or grammatical impossibility is presented as factual impossibility; not that such an interpretation would be quite evident, but it might be good to have a test. We can come by one if we realize that *book* not only cannot be the Object of *elapse*, but that that Verb, being intransitive, cannot have any Object at all. How would one, as a parallel expression to *One cannot elapse a book*, express this? By *One cannot elapse something* or by ?**One cannot elapse anything*? The latter looks suspiciously like a deviant sentence, but that is, I submit, because, by reason of *anything*, it would be the expression relating to factual impossibility, while the use of *something*, which can be strongly generalizing in meaning, rather indicates the semantic (grammatical) impossibility. If so, it is the semantic impossibility which is being expressed, but not transferring it to a factual level, and we have therefore a true case of noumenalization. Yet *elapse* is not a true case of self-reference, for then it would be nominalized (*Elapse is not a word that* [...]). Again, then we have a case of noumenalization which is not self-referential.

As a final case in this series I mention a word like Latin *seu*, 'or', which differs from *vel* and *aut*, in that *vel* and *aut* (differently, otherwise) are related to the choice between objective alternatives, while *seu* only links synonymous phrases equally valid semantically without constituting any alternative other than between parts of utterances. *Seu*, therefore, links utterances, or segments thereof; the same holds for Dutch *oftewel* versus *of*, 'or' as an "objective" alternative. I will now bypass in how far anaphoric reference fits this picture also, beyond saying that contextual reference is not enough to constitute noumenalization, but one might doubt about expressions like *(the) former* and *(the) latter*. One might also hesitate about enumerations *(He visited Mary, Kenneth, and John)*, which, though they certainly do not necessarily reflect factual order in the grammatical device of word order, do reflect it when a phrase like *in that order* is added; perhaps then *that* in *in that order* is a case of noumenalization.[4] There must, however, be more to the relation between grammatical and real order, or else the stylistic device known as *hysteron proteron* (which often constitutes a case of noumenalization) could not be a stylistic device.

Now to a new and possibly more significant type of problem. What if grammar, in the form of predication, forms the basis for an expression being noumenal? Note, "noumenal," not "noumenalizing;" also, I speak about the noumenal entailed in predication, but I am not committed to the claim that all predication entails the noumenal. Further, as this is not the place to develop a full Subject-Predicate structure theory, let me state a few assumptions.

First, Predicate as a notion should be taken extensively enough, in certain cases (which I cannot now specify) including certain types of

Complement. One Complement always included is a Nominal Phrase following a Copula; that is, that phrase plus the Copula is the Predicate. A Predicate may extend or narrow down the meaning conveyed by the Subject; for example, in *This is a table*, and *This table is too low*, respectively. Both cases I shall call "specification". Therefore, the meaning of (whatever happens to be) the Predicate specifies the meaning of (whatever happens to be) the Subject. I shall further assume that both Subject and Predicate, each considered in itself, are referential. We now have mS (the meaning of the Subject), rS (the referent of the Subject), mP (the meaning of the Predicate), and rP (the referent of the Predicate). I shall further say that, in the mind of the speaker, rS and rP are inter-related by way of a "connection". Furthermore, mP is applied to rS, not to mS.[5] Application, then, as a notion, is ambiguous: we must distinguish referential application and predicative application. The only relation not given a name now is that between rP and mS; I am not sure there is a relation of interest to the linguist there, but if there is it has no bearing on my present topic. Finally, note that all relations are uni-directional, except the connection, which is bi-lateral. Truth will depend upon a further determination of the connection, that is, in sentences which are suitable for assignment of truth values in the first place. This aspect, however, does not belong to the province of the linguist, any more than the connection itself. The following diagram may help visualize the above:

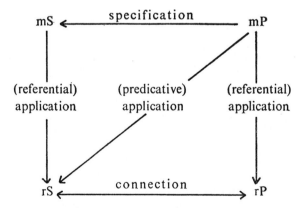

Now consider the sentence *Oculist is eye-doctor*. Note that both S and P are used self-referentially, and therefore noumenalizingly; or, the referential application takes the form of noumenalization. Since mS and mP have now become rS and rP, what we have extra-lingually is a connection; lingually, however, we have a specification. It can also be proved that we must take the lingual point of view (apart from reasons of limitation of my topic, that is), for a connection is bi-directional while a specification is uni-directional. However, if bi-directionality applied *Oculist is eye-doctor* would be the same as *Eye-doctor is oculist*, which cannot be the case by reason of a difference in topicalization. That is, while all speakers of English would know the meaning of *eye-doctor*, not all might know the meaning of *oculist*; so that, for the topicalization entailed in *Eye-doctor is oculist*, there has to be a special reason, for example the pedagogical introduction of unfamiliar words through familiar ones. This stated, the question is if we have noumenalization here not only by referential, but also by predicative application. I submit that we do not. Indeed since mS functions, referentially, as rS, and the *terminus a quo* of predicative application is mP and not rP, there is no self-reference predicatively (or, philosophically, there is no tautology), in spite of what one would have to say from the point of view of synonymy. There *is*, however, in *An oculist is an eyedoctor*, by reason of the article. In English, whenever the indefinite article is not used self-referentially, it has a meaning paraphrastically expressible as 'a certain', which would make nonsense of our sentence if entering the meaning of *an*. It is the occurrence of *an* in P-position which makes the predicative application a noumenalizing one, not its occurrence in S position, for predicative application has only (m)P for its *terminus a quo*. This appears from the fact that we may leave out *an* in S-position, but not in P-position, for *Oculist is an eye-doctor* is all right, while **An oculist is eye-doctor* is deviant.

A last example. Consider the sentence *Nixon has become a household word on campus*. One might, perhaps, be tempted to argue that *Nixon* is used self-referentially here, for such use would indeed make it worthy for S to predicate *(household) word*. *Word* would then itself not be used self-referentially. However, if *Nixon* is used self-referentially, could one substitute *he*? Yet, *He has become a household word on campus* is perfectly all right. Therefore, *Nixon* is not used self-referentially. It would still be true that *(household) word* would not be a case of self-reference either; but yet, because of the very meaning of *word*, or, more specifically, of *household word* (paraphrasable as 'familiar expression in frequent topical use') the noumenal would come in by way of predicative application; not because *a* meaning is (predicatively) applied to S (this is normal), but because of the (partly) noumenal *content* of the phrase filling *this particular predicate*; after all (expressing the same thing in terms of the

"connection"), Nixon (as distinct from *Nixon*) *is not* a word! Therefore,
predicative application here constitutes a case of noumenalization, even
though (and here it differs from the *oculist* sentence), neither S nor P
present a case of noumenalization in terms of referential application.
Sentences like this one occur regularly even though not frequently:
That vehicle is John's idea of a nice car, or *That country is my ideal of a
guided democracy*, or *Peter has become the epitome of all that is inefficient*.

To the extent that analyses like these will turn out to be firmly enough
founded, the issues raised for linguistic theory are far-reaching. I have
elsewhere argued that, if we recognize the grammaticalization of the
lexicon (in the way of transformational grammar) for the fallacy it is,
and if therefore we have to recognize rules of "lexical collocation"
which are not grammatical while yet affecting "sentence meaning"
(see Verhaar 1972) at least in cases of specific kinds of meaning application such as those of metaphor, we also have to recognize that the kind
of "collocation" described above is undoubtedly grammatical, though
wholly unrelated to the selectional restrictions approach in the manner
of Chomsky. As of now, I have no answer except for the significant fact
that such examples as given above appear to be limited to sentences
with a Copula. This, however, is (almost?) uniquely limited, typologically,
to Indo-European languages, which may, therefore, be unique in having
collocational rules not all of which are exempted from grammar. Non-
verbal predicates are found, for example, in certain Semitic, Chinese,
and Austro-Polynesian languages. Though presumably the predicative
relation between S and P in those languages is still uni-directional from
S to P, one may wonder if that relation is an applicational one; that is, if
it moves from m(P) to r(S). For non-verbal sentences in Indonesian I am
satisfied that the relation is not from m(P), though I cannot deny that
it would be to r(S). I propose to make results of my research in this
respect available as soon as they are somewhat more mature, and I
will now merely mention what I suspect the S-P relation in that language
(and others) to be. It would be what I would call "juxtapositional",[6]
that is, the language user's orientation towards the "situational component" (Verhaar 1971, 1972) would make meaning as distinct from
referent less functional, in favor of the referent; and this, once it would
appear to be true of the S-P relationship, would hold for verbal predicates
as well as for non-verbal ones. There are a few elements in the Indonesian
verbal system which point in this direction, such as the low functionality
of transitivity of transitive verbs, which are used far more frequently
"absolutely" (this means what other theories unfelicitously call "with

Object deletion") than in Indo-European languages, in many cases even raising doubts about the verbal status of what morphologically looks like a Verb (morphology being in those cases a poor criterium of word class membership). A strongly corroborating feature for this approach, which amplies that noumenalization is much less characteristic of such a language as Indonesian than it is for Indo-European languages, is that noumenalization through self-reference would be deviant in a number of samples I have reviewed.

Universitas Indonesia. Jakarta   [November, 1971]

NOTES

* While working on an earlier version of the present paper I profited from discussions with Dr C. Verhaak, S. J., of the *Sekolah Tinggi Filsafat "Drijarkara"*, Djakarta, and with Professor Leslie Dewart, of the University of Toronto; the term "uni-directional". as used for the P to S relation, is due to Professor Dewart.

1 I will use no quotation marks for cases of self-reference occurring in the material, as they would prejudge certain cases; in my opinion, they cannot be used consistently, and it seems better, for my purposes, to have written representation more in keeping with the oral-aural experience of language use. – Outside the material (which will appear italicized), quotation marks (double) will be used according to the usual conventions, including the "scare quotes" with an eye on (as Bertrand Russell once expressed it) the "thought police", as in these very instances. Single quotes enclose glosses, and paraphrases.

2 See Reichling 1967. – I consider Austin 1961 to be extremely vulnerable, but to refute it would be a fairly detailed job, and for the present paper I must decide against it.

3 In view of the language-typological remarks at the end of the paper the reader may be interested in turning to Staal 1965, Alexander 1953, and Verhaar 1969:25-9.

4 De Vries 1971 argues that Dutch *want* 'for', and *omdat* 'because', differ in that *want* may be paraphrased as 'and I say this because [.....]'. *Want* could therefore count as noumenalized *omdat*. So far as I can see, exactly the same holds for the English glosses just given.

5 This point has been clearly made by Geach 1962:22-3; my terminology is slightly different here.

6 As for possible parallels of this (if true) for the logic of classes as different from the logic of predicates, *videant logici*!

REFERENCES

Anon. 1965. Logic and philosophy: Essays in Honour of I. M. Bochenski. Amsterdam: Noordhollandse Uitgeversmaatschappij.
Austin, J. L. 1961. The meaning of a word. In: Urmson and Warnock 1961:23-43.
de Groot, A. W. 1949. Structurele syntaxis. Den Haag: Servire.

Garvin, Paul L. (ed.) 1970. Method and theory in linguistics. The Hague: Mouton.

Geach, Peter Thomas. 1962. Reference and generality. Ithaca, New York: Cornell University Press.

Natanson, Maurice (ed.). 1973. Phenomenology and the social sciences. 2 vols. Evanston, Illinois: Northwestern University Press.

Reichling, A. J. B. N. 1967. Het woord. Een studie omtrent de grondslag van taal en taalgebruik. Zwolle (or. 1935): W. E. J. Tjeenk Willink.

Staal, J. F. 1965. Reification, quotation and nominalization. In: Anon. 1965:151-87.

Urmson, J. O., and Warnock, G. J. (eds.). 1961. J. L. Austin. Philosophical papers. London: Clarendon Press.

Verhaar, J. W. M. 1963. Some relations between perception, speech, and thought. Assen: van Gorcum.

—. 1969. Language and theology. Continuum 7.3-39. Reprint of: Some notes on language and theology. Bijdragen 30.39-65, which is less accessible than the reprint.

—. 1970. Method, theory and phenomenology. In: Garvin 1970:42-91.

—. 1971. Philosophy and linguistic theory. Language Sciences 14.1-11.

—. 1973. Phenomenology and linguistics. In: Maurice Natanson 1973:1.361-464.

de Vries, J. W. 1971. Want en omdat. De nieuwe taalgids 64.414-20.

IN DEFENSE OF THE FAMILY TREE
(WITH SUPERIMPOSED TYPOLOGY)

C. F. AND F. R. VOEGELIN

Debate over whether there is such a thing as a 'mixed language' (*Mischsprache*) should by now be a dead issue, but it turns out that this issue is unexpectedly alive, as we are discovering in our survey of alternative genetic classifications of the world's languages — as though there were a genuine competition between genetic classification and typological change. In the autonomous approach to language change, whether by Sturtevant in 1917 or by King in 1969, or by Hoenigswald or Lehmann in the intervening half century, rule mechanisms account for change from generation to generation of speakers in the evolution of a single language; but once a whole language is classifiable as belonging to a given family, it may change typologically but not genetically. It is never the case that a natural language is found at one time period to be descending from one proto-language, but at a later period to shift and descend from another proto-language in another language family. Put another way, THERE ARE NO MIXED LANGUAGES IN GENETIC CLASSIFICATION in which languages are displayed on a family tree showing all terminal nodes dominated by a single apex node.

Some linguists say they prefer the wave-theory explanation of language change, as though it were in competition with genetic classification.[1] Now the wave-theory requires a kind of typology which is — to use Benveniste's expression — 'superimposed' on a genetic classification. To typologize languages first, and then reckon lines of descent from proto-languages, leads chiefly to controversy over alternative proto-language candidates, as in the history of classifications of African languages.

If the rule mechanisms mentioned were constantly active, an agglutinative language might become an inflectional language, as was claimed in the last century. Conversely, if the rules followed in one generation were followed without change in every succeeding generation, a given type of language might be classifiable as forever belonging to that type.

Neither alternative has ever been encountered. Put another way, ALL LANGUAGES ARE TYPOLOGICALLY MIXED. The 'too famous classification' of whole languages as being exclusively agglutinative, inflectional, or isolating does a disservice to subsystem typologies which account for what is actually encountered — both in the last century and in this. For example, both Johannes Schmidt's wave-theory in the 19th century and 20th-century concern with language universals belong to the class of sub-system typology.

Beside (a), the class of sub-system or grammatical typology, some other typological frames of reference are relevant to language change, such as (b) cognitive typologies of anthropology and psycholinguistics; (c) social typologies, as the network of social relations in British Social Anthropology, and as diglossia in sociolinguistics; and (d) cultural space typologies, as in cultural anthropology and geography.

(b) The relevance of cognitive typology to language change (now being explored in psycholinguistics) involves three kinds of tacit (intuitive) language knowledge: (1) how to produce sentences; (2) how to understand sentences; (3) how to predict (or generate) new sentences, and self-correct violations of rules, as every three-year-old does — or, in the words of Bever and Langendoen, (1) external structures, (2) perceptual mechanisms, (3) internal structures. These three kinds of language knowledge are relevant to evolutionary change in grammatical typology — in English, for example, which was once much more inflectional than it is now; hence Modern English has fewer lexical classes and fewer suffixes than Old English. This makes it easier to learn — i.e. to produce grammatical sentences; but harder to understand, for understanding requires additional syntactic interpretation in lieu of the redundant information formerly supplied by inflectional suffixes especially.

(c) The relevance of social typology to language change is traditionally stated in terms of prestige dialects spoken by an old elite whose dialect serves as a model for the non-elite until the entire speech community speaks like the old elite; then a new elite innovates, thereby initiating non-ending cycles of language change. It remains to be discovered how language change takes place in egalitarian societies which do not distinguish superordination from subordination dialectically. Current work in sociolinguistics is in a discovery phase rather than in an explanatory phase. Spatial terms in popular usage, as well as those used in social anthropology, are metaphorically rather than literally referential. Thus, 'high society' may exist in a valley while 'low life' may be found in attics as well as in basements; observe also 'social distance', 'the network of social relationships', and the metaphorical spacing of castes and other hierarchical classes from 'upper' to 'lower', down to the 'subproletariat' and the 'outcaste' who are 'widely' separated from 'in-groups'.

(d) Spatial terms in cultural anthropology are quite literally three-dimensional spaces rather than metaphorical spaces. Cultural-space typology classifies such spaces according to the activities that go on in them. For example, in the 'household' there are family activities (quite contrastive activities when Japanese households are compared to Hopi households; or, in the same society, the households of the colonel's lady and Rosie O'Grady may also be contrastive). In 'plazas' of Southwest pueblos, the characteristic activity is ceremonial dancing, well rehearsed for the public domain, while in the 'kivas' the dances are privately rehearsed — among other ritual activities. But the kivas are 'closed' rather than 'open' to the public. Something like the 'culture area' of yesterday's cultural anthropology (a rather homogeneous geographic area in which are found subsets of somewhat similar tribal cultures) is being revived in modern ecological anthropology, with its 'niches' and 'ecosystems' and ethologically inspired 'territorialities'. For each of the cultural spaces here exemplified (e.g. in the 'kiva'), there is some way of talking appropriately that would not be appropriate in another cultural space (e.g. in the 'plaza') of the same society.

A relationship of change in culture space with change in language is less commonly encountered. One clear instance of such a relationship is that of dialect leveling among speakers of American Indian languages who have been relocated in post-Discovery days, in contrast to the persistence of dialect differences among languages whose speakers remain in the same cultural spaces that were occupied by their forbears in pre-Discovery days. Thus, the dialect differences in the Hopi language are particularly discernible between three village mesas which are not more than forty miles apart. In contrast, there are no consistent dialect differences today among the Shawnee whose great-grandparents were removed to Indian Territory (now Oklahoma). When they were in Ohio, it is said, the Chilacootha Shawnee had a different way of speaking than the Pekowi Shawnee. The descendants of the Chilacootha, Pekowi, and other political bands are now in Oklahoma where those who speak Shawnee at all speak in one leveled dialect.[2]

Massive lexical borrowing commonly occurs between languages in contact, but may also occur as a consequence of some unusual social situations — e.g. the cases in which some few speakers serve as transmitters of the donor language by entering the cultural spaces of bilinguals in a far distant country. In fact, the languages may be separated by a vast ocean; Mary Haas' example is that of the flood of loans from English in the modern Japanese lexicon.

FAMILY-TREE AND/OR WAVE-THEORY

Now it appears to be the case that classification either by social typology (c), or by culture space typology (d),[3] can contribute to an understanding of language change — but not autonomously so; in contrast, classification by family-tree can, quite by itself, reveal the single line of descent taken after separation from a proto-language. But when single-line-of-descent information is supplemented typologically — especially by wave-theory information — the additional kinds of information can account for additional aspects of language change.

The wave-theory claim is that linguistic change can be represented as waves, or as a series of successive waves — isoglosses and networks of isoglosses in the case of dialect geography; and 'special resemblances', as Bloomfield put it, between related languages in the case of separate languages in contact in two different but neighboring branches (as Germanic and Celtic) of one language family (as Indo-European). But the 'special resemblances' in wave-theory typology are dense only between languages in geographic proximity; they are less numerous between geographically distant languages — or even lacking entirely then. Like the family-tree model, wave-theory was formulated in the 19th century, but a full half-century after the family-tree formulation.

The claim of earlier family-tree formulations was that linguistic change takes place in consequence of a lack of continuing contact among speakers who separated after sharing an idealized homogeneous proto-language. Here it is the lack of continuing contact that is conducive to linguistic change — dialects of a single language, upon discontinuing contact, become separate languages (family-tree) — while in the wave-theory it is the resumption of contact that is conducive to linguistic change. In no sense, even when put as a matter of extreme contrast, can the wave-theory way of explaining linguistic change be said to be a counterexample to the family-tree theory. The claims of the two theories are not contradictory; they are complementary.

Rule changes can be reconstructed so that the rules operating when the proto-language was spoken are restored. This restoration or reconstruction serves as the point of departure for stating rule changes in the languages which have separated in space and descended in time from the proto language. The direction of change of rules, including sound correspondences, is from proto-language to daughter languages in the family-tree theory. However, all descending dialects and languages that encounter each other may in consequence undergo the kind of rule change that is accounted for by wave-theory.

It turns out then that family-tree theory is dependent upon the wave-theory, and vice versa. Taken by itself, the family-tree theory is not strong enough to calculate time elapsed between a proto-language and its own present-day descendent languages; and even its genuine strength – to classify present-day languages genetically – is offset by its weakness or inability to account for just those rule changes that occur when the descending languages encounter each other in the intervening period between separation from their common proto language and the time they are studied. Though the wave-theory has the strength to do precisely this, it is thereby dependent upon a prior genetic classification stated in terms of family-tree – as Indo-European with nodes for main branches, as Germanic and Celtic and Italic and Slavic – in order to show how 'special resemblances' diffuse between languages in different but adjacent branches.

As Benveniste has put it, typology is not opposed to but may be, rather, superimposed upon genetic classification. So also, to demonstrate diffusion of typological features between different families of languages in areal linguistics, the order of research is irreversible; a genetic classification must be made before historical conclusions can be drawn about the typological classification. Thus, Emeneau's demonstration that Indic languages could not be the donor of the retroflexion feature in India could not have been made without prior genetic classification of Dravidian, Munda and the Indo-European languages.

WHOLE LANGUAGE AND/OR SUBSYSTEM TYPOLOGIES

Several good summaries of typological classifications in this century were made in the decade between 1952 and 1962.

Almost half of Hockett's *A Manual of Phonology*, written in 1952, is devoted to the second chapter, "A Typology of Phonological Systems" of which Hockett says (p. 1), "The typology developed in §2 of the present manual is not supposed to be arbitrary, and it is considerably more complex than either Trubetzkoy's or Voegelin's; but I am sure that it falls far short of what we must eventually develop." Any 'phonological system' is, by definition, a subsystem of the language of which it is a part, whether or not 'sub-' is prefixed to 'system'. The subsystem approach in 20th-century typology was generally felt to be convenient – i.e. an enabling device for comparing parts of language irrespective of whether the languages compared are genetically related – but vulnerable to arbitrariness.

It may be the general case that smaller sybsystems were preferred to larger or more comprehensive ones. Thus, Hockett was in good company at mid-century when he typologized vowels and consonants separately, as two subsystems, just as Trubetzkoy had done earlier. But between the typologies of Trubetzkoy and Hockett, Roman Jakobson introduced a distinctive feature approach which permits typologizing vowels and consonants in a single subsystem; nevertheless, vowel systems and consonant systems continued to be treated as two separate systems in most subsystems typologies.

One chapter each in Martinet's 1962 book and in Lehmann's 1962 book is devoted to typology, with emphasis on subsystem and whole-language typology, respectively.

The *International Journal of American Linguistics* for July, 1960, published four papers on typology, including Greenberg's 1954 revision of Sapir's 1921 typology, and Kroeber's enthusiastic endorsement of this mid-century attempt, long after Sapir had tried – apparently in vain – to revive 19th-century typology.

Unlike his predecessors, Sapir refused to rank some types of languages low on an evolutionary scale, or on any evaluation scale, on the grounds that such scaling was at bottom ethnocentric. Like Meillet, Sapir had no confidence in former typologies which characterized whole languages by single labels, as in the 'trop fameuse classification' of *agglutinative, isolating,* and *inflectional* types.

Instead, Sapir classified languages within or under the rubrics of three axes or parameters, as follows:

(1) Complexity of word; this permits rating languages along a scale from minimum word complexity – designated *analytic* – to *polysynthetic* for maximum word complexity.

(2) Technique of juxtaposing constituents within a word; this permits rating languages from those whose technique is *agglutinative* – those whose juxtaposed constituents are not much or not at all changed as a consequence of juxtaposition – to those whose constituents are *fused*

to such an extent that segmentation of constituents becomes difficult after juxtaposition, as in *inflectional* types.

(3) Types of concepts; these permit distinguishing what is language specific from what is universal to all natural languages. Two types of concepts are surely universal – i.e. every natural language includes constituents with *concrete* meanings, as 'table' or 'to eat' (type I), as well as constituents which 'serve to relate the elements of the proposition to each other', as case markers do (type IV or *pure relational*). The intervening types between I and IV are expressed in some languages but not in all – i.e. either type II, *derivational*, or type III, *concrete-relational*, or both II and III, or neither II nor III serve to distinguish what is language specific among natural languages.

In summary, one aspect of Sapir's whole language typology is that it represents an anticipation of current work in the transformational-generative framework: the distinction between what is language specific – what is heterogeneous in the world's languages – and what is universal, or homogeneous in the world's languages. But one weakness offsets what is admirable in Sapir's revision of 19th-century typology, and in Greenberg's revision of Sapir's typology; this is the fact that all whole-language typologies, so far, suffer from the logic of metonomy: just a few aspects or features of a language – even if not just a single one – are allowed to represent the whole.

Obviously, subsystem typology does not suffer in the same way. The limitation of subsystem typology is that it provides no way of relating or correlating the various subsystems found in a given language into a coherent single system, a single language. This is ideally the province of grammar rather than of typology. But a grammar of any one natural language which shows how sounds, syntax, and semantics are integrated cannot then be classified as a whole with any other natural language; some such attempts were made in the name of 'contrastive grammars', which were meant to contribute to pedagogy rather than to theory.

Research aims have shifted from 1911 – from Franz Boas' expectation of finding unrestricted heterogeneity among the world's languages – to the present decade, when the expectation of two centuries ago – to find a way to state universals – again looms large. It is now realized that universals can be captured only when they are segregated from what is language particular; and it is subsystem typology which serves to distinguish one language from another, irrespective of whether the languages are related (dominated by the same proto-language as apex node) or unrelated (dominated by different apex nodes in the family-tree display).

Interest in the dimension of heterogeneity among the natural languages and interest in their homogeneity (language universals) are complementary aspects of the languages-of-the-world problem. Exclusive focus on heterogeneity permits the ethnocentric claim that some languages – such as creoles, as well as unwritten languages or dialects – are inferior by virtue of being less complex, efficient, or adequate than languages with a written tradition. Increased knowledge of language universals provides motivation for the thesis that an equality exists among all natural languages, irrespective of whether such languages are spoken in simple societies or in complex societies. This thesis about the equality of all human languages has often been expressed intuitively, but never since 1921 more eloquently than by Sapir ("When it comes to linguistic form, Plato walks with the Macedonian swineherd, and Confucius with the headhunting savage of Assam."),[4] nor more convincingly than by Arch Hill in his paper on the conceptualization of 'washing' in Cherokee.

Indiana University

NOTES

[1] It may well be, as Fred Householder suggests, that Johannes Schmidt regarded his wave-theory to be a critique of, if not in competition with, the family-tree image of Indo-European. Nevertheless, we accept Bloomfield's explication: wave-theory supplements the image of family-tree single-line descent.

[2] Inconsistent traces of former dialects are still discernible among the Shawnee, as well as among speakers of other languages relocated in Oklahoma. Thus, an Iowa woman married to an Oto man claimed to speak Iowa-Oto differently than her husband; but after a week of investigation the dialect differences appeared to be exchanged freely between them without revealing which were Iowa and which Oto.

[3] For this century, training and continuing contacts with linguistic developments can be said to be part and parcel of cultural anthropology but, until recently, to be foreign to social anthropology; Hymes gives abundant references (1971b:254ff.).

[4] For another interpretation of this glittering sentence, see Hymes 1971a; dubiousness in interpretation is the price that Sapir had to pay for glittering as he talked.

REFERENCES

Benveniste, Emile. 1966. Problèmes de linguistique générale. Paris: Gallimard. English translation by Mary Elizabeth Meek, Coral Gables: University of Miami, 1971.

Bever, T. G., and D. T. Langendoen. 1971. A dynamic model of the evolution of change. Linguistic Inquiry 2.433-63.

Bloomfield, Leonard. 1933. Language. New York: Henry Holt.

Boas, Franz. 1911. Introduction. Handbook of American Indian languages I. Bureau of American Ethnology Bulletin 40. Washington, D. C.: Smithsonian Institution.

Emeneau, Murray B. 1956. India as a linguistic area. Lg. 32.3-16.

Greenberg, Joseph H. 1954. A quantitative approach to the morphological typology of language. Method and perspective in anthropology, ed. by Robert F. Spencer. Reprinted in International Journal of American Linguistics 26.178-94 (1960).

Haas, Mary. 1971. Personal communication when a preliminary version of this paper was read at the 10th Conference on American Indian Languages, American Anthropological Association meeting, Nov. 18-21, 1971.

Hill, Archibald A. 1952. A note on primitive languages. International Journal of American Linguistics 18.172-7.

Hockett, Charles F. 1955. A manual of phonology. Indiana University Publications in Anthropology and Linguistics 11 (IJAL Vol. 21, No. 4).

Hoenigswald, Henry M. 1960. Language change and linguistic reconstruction. Chicago: University of Chicago.

Hymes, Dell. 1971a. Foreword. The origin and diversification of language, Morris Swadesh. Chicago, New York: Aldine, Atherton.

—. 1971b. Linguistic method in ethnography. Method and theory in linguistics, ed. by Paul Garvin. The Hague: Mouton.

King, R. D. 1969. Historical linguistics and generative grammar. Englewood Cliffs: Prentice Hall.

Kroeber, A. L. 1960. On typological indices I: Ranking of languages. International Journal of American Linguistics 26.171-7.

Lehmann, Winfred P. 1962. Historical linguistics: An introduction. New York: Holt, Rinehart and Winston.

Martinet, André. 1962. A functional view of language. Oxford: Clarendon.

Sapir, Edward. 1921. Language: An introduction to the study of speech. New York: Harcourt, Brace.

Schmidt, Johannes. 1872. Die Verwandtschaftsverhältnisse der indogermanischen Sprachen. Weimar.

Sturtevant, E. H. 1917. Linguistic change. Chicago: University of Chicago, Press.

Trubetzkoy, N. S. 1969. Principles of phonology. Translated by Christiane A. M· Baltaxe. Berkeley and Los Angeles: University of California Press.

Voegelin, C. F. 1954. Inductively arrived-at models for cross-genetic comparisons of American Indian languages. Papers from the symposium on American Indian linguistics held at Berkeley July 7, 1951, 27-45. (University of California Publications in Linguistics 10.)

NATURAL AND
UNNATURAL RULE ADDITION

JOSEPH B. VOYLES

1. A comparatively recent insight into the nature of so-called 'sound' change has been to consider it the result of some sort of alternation in the phonological component of a grammar. The phonological component has been observed to change in four basic ways: rule reordering, rule loss, rule simplification, and rule addition (on this see King 1969, esp. 39-63 and 157-75). Several examples of rule reordering have been noted (e.g., in Kiparsky 1968). We shall not repeat Kiparsky's examples here. He has proposed convincing explanations for these changes in terms of 'reordering tendencies' which may be subsumed under the general principle that (Kiparsky 1968:200) "Rules tend to shift into the order which allows their fullest utilization in the grammar". Two examples of rule loss are the deletion from the grammar of Yiddish of the original rule for the devoicing of word-final consonants and the deletion from Gothic of the rule for Verner's Law in the strong verb paradigm (King 1969:47-8). An example of rule simplification is to be found in the development of word-final consonant devoicing in certain German dialects. At the earliest attested stage (say, in Old Saxon) only continuant consonants were devoiced in final position. Hence the rule was

$$\begin{bmatrix} -\text{sonorant} \\ +\text{continuant} \end{bmatrix} \rightarrow [-\text{voiced}] \ / \ - \ \#.$$

At a later stage all consonants were devoiced in this environment: the specification +continuant was deleted from the rule. Finally, the addition of a new rule onto (or its insertion into) the phonological component of a grammar may well be the most frequently occurring of the four types of phonological change listed above. We shall consider some instances of this type of change directly.

A purely formal analysis of these types of change is, however, an insufficient account of their operation. For example, in the OS rule cited above, there is no formal reason why the feature −sonorant could not have been deleted instead of +continuant. This would have resulted in the devoicing of [l, r] as well as all vowels in final position. Such a change has probably never occurred – or, if it has occurred, it is doubtless much less frequent and less expected than the devoicing of final stop and continuant consonants. Thus to say that one type of phonological change is rule simplification is not enough. A complete theory of phonological change must also specify in what kinds of rules what kinds of features are likely (or certain) to be deleted.[1]

The same problem exists with rule addition: only certain kinds of rules are likely to be added to a grammar. We shall consider here one of the early vocalic changes of Old Icelandic which would seem to represent the addition of an 'unnatural' rule to the grammar. In describing this change, we shall first formulate the pertinent OI phonological rules. Then we shall propose an explanation for this change based on the functional unity or general effect of rules in a grammar – a notion which will be further explicated below.

2. The systematic phonemics and phonetics for the vowels of Old Icelandic at around 1200 AD were these:

/ ĭ ĕ ǎ ŏ ŭ /, i.e., ĭ   ŭ

	ĭ	ĕ	ǎ	ŏ	ŭ
vocalic	+	+	+	+	+
high	+	−	−	−	+
low		−	+	−	
back	−	−		+	+
round					
	−	−	−	−	−
long	+	+	+	+	+

       ĕ   ŏ
         ǎ

[ĭ y̆ ĕ ø̆ ǎ æ̆ ǫ̆ ŏ ŭ], i.e., ĭ, y̆   ŭ

	ĭ	y̆	ĕ	ø̆	ǎ	æ̆	ǫ̆	ŏ	ŭ
vocalic	+	+	+	+	+	+	+	+	+
high	+	+	−	−	−	−	−	−	+
low	−	−	−	−	+	+	+	−	−
back	−	−	−	−	+	−	+	+	+
round	−	+	−	+	−	−	+	+	+
	−	−	−	−	−	−	−	−	−
long	+	+	+	+	+	+	+	+	+

      ĕ,ø̆   ŏ
       æ   ǎ ǫ̆

There is general agreement on the systematic phonetics: we adopt here the analysis of Benediktsson (1959) as well as that implicit in Noreen (1903). Our analysis of the phonemes, for which we shall adduce arguments below, is the same as that for Modern Icelandic assumed by Anderson (1969:71).

The phonological component of Old Icelandic at this time contained two major vowel mutation rules. These are referred to in the traditional sources as *u*-umlaut and *i*-umlaut. The rule of *u*-umlaut is this:

(I)   V → [+round]

$$/ \begin{Bmatrix} \text{a.} \begin{bmatrix} +\text{low} \\ \underline{} \end{bmatrix} \begin{Bmatrix} (C_1) \\ (+) \end{Bmatrix} \left(\begin{bmatrix} V \\ +\text{low} \\ -1\ \text{stress} \end{bmatrix} \right)_0 \\ \text{b.} \begin{bmatrix} 1\ \text{stress} \\ \underline{} \end{bmatrix} C_0 \end{Bmatrix} \begin{Bmatrix} \begin{bmatrix} V \\ +\text{high} \\ +\text{back} \end{bmatrix} \end{Bmatrix}$$

(We shall use the symbol V for the feature +vocalic and C for +consonantal. C_1 is a sequence consisting of at least one consonant; C_0 is a sequence of at least 0 consonants – i.e., the presence of the sequence is optional.) That is, (environment a.) /ǎ/ → [ǫ̆] if followed by at least one consonant (C_1) or a morpheme boundary (+), either of these being followed in turn by the high back vowel /ŭ/. E.g., /kall+ūm/ 'we call' → [kǫllūm] (eventually [kǫllum] by rule B in the appendix to this paper); /āt+ūm/ 'we ate' → [ǭtum]; /grā+ūm/ 'grey' (dat. pl.) → [grǭ+um] (eventually [grǭm] by a rule of vowel syncopation which we shall not consider here). In other instances the dat. pl. ending is /-ūm/, e.g., /spak+ūm/ 'wise' → [spǫkum]. We have included the specification (+) in this rule because the diphthong /au/ in a form like /flaut/ 'flowed' seems to have been phonetically [flaut]. Later, however, the specification (+) seems to have been dropped from the rule when the form [flǫut] occurred. (On this see Benediktsson 1959:288, footnote.) Environment (a.) further specifies that /ǎ/ is rounded if followed by any number of unstressed syllables with vocalic nucleus /ǎ/ – i.e.,([V, +low, −1 stress])$_0$ – in turn followed by /ŭ/. E.g., /mānaþ+ūm/ 'months' (dat. pl.) → [mǭnǫþum].[2]

Environment (b.) of rule I says that any vowel with primary stress, if followed by any number (including 0) of consonants and /ŭ/, is rounded. E.g., /rer+ū/ 'they rowed' → [rǫru]; /fē+u/ 'money' → [fø] (with the deletion of /u/ by rule A given in the appendix); /þrisk+u+a/ 'to thresh' (eventually) → [þryskwa] (later [þryskva]), and the same verb with a different inf. suffix /þrisk+i+a/ (eventually) → [þriskja]; /suīk+u+a/ 'to deceive' → [suȳkua] (eventually, since /u/ is dropped before a rounded vowel) → [sȳkwa], also /suīk+i+a/ 'to deceive' → [swīkja].

The existence of double orthographic forms such as *miklum* and *myklum* 'many' (dat. pl.) from /mik-il+ūm/ may mean that the effects of this rule tended in some instances in the course of time to be leveled out by other non-umlauted forms in the paradigm (for the particular case just cited, forms such as nom. sing. masc. [mikill], acc. sing. masc. [miklan], etc.). As Noreen (1903:60) remarks, "Doppelformen sind entstanden, z.b. *hǫll*, selt. *hall* saal aus nom. *hǫll*, gen. *hallar*. ..." In any event, the automatic nature of this rule – at least in its earlier stages at around 1200 AD – is evident: any unrounded vowel fitting the environmental description (and in any paradigm) becomes rounded.

In certain cases the /u/ in the environmental statement for this rule is deleted (e.g., /hall+u/ → [hǫllu] → [hǫll]). As will be seen directly, an analogous situation prevails for the /i/ which causes *i*-umlaut: in certain instances it must be deleted after the rule for *i*-umlaut has applied. In Old Icelandic this can be accounted for in a manner similar to that of Anderson in his consideration of Modern Icelandic (1969, esp. 55-7). The solution for Old Icelandic in outline is this: there is an OI rule whereby all vowels in unstressed position are −long. Now if those /i/'s and /u/'s which must be deleted are marked −long and those which remain are marked +long, the deletion rule (which follows the rules of *i*- and *u*-umlaut) is somewhat like this:

$$
(A) \quad \begin{bmatrix} V \\ +\text{high} \\ -\text{long} \\ -\text{stress} \end{bmatrix} \rightarrow \emptyset
$$

I.e., /i, u/ → ∅ in certain environments, e.g., __ C or #, or after long verb stems (such as /draum+i+a/ 'to dream', eventually [dreyma], as opposed to /tal+i+a/ 'to tell', eventually [telja]). After rule A the rule shortening vowels in unstressed position applies changing the remaining /ī/'s and /ū/'s to /i/ and /u/. (These /i/'s and /u/'s, if occurring before a vowel, are changed by a later rule to [j] and [w].)

The positing of an underlying vowel which is later deleted is necessary for other reasons besides triggering the rules for *u*- and *i*-umlaut. For example, there is an OI rule whereby consonants are devoiced in the environment __ ※, but only in the past singular forms of strong verbs: inf. [binda] 'tie', [gjalda] 'pay', and [ganga] 'go', as opposed to the past sing. forms [batt] (derivation: /band+∅/ → [bant] by the consonantal devoicing rule, → [batt] by a rule of nasal assimilation before voiceless consonants), [galt], and [gekk] (from [genk] by the same rule of nasal assimilation). A less immediately obvious instance of this rule is the past sing. of [stīga] 'climb', [stē] (derivation: /stēg+∅/ → [stēx] → [stē] by a rule of [x]-and-[h] deletion which applies in word-internal position).

Now the only strong verbs which do not undergo this rule of consonantal devoicing are those which show *u*-umlaut in the past singular: inf. /slingu+a/ → [slyngwa] 'throw', past sing. /slangu+∅/ → [slǫng]. The occurrence of [slǫng] instead of *[slǫkk] may be accounted for by the fact that the consonantal devoicing rule applies before /i/-and-/u/ deletion (rule A) apply yielding [slǫng].

The rule for *i*-umlaut is this:

(II)   V → [−back]

$$/ \left\{ \begin{matrix} \text{a.} \begin{bmatrix} +\text{stress} \\ \left\langle \begin{matrix} +\text{low} \\ -\text{long} \end{matrix} \right\rangle \\ \rule{1cm}{0.4pt} \end{bmatrix} \\ \text{b.} \begin{bmatrix} V \\ +\text{low} \\ +\text{stress} \end{bmatrix} \begin{bmatrix} -\text{stress} \\ \rule{1cm}{0.4pt} \end{bmatrix} \end{matrix} \right\} \left\{ \begin{matrix} \text{a.} \left\{ \begin{matrix} (/\breve{u}/)C_0(/\breve{u}/) \\ \langle \emptyset \rangle \end{matrix} \right\} \begin{bmatrix} +\text{high} \\ -\text{back} \\ \langle C \rangle \end{bmatrix} \\ \text{b.} \begin{bmatrix} +\text{coronal} \\ +\text{strident} \\ +\text{voiced} \end{bmatrix} \end{matrix} \right\}$$

That is, (environment a.a.) any vowel with primary or secondary stress is fronted if followed optionally by /ŭ/, and (or) a sequence of consonants, and (or) another optional /ŭ/ – all of which must be followed by the high front vowel /ĭ/ : i.e., /ǎ, ǒ, ŭ/ → [æ̆, ǒ̈, y̆]. For example, /tam+ia/ 'to tame' → [tæmja] (eventually by rule C which we shall consider later) → [temja]; past /tam+þa/ → [tamþa]; /lāt+ir/ 'you (sing.) let' → [lætr]; /son+īr/ 'sons' →[sønir]; /blōt+ir/ 'you (sing.) sacrifice' → [bløtr]; /full+ing/ → [fylling] 'a filling'; /lūk+ir/ 'you (sing.) close' → [lȳkr]. Environment (a.a.) also fronts the initial vowel in the diphthong /ai/ to [æi]; and the /a/ in the diphthong /au/ – if followed by /ĭ/ – is fronted to [æu]. The /u/ in this diphthong is fronted by environment (b.a.) resulting in the final output [æy] (eventually by rule C) → [ey]. E.g., /draum+ia/ 'to dream' → [dræymia] (C) → [dreymia] (eventually by rule A) → [dreyma] as opposed to the noun /draum+r/ → [draumr] 'a dream'.

Thus the only initial vowel in a diphthong to undergo this rule is /a/ : /au/ → [æy] (C) → [ey] and /ai/ → [æi] (C) → [ei]. This fact is accounted for by the specification +stress in environment (a.) of rule II: by an earlier stress rule (which we shall formulate and discuss directly) only diphthongs with an initial low or back vowel have stress on their first segments. Otherwise OI diphthongs are 'falling'; i.e., they have the main stress on the second vowel. For example, /dreup+a/ 'to drip' (stress rule) → [dreúpa] (eventually) → [drjúpa].

Environment (a.a.) also stipulates that short /a/ (specified in rule II as ⟨−low, −long⟩) followed immediately (specified by ⟨∅⟩) by the high back consonants (specified by ⟨C⟩) is fronted to [æ]. The high back consonants are the /k/'s and /g/'s which are palatalized before front vowels. In the traditional accounts, *i*-umlaut is described as occurring before *i* or *j*; and so-called velar umlaut occurs before *k* or *g* when followed by a front vowel. E.g., /tak+en+r/ 'taken' (past part.) → [tækenr] (eventually) → [tekinn] as opposed to the past part. form of another verb in the same class, /far+en+r/ 'traveled', which is [farinn].[3]

Environments (a.b.) and (b.b.) of rule II also front back vowels (and the diphthongs /ai, au/) before [z]. This [z] represents an intermediate stage in the derivation between phonemic /s/ and phonetic [r]. Positing this environment for rule II may be justified as follows. There is a rule (the reflex of Verner's Law) in the OI grammar whereby continuant consonants in certain strong verbs are voiced in the past pl. and past part. forms. The immediate effects of this rule are often obscured by later rules. For example, /slax+a/ 'to strike' (eventually by /x/-deletion and vowel contraction) → [slā]; likewise the past sing. /slōx/ → [slō]. But past pl. /slōx+ūm/ (by Verner's Law) → [slōgum]. Similarly for the verb /frVs-/ 'to freeze': inf. [frjōsa], but past pl. /fros+ūm/ (by Verner's Law) → [frozūm] (II) → [frøzum] (eventually) → [frørum]. It should be noted that rule II does not front vowels before any surface [r]. Rather, it fronts vowels only before those [r]'s which are derived from underlying /s/ (→ [z] → [r]): cf. past part. [borinn] 'carried' from /bor+en+r/ as opposed to [frørinn] from /fros+en+r/.

We note also that at this time (1200 AD) the following rule was in the OI grammar:

$$(B) \quad \begin{bmatrix} V \\ -\text{stress} \\ \left\{ \begin{matrix} [-\text{back}] \\ \begin{bmatrix} +\text{back} \\ +\text{round} \end{bmatrix} \end{matrix} \right\} \end{bmatrix} \rightarrow \begin{bmatrix} +\text{high} \\ \alpha\text{back} \\ \alpha\text{round} \end{bmatrix}$$

That is, any unstressed −back vowel is [i]; any unstressed +back and +round vowel is [u]; and a +back, −round vowel (i.e., /a/) is not affected by this rule. Thus the only vowels permitted in unstressed position are [i], [u], and [a].[4] This rule must follow the umlaut rules. It accounts for the fact that there are surface [i]'s and [u]'s which do not cause umlaut, e.g., nom. sing. masc. weak adj. declension [langi] 'long' instead of *[lengi]. Derivation: /lang+e/ (where *i*-umlaut does not apply, but rule B does) → [langi].

There was also at around 1200 AD the following rule in the grammar of Old Icelandic (see also Benediktsson 1959:290):

(C) $$\begin{bmatrix} V \\ -\text{back} \\ \left\{\begin{matrix} [-\text{long}] \\ [+\text{round}] \end{matrix}\right\} \end{bmatrix} \rightarrow [-\text{low}]$$

That is, a front vowel, if it is −long or +round (either one or both), must be −low. Rule C must follow the umlaut rules. Hence by the *i*-umlaut rule (II), /a/ → [æ], which, by rule C, is raised to [e]. Similarly, there is in the OI vowel system no +low, +round, −back vowel [ø], either long or short. As we shall see later, we shall need rule C to exclude such a vowel by raising it to the −low [ø].

A complete survey of all the OI phonological rules pertaining to vowels is well beyond the scope of this paper. However, even on the basis of the above outline one may make certain generalizations about the OI vowel system. One of these is the observation that the two umlaut rules (I and II) constitute a unity in that they are the only productive vowel mutation rules in the language. They apply to any forms in any paradigm. Rules I and II are unordered with regard to each other (although both must occur before rules A, B, and C). For example, the derivation of the verb [gørwa] 'to make', past [gǫrþi], past part. [gǫrr], is as follows: inf. /garu+i+a/ (I: *u*-umlaut) → [gǫruia] (II: *i*-umlaut, environment a.a., specification — C_0 /u/ /i/) → [gøruia] (C) → [gøruia] (eventually by rule A which deletes the [i] after long-syllable verb stems) → [gørwa]. The past tense and past part. forms are derived by the *u*-umlaut rule (I) from the underlying forms /garu+þ+e/ and /garu+r/, respectively. (In these cases rule A deletes the [u].) The derivation of the infinitive is the same if rule II applies before rule I instead of the other way around: /garu+i+a/ (II) → [gæruia] (I) → [gøruia]. (The rule of *u*-umlaut, I, when it rounds [æ], results in the low, front, round [ø].) Finally, [gøruia] (C) → [gøruia], eventually [gørwa].

We have noted that rules I and II are the only generally applicable vowel mutation rules in the phonology of Old Icelandic. There are, of course, other OI rules which change vowels in certain relatively restricted environments. One obvious example of such a rule is furnished by the vowel alternations in strong verbs such as [fara, fōr, fōrum, farinn] 'travel' or [bresta, brast, brustum, brostinn] 'break'. But the rule for these alternations would, unlike rules I and II, apply only to a particular class of verbs. Another instance of a vowel mutation rule with a restricted domain is the process known as 'breaking'. We shall not give a detailed formulation of this rule. Suffice it to say that it is basically this:

$$/e/ \rightarrow [ea] \; / -- C_1 \begin{bmatrix} +\text{vocalic} \\ +\text{back} \end{bmatrix}$$

but only in certain forms. E.g., /geld+a/ 'pay' → [gealda] (eventually by the rule of stress mentioned earlier – on page 387 – whereby the second segment in a diphthong like [ea] receives primary stress, then by rule B which raises [e] to [i], and finally by a rule which devocalizes [u] and [i] before vowels to [w] and [j]) → [gjalda]. The derivation of the first pers. pres. indic. form is /geld+∅/ → [geld] where breaking does not apply since there is no following back vowel. The breaking rule must precede the rule of u-umlaut (I): cf. the derivation of the first pers. pl. indic. /geld+ūm/ (breaking) → [gealdūm] (I) → [geǫldūm], eventually [gjǫldum]. But the breaking rule, unlike rules I and II, does not apply generally in Old Icelandic. Noreen (1903:74) notes, "Wo in einem paradigma oder einer gruppe von verwandten wörtern gebrochene und ungebrochene formen wechseln sollten, ist oft ausgleichung eingetreten, so dass entweder der gebrochene vokal durchgeht, z.b. *bialke* [i.e., [bjalke]] balken nach obl. *bialka* ...; oder endlich sind doppelformen entstanden, z.b. *biarg* und *berg* gebirge, ... *spiall* und *spell* schaden. ..."

Thus only the umlaut rules I and II – as opposed to all the other vowel-changing rules in the phonology of Old Icelandic – are generally applicable. They constitute automatic alternations in that they apply to any forms in any paradigm of the language. Since they are the only such rules, they represent a unity of sorts in the phonology of the language. We shall return to this point directly. But for the moment we shall consider certain of the principal diachronic changes in the OI vowel system.

3. Our account of the chronology of these early changes in the development of the OI vowel system to that of Modern Icelandic is based on Benediktsson (1959). By 1200 AD the OI vowel system was as we have outlined it above with the systematic phonemes /ă, ĕ, ĭ, ŏ, ŭ/ and the phonetics [ă, ĕ, ĭ, ŏ, ŭ, æ, ǭ, ў, ǫ̆]. Short [æ] (by i-umlaut from /a/) had by this time merged with [e] and the formerly phonemically distinct nasal vowels had become nonnasal (Benediktsson 1959:290, 293).

We shall first give a superficial outline of the changes, then turn to a consideration of the underlying rule alternations involved. All page references in the following are to Benediktsson 1959.

(1) [ā] > [ǭ]. Benediktsson considers this the earliest change in this series. He gives no precise data for it; but it would seem to have been in the OI grammar by the end of the 1100's.

(2) [ǫ] > [ø] (end of the 1100's or beginning of 1200's: p. 295).

(3) [o] > [ǫ] (either contemporaneous with or somewhat later than change 2: p. 296).

(4) [ø̄] > [ǣ] (about 1250: p. 297).

(5) Diphthongization: [ē, ǣ, ō, ǭ] > [eę, aę, oǫ, aǫ] (soon after 1250: p. 298).

(6) [eę] > [je] (about 1400: p. 298).

(7) [y, ȳ] > [i, ī] (between 1400 and 1600: p. 300).

(8) [u] > [y] (after 1600: p. 300).

First, we shall consider what are the more usual types of change in this series, namely changes 1, 4, 5, 6, and 7. Then we shall treat of changes 2, 3, and 8. To begin with change 1, it would seem to have been caused by the addition of the following rule to the grammar:

(1)
$$
\begin{bmatrix} V \\ +\text{low} \\ -\text{back} \\ +\text{long} \end{bmatrix} \rightarrow [+\text{round}]
$$

I.e., [ā] > [ǭ]. The addition of such a rule to a grammar is a change of a frequently occurring type. It thus constitutes a 'natural' kind of rule. (There are several instances of this change occurring in contemporary German dialects: see Keller 1961:169.) If, as seems likely, this rule was originally optional and then later became obligatory, its becoming obligatory meant in effect that the OI phonemic inventory was restructured: original /ā/ became /ǭ/; and [ǭ] was thus no longer a derived vowel.

Change 4 would also seem to have been occasioned by the addition of a rule to the grammar:

(4)
$$
\begin{bmatrix} V \\ -\text{high} \\ -\text{back} \\ +\text{round} \\ +\text{long} \end{bmatrix} \rightarrow \begin{bmatrix} +\text{low} \\ -\text{round} \end{bmatrix}
$$

I.e., [ø̄] > [æ]. Although such a rule is perhaps not so frequent a change as the preceding one, it is nonetheless attested (e.g., in the Luxemburg dialect of German where [ø] > [æ]; cf. Standard German *Frösche* [frøšə] 'frogs', Luxemburgish [fræš]: Keller 1961:257).[5]

Change 5, diphthongization, was caused by the addition to the grammar of a rule like the following:

$$
(5) \quad
\begin{bmatrix}
V \\
-high \\
+long \\
\begin{bmatrix}
\alpha back \\
\langle \ \alpha round \rangle \\
-low \\
\alpha back \\
\langle \ \alpha round \rangle \\
+low
\end{bmatrix}
\end{bmatrix}
\rightarrow
\begin{bmatrix}
V \\
-high \\
-long \\
\begin{bmatrix}
\langle \ \alpha back \\ \quad \alpha round \rangle \\
\langle +back \\ \ -round \rangle
\end{bmatrix}
\end{bmatrix}
\begin{bmatrix}
V \\
?-high \\
-low \\
\alpha back \\
\alpha round \\
?+tense \\
-long
\end{bmatrix}
$$

i.e., [ē, ǣ, ō, ǭ] > [ee̦, ae̦, oo̦, ao̦]. We assume that the second segments in the resulting diphthongs were originally somewhat higher than the usual OI [e] or [o] but lower than [i] or [u]. We have considered them —high and +tense and have transcribed them as [e̦] and [o̦]. But the precise phonetic nature of the resultant diphthongs need not concern us here. In any case, they seem to have been, at least in their initial stages, different from the older diphthongs [ei] (from /ai/ by *i*-umlaut) and [au] (underlying /au/).[6] Although in our formulation this rule looks somewhat complex, it is nonetheless a type of change which has often been observed: Keller has several instances of this kind of change in the German dialects (e.g., 1961:211, 259-60, 347-8). In its later version, this rule seems to have become more general and to have included in its domain the high vowels /ī/ and /ū/. (It corresponds to Anderson's rule VIII for Modern Icelandic given in 1969:66.)

Change 6, [ee̦] > [je̦], was caused by a reordering of rules in the grammar. As was mentioned earlier (p. 387 of this paper), there was a stress rule in Old Icelandic whereby only diphthongs with an initial low or back vowel had primary stress on the first segment:

$$
\begin{bmatrix}
V \\
-back \\
-low \\
+stress
\end{bmatrix}_1
\begin{bmatrix}
V \\
-stress
\end{bmatrix}_2
\rightarrow
\begin{bmatrix}
V \\
-back \\
+low \\
-stress
\end{bmatrix}_1
\begin{bmatrix}
V \\
+stress
\end{bmatrix}_2
$$

(This rule corresponds to the Modern Icelandic rule VII in Anderson 1969:65). We have already cited some examples of the application of this rule: /géld+a/ 'to pay' (breaking) → [géalda] (stress rule) → [geálda] (B) → [giálda], eventually [gjálda]. For some time it would seem that the stress rule preceded the rule for change 5 in the grammar. However, by about 1400 the tendency toward maximum utilization of rules had asserted itself. (This tendency has been discussed in Kiparsky 1968, esp. 200.) This resulted in the reordering of the rule for change 5 and the stress rule so that the output of rule 5, [eẹ], served as input to the stress rule and rule B. This situation eventually produced [je] from [eẹ].

Change 7, the unrounding of [y, ȳ] to [i, ī], seems to be an instance of rule addition of a fairly frequent type. It is attested in several German dialects (see Keller 1961:168) and also occurred in the development from Old to Modern English (e.g., OE [kynn] 'family', ModEng. [kin]).

The changes considered so far would seem to have been rule additions of a fairly common type (or, if not frequent, at least attested elsewhere as in the case of change 4, [ȫ] to [ǣ]) as well as one case of predictable rule reordering (change 6, [eẹ] to [je]). But this cannot be said of change 2, [ǫ] to [ø]. (The vowel is written ö in Modern Icelandic, e.g., dat. pl. dögum 'days' as opposed to the regularized OI spelling dǫgum.) This change has appeared unusual to various scholars and in need of some sort of explanation. Benediktsson offers none of his own, but mentions one such attempt (1959:297-8, footnote): "The opinion has been expressed, e.g., by M.I. Steblin-Kamenskij, "A Contribution to the History of the Old Icelandic Vowel System," Časopis pro moderní filologii XL (1958), no. 3, p. 79, that the merger of ø and ǫ was caused by the low functional yield of this opposition. On the whole ǫ was indeed a comparatively rare phoneme. Nevertheless, there is a considerable number of minimal pairs with ø vs. ǫ, probably not fewer than for most of the other oppositions in which ø participated. Among these pairs are: ørr ('a scar') vs. ǫrr ('swift, ready'); høgg (1st sg. pres. of hǫggua 'to strike, smite') vs. hǫgg ('a stroke'). ..." (The first two forms cited above – OI [ørr] 'scar' and [ǫrr] 'swift' – both appear as [ør], written ör, in Modern Icelandic.) On the basis of these many contrasting pairs, Benediktsson concludes (p. 298) that "The hypothesis that the cause of the merger of ø and ǫ was the exceptionally low functional yield of the opposition is therefore not convincing."

It would seem that the immediate cause of this change was the addition of the following rule to the grammar:

(2) $\begin{bmatrix} V \\ +low \\ +back \\ +round \\ -long \end{bmatrix} \rightarrow [-back]$

That is, [ǫ] (from /a/ by *u*-umlaut) is realized as −back, +low [ø̨]. Rule 2 was inserted in the grammar after rule I (*u*-umlaut) and before rule C. Rule C then automatically raises +low [ø̨] to −low [ø]. We are assuming that this change was the result of rule addition (as opposed to, say, some sort of modification of rule I: *u*-umlaut), primarily because the reflex of our OI rule 2 appears in the modern language as a separate rule − though in a slightly simpler version (Anderson 1969:59, rule Vb). This Modern Icelandic rule not only fronts [o] (from /a/ by *u*-umlaut) to [ø]; it also fronts /u/ to [y]. Thus it would seem that the later change (8) of [u] to [y] was caused by the simplification of the chronologically earlier rule 2.

Change 3 of [o] to [ǫ] would also seem to have been caused by the addition of a rule to the grammar. Such a rule lowering [o] to [ǫ] is elsewhere attested (e.g., in Keller 1961:90) and doubtless constitutes a fairly frequent type of change. The rule is of an obvious enough nature so that we shall not formulate it here. The Modern Icelandic rule corresponding to change 3 is given in Anderson (1969:59, rule Va) as an alpha-switch rule preceding rule Vb (our change 2) whereby original −low /o/ becomes +low [ǫ] and original +low [ǫ] (from /a/ by *u*-umlaut) becomes −low [o]. This [o] is then fronted to [ø] by Anderson's rule Vb.

To summarize the situation, our analysis for this early stage of Old Icelandic has been as follows: (2) [ǫ] (from /a/) → [ø̨] (which is then raised to [ø] by rule C). (3) /o/ → [ǫ]. Anderson's analysis for Modern Icelandic is the following: (Va) /o/ → [ǫ] and [ǫ] (from /a/) → [o]. (Vb) [o] (from [ǫ] from /a/) and /u/ → [ø] and [y], respectively. We are of the opinion that our analysis is correct for Old Icelandic and that Anderson's is for the modern language. However, even if one were to tailor Anderson's analysis to fit the OI situation (so that the order of rules in the OI grammar was 3,2 instead of 2,3) one would still have to posit for this stage of Old Icelandic an unnatural rule. This is of course rule 2.[7]

4. By an 'unnatural' rule we mean that, as far as we know, no such change has ever occurred in the historical development of any other

Gmc. language. Further, this change may well be unique to Old Icelandic and as such represents a type of change which no other natural language may be expected to undergo. To be sure, there have been changes which superficially resemble our change 2. For example, so-called *i*-umlaut whereby early [o] appears later as [ø]. The traces of this change are present in every contemporary Gmc. language. Of course, *i*-umlaut, which affected [a] and [u] in addition to [o], is an instance of a fairly frequent type of change. It originally occurred in the environment – C_0 /ĭ/ and thus is an instance of assimilation of the feature —back from /ĭ/ to the preceding vowel. Even a change from [e] to [ø] as in MidHG [tswelf] 'twelve', ModHG [tsvølf], is obviously an assimilatory change. The rounding of [w] was transferred to the [e] and resulted in [ø]. But these cases are clearly not the same as the nonassimilatory OI change from [ǫ] to [ø].

We should add that one of the principal factors in this change which makes it so anomalous is the fact that it all took place in a single step. A change such as [o] to [i] is, we suggest, impossible in a single step. On the other hand, if it occurs as a series of changes, it is completely plausible: [o] to [u], then [u] to [y], and finally [y] to [i]. But the OI change of [ǫ] to [o] would not even seem plausible if construed as a series of steps, much less as a single event.

The obvious question to ask in such a case of unnatural rule addition is what could have occasioned the incorporation of such a rule into the grammar – a rule of a type hitherto unattested. We suggest that the reason for the addition of this particular unnatural rule to the grammar is not to be found in a consideration of the formal properties of the OI phonological rules, but rather in their over-all functions and tendencies. Kisseberth (1970:293) has explicated the notion of the functional unity of two or more formally different phonological rules as follows: "The standard theory says there is no other way in which rules can be the 'same' except structurally. This position can, I believe, be demonstrated to be incorrect. The unity of a set of rules may not rest upon the similarity of their structural descriptions, but rather upon the similarity of their FUNCTION. Or to put the point in a slightly different way, rules may be alike in having a common EFFECT rather than in operating upon the same class of segments, or performing the same structural change, etc." Kisseberth then turns to a consideration of Yawelmani (a dialect of Yokuts) where, he shows, certain structurally dissimilar rules all function together and have the ultimate effect of preventing certain types of consonantal clusters in the language.

Let us now consider the phonological rules of Old Icelandic from this point of view. As we have noted above, rules I and II are the only generally applicable vowel mutation rules in the language. As such, they form a unity. They derive from the systematic phonemes /ă, ĕ, ŏ, ŭ/ the phonetic segments [æ, e, ǿ. ў, ǫ̃]. The systematic phonemes are the basic vowels and the phonetic segments the derived or secondary vowels.

This was the situation when the rule which we have labeled 1 ([ā] > [ǭ]) was added to the grammar. As we have noted, after this rule became obligatory, this meant that the phonetic inventory was restructured so that instead of underlying /ā/ (eventually surface [ā] and [ǭ] by rule I: *u*-umlaut), one had only underlying /ǭ/ (surface [ǭ]). After change 1, rule I in effect no longer derived [ǭ] from underlying /ā/. The vowel [ǭ] was no longer a derived or secondary vowel in paradigms. Alternations which had originally been between [ā] and [ǭ] – such as [gālgi] 'gallows' (nom. sing.) and [gǭlgum] (dat. pl.) – after change 1 were leveled to [gǭlgi] and [gǭlgum] with no change in the vowel.

After change 1 the derived or secondary vowels – i.e., the vowels produced by the block of rules I and II from the phonemes – were [æ, e, ǿ, ў, ǫ]. At this time then the general effect of rules I and II could be described as follows: "The generally applicable vowel mutation rules (I and II) produce derived vowels, all of which are —back – except for the vowel derived from /a/ by rule I." In view of this, change 2 – the addition of a rather unusual, complicated, or expensive rule to the grammar – appears not to have been so much of a complication in the formal structure of the grammar. Rather, rule 2 would seem to have effected a simplification in the over-all function of rules I and II. This new function may be stated as follows: "The generally applicable vowel mutation rules (I and II) produce derived vowels, all of which are —back." That is, the feature —back became in effect the mark of a derived vowel at this stage of Old Icelandic. It is this fact, we suggest, which accounts for the addition of the anomalous rule 2 to the grammar.

5. An adequate theory of language and linguistic change must segregate those types of rules which can be and have been added to historically attested grammars as changes from those types of rules which are impossible. This is, of course, an empirical question: to answer it, one must observe numerous instances of rule addition from various attested natural languages. Further, in the formulation of such a theory of natural as opposed to unnatural rules, one must segregate those instances of 'spontaneous' rule addition from those cases where the

form of a particular rule added to a grammar is conditioned by already existent rules in the grammar. As noted by Kisseberth (1970:306), "The kinds of rules which are added to a grammar are to some extent determined by the rules which are already in the grammar."

It would seem that the type of rule addition discussed here, namely change 2 whereby [ǫ] > [ø], is an instance of unnatural rule addition. This rule was added to the grammar of Old Icelandic because it simplified the general functional effect of a block of rules (I and II) already in the grammar. We would add that if the simplification of the general function of rules is a factor in phonological change, then it is likely that instances of hitherto unattested types of phonological change are yet to be discovered. One of these may well be rule complication.

University of Washington

APPENDIX

The following are the principal OI phonological rules which we have considered. They were in the grammar at the time when the series of changes enumerated in the second paragraph of section 3 began. Rules I and II must precede rules A, B, and C.

(I) / ă, ĕ, ĭ / → [ǫ̆, ø̆, y̆] (*u*-umlaut).
(II) / ă, ŏ, ŭ / → [æ̆, ø̆, y̆] (*i*-umlaut).
(A) / i, u / → Ø in certain environments.
(B) Unstressed V → [a], [i], or [u].
(C) / æ, ø̆ / → [e, ø̆], i.e., all front vowels, if either short or round (or both), are -low.

NOTES

[1] This problem and those treated of in the remainder of this paper are in effect the same as the questions of markedness and of 'linking' rules discussed in Chomsky and Halle 1968, esp. 400-35.

[2] In accordance with a convention proposed for the corresponding Modern Icelandic rule by Anderson 1969:58, we assume that rule I, environment (a.), applies to all instances of /a/ simultaneously. Hence the second /a/ in /mănaþ+ūm/ is changed to [ǫ] at the same time that the first /ā/ is changed to [ǫ̆].

[3] Anderson (1969:69) treats of velar umlaut in Modern Icelandic. We have adopted for Old Icelandic the conventions suggested by him, e.g. "... we assume ... that the rule of VELAR FRONTING [i.e., of back /k, g/ to front [k', g']] is not a part of the grammar of Icelandic at all, but rather one of the universal marking conventions. ..."

[4] Anderson 1969:58, offers a different formulation of this rule for Modern Icelandic.

[5] This change is perhaps best formulated as an alternation from −low to +low. The specification −round is then assigned automatically as a 'linking' convention by the rule in Chomsky and Halle (1968:405) labeled (XI) (b) whereby +low vowels are −round.

⁶ Cf. Benediktsson 1959:298: "... these diphthongs remained distinct from the three original diphthongs *ei*, *ey*, *au*." In the modern language [ae̜, o̜o̜, ao̜] have become [aj, ow, aw] spelled conservatively *ae*, *ó*, and *á* (cf. Anderson 1969:53).

⁷ If the order of rules in the OI grammar were 3-2, then rule 3 would have to be an alpha-switch rule like Anderson's whereby /o/ → [o̜] and [o̜] → [o]. Then rule 2 would be as we have formulated it except that it would have the feature −low instead of +low. Such a rule where [o] changes to [ø] is virtually the same as one where [o̜] changes to [ø̜]. And, we suggest, they are the same in one respect: the one is just as unnatural as the other.

REFERENCES

Anderson, S. R. 1969. An outline of the phonology of Modern Icelandic vowels. Foundations of Language 5.53-73.

Benediktsson, Hreinn. 1959. The vowel system of Icelandic: A survey of its history. Word 15.282-313.

—. 1965. Early Icelandic script. Icelandic manuscripts. Series in Folio. Volume 2. Reykjavik: The Manuscript Institute of Iceland.

Chomsky, Noam, and Halle, Morris. 1968. The sound pattern of English. New York, Evanston, and London: Harper and Row.

Keller, R. E. 1961. German dialects: Phonology and morphology with selected texts. Manchester: Manchester University Press.

King, Robert D. 1969. Historical linguistics and generative grammar. Englewood Cliffs, New Jersey: Prentice-Hall.

Kiparsky, Paul. 1968. Linguistic universals and linguistic change. Universals in linguistic theory, ed. by Emmon Bach and Robert T. Harms, 171-205. New York: Holt, Rinehart, and Winston.

Kisseberth, Charles W. 1970. On the functional unity of phonological rules. Linguistic inquiry 1.291-307.

Noreen, Adolf. 1903. Altisländische und altnorwegische Grammatik. 2nd ed. Halle: Max Niemeyer.

G. W. LEIBNIZ:
A SEVENTEENTH-CENTURY ETYMOLOGIST

JOHN T. WATERMAN

Etymology to Leibniz was primarily a research tool. Contrary to many intellectuals of his age, for whom it was almost a parlor game, Leibniz was keenly interested in using the history of words to help reconstruct the history of people. In a letter dated January 20, 1692, he wrote: "Ex linguarum connexionibus illustrari origines cognationesque populorum indubitata res est, imo eam unicam superesse arbitror viam in abdita antiquitate."[1] Or again: "... les langues sont les plus anciens monumens du genre humain, et qui servent le mieux à connoistre l'origine des peuples".[2]

He also recognized the value of etymology in getting at the semantic essence of a word and at the historical development of ideas. Indeed, one of the major projects of his latter years was the preparation for printing in book form a collection of essays written by contemporary scholars on etymological themes. The book was to be in two parts, the first one containing mostly works by Leibniz himself: of 314 pages, 161 are written by him. Part II, pp. 1-544, consists for the most part of edited correspondence in the form of what we today would call 'articles'.[3]

Though his linguistic interests led him in thoughts far afield – to all the countries of Europe, to Africa, to Asia, and even to the Americas – his own attempts at etymologizing were restricted to Celtic (which he defined in approximately our own sense of the term), French, and German. He actually busied himself more with French, partly because the French language had been much studied; there was a body of critical literature dealing with French (and Romance) philology. Then, too, Leibniz, who was after all a German (and often quite chauvinistic), may have wanted to point up the rather large number of Germanic words which he believed had been taken into the French language over the centuries. Several scholars from German-speaking lands had anticipated his attempts. One of them by the name of Johann Heinrich Ott, a Swiss literary historian, had published an etymological work called *Franco-Gallia* in 1670.

Leibniz, in fact, prepared an addendum to Ott's lexicon, wherein he listed alphabetically either those loanwords not given by Ott, or, if listed, not in his opinion accurately explained.

His conviction that the Romance languages ought to yield a rich harvest of German loanwords is expressly stated in his "Unvorgreifliche Gedanken": "Es ist handgreiflich und gestanden, daß die Frantzosen, Welschen [Italians] und Spanier (der Engländer, so halb Teutsch zu geschweigen) sehr viele Worte von den Teutschen haben und also den Ursprung ihrer Sprachen guten Theils bei uns suchen müssen."[4] He then goes on to list a good many examples of what he took to be German loanwords common to the French of his day. I select a few of them:

French	German
agrafe 'hook'	*Griff* 'grip'
coucher 'to put to bed'	*küssen* 'to kiss'
digue 'dike'	LG *dīk*; in High German the pond itself is meant rather than the surrounding wall.
écrevisse 'crayfish'	*Krebs* 'crab'
écrou 'screw'	*Schraube* 'screw'
fourrage 'fodder'	*Futter* 'fodder'
haras 'stud farm'	Leibniz inaccurately suggests Ger. *Härde* 'herd' or perhaps *Heer* 'a [mounted] army'. In either case his guess is wrong.
guerre 'war'	*Wehr* 'armed resistance'
guider 'to guide'	*weisen* 'to direct'
laid 'ugly'	*Leid* 'sorrow'
maquereau 'mackerel'	*Makrele* 'mackerel'
mare 'pool, puddle'	*Morast* 'morass, bog'.[5]

In the *Journal des savants* of 1692, Leibniz devotes an entire article to a study of Fr. *blason* 'coat of arms, blazon', attempting in vain to trace its origins to Low Saxon *bles*, HG *Blesse* 'a white fleck on the forehead of an animal' [such as a cow or a horse]. He tried, also without success, to establish a line of relationship to Fr. *blesser* 'to wound'.

Leibniz also sought to establish still more remote linguistic relationships, attempting to align French with what he called 'Celto-Scythian', which is quite close to what many of us mean today by the term 'Indo-

European'. An example of this sort is afforded by Fr. *feu* 'fire', which he relates to Ger. *Feuer*, Cimbrian *fyr*, and Gk. *pȳr*. Unfortunately, the only false cognate in this set is the French one, *feu*, which derives from Lat. *focus* 'fire-place'.

He worked intermittently on his *Collectanea* for years. So sure was he of finally finishing it within the year that he had included the title in the catalogue of the 1716 book fair held annually at Leipzig. However, he died before the year was quite out. His personal secretary and assistant, Johann Georg Eckhardt, did manage within a year after his master's death to complete the volume and get it published in 1717. The full title is given in footnote 1; the volume is referred to simply as Leibniz' *Collectanea*.

He had begun publishing his own treatises on languages roughly at the turn of the century, leading off with *Cogita ad lexicon Cambro-Britannicum sive glossarii Celtici*. During these years, from about 1690-1700, appear most of his French etymological studies. A comparison of his work with that of Johann Clauberg's (*Ars etymologica Teutonum*, 1663) led him closer and closer to the conclusion that Germanic did indeed represent the oldest of all the languages known to the scholarly world of his day. The Germanic roots he held generally to be of the greatest antiquity. That there was an *Ursprache*, and that this language primeval could not have been biblical Hebrew, Leibniz was now willing to accept (how could one otherwise explain away the contemporary Egyptian?). Finally, in his *New essays concerning human understanding*, he allows himself to speculate as follows: "... the strange and often ridiculous etymologies of Goropius Becanus, a learned physician of the sixteenth century, have passed into a proverb, although otherwise he may not have been excessively wrong in claiming that the German language, which he called Cimbric, has as many, yes, more, marks of a primitive character than the Hebrew itself. ... It is certain at least that the Teutonic language and antiquities enter into the majority of the researches into European origins, customs, and antiquities."[6]

Leibniz tried to work out an objective and controllable system for examining possible etymological relationships between words: 1) He insisted on using the oldest recorded versions of all manuscripts and inscriptions then available; 2) He also insisted on including all material from every accessible living dialect, even from those specialized dialects of the arts, the trades, the hunt, agriculture, and so forth. The works of the Old High German and of the Middle High German poets especially interested him, because he saw in their idiom a reliable source for comparing linguistic change down through the centuries.[7]

Leibniz also took issue with many of the learned men of his day – in this case most of them Scandinavians – who would consider the ancient language of the Bible translation of the Gothic bishop Ulfilas (311-82) as preserved in the so-called Codex argenteus (an early sixth-century copy),[8] to be a direct and practically unadulterated descendant from the dialect-free Primitive Germanic. On December 20, 1692, he wrote to his friend Spanheim: "Le dialecte du codex argenteus est fort different de tous les autres dialectes Allemends; et même de l'ancien langue suedois; et s'il est Gothique, il ne s'est pas à mon avis à confirmer la pretension de Messieurs les Suedois qui veuillent que les Goths soyent sortis de chez eux. L'ancien suedois, qui est l'islandois moderne, a bien plus de rapport à l'ancien Saxon, aussi bien que le Danois. Au lieu qu'il y a bien des choses dans le Codex Argenteus, qui paroissent tenir du Latin et du Grec; et entre autres il est digne de consideration que l'Allemand de ce Codex n'a presque point de verbes auxiliaires. Ainsi il pourroit bien estre de ces peuples Goths establis dans le Moesie ou dans la Pannonie [roughly present-day Rumania and Hungary]."[9]

As mentioned earlier, although etymology was something of an intellectual hobby to many scholars of his day, Leibniz in fact saw written on those fragile and beautiful folio pages of the Silver Codex another dialect of an ancient but authentic Germanic language. In his *Otium Hanoveranum*, he writes: "And notwithstanding the fact that our brethren to the north apparently want to belittle almost all our modest accomplishments so far made, why should it now not be just as important to us that we seek things of value among the Cymbrians [a German tribe once inhabiting the lower reaches of the Elbe], or the Germanic and Teutonic roots that are not only established now in Scandinavia and Iceland, but also in England, or in Ulfian Gothic, or even among the Franks of Otfried, or wherever else their remains may be found?"[10]

He did not, as so many of his contemporaries did, urge that the Gothic of the Silver Codex be accepted as an example of Primitive Germanic. He noted similarities which the language shared with English, Danish, High German, Low German, and Swedish, but he cautiously comments: "Sed etsi paucula vocabula consentirent, ipsa tamen idiomatis structura multum abit" (Dutens, vol. VI, Part II, p. 101).

As any etymologist worth his salt, Leibniz was interested in recording for posterity the even then fast-dying dialects of Europe, Russia, and the Orient. He urged upon his royal friend, Peter the Great (1682-1725),

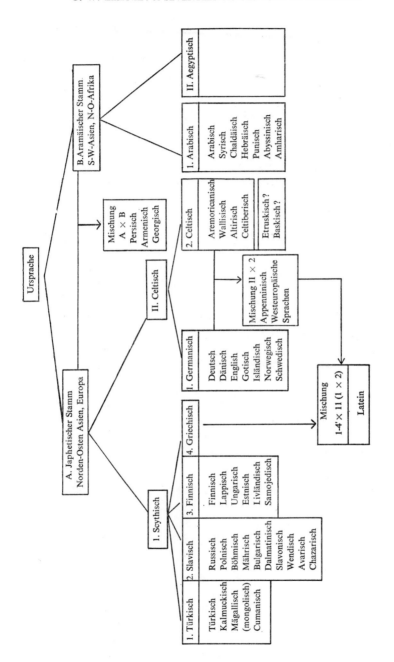

Leibniz' proposed pedigree of the languages of the world

to have studies made of all the many languages spoken within the Russian Empire, to have them reduced to writing (in the Roman alphabet!), and to have dictionaries (copiously illustrated) and grammars prepared. Leibniz' own ingenious classification of the languages of the then-known world – arrived at largely by etymological studies – was printed in 1710 as part of the first memoire of the young Berlin Academy – of which he was one of the founding fathers (and first president) in 1700 – and which exists to this very day as *Die Deutsche Akademie der Wissenschaften.* Liselotte Richter, in her monograph *Leibniz und sein Russlandbild* (Berlin, 1946), tries with considerable skill and acumen to determine Leibniz' ideas of how the languages of the world were in fact related. In an article of my own, which reasons of space do not permit me to dwell upon here, I also attempt a tabular schematization based to some extent upon Dr. Richter's. The publishers of this article, The Washington University Press (St. Louis), graciously consented to a reproduction of the schematization here.[11] Turning now to the chart, an inspection will reveal that Leibniz worked out a detailed classification only for the languages of Europe and north-eastern Asia, namely, for those which he subsumes under the title JAPHETIC. It will furthermore be noticed that the immediate subdivisions of Japhetic are Scythian and Celtic. The vast area to the north through the mountain passes that lay between the Black and the Caspian Seas, unfolding indefinitely eastward as Inner Asia, he called SCYTHIA, expanding the term to include much more territory than it traditionally encompassed.

As mentioned earlier, Leibniz' own attempts at etymologizing were limited more to French than to German. At least part of his reluctance to dwell on German was a knowledge of his own limitations; he recognized scholars such as Gerhardt Meyer and his own assistant, Johann Eckhardt, as having a better command of the older German dialects and as being more conversant with the older literature. He encouraged both of them – and others – to work independently, asking them to observe only two major principles: (1) always to use the oldest sources available; and (2) to make constant reference to the living dialects, no matter how humble or crude they might seem to be.[12]

Leibniz' only personal effort to publish an etymological dictionary of sorts was based upon some material furnished him by a certain Canonicus Kelpius of the Duchies of Bremen and Werden. He organized his material into an alphabetically arranged "Notae ad glossarii Chaucici specimen". To this collection of Low German words and phrases he adds information from other dialects, both from the Low and from the

High German speech areas. The entire article, covering pages 33 to 56 of the *Collectanea*, shows not only a command of but also a creative and poetic sense for the Low German.

University of California, Santa Barbara

NOTES

[1] *Leibniz Briefwechsel*, Leibniz an Tentzel, 20.1.1692. The correspondence, hereafter referred to by the abbreviation LBW, is part of the Leibniziana in the Niedersächsische Landesbibliothek in Hannover. The letters are stored in gatherings and arranged alphabetically by correspondent. The late Eduard Bodemann catalogued most of the Leibniz Nachlaß. See Bodemann 1889:1895. Another valuable bibliographical source is Ravier 1937.

There is as yet no edition of Leibniz' complete works. However, such a project has long been underway. Begun in 1901, it has remained under the auspices of the Deutsche Akademie der Wissenschaften zu Berlin. The short title of the edition is *Sämtliche Schriften und Briefe* (Darmstadt, 1923ff.). It is usually referred to as the *Akademie-Ausgabe*. Of an anticipated fifty volumes, less than half are completed (some, indeed, are already out of print). See Schröter 1969. Scholars must therefore frequently use older and – their titles notwithstanding – incomplete editions, chief among which are Ludwig Dutens, *Gothofredi Guillelmi Leibnitii Opera Omnia* (Geneva, 1768), 6 vols., and Foucher de Careil, *Oeuvres de Leibniz* (Paris, 1861-75), 7 vols. Also valuable is Gottschalk Eduard Guhrauer, *Gottfried Wilhelm Leibniz: Deutsche Schriften* (Berlin, 1838; rpt. Georg Olms Verlagsbuchhandlung, Hildesheim, 1966), 2 vols.

For a work which treats specifically of Leibniz' interest in language and etymology, see Neff 1870. Of interest to students of German is Pietsch 1907-1908. Leibniz' essay "Unvorgreifliche Gedancken, betreffend die Ausübung und Verbesserung der Teutschen Sprache" is in Pietsch 1908:327-56. Another of his better known German essays, "Die Ermahnung an die Teutsche, ihren Verstand und ihre Sprache besser zu üben", is reprinted in Pietsch 1907:292-312. At least one article should be mentioned: Hans Aarsleff 1969.

Of Leibniz' own works on language two must be cited: "Brevis designatio meditationum de Originibus Gentium, ductis potissimum ex indicio linguarum", in *Miscellanea Berolinensia* (Berlin, 1710), pp. 1-16. The second item – which he did not live to see in print – was edited for publication by his associate and private secretary, Johann Georg Eckhardt: *Illustris Viri Godofr. Guilielmi Leibnitii Collectanea Etymologica* (Hannover, 1717).

The recently founded Gottfried-Wilhelm-Leibniz Gesellschaft held its first international congress in 1966 in the city of Hannover, where Leibniz is buried; see Schneider and Totok 1968. The society publishes a journal entitled *Studia Leibnitiana*. It also issues occasional hard-cover *Supplementa*.

[2] *LBW*, Leibniz an Bignon, 16.1.1694.

[3] Referred to is the *Collectanea Etymologica* mentioned in n. 1. In this volume is the first of two posthumously printed essays written in German: "Unvorgreifliche Gedancken, betreffend die Ausübung und Verbesserung der Teutschen Sprache". His is also the "Ad glossarii Chaucici [a Low German tribe that once lived between the lower Ems and the Elbe rivers] specimen notae", pp. 33-56, a curious etymological dictionary that should one day be reprinted. Furthermore, he is the author of a longish essay-dictionary (pp. 56-154), presumably written to Eckhardt, entitled "Celtica".

[4] My judgment may be too harsh, but I think he fails to make his point that German had contributed heavily to the French vocabulary. Authorities estimate that there were from about 300 to 400 German loanwords in the French language of that time. Compare the number of Americanisms current in either French or German today!

[5] It is odd that Leibniz does not cite Fr. *marais* 'bog'. Fr. *mer* is the cognate of Lat. *mare* 'sea', which Leibniz for some reason chooses to ignore. Kluge 1960 s.v. *Morast*, does explain Fr. *marais* as coming from a Frankonian **marisk*, which in turn he takes to be a derivative of **mari*.

[6] Tr. Alfred Gideon Langley, 2nd ed. (The Open Court Publishing Company, Chicago and London, 1916), Book III, chap. 2, par. 1.

[7] Dutens, Vol. VI, Part I, p. 311.

[8] The 'Silver Codex'. Leibniz probably saw this beautiful and celebrated work of art – the leaves dyed a royal purple, the half-uncials done in silver ink, the uncials in gold – sometime after the manuscript had been brought to Holland in 1655. In 1662 the entire bundle of fascicles (originally totalling 330 leaves, but reduced to many less by then; today there are but 187 folios in existence) was bound in silver, though the name in the title refers to the ink rather than to the binding.

[9] *LBW*, Leibniz an Spanheim, 20.12.1692.

[10] Ed. Joachim Friedrich Feller (Leipzig, 1718), p. 44. Translation my own.

[11] "The Languages of the World – A Classification by G. W. Leibniz", reprinted from *Studies in Germanic Languages and Literatures* (Washington University Press, St. Louis, 1963), p. 34.

[12] *LBW*, Leibniz an Cuper, 23.1.1703.

REFERENCES

Aarsleff, Hans. 1969. The study and use of etymology in Leibniz. Studia Leibnitiana Supplementa, 3.173-89. Wiesbaden: Franz Steiner Verlag.

Bodemann, Eduard. 1889. Der Briefwechsel des Gottfried Wilhelm Leibniz. Hannover.

—. 1895. Die Leibniz-Handschriften der Königlichen Öffentlichen Bibliothek zu Hannover. Hannover.

Kluge, Friedrich. 1960. Etymologisches Wörterbuch der deutschen Sprache. 18th ed. Berlin: W. de Gruyter.

Langley, Alfred Gideon. 1916. New essays concerning human understanding, by G. W. Leibniz. Translation, 2nd. ed. Chicago and London: The Open Court Publishing Company.

Neff, Landolin. 1870. Gottfried Wilhelm Leibniz als Sprachforscher und Etymologe. 2 vols. Heidelberg.

Pietsch, Paul. 1907-1908. Leibniz und die deutsche Sprache. Wissenschaftliche Beihefte zur Zeitschrift des Allgemeinen Deutschen Sprachvereins, Series 4, vol. 29 and 30. Berlin.

Ravier, Emile. 1937. Bibliographie des oeuvres de Leibniz. Paris: F. Alcan.

Schneider, Rolf, and Totok, Wilhelm. 1968. Leibniz: Der Internationale Leibniz-Kongress in Hannover. Hannover: Verlag für Literatur und Zeitgeschehen.

Schröter, Karl. 1969. Bericht über den Stand der Leibniz-Ausgabe der Deutschen Akademie der Wissenschaften zu Berlin. Studia Leibnitiana Supplementa, 3.209-16. Wiesbaden: Franz Steiner.

Waterman, John T. 1963. The languages of the world: A classification by G. W. Leibniz. Studies in Germanic languages and literatures. In memory of Fred O. Nolte. A collection of essays written by his colleagues and former students, ed. by Erich Hofacker and Liselotte Dieckman, 27-34. Saint Louis: Washington University Press.

DECIPHERING IN LINGUISTICS:
A NINETEENTH-CENTURY EPISODE

RULON WELLS

[Inasmuch as my acquaintance with Archibald Hill began with a common attempt (quite unsuccessful on my part) at cryptanalysis and went on through the years with a common interest in linguistics, a topic which considers the two enterprises jointly seems appropriate for his Festschrift.]

In November 1882 Charles Peirce indulged himself in extrapolating from history to prophecy. He wrote (*Collected Papers* 7.66): "... The higher places in science in the coming years are for those who succeed in adapting the methods of one science to the investigation of another. That is what the greatest progress of the passing generation has consisted in. Darwin adapted ... the methods of ... the economists; Maxwell ... the doctrine of chances. Wundt adapts to psychology the methods of physiology; Galton adapts to the same study the methods of the theory of errors. ... The philologists have adapted to their science the methods of the decipherers of dispatches. ..." Like most historians, Peirce was a better historian than prophet, but my present question concerns his powers as a historian. When he spoke of the philologists' adapting the methods of decipherers, to what was he referring?

The answer offered in the present paper is far from definitive; I offer a hypothesis and argue that it is plausible. The hypothesis leans upon two considerations. One is that Peirce does not intend that the adaptation must be conscious and deliberate. The example of Darwin shows this; Darwin acknowledged the influence of Malthus (who might, perhaps, in a loose sense, be called an economist), but his leading conscious model was plant and animal husbandry: natural selection operates like the artificial selection of the breeders. The other consideration is that Peirce has his facts wrong: Cryptanalytical methods had not by his time played, and have not since come to play, any leading part in 'philology' (Ventris's decipherment of Linear B is a spectacular exception);[1] even in that small branch of linguistics which concerns us here, and which

Peirce would have subsumed under philology, namely the decipherment of dead languages, methods of decipherment previously used by crypt-analysts have played a substantial but still minor part. Any hypothesis, then, that such and such were the sources of Peirce's statement must account for the fact that these sources were in error or at least led him into error.

George Boole's *The laws of thought* (1854) is a book with which Peirce was intimately familiar. In Chapter 16, §31, p. 245 Boole writes: "... Events of a given species ... tend to recur with definite frequency, whether their true causes be known to us or unknown. Of course this tendency is, in general, only manifested when the area of observation is sufficiently large. The judicial records of a great nation, its registries of births and deaths, in relation to age and sex, etc., present a remarkable uniformity from year to year. In a given language, or family of languages, the same sounds, and successions of sounds, and, if it be a written language, the same characters and successions of characters recur with determinate frequency. The key to the rude Ogham inscriptions, found in various parts of Ireland, and in which no distinction of words could at first be traced, was, by a strict application of this principle, recovered. The same method, it is understood, has been applied to the deciphering of the cuneiform records recently disentombed from the ruins of Ninevah by the enterprise of Mr. Layard." A footnote explains that "The discovery [of the Ogham key] is due to the Rev. Charles Graves, Professor of Mathematics in the University of Dublin. – Vide *Proceedings of the Royal Irish Academy*, Feb. 18, 1848. Professor Graves informs me that he has verified the principle by constructing sequence tables for all the European languages." And the next footnote explains that the application to the deciphering of cuneiform is "by the learned Orientalist, Dr. Edward Hincks".[2]

In this passage there is no suggestion that Graves and Hincks were consciously adapting the methods of cryptanalysis; the word 'decipher', applied to cryptanalysis since 1545,[3] had since 1710 been used metaphori-cally in speaking of deciphering difficult handwriting, etc.

If we follow up these references to Graves and to Hincks, we find our-selves rewarded in the one instance and disappointed in the other.

Charles Graves (1812-1899; eventually Archbishop of Dublin)[4] published in Volume 4 (1850, for the years 1847-50), pp. 70-3, of the *Proceedings of the Royal Irish Academy* a paper "On a general method of deciphering secret alphabetic writings", read on 14 February 1848. Here the very title, by its reference to 'SECRET writings', shows that deciphering in the literal sense is intended. This clue is valuable, because there is no indication in the paper, explicit or implicit, that Graves is adapting a method previously used elsewhere. On the contrary, the paper presents its method as a novelty.

Graves offers a general formulation of his principle, but what he has in mind is better shown by the immediately following passage. This calls (p. 71) for "the construction of a table, which shows how often, on an average, each letter is followed by each of the remaining ones, in a passage of some determined length. ... With such a table at hand, it is not difficult to assign their proper powers to the secret characters or ciphers in which a document in that language is written. We have merely to tabulate the sequences of the ciphers; and, by comparing their tendencies to repetition and combination with those of the known letters, we readily arrive at a knowledge of their respective powers. It is here assumed that the document to be deciphered is of a reasonable length. This condition is indispensable. ..."

Graves, then, proposes tables of what would now be called transitional probabilities. And he goes on to note that such tables "would be valuable, not merely for the purpose of deciphering, but also in connection with philology"; as showing, e.g., (a) how languages change, and (b) "general principles of euphony, prevailing amongst all languages, and founded on the very nature of our organs of speech and hearing" (p. 72). Returning to decipherment, Graves says that "considerable progress might be made towards the deciphering of purely alphabetic writings" – the precision of his mathematical mind displays itself here, in specifying limitations; not all writings, by any means, are purely alphabetic – "in a language wholly unknown". His concrete examples are that such tables could distinguish vowels from consonants; could pick out certain subclasses of consonants, especially the liquids; and could identify "the letters of the same organ" as those "which enter *similarly* into combination".

Next, "Mr. Graves suggested that this method of tabulating might be employed with advantage in the case of the cuneiform writings. ... Nay, more, it seems that we might thus ascertain whether any giving writing, of which there existed considerable remains, were phonetic or ideagraphic [sic]. ..." In this paragraph there is no mention of Hincks or anyone else, but Graves displays a clear awareness that some of the Persian cuneiform texts (those in Old Persian) were closer than others (those in Akkadian) to purely phonetic writing.

If Edward Hincks (1792-1866)[5] took any account of this suggestion, I find no record and no evidence of it. Boole's report expressly refers to the finds at Ninevah;[6] now already before these reached him, through his work on the inscriptions at Behistun, Van, etc., Hincks had settled upon his methods of work and on his main thesis that the Akkadian cuneiform is primarily phonetic, not ideographic. He made a major contribution to the final breakthrough of 1857,[7] second, I gather, only to Rawlinson's, but I have not in perusing his very minute and personal progress reports found any allusion to the method ascribed to him by Boole and proposed by Graves. One sees from rereading Boole's account that the information about Hincks came to him at second hand, and I tentatively conclude that it was inaccurate.

In any case, Graves's method or something like it was used on unknown writings over a quarter of a century before be wrote, namely by Champollion on Egyptian hieroglyphics. Shortly before his decipherment in December 1821, Champollion noticed – I translate Friedrich (1966: 22) – "that the preserved hieroglyphic part of the Rosetta Inscription contained about three times as many signs as the Greek text contained words. It was therefore quite unthinkable that each hieroglyphic sign should represent a whole word." And in the same volume as contains Graves's paper, the Reverend C.W. Wall (p. 26, 12, 13, December 1847) made a similar observation about the cuneiform trilinguals.[8]

So far, we have evidence of linguists using in their decipherments considerations of frequency such as cryptanalysts had employed long before (as early as 1685, see below) But we have as yet no evidence that they were wittingly influenced by cryptanalysts.

The possibility suggests itself that Poe's story "The gold bug" (1842) may have been an influence upon Graves. This cannot be more than a conjecture until a sufficiently thorough literary-historical study shall have determined the probability that Graves was acquainted with this story. I can cite only the general impression that Poe's story became widely known.[9] But the conjecture, especially when taken in conjunction with the last point that I shall mention, has enough initial plausibility so that it will be worth while to amplify upon it.

It appears from Wimsatt's investigation[10] that Poe relied for his knowledge of enciphering and deciphering chiefly upon William Blair's article "Cipher" in Abraham Rees's *Cyclopaedia*, published in 1819.[11] It appears that the article was actually written twelve years earlier, but that doesn't matter here. At present three points are germane. First, in discussing frequency as a cryptanalytical clue, Blair (1973) mentions three predecessors – Falconer (1685),[12] Breithaupt (1737), and Conrad

(1739). Second, for Blair frequency is only one of many clues; he gives it nothing like the prominence that Poe does. (Here a slight correction of Wimsatt's account is in order: for better or worse, Poe was not wholly unoriginal.) Third, there is a notable difference between Blair and Poe on the one hand and Graves on the other: they speak only of most probable, second most probable, etc., he speaks of numerical ratios; their mathematics is serial, his is quantitative.

It is obvious that Graves may have known of Blair's article directly, whether or not he knew of Poe's story (or of Poe's other writings on ciphers). Blair mentions Ogham writing on columns 10A and 12B. The present article does not investigate this possibility.

There is something more to be said about the antecedents of Graves and of Poe. Colin Cherry, in the 'historical review' (Chapter 2) of *On Human communication*, remarks (1957:35) that "with the introduction of the famous dot-dash code, by S. F. B. Morse in 1832,[13] the STATISTICAL aspect of language economy seems to have been realized". Morse noticed, we are told,[14] that in a typical printer's type-font the different letters were represented by different numbers of pieces, about sixty times as many being needed (for example) in English for E as for Z. The hypothesis is worth considering that publicity connected with Morse helped to make Poe, or Graves, or both, sensitive to frequency as a fact of language. Morse's telegraphic device was publically demonstrated in 1844, after "The gold bug" but before Graves's paper.[15] How much public knowledge there was of Morse's code, before the public demonstration of his device using the code, I do not know. To whatever extent Morse contributed directly or indirectly to Graves's idea, we should qualify Peirce's generalization, since neither the printers who discovered empirically the fact of differential frequency nor Morse, who took it into account in devising his efficient code, were cryptanalysts.

Peirce's generalization, it appears, greatly exaggerated the facts. But the case of Graves (and, to a lesser extent, Champollion) shows that it may not have been wholly false. The hypothesis that Boole was the source of Peirce's misapprehension is far from confirmed, since no thorough attempt to find other possible sources has been made. But although not confirmed, the hypothesis is compatible with all the facts known to me. In any event it has supplied an episode in the history of mathematical linguistics.

Yale University

NOTES

[1]   See Chapter 25 of David Kahn's magnificent book, *The Codebreakers* (New York, 1967).

[2]   Joshua Whatmough (1958:63) cites Boole.

[3]   *New English Dictionary* 3.95-6.

[4]   *Dictionary of National Biography* 22 (Supplement).770-1. On the Ogham alphabet (besides the often-cited discussion in Pedersen 1931:229-39), see Diringer 1968: 1.398-417, with bibliography. Apparently there is still not agreement as to whether Graves's decipherment was right in the main or not.

[5]   *DNB* 9.889-90; Edward Hincks, ... *Correspondence* (0000).

[6]   1845-47, 1849-51 (Pedersen 1931:160).

[7]   Friedrich 1966:56; also Kahn 1967:913.

[8]   F. Münter (1802) seems to have been the first to make this observation (Pedersen 1931:156).

[9]   Preliminary evidence in Kahn 1967:792-3.

[10]   Wimsatt 1943; discussed by Kahn 1967:783ff. and notes.

[11]   In Volume 8. The pages are not numbered. The article occupies thirty-one pages, and I will make references to it as if paginated pp. 1-31 inclusive. P. 5 corresponds to signature 'A a'; p. 31 to signature 'D d 2'. The author tells us (5B, second paragraph) that the article was written in 1807; his interest in the subject was aroused, in 1804, by the Ogham-like cipher of Charles I (10A, third paragraph). Blair's article is cited for its table of factorials by W. Stanley Jevons, *The Principles of Science* (Second edition, London 1879), 179. See further Galland 1945:24-5 (Blair); 70 (Friedman, last article, on Blair); 153-4 (Rees). But the date of 1802 appears to be mistaken.

[12]   Kahn 1967:155 says that the 1685 volume is posthumous and that the 1692 volume is a mere reissue with new title page.

[13]   Kahn 1967:741 gives the date as "about 1838".

[14]   *Ibid.*

[15]   Accordingly, Graves should be added to Guiraud 1954.

REFERENCES

Cherry, Colin. 1957. On human communication: A review, a survey, and a criticism. New York: John Wiley and Sons, and London: Chapman and Hall.

Diringer, David. 1968. The alphabet: A key to the history of mankind. 3rd ed. 2 vols. London: Hutchinson.

Friedrich, Johannes. 1966. Entzifferung verschollener Schriften und Sprachen. 2nd ed. Berlin, Heidelberg, New York: Springer.

Galland, Joseph S. 1945. An historical and analytical bibliography of the literature of cryptography. Northwestern University Studies in the Humanities. Nr. 10. Evanston, Ill.: Northwestern University Press.

Guirand, Pierre. 1954. Bibliographie critique de la statistique linguistique. Utrecht: Spectrum.

Kahn, David. 1967. The codebreakers. New York: Mac Millan.

Pedersen, Holger. 1931. Linguistic science in the 19th century, translated by John Webster Spargo. Cambridge, Mass.: Harvard University Press.

Whatmough, Joshua. 1958. Mathematical linguistics (Report). Proceedings of the Eight International Congress of Linguists, Oslo 1957, ed. by E. Sivertsen, 62-91. Oslo: Oslo University Press.

Wimsatt, William K., Jr. 1963. What Poe knew about cryptography. Publications of the Modern Language Association 58.754-78.